CW00821414

ARCHITECTURE, MEDIA, POPULISM... AND VIOLENCE

The 'Storming of the Capitol' was, for many, the culminating media performance of the four-year presidency of Donald Trump. His presidency, and its 'final act', bore all the hallmarks of a 21st century form of populism and media-politico spectacle that may yet come to dominate the political scene in the US, and worldwide, for years to come. The questions that such events raise are complex, varied and operative across a multitude of disciplines. This book engages with these vexed questions in the broad fields of politics and media, but does so, uniquely, through the prism of architecture.

This book does not, however, limit its view to the recent events in Washington DC or the United States. Rather, it seeks to use those events as the starting point for a critique of architecture in the tapestry of mediated forms of protest and 'political action' more generally. Each chapter draws on case studies from across timeframes and across nations.

The book sharpens our critique of the relationship between direct political action, its media representation and the role it assigns to architecture – as played out globally in the age of mass media. In doing so, it opens up broader debates about the past, present and future roles of architecture as a political tool in the context of international political systems now dominated by changing and unpredictable uses of media, and characterised by an increasingly volatile and at times violent form of political activism. It is essential reading for any student or researcher engaging with these questions.

Graham Cairns is an academic and author in the field of architecture who has written extensively on film, advertising and political communication. He has held Visiting Professor positions at universities in Spain, the UK, Mexico, the Gambia, South Africa and the US. He has led academic departments in the

UK and the US. He has worked in architectural studios in London and Hong Kong and previously founded and ran a performing arts organisation, Hybrid Artworks, specialised in video installation and performance writing. He is the author and editor of multiple books and articles on architecture as both a form of visual culture and a socio-political construct, including the Routledge volume that preceded this one *Reification and Representation – Architecture in the Politico-Media-Complex*. He is currently Director of the academic research organisation AMPS (Architecture, Media, Politics, Society), and Executive Editor of its associated journal *Architecture_MPS*.

ARCHITECTURE, MEDIA, POPULISM... AND VIOLENCE

Reification and Representation II

Edited by
Graham Cairns

Routledge
Taylor & Francis Group

LONDON AND NEW YORK

Cover image: Photo by Colin Lloyd on Unsplash

First published 2023
by Routledge
4 Park Square, Milton Park, Abingdon, Oxon OX14 4RN

and by Routledge
605 Third Avenue, New York, NY 10158

Routledge is an imprint of the Taylor & Francis Group, an informa business

© 2023 selection and editorial matter, Graham Cairns; individual
chapters, the contributors

The right of Graham Cairns to be identified as the author of the
editorial material, and of the authors for their individual chapters, has
been asserted in accordance with sections 77 and 78 of the Copyright,
Designs and Patents Act 1988.

All rights reserved. No part of this book may be reprinted or reproduced
or utilised in any form or by any electronic, mechanical or other
means, now known or hereafter invented, including photocopying and
recording, or in any information storage or retrieval system, without
permission in writing from the publishers.

Trademark notice: Product or corporate names may be trademarks
or registered trademarks, and are used only for identification and
explanation without intent to infringe.

British Library Cataloguing-in-Publication Data
A catalogue record for this book is available from the British Library

Library of Congress Cataloging-in-Publication Data
A catalog record has been requested for this book

ISBN: 978-1-032–22318-6 (hbk)
ISBN: 978-1-032–22321-6 (pbk)
ISBN: 978-1-003–27207-6 (ebk)

DOI: 10.4324/9781003272076

Typeset in Bembo
by codeMantra

This book follows on from the 2018 Routledge publication, *Reification and Representation — Architecture in the Politico-Media Complex*, authored by Graham Cairns.

The editor would like to thank the team at the research organization AMPS (Architecture, Media, Politics, Society) for its support and advice in the production of this book.

CONTENTS

CONTRIBUTORS

Eva Branscome works at the Bartlett School of Architecture, University College London, from which she also received her PhD. Originally trained as an interior architect, her research and teaching have two main strands: the first engages with links between built heritage and cultural practices in contemporary Western cities, whether expressed through cultural institutions or counterculture and street art; the second is in the 19th- and 20th-century architectural history of Central Europe, focusing upon Austria and other regions in the former Austro-Hungarian Empire. She has published extensively, including *Hans Hollein and Postmodernism* (Routledge, 2018), the first major monograph on that architect-artist.

Peggy Deamer is a Professor Emerita of Yale University's School of Architecture and Principal of Deamer, Studio. She is the founding member of the Architecture Lobby, a group advocating for the value of architectural labour. She is the editor of *Architecture and Capitalism: 1845 to the Present* and *The Architect as Worker: Immaterial Labor, the Creative Class, and the Politics of Design* and the author of *Architecture and Labor*. Her theory work explores the relationship between subjectivity, design and labour.

Annie Dell'Aria is an Associate Professor of Art History at Miami University in Oxford, Ohio. Her research concerns the intersection of public space, screen media and contemporary art. She is the author of *The Moving Image as Public Art: Sidewalk Spectators and Modes of Enchantment* (Palgrave Macmillan, 2021) as well as articles in publications such as *Afterimage, Moving Image Review and Art Journal*, and *Public Art Dialogue* and chapters in the books *Screening the Art World* (Amsterdam University Press, 2022) and *Teachable Monuments* (Bloomsbury, 2021).

Bram De Maeyer is currently working as a PhD student at KU Leuven, Department of Architecture. In 2017, he obtained his Master's degree in History at the University of Antwerp with a dissertation on the Council of Flanders during the First World War, which has been published in the *Journal of Belgian History*. His research interests primarily lie in the examination of national and political representation in a foreign context. This book chapter is part of the ongoing PhD project *Designing Embassies for Middle Powers: The Architecture of Belgian Diplomacy in a Globalizing World* which sheds light on the embassy building policy of the Belgian Ministry of Foreign Affairs.

Murray Fraser is Professor of Architecture and Global Culture at the Bartlett School of Architecture, University College London, and also the current Chair of the Society of Architectural Historians of Great Britain. In 2008, his book *Architecture and the 'Special Relationship'* won the RIBA Research Award and CICA Bruno Zevi Book Prize. With Catherine Gregg, he edited the 21st Edition of *Sir Banister Fletcher's Global History of Architecture* (2020), which was awarded the SAHGB's Colvin Prize. He received the 2018 RIBA Annie Spink Award for Excellence in Education.

Jeffrey Kruth is an urbanist and teaches at Miami University in Oxford, Ohio. At Miami, he teaches courses on urban design history and theory and works closely with the Miami University Center for Community Engagement in Over-the-Rhine.

Nadir Lahiji is the author of *Architecture in the Age of Pornography: Reading Alain Badiou* (Routledge, 2022). His previous publications include *Architecture, Philosophy and Pedagogy of Cinema: From Benjamin to Badiou* (Routledge, 2021), *Architecture or Revolution: Emancipatory Critique after Marx* (Routledge, 2021), *An Architecture Manifesto: Critical Reason and Theories of a Failed Practice* (Routledge, 2019) and *Adventures with the Theory of the Baroque and French Philosophy* (Bloomsbury, 2018 [2016]). He has co-authored *The Architecture of Phantasmagoria: Specters of the City* (Routledge, 2016). His edited books include *Can Architecture Be an Emancipatory Project: Dialogues on Architecture and the Left* (Zero Books, 2016), *The Missed Encounter of Radical Philosophy with Architecture* (Bloomsbury, 2015 [2014]), *Architecture against the Post-Political: Essays in Reclaiming the Critical Project* (Routledge, 2014) and *The Political Unconscious of Architecture: Re-Opening Jameson's Narrative* (Ashgate, 2012 [2011]).

Joern Langhorst, currently an Associate Professor and Interim Chair of Landscape Architecture at the University of Colorado Denver, was educated in Landscape Architecture, Architecture and Urban Planning in Germany and Europe, and has taught in Landscape Architecture, Architecture, Urban and Regional Planning and Urban Design in the US and abroad. His practice has focused on projects in highly contested situations, such as redevelopment and remediation in post-industrial cities, brownfield sites and post-disaster recovery, and he is consulting on these issues nationally and internationally. His research and teaching are exploring the processes and actors that make and unmake place, space and landscape, focusing on places of incisive and radical change such as post-colonial, post-industrial and post-disaster cities. His approaches involve multiple perspectives and disciplines, and establish a methodology he calls 'landscape forensics'. He examines how concepts such as social and environmental justice, resilience and sustainability are conceived and implemented, arguing for a 'right to landscape'. Langhorst scrutinises the role of emergent technologies, alternative processes and the relationships between traditional and new actors and agents, and foregrounds contestation and conflict as unavoidable processes central to landscape and place change.

Isaac Leung is a practicing artist, curator and scholar in art and culture. In 2003, Leung received an Honorary Fellowship of a Bachelor of Fine Arts at the School of the Art Institute of Chicago. During 2013 and 2020, Leung was appointed as the Chairman of Videotage. During his tenure, he initiated and participated in projects that included exhibitions, workshops, lectures, publications, online projects and symposia. He is currently an Assistant Professor in the Faculty of Arts of the Chinese University of Hong Kong and Board Director of the Hong Kong Jewish Film Festival.

Alfie Peacock studied architecture at the University of Brighton in 2016 in Studio 12, before presenting at the AMPS Conference in Liverpool on his paper 'Social Constructs of Social Housing'. After working for two housing architecture practices in London, he moved to Copenhagen to study 'Political Architecture: Critical Sustainability' MA at the Royal Danish Academy. Since returning to the UK, Alfie has been working for a local government housing management organisation in London.

Malcolm Rio is a graphic and architectural designer and thinker living in Providence, RI. He is an Assistant Professor in the Department of Architecture at the Rhode Island School of Design and a PhD candidate at Columbia University. His scholarship, criticism and interviews have appeared in *Thresholds, Avery Review, The New York Review of Architecture, Architecture_MPS* and *Pidgin*, as well as within forthcoming books such as a volume on sexuality, gender and architecture titled *Living Room* being edited by Sophie Hochhäusl.

Charlotte Rottiers is working as a PhD researcher at the KU Leuven's Faculty of Architecture in Ghent from 2020 onwards. She obtained her Master's degree in Art History at the University of Ghent in 2018 with great distinction, and a Bachelor in East European Languages and Cultures with distinction in 2021. Her interests lie in architectural history, cultural and political representation combined with the formation of identity through art and architecture. This book chapter is part of her project *Housing the Nation Abroad. The Belgian Diplomatic Representation through Architecture and Interior Decoration, 1831–1940*, supervised by Anne-Françoise Morel and Fredie Floré.

Ian Volner is a freelance writer and critic on architecture, design, art and urbanism based in New York City. He is a contributing editor at *Architect* and *Architecture Today* (UK); and a contributor to *The Wall Street Journal, The New Republic, The New Yorker, New York Magazine, The Washington Post, Artforum* and *Architectural Record* (amongst many others). He is the author of *Jorge Pardo: Public Projects and Commissions, Philip Johnson: A Visual Biography, The Great Great Wall, Michael Graves: Design for Life* and *This Is Frank Lloyd Wright*.

WEAPONISING ARCHITECTURE

Graham Cairns

Setting a Scene: The Capitol Riot.....

On Wednesday, January 6, 2021, the United States Congress sat in session presiding over the count of electoral college votes that would clear the way for the inauguration of Joseph Robinette Biden as the 46th President of the United States. A little over one mile away the incumbent President Donald Trump addressed a crowd of supporters gathered at the 'Save America' rally in protest at the results of the November 3rd Presidential Election. Within two hours what has been variously described as a 'mob', 'a band of revolutionaries', 'US patriots' and 'good people on the right side of history' were storming the Capitol building which, within minutes, would be the site of vandalism, desecration and riot.

All seen in real-time on internet streaming platforms, photographed and posted 'as it happened' on social media outlets, and screened live on news channels across the United States and further afield, the 'Storming of the Capitol' was, for many, the culminating media performance of the four-year Presidency of Donald Trump. Initiated by a 2016 election campaign itself played out through social media channels like never before, his Presidency and its 'final act', bore all the hallmarks of a 21st-century form of populism and media-politico spectacle that may yet come to dominate the political scene for years to come.

The issues these events raise in the field of political science are complex. The questions they pose for the discipline of political communication are equally intricate. The problems posed by all this for the media are openly debated, while the concerns found within the arena of communications studies are burgeoning and increasingly polemic. This book engages with these vexed questions in the broad fields of politics and media through the prism of architecture. It seeks to critique the role of the (often symbolic) architectural settings in such events and explore the deeper social and cultural issues the role of architecture in them can reveal.

DOI: 10.4324/9781003272076-1

Is it simply the historic and symbolic status the Capitol building has for United States politics that marks this particular event as unique? Is it the visceral display of a populist rejection of the established modes of government and all its paraphernalia, including its architecture, that marks this event as significant globally? Where does the preference for neoclassical architecture in the United States espoused by Donald Trump himself stand now, given that its status as a symbol for disconnected government seems set in the 'populist' imagination? Thinking more broadly, why did these images have more 'political' impact than the imagery of urban rioting and Black Lives Matter protests that had been evidenced across the United States in previous years? What importance does the political architectural backdrop to such media images have in determining their power and impact on politicians and citizens alike? What, if anything, do the events of January 6, 2021 in Washington DC tell us about populism as a political movement more generally? How do these events shed light on other instances of architecture's imbrication in political discourse and action evident globally? Indeed, what can other acts of politicised violence historically reveal about recent populist events in the United States and beyond?

Using the January 6th riot in Washington DC as its starting point and provocation then, this book seeks to sharpen our focus on the role architecture can, and does, play in populist political-cultural discourse. It opens up debates about architecture's role in the machinations of a contemporary politics played out through a complex array of media: the mainstream established press, radical independent online platforms and global social media, to name but three. It asks questions about historical precedent for political movements and their appropriation of architecture as both symbol and site of power. It also critiques how acts of force staged in definable place form feedback loops in debates about design and spatial practice. It does so through a series of international case studies in which architecture has become a site of political protest and violence from across the 20th and 21st centuries. It uses examples of housing, infrastructure, city streets, embassies and, of course, the Capitol Building itself.

Each of the essays in this book then, take the events of January 6, 2021, as a starting point for their own debates and critiques of how architecture is folded into the symbolic games of populist politics – often through a veil of violence. The authors of each essay were invited to critique the role, and future role, of architecture as a political tool in the context of a political system dominated by changing and unpredictable uses of media from their particular discipline perspectives: architectural history, cultural theory, political communication, sociology, human geography and media studies.

The book itself is a follow-on from the 2018 Routledge publication, *Reification and Representation – Architecture in the Politico-Media Complex*. That book examined the role given to architecture in the political campaign imagery of the United States and the United Kingdom and, more significantly, how that reveals underlying issues of the Neoliberal turn of the late 20th and early 21st centuries. Among its case studies were examples taken from the 2008 Presidential campaign of Barack Obama; the 2000–2008 administrations of George W. Bush; the 2010 election campaign of the Tory Party in the United Kingdom, related to the Brexit campaign six years later; the 1979–1983 Conservative Party Government under the leadership of Margaret Thatcher; and the 1997 election campaign of New Labour and its immediate period of policy launches related to issues of the built environment. It also included what we can define as the opening act of the Donald Trump Presidency, the theatrical launch of his Presidential campaign in June 2015 in the lobby of Trump Tower. Using the closing 'spectacle' of his Presidency at the Capitol Building, Washington DC on January 6, 2021, to open debates about the role of architecture in the mediated arena of populist politics more broadly, this book also highlights how this is all too easily laced with violence and conflict.

In the introduction of the first book, the conceptual framework applied to its readings of architecture as a communicative device was identified as being influenced by several key theoretical constructs. They included an intellectual structuring of architecture's role in politics that drew on Louis Althusser and Antonio Gramsci, both thinkers who are cited by the authors in this publication. From Althusser, Book One borrowed his schemata of Ideological State Apparatus and Repressive State Apparatus, while from Gramsci, it borrowed his definitions of Civil and Political Societies. Within these schemata, that book's interest in the imagery of political communication campaigns saw architecture as imbricated in the mediatic constructs of the political communicative process and, as a result, as a constituent part of the mechanisms of the *Ideological* and the *Civil*, respectively. Set within this conceptualisation, the 'desecration' of the architectural symbol of US democracy on January 6th remains part of what Althusser defined as ideological apparatus, and what Gramsci calls the realm of the Civil. More precisely, and picking up on a theme Murray Fraser will return to in his chapter, *Germania-on-Thames*, is part of a that 'desecration' can be said to form part of a 'cultural' War of Position – whereby political actors continue their fight to influence political beliefs and behaviours at what may be reductively defined as the *level of culture*.

This definition, albeit admittedly partial, is useful in understanding a particular strand of resurgent debates in the past decade on the phenomenon of 'culture wars', whereby entire belief systems, and the symbolic and formative models that set them, are seemingly treated as sites of contestation between opposing political world (or nation) views. In this framework, religion, history, anthropology science and mores, are all 'fought over' as much as the curricula of schools, socially admissible modes of expression and language, political and human rights, and a whole array of symbolic cultural artefacts, including architecture and its associated interpretations. If we accept the nomenclature of 'culture war' and permit its extension, we open the possibility of defining the tools of these wars as their *cultural weapons*, architecture included.

While the majority of the authors in this book will reiterate variations on this standpoint, it is also worth noting a line of argumentation that suggests the events of January 6th could function as precursors to ever greater violence in the practice of democracy in the United States and elsewhere in the years to come. With an eye on the 2024 US Presidential election, it is not inconceivable that what we witnessed in 2021 represents a step on a road to greater violence that – at least momentarily – threatens to become integral to the mechanics of US democracy. Whether manifest in the intimidation of voters at polling stations, the forcible occupation of the streets, the targeting of activists in their homes, or the ransacking of the architectural icons of the political system itself, it is currently difficult to imagine the Presidential elections of 2024 in the United States not being accompanied by acts of coercive violence in one form or another. If such activity remains tacitly accepted and condoned by the country's political elite, it is feasible that the January 6th riot will be viewed in hindsight not only as the wielding of architecture as a 'cultural weapon' at a specific moment in time, but as the explicit emergence of something else: the repressive apparatus of a proto-state and the direct actions of a proto-political society, to paraphrase both Althusser and Gramsci.

Whether January 6, 2021 and the threats of the far-right in the United States prove to be empty symbolic acts of defiance and diffused anger, or develop into something more sustained, remains to be seen. The third book in this series will follow what promises to be the 2024 litmus test of US democracy's descent into randomised violence: a violence bolstered by party political imagineering and administrative manipulation of verifiable news, media representations, voting rights, congressional investigations and architectural symbolism, amongst other things. That book may well be forced to return to these points of departure to explore subsequent and related issues of ever greater severity post-2024. Whether it does so or not will depend on many things, including the continued evolution of the 'culture war' in the United States and its potential weaponising of everything from religion to social media, party politics to free speech, and law enforcement to architecture.

Exploring Responses: Beyond the Riot Part One....

Returning to this book, given the range of questions the January 6th riot potentially opens up, it should not be surprising to the reader that the essays contained within it are diverse. Each author has been asked to respond to the provocation of the Capitol Riot and has done so through a series of essays that examine architecture as experienced and presented in the context of mediated acts of violence and populist rhetoric. In doing so, they open doors to a variegated set of perspectives on architecture as image and material object in the political arena globally and over time. They are structured in two main parts, broadly definable as contemporary and historic case studies, and are linked by a sideways look at the issues at play in the 'intersection' text of Peggy Deamer and Ian Volner. They are bookended by two pieces that specifically engage with the Capitol Riot as an act in and of itself, Nadir Lahiji's *The Pornographic Scene of Insurrection* in closing, and Annie Dell'Aria's *Screening the Capitol Riot*, to open.

Dell'Aria's text begins with Donald Trump's second impeachment trial in February 2021 and the mediated imagery filmed at the riot as shown in Congressman Jaime Raskin's opening debate. Centring from the outset on the multifaceted widescreen, televisual and vertical smartphone footage of Raskin's montage, she frames the event, and her consideration of it, squarely as a mediated phenomenon in which the site and its symbolism are largely subservient to the social networks on which the imagery was played out as a global event. In so doing she uses as historic touch points, Walter Benjamin and his arguments related to the aestheticisation of politics as explored in relation to 1930s fascism, and the Nikolai Evreinov directed film, *The Storming of the Winter Palace, 1920* references that directly and indirectly reappear in the closing essay of Nadir Lahiji.

In Dell'Aria's opening, these references connect us to contemporary political readings of the Capitol Riot as spectacle and, interestingly, contemporary artworks from Arthur Jafa and the collective LaBeouf, Rönkkö & Turner. Aesthetically, it is also a reading that underlines the discrepancies between the aesthetic tropes of the architectural setting; its mainstream media filmic presentation; the dense aesthetic of shaky, multiply formatted and often cacophonous visual and audio manifestations available online; and in Raskin's rendition of them presented in the Senate. The conglomeration of imagery with which we are now familiar is a visualisation of space and event that, Dell'Aria suggests, can be read as *placeless* and *untethered* and simultaneously a *specific, surgical,* and multi-layered production of place.

While Dell'Aria begins with Raskin's filmic projection screened just weeks after the Capitol Riot, Malcom Rio takes a wider perspective on the violence often connected to populist politics in his chapter, *Housing Populism: Constructing the 'Little Man's' House, Deconstructing the 'Queer' Home.* He considers parallels between underlying issues of race and social normalisation evident in the events screened by Raskin in the Senate in 2021, and those that have manifest themselves for over a century around the issue of housing, race and familial structures in the United States. Opening with imagery of white middle-class American's 'defending' their 'housing' vis-à-vis the Bundy and McCloskey standoffs in 2014 and 2016, respectively, he critiques how the January 6th storming of the Capitol, *also commonly known as the 'People's House,' deployed rhetoric of the home, ownership, and property to legitimise the voting power of 'real Americans'.*

Through this trope, he not only explores the experience of racial and queer communities in the United States since the Second World War, but also how underlying prejudices are facilitated by the mechanics of policy and cultural mythology premised on what he defines as the privilege of white land-holding heterosexual men. Through examples such as the GI Bill's exclusion of financial support for homosexual veterans and the racial intimidation of the Myerses, the first black family in the Levittown, Pennsylvania, he links the claims of 'taking back' the People's House heard throughout the four-hour 'siege' of the Capitol, with the barely concealed racial narratives of what is considered to be the *'Ordinary American'* in the frameworks currently set by America's political Right.

Malcom Rio ends his essay citing MSNBC News anchor Joy Reid's commentary on the apparent relationship between protestors at the Capitol Riot and the police charged with protecting it. Reid underlines the enormous discrepancy between the apparent cordial interplay of those actors in comparison to the militarised and violent police responses across the United States over the previous decade in relation to Black Lives Matter protests. Similar themes are brought up in Jeff Kruth's work, *Representation and Refusal: From State Architecture to Highway Protests*. Kruth explicitly compares the Black Lives Matter protests and their mediated aesthetic and spatial tropes with those of far-right movements such as the Proud Boys and, more precisely, the Boogaloo Movement.

His analysis starts by identifying the *reflexive relationship* between the architectural points of reference used by Trump, and by extension his supporters, in both imagery and as backdrops to action in the years prior to the Capitol Riot. To paraphrase, he examines the Right's tendency to use the clearly defined sites of power as sites of action and image production, including the US Capitol on January 6th, and compares that to how the Black Lives Matter movement favoured the less visually and symbolically notable infrastructure of the United States Highway system as its place of appearance and action.

His examples include the occupying of Interstate 70 in Ferguson, Missouri, in protests related to the death of Michael Brown in 2014. He cites the June 2020 march between the Minnesota State Capitol building in St. Paul to Minneapolis that blocked the I-94 highway in response to the murder of George Floyd. He also pinpoints the blockades of the I-630 in Little Rock, the I-40 in Memphis and the I-75 in Cincinnati as similar modes of protest. These spatial practices are linked to an aesthetic of dress that, more importantly, also helps move his critique into the field of digital surveillance and counter acts of invisibility employed by both activists on the Left and Right, respectively. In particular, he introduces Simone Browne's work on the surveillance of black activists and her notion of dark sousveillance – '*the tactics employed to render one's self out of sight*' and a way of '*contending with antiblack surveillance*'. It is an essay that interlinks the use of digital media in protest, an emerging area of research into the spatial practices of protest and an awareness of the aesthetics of image production embedded in both.

In its focus on transport infrastructure as a site of protest, and its critique of the reflexive image relationship evident in the imagery manufactured by the Donald Trump Administration and his proto-political support network, Kruth's essay connects to themes evident in our next text. In *Architecture and Disciplinary Knowledge*, Isaac Leung discusses the 2019 and 2020 protests in Hong Kong against the Fugitive Offenders Amendment Bill and identifies both the strategic use of streets in the city by protestors and the manufacture of 'reflexive' imagery by the media. He does so in a broader conversation about how, in recent years, the infrastructural and architectural heritage of Hong Kong has entered into the political terrain of contestation over Hong Kong's colonial past and its future as part of the economically hybrid communist state structures of China.

Leung's entry point into his argument is to underline how, as with the Capitol Riot which serves as this book's point of departure, the politically symbolic role of architecture in Hong Kong is increasingly complex to decipher. His case in point is the renovation of the Tai Kwun, the main British Police Station and prison cells built in 1864 and now the site of a museum and cultural complex exploring the history of Hong Kong as part of the broader tourist-focused cultural offerings of the city. Located within the area of unrest during the protests of 2019–2020, Tai Kwun serves as his vehicle for exploring how China is, in the context of Hong Kong, managing narratives about its past, present and future. In discussing it, Leung identifies a definition of Hong Kong, its particular architectural case study and the broader site of protest surrounding it, in the Foucauldian terms of heterotopia.

The simultaneous conflation of narratives, acts, people and medias in his sites of interest are revelatory with regard the ascribed role of architecture and place in protests, and their wider political narratives. For example, while arguing that for the protestors of 2019–2020 their sites of action were, by and large, primarily infrastructural locales of action, he also underlines how in the photography of those acts that found its way into mainstream news outlets, a very specific and particular spatio-symbolic narrative was imposed: that of *contradiction* politically spun or, to paraphrase Leung's use of Foucault, heterotopic imagery politically spun. Examples include the local *Shing Tao* newspaper which ran with images of post-demonstration destruction in front of the Emporio Armani, replete with a suited ex-pat carrying his briefcase. Internationally, he highlights similar tropes employed by *Time* magazine who used the deliberately provocative image of protestors arrayed in front of the Louis Vuitton store for the same contradistinctive aims.

In Leung's text then, we see both the seemingly strategic and reflexive use and portrayal of space that Kruth explores, and the broader tapestry of sociocultural and political issues Malcolm Rio examines in his contribution. Considered in the politically charged context of Hong Kong right now, it not only encompasses the heterotopia of Foucault, but also Zygmunt Bauman's ideas of Liquid Modernity – both concepts key to the thinking of Joern Langhorst in the subsequent essay, *Mediating Consensus and Enacting Dissensus*. Langhorst takes the Capitol Riot of 2021 and the 2013 street protests in Rio de Janeiro as *bookends* in his wide-ranging consideration of contemporary democracy and the role of conflict within it. Encompassing not only these two moments and sites of protests, Langhorst also references the Black Lives Matter protests, the Arab Spring and the Occupy movements. He defines them as a *spectrum of political and politicised, spatial and spatialised acts* through which he attempts to investigate and explain how *architecture and its spatial/material manifestation in (public) space [is] influence[d] and affected by political and politicised acts of protest.*

Theoretically, his essay considers the interplay of consensus and dissensus via Chantal Mouffe's notion of agonism, whereby politics itself is defined as a continual interplay of conflictive forces whose very acts of conflict are necessary components of a truly active democracy. He sees these conflicts as currently heightened by a climate of *existential crises* related to a fear of the loss of identity on the political Right in the United States and, by extension, significant portions of the populace in Western democracies more widely. He thus reinforces the argument that underlying the spectacle at the Capitol Riot was, ultimately, a sense of *instability, ambiguity and disappearance of what appeared to be stable or solid categories of identity* as captured by Bauman. In the framework of analysis suggested by Mouffe (and Baumen) then, Langhorst suggests the Capitol Riot can be defined not as wholly negative, but rather as a visualisation of struggles at the heart of political consensus and dissensus, currently manifest through Right-Wing Populism, amongst other things.

Related to these readings, Langhorst also identifies how the concomitant cell phone filmed, and social media distributed, images and narratives from events such as the Capitol Riot can, and do, function as alternate channels for narrative construction that can be defined as resisting the potentially hegemonic single perspectives of mainstream media. In addition to being a line of thought that comes through Mouffe, and indeed Ernesto Laclau, it can be highlighted in a whole range of theorists who also critique the typically homogenising narratives that safeguard the workings of contemporary capitalist democracies from fundamental questions related to its validity, from Noam Chomsky to Alain Badiou and Raymond Williams to Jacques Rancière, to name but a few.

While Langhorst's paper ends the first part of this book, his commentary on the limited perspectives that come through mainstream media in relation to critiques that fundamentally challenge capitalism itself, finds its own echo in Peggy Deamer and Ian Volner's text, *Architecture Journalism and the Proto-Political*. This contribution functions as a form of intersection in the book's structure, with Deamer and Volner taking us outside our primary frames of reference – the use of architecture as an image-framed political tool and site of protest. Via nods to Walter Benjamin, they draw attention to the range of issues that condition the general public to accept the use of architecture as a symbolic part of the contemporary political ensemble or, to use their term, *symbolic pantomime*. In their reading, the events at the Capitol building on January 6th, *just like the attack on the World Trade Center in 2001, offered a chance for the media to foreground architecture-cum-symbol* and, as such, represent just another example of how architecture is artificially framed for the general public. Their angle of enquiry then, is not the attack itself, or its particular use of architecture as symbol, but rather the *collective imaginary* of the American public that the events played into – an imaginary they argue that has been *primed* to see architecture in almost exclusively 'symbolic' terms.

Within this context, Deamer and Volner focus their attention not on the images of architecture as they appeared in social media and in news coverage of the January 6th events, but rather on the pages of architectural criticism across a slew of mainstream and professional media outlets. The work of Michael Kimmelman in particular is brought into focus. The mainstream media engagement and presentation of architecture, they argue, revolves around its object status and, at a stretch, the sensorial and aesthetic responses it is capable of inducing in an interested observer. Embedded in this critique are considerations on how the use of the word architect itself helps form this *primed* public mentality of object status consumption. In its worst manifestations it results in what they see as the profession's portrayal as something mysterious, and its practitioners as esoteric – *somewhere between a James Bond villain and the Wizard of Oz*. The serious implications of this relate to how it deflects almost all public engagement with architecture away from the labour involved in its design and production, and onto its finished 'symbolic' form.

In exploring the financial underpinnings of architectural criticism as practice in mainstream media they reveal a number of issues discussed at length in more generic critiques of the media over the past two decades: the ever decreasing financial backing of investigative journalism; the reliance of newspapers in particular on advertising revenue; the increasing reliance on 'interested' third party sources for copy, and more. As in other journalistic fields, Deamer and Volner identify that it leads to superficial journalism for easy consumption. When only the surface veneer of architecture is ever presented and discussed in public, they suggest, it is hardly surprising that it is only publicly understood role in the collective imaginary is similarly superficial – as a backdrop laden with deep, but loosely ascribed, cultural meaning. In the case of the Capitol, it lends itself to those who wish to use it as a messaging system about democracy, tradition and the authority of 'the people'.

Beyond the Riot. Part Two....

Picking up expressly of Deamer and Volner's investigation of architecture as it appears in the media, Eva Branscome's essay opens Part Two of this book and is the first that explicitly takes a step back in time. In *The Press Photography of 'Red Vienna', 1929–1938*, she examines how images of the architecture of Red Vienna were, during the pre-Second World War conflicts in 1930s Austria, variously appropriated and assigned meaning from at least three differing political perspectives. For Branscome, the events of January 6th in the United States resonate directly with one precise act in the period of fascist conflict in Austria in the 1930s, the storming of the Federal Chancellery by Austrian fascists on July 25, 1934. However, the focus of her essay lies in the architecture for which Vienna of the period is better known, its social housing.

Branscome examines the way in which media representations of the housing complexes of Vienna informed the coverage of the build-up to the Second World War by international journalists, particularly those of the United States. A 'symbol' of the socially oriented political policies of the Social Democrat Party up to 1934, her examination of the press photography and coverage at the time reveal that housing estates such as Karl-Marx-Hof, were also used as political symbols for other ends. They were presented as fortresses of resistance during the

1934 civil war when they became strongholds for communists and socialists engaged in armed conflict with Austria's Nazi forces. They were also presented in 1938 as pictorial symbols of the social support provided by the Right after Austria's annexation by Nazi Germany, when Karl-Marx-Hof operated as a feeding station for desperate local civilians.

Demonstrating the slippages of meaning easily ascribed to architecture reduced to image, her work underlines the role of the image in *the history-making process helping to forge a common sentiment that triggered an Allied reaction once the Second World War broke out.* It is a line of argumentation that brings up the issues of authenticity as rehearsed by Roland Barthes and Susan Sontag with respect to photography and it obliges us to consider the image as what she terms, a *social construct.* In many ways, these arguments reinforce a number of the issues raised by Deamer and Volner in relation to contemporary architectural criticism, but also by Joern Langhorst in relation to the power of the image to construct narratives. However, her essay also does something else that links it to the variegated themes threaded throughout this book. Branscome underlines the emerging technologies at play in 1930s press photography (hand-held cameras, flashbulb technology, etc.) and how they were causing 'political concern' about the control of political messaging. Her essay thus also operates as a reminder that current concerns about social media, web-based sites of political activism, and their presentation of political messaging and symbols (architecture included) is far from new.

Branscome's step back to the 1930s is echoed in the following chapter by Charlotte Rottiers and Bram De Maeyer who segway into their essay, *Diplomacy Under Siege,* via the response of former US President George W. Bush to the Capitol Riot on January 6, 2021. That response they highlight reflected Bush's response to previous attacks on sites of United States political power on foreign territory in 2006 – specifically protests and attacks on US and allied Embassies in response to Western political support for the newspaper published caricatures of the Prophet Muhammad initiated by the *Charlie Hebdo* satirical magazine on the 9th of February that year. Both those 2006 attacks, and the January 6th riot at the Capitol building, they argue function as *recent reminders of the ambiguous relationship between political architecture and the popular masses.* They also remind us how the symbolic role ascribed to architecture is malleable and capable of functioning in multiple ways simultaneously, and of being inverted instantly.

Their case studies are the destruction of the Belgian Legation in Beijing during the Boxer rebellion of 1900 and various attacks on Belgian embassies in Poland, Yugoslavia, India and the one they examine in detail, Cairo, Egypt, in 1961. In each scenario, they examine the use of embassy buildings as *architectural surrogates* for state actors on foreign soil and, via Robert Bevan, underline that this type of 'attack on buildings' has been defined in recent years as a form of *lingua franca of nationalist and regionalist terror groups.* Importantly, they also distinguish between terrorist and mob attacks, like the one used as the touchstone in this book, and identify that, in the case of Belgium, the destruction of their legation in Beijing in 1900 had unexpected consequences: it actually drew the attention of the Belgian government to the heightened symbolic role the architecture of their embassies could play in furthering Belgium's political visibility and apparent importance globally. In this light, the attacks and destruction of their Embassy in Cairo in 1961 in response to Belgium's role in the kidnap and assassination of Congo's President Lumumba, represent the flip side of this architectural symbolic coin: the instant conversion of their architectural paraphernalia into a *tool of retaliation*.

If Rottiers and De Maeyer identify the architecture of embassies as a 'political tool' in the context of international politics, in *Social Infrastructure & Disintegration, Statecraft & Democracy*, Alfie Peacock underlines something analogous in relation to public housing in the United Kingdom – specifically the Broadwater Farm Housing Estate in London. While revisiting housing, as per the essay of Eva Branscome, this text focuses on a different time and place, 1980s Britain and the internal political wranglings of UK domestic party politics. For Peacock, the 'political' violence that emerges in and around architectural settings, whether the Capitol Riot in January 2021 or the 1985 riots that came to frame thinking about Broadwater Farm for decades, needs to addressed politically. His suggestion is that, on the contrary, it has too often been considered an issue of design and environmental determinism.

In focusing on this Peacock seeks to move debates about Broadwater Farm away from the issue of violence, and the stigma it has brought to its community for over 30 years, and focuses his critique on the political response and causes of the problems that culminated in the 1985 riots. He particularly takes issue with what he defines as the social determinism ascribed to architecture and environmental design discernible in the theories of Oscar Newman and, in the UK context, Alice Coleman. The influence of these ideas is still felt today through the UK's *Secured by Design* agenda, its integration of policing into design debates and, more recently, the 'enshrinement' of security and policing in the actual Building Regulations of the United Kingdom.

This essay argues that the particular political climate in the United Kingdom in the mid-1980s facilitated the elision of the riots with other issues politically relevant at the time. For example, the racial component of the unrest was easily connected to concerns about immigration embedded in Right-Wing thinking since Enoch Powell's 1968 *Rivers of Blood* speech, and still evident in Margaret Thatcher's more anodyne repetition of its core themes in 1978. Similarly, Peacock also underlines how housing as an issue was, throughout the 1970s and still in the 1980s, highly politicised and at the centre of wranglings between the then Central Tory Government and local Labour administrations responsible at that juncture for the borough in which Broadwater Farm is located.

The elision of party politics, racial tensions, civil unrest and architectural design then, represent for Peacock a cauldron of confusion and competing agendas that, as is to be expected, have harmed the community of Broadwater Farm for decades. It is a concoction of competing agendas that, he reminds us, is still at play and was clearly evident in the discourses that followed the 2011 riots across London and the United Kingdom more widely.

In bringing us to the United Kingdom and London in particular, Peacock's essay on architecture and its political context in the late 20th century connects us to the last essay in this section, Murray Fraser's *Germania-on-Thames*, which discusses the emergence of fascism in 1930s Britain. It draws parallels between the storming of the Capitol and fascist spectacles of the 1930s in Germany and Britain in various ways, including the identification of two spatial strategies – the *frontal march and assault* on a symbolic location, and the deployment of the 'political rally' as a mode of engagement. Fraser's essay looks at the themes of this book in a way that does not shy from highlighting pseudo-fascist tendencies in the US political administration of 2016–2020 and identifies them, as echoing trends in the United Kingdom today. His primary concern is, however, the documentation of fascism in the United Kingdom in the 1930s and, more precisely, the incorporation and alignment of certain British architects in the fascist fold during that period. He does this through a detailed examination of the aesthetics of fascism as manifest in the UK context, and a thorough documentation of the relationship between British architects of the 1930s and the country's principal fascist political party, Oswald Mosley's British Union of Fascists.

Fraser's essay highlights the most conspicuous aesthetic manifestations of British Fascism in the British Union of Fascists rallies at the Olympia exhibition centre, June 7, 1934, and at Earl's Court on July 16, 1939. He critiques both events within the frames of reference of Benjamin's warnings on the aestheticisation of politics under fascism and highlights the communicative modes of spectacle employed: theatrical, cinematic and rhetorical. The associated 'politicised violence' of British Fascism may have been insignificant in comparison to other countries at the time but nevertheless, as Fraser also points out, it was there at every turn. It was manifest in manufacturing a climate of fear for small-scale political speeches and rallies by Mosley; in the police-protected stand-off with anti-fascist demonstrators at the Battle of Cable Street; and in the silencing of hecklers at the spectacles of Olympia and Earl's Court themselves. Similarly, at play in British Fascism, Fraser reminds us, was the cult of the leader who through his narratives of brutishness and his call to 'keep Britain great' eerily echoed the manners and rhetoric of Donald Trump and demonstrators at the Capitol building.

In linking the politics of 1930s Fascism in Britain with the practice of architecture, Fraser also discusses the aesthetic influence of both Mussolini's brand of fascism and that of Hitler's Nazi Germany. Aesthetically, the unique conditions of Britain as a declining Imperial power and constitutional monarchy meant its engagement with the aesthetics of modernism – as 'symbolic' of the new political age – were always tempered by a respect for tradition that resulted in a complex position with regard to culture and design. He also highlights how these debates fed into the mainstream professional press via the *Architect's Journal* and the commissions obtained by those architects associating themselves with the British Union of Fascists, as well as through sympathisers outside the activist fold.

Fraser's theoretical mode of analysis for this is Benjamin and, significantly, Gramsci, from whom he borrows critiques filtered through the aestheticisation of politics and the War of Position. In doing so, he connects with two of the key thinkers that inform the final essay in the book, Nadir Lahiji's *The Pornographic Scene of Insurrection*. Lahiji returns us to a direct examination of the January 6th 'act' presented to all the book's authors as a provocation for thought. As with Murray Fraser, Lahiji holds no punches in his critique of these events and the figures at the symbolic head of them, drawing on the definition proffered by Alain Badiou of the *Berlusconis, the Sarkozys, the Le Pens, and the Trumps*, as the new political figures of *democratic fascism*. Indeed, it is from Badiou that Lahiji draws his title.

Badiou critiques our understanding and employment of the notion and mechanisms of democracy, suggesting that the term hides the contradictions and fallacies of a system of exploitation and embedded hierarchy and inequality. To begin a serious critique and debate about politics in this theoretical scenario Badiou, followed by Lahiji, suggests it is necessary to reveal and deconstruct the imagery that surrounds it, to *disimage* or *disimagine* it. In starting from this point, Lahiji proposes a critique of what he calls the *pornographic scene* of the media-saturated Capitol Riot. The tool he employs in that critique is an image-based parallelism with another 'revolutionary' scene captured as moving image some 100 years earlier, the staircase massacre from Sergei Eisenstein's *Battleship Potemkin*.

In bringing into his thinking the Soviet avant-garde in film, he references – albeit through a different artefact – ideas found in Annie Dell'Aria's opening text which also centred on the January 6th riot as a mediated spectacle. In some ways bringing us full circle, Lahiji also closes with a call that could be seen as directed to the artists and filmmakers referenced in our opening chapter, to create a film that *reconstructs* and *cinematographically* records the *January 6th insurrection* in such a way that it allows us to see the *political ideology* behind the neoclassical architecture and the events themselves. Lahiji then, ends the book by not only identifying the events of January 6th as political theatre, but suggesting that a variation on their current mediated representation may well be necessary, and indeed could well be a useful cultural tool – *or weapon* – in unmasking the theatrical and illusionary aspects of Western democracy itself.

The range of perspectives offered by the authors of this book then is varied. They are historical and contemporary, conceptual and practical, and focus attention on the question of politics, media, sociology and, of course, architecture. As such, they reveal much about what we defined at the outset as architecture's imbrication in political discourse and action, and how that takes on particular hues when framed within the rhetoric and tactics of populist politics. In one way or another, they all identify a certain 'weaponising of architecture' through which buildings take their place in an ideological construct – whether that be long term as a form of inclusionary or exclusionary 'socialised' built object, or momentarily in an act of symbolic image making or physical violence. They thus all point to the role of architecture as a tool in a broader 'culture war' played out in physical space and, as considered in the book that preceded this one, *Reification and Representation – Architecture in the Politico-Media Complex*, a space we can define as mediated. Whether this 'weaponising' of architecture becomes increasingly literal as it is employed in an ever more 'populist' political context, or whether it remains somewhat more symbolic in a form of Gramscian War of Position, remains to be seen.

PART ONE

1

SCREENING THE CAPITOL RIOT

Annie Dell'Aria

> Poor images are thus popular images—images that can be made and seen by the many. They express all the contradictions of the contemporary crowd: its opportunism, narcissism, desire for autonomy and creation, its inability to focus or make up its mind, its constant readiness for transgression and simultaneous submission.
>
> Hito Steyerl, "In Defense of the Poor Image"

Introduction

Inside the Capitol building on February 9, 2021, Democratic Congressman Jaime Raskin opened the second impeachment trial of Donald J. Trump by arguing that failing to impeach the former president for inciting the Capitol Riot would "risk allowing January sixth to become our future." "And what will that mean for America?" he continued, "I'll show you." Then, in the very same place, the events occurred a month before, Raskin and the Democrats screened a harrowing 13-minute video of the January 6 breach of the Capitol building. This chaotic collage, arranged in chronological order, featured shaky, handheld video cross-cut with news coverage of Trump's rally, C-SPAN footage of the House and Senate floors, and sober intertitles. The angry roar of the mob, including profanities that transgressed the rules of both the Senate chambers and the many media outlets that carried the trial, scored a video that was violent not only in terms of the actions captured within the frame but also visually through its disorienting camera movement and an aspect ratio that fluttered between widescreen, televisual, and vertical smartphone. Each individual clip could be seen as what filmmaker Hito Steyerl calls a "poor image"—video ripped from its original source, distributed with incredible speed through a variety of online networks, and repurposed.

DOI: 10.4324/9781003272076-3

Many commentators, journalists, and legislators remarked that the video was traumatic, shocking, and deeply upsetting. The footage, however, was nothing new. Clips screened on individual phones, laptops, and television screens on January 6th as events unfolded. In the weeks that followed, law enforcement, pundits, journalists, and others replayed these clips hundreds of times, freeze-framing, reversing, and dissecting footage for analysis. When these separate videos coalesced for screening at the impeachment trial, they "def[ied] the thermodynamic law of the Internet age" and actually became "*more* compelling with time" rather than forgotten.[1]

Raskin's screening set the tone for a trial that centered video as evidence, pointing to how the circulation, accumulation, and assemblage of digital video from surveillant gazes both participatory and institutional have become primary agents of both policing and politics in the 21st century. On-the-ground video footage from an array of sources coalesces into a dense montage at the same time that it is parsed out, analyzed, slowed down, and used as spatial evidence for media, prosecutors, and online communities. These two operations—the affective aggregation and the analytic dissection—occur together, and just below the impeachment video's drama as short film and richness as evidence lay a host of contradictions and conundrums about how digital media, visual culture, and the built environment intersected during the Trump era. This essay is an attempt to tease out some of these underlying questions, probing the "contradictions of the contemporary crowd" expressed in poor images. I do so by exploring the theme of density along three readings of the insurrection's digital evidence: as performative utterance of the crowd, as material evidence, and as assemblage. I conclude each section by exploring the work of contemporary artists in and around the Trump era that tackle these problematics head-on rather than sublimating them for the sake of narrative cohesion or evidentiary clarity: *HEWILLNOTDIVIDE. US*, a participatory artwork by LaBeouf, Rönkkö & Turner; the research practices of Forensic Architecture; and the video collages of Arthur Jafa.

Casting Call

Following months of baseless claims of election fraud, Donald Trump planned the "Save America" rally on the day of the Electoral College certification of his defeat. Trump's supporters gathered to hear him speak from a stage on the Ellipse, a 52-acre park just south of the White House and bordering Constitution Avenue, the street that leads to the Capitol. Spurred by the erroneous suggestion that somehow the election results could be overturned on this day, an increasingly agitated base of supporters descended on Washington, D.C. from all over the country, some with violent intentions. As subsequent investigations and articles have found, numerous intelligence threats pointed to the potential for violence, particularly through chatter on far-right online networks. The increased security necessary to meet this threat was not granted, something strikingly at odds with the visible presence of militarized local and federal law enforcement officers during protests against racism and police brutality the previous summer. The density of the crowd, agitation spurned by Trump, and decreased security bred conditions for the most dramatic realization of how "post-truth is pre-fascism."[2] Lawmakers supporting impeachment maintained that the person most responsible for inciting the riot was Trump himself, looking to his tweets and his words on the Ellipse, which were intercut with footage of violence in the impeachment montage.

The Capitol building, one of the most iconic structures in Washington and site of the political process protestors attempted to disrupt, symbolized both the government they sought to "take back" and the empire grounded in whiteness that they believed they should rightfully inherit, prompting scholars of art and architectural history to weigh in. As Reinhold Martin argues, the appropriation of government's classical buildings as backdrops for right-wing protest is part of the same "anti-democratic performance" enacted by the National Civic Art Society (NCAS), the conservative organization that fetishizes these same buildings and seeks to standardize classical architecture across the government.[3] Martin cites the imperial origins of the Roman Pantheon—inspiration for both the Capitol building and Thomas Jefferson's Rotunda at the University of Virginia (the site of 2017's deadly "Unite the Right" rally)—to ask if the actions of rioters like the infamous "QAnon Shaman" weren't in a way auditions for parts in this theater of empire rather than acts of iconoclasm against it.

> His spear-as-flag, his costume, his gestures, and his chants did not desecrate the Senate chamber; rather, they re-sacralized it, like a conquered mosque converted into a Christian church, replacing one deified if time-worn 'founding father' with another, more entertaining model.[4]

Calling such acts "performatives"—speech acts that bring about what they claim (a concept borrowed from J.L. Austin)—Martin maintains that actions like the Capitol breach or armed demonstrations at state capitol buildings the summer before "affirm the power of the theater itself—that is, the stage on which the weapon-as-prop acquires meaning in the first place."[5] Understanding the riot as performative speech encapsulates both its theatrical components and its actual danger. Martin's reading also complicates claims that rioters' actions "desecrated" or "disrespected" an otherwise coherent symbol of democracy, a finding echoed by many other scholars of American art and architecture who pointed out how the event "implied uneasy echoes between the violence of January 6th and past centuries of American history."[6]

For Sven Lütticken, the attack on the Capitol was a fascist appropriation of *The Storming of the Winter Palace* (1920), a participatory mass spectacle in the Soviet Union that reenacted the 1917 October Revolution for an audience of over 100,000.[7] Both events featured thousands of participants as actors, used the grand architecture of the state as a stage, and played to the camera's gaze, but the more unpredictable descent into violence realized on January 6th might better be compared to an earlier participatory spectacle: Futurist theater. As Claire Bishop describes, the Futurist *serate* (Italian for "evening parties") were loosely scripted variety shows that drew from working-class entertainment, deployed populist communication strategies to advance leader F.T. Marinetti's fascist politics, and—most importantly—stirred up lively and even violent audience participation.[8] The *serate* fulfilled audiences' desire to "be part of a work of art and feel legitimated to participate in its violence." For Marinetti, their participation represented "total commitment to a cause," and as Bishop points out, paraphrasing Walter Benjamin, "Fascism is precisely the political formation that allows people to participate in, and enjoy, the spectacle of their own destruction."[9]

The New Yorker reporter Luke Mogelson, who captured some of the most harrowing moments of the riot used in the impeachment montage, recalls a similar moment after Trump summarized the alleged fraud against him as "bullshit":

> It was a peculiar mixture of emotion that had become familiar at pro-Trump rallies since he lost the election: half mutinous rage, half gleeful excitement at being licensed to act on it. The profanity signalled a final jettisoning of whatever residual deference to political norms had survived the past four years.[10]

The impeachment video opens with this appeal to the crowd (minus the curse word). In a medium shot, Trump stands at a podium bearing the presidential seal and behind bulletproof glass claiming "We will stop the steal" and telling the crowd he will "be there with" them as they walk to the Capitol (Figure 1.1). The next shot features vertically framed cell phone footage of the rally from behind the crowd with shouts of glee and "Let's take the Capitol!" (Figure 1.2). This cut from medium shot to extreme long shot shifts the viewer's perspective from the televisual to the handheld smartphone, at once removing them from Trump and placing them within the density of the crowd. Trumpism's participatory self-destruction (similar to what Jonathan Metzl calls "dying of whiteness")[11] certainly makes use of the affordances of new technologies and fetishizes both war and nation, like the Futurist *serate*, but does so not through the destruction of the past and an embrace of the future but rather with an obsessive desire to repeat the past and refortify its structures of white supremacy—to "take back" or "make...again."

Though rhetorically aligned with the past, Trumpism's violent crescendo can also be associated with the narcissistic collapse within the present frequently associated with digital media and social networks, as well as its related performance of identity. What Martin calls the "aggrieved cry of emasculated power, weaponized" from which Trumpism derives "existential meaning"[12] was cultivated largely through technologies of simultaneity—the 24/7 news networks (some peddling conspiracy theories and misinformation); the up-all-night, algorithmically programmed YouTube rabbit holes that take viewers further into

FIGURES 1.1 AND 1.2   Video stills from House impeachment trial video, 2021.

"alternative truths" and fabrications; and the temporal and spatial ubiquity of digital social networks that not only create the oft-maligned "echo chambers" that isolate and divide but also monetize extremism through clicks and comments.

In many ways, the rioters seemed to be participating through and for social networks as much as in the physical and symbolic space of the Capitol. They took selfies, recorded video, and even live-streamed their crimes as they unfolded, clips of which feature a stream of likes and comments, melding the visual space of gamers with the material space of the Capitol.[13] Building on Wendy Hui Kyong Chun's analysis of how social media's hyper-individualization, dispersed networks, and echo chambers fracture our experience of time and space, Lütticken claims the riots realized that the space and time of the nation are themselves becoming increasingly divided and fractured…imagined networks giv[e] rise to communities that reimagine the history of the nation, becoming parallel societies; in the process, the space of networks seeps into physical space.[14]

If the riot at the Capitol dramatized the seepage of network space into physical space at the end of Trump's presidency, a participatory artwork in Queens, New York did so at its very beginning. *HEWILLNOTDIVIDE.US* (2017–2021) by the artist collective LaBeouf, Rönkkö & Turner originally featured a webcam and microphone attached to an external wall of the Museum of the Moving Image (MoMI) (Figure 1.3). Sound and video streamed to the work's titular website, whose words appeared as mantra printed in black letters on the plain white wall that hosted the recording devices. The work began on January 20, 2017, Trump's inauguration day, with the stated intention of remaining throughout the Trump presidency. The site in Queens, however, lasted only a mere three weeks. The work received a fair amount of press, in part due to the involvement of Hollywood actor Shia LaBeouf, and eventually became a viral topic on internet communities such as the far-right hub 4chan. Within the project's opening days, conflicts arose and hate speech started to appear, most often with reference to alt-right memes that give certain behaviors the veneer of irony and humor or the inscrutability of in-group codes, such as drinking milk as a sign of white supremacist identity.[15] Though controversy garnered most of the attention, the participation captured within the static mise-en-scene of the security camera was actually a mixed bag. Regular samples at every hour indicate far more downtime than agitation, and even moments of genuine discussion and debate.[16] Situated at

FIGURE 1.3 LaBeouf, Rönkkö & Turner, *HEWILLNOTDIVIDE.US*, 2017–2021. Video still from day one 2017.

the intersection of surveillance and celebrity, the work overlapped the digital and physical public spheres to bring a fractured commons into focus. The artwork's failure to persist as a stable site of open participation foregrounds how quickly digital spheres where Trumpism thrives threaten the physical and social spaces of democracy and public speech.

Shooting Video

Just as Raskin prefaced the impeachment screening with "I'll show you," he followed it by pointing to the screen and claiming, "You ask what a high crime and misdemeanor is under our Constitution, that's a high crime and misdemeanor," conflating the video compilation with the act itself. Laura Saltzman contends that video's ontology is rooted in its etymology—the Latin *video* or "I see."[17] Countering Rosalind Krauss's theorization of video as rooted in narcissism, Saltzman instead looks to the social function of a recorded video's delayed screening. In these moments, when video "asks that we bear witness to its act of witness," its declaration moves from "I see" to "I saw."[18] This function of video as witness is perhaps why the site-specific screening in the Capitol Building carried the affective weight of emotional testimony while also providing concrete evidence of events.

The on-the-ground, handheld footage joins a genealogy of home movies of significant acts of violence in U.S. history from the Zapruder film to the George Holliday videotape to Darnella Frazier's cell phone, though, as we shall see, the presence of the camera did more than merely capture events from the bystander's perspective.[19] The sheer density of cameras present provided opportunity for analysis in the aggregate as well as within the frame. Theories of digital media often assume a lack of indexicality, its "immaterial" or "disembodied" nature, but, as Jennifer Malkowski maintains, "this drama of referentiality seems surprisingly irrelevant in the reception of digital documentary" and its capacity to communicate embodiment in scenes of violence.[20] Indeed, the Capitol screening could be read through the bodies of its spectators: journalists remarked how the footage made them feel physically ill and Republican senators still aligned with Trump and seeking to downplay the event's severity noticeably shifted in their chairs, averted their gazes, or busied themselves with paperwork.

During the events of January 6th one death was captured on video, that of U.S. military veteran and avid Trump supporter Ashli Babbitt. Available footage of the shooting was captured from the rioter's side of a makeshift barricade erected by security to protect the entrance to the Speaker's Lobby, where members of Congress were steps away. In a two-minute video analyzed by *The Washington Post*, part of which was included in the impeachment montage, the camera moves with relative ease through a few rows of people to blocked doors protected by two unarmed Capitol policemen that members of the crowd berate and taunt.[21] As the confrontation escalates, rioters begin punching and shattering a glass pane on the wooden doors in front of the barricade. As the two unarmed officers move out, the protesters smash the window and chant "break it down." As the confrontation escalates, the handheld camera moves closer to the door and periodically pans back to survey the group, creating a visual juxtaposition between a sea of "Make America Great Again" hats at the bottom of the screen and two formal portraits of former statesmen on the wall above. As the glass shatters, the camera pans back to the barricade and a gun emerges on the left side of the frame; the videographer points and shouts "there's a gun!" followed by a shot. The camera follows the shot and Babbitt as she falls back, the footage mercifully blurred.

The evidentiary content of the footage is robust, being used in both legal and journalistic accounts, though its ethics as documentary footage is murkier. In terms of the position inscribed within the clip, the gaze is both "accidental" and "helpless," drawing from Vivian Sobchack's taxonomy of acceptable ethical gazes in footage of death.[22] The death was unpredicted and the camera operator is clearly blocked from intervening once the danger arose. Looking to the video's source, however, complicates the camera's presence. Most of this footage was taken by John Earle Sullivan, known on social media as "Jayden X" (his watermark overlays footage he shot in both the *Washington Post* video and the impeachment montage). Sullivan is a controversial figure and self-proclaimed activist, though he was publicly disowned by groups such as Black Lives Matter Utah for being an instigator and troublemaker before the events of January 6th. Many have concluded that he is largely self-interested since he monetizes his footage and seems to have only tenuous ties to any activist group.[23] Following analysis of Sullivan's footage and that of others that captured his presence, he was arrested by federal agents on charges relating to participation in the riot, and $90,000 in payments from mainstream media outlets was seized from his account (Figure 1.4).[24]

FIGURE 1.4 Video still from House impeachment trial video, 2021.

If Sullivan allegedly participated in and even stoked the anger of the unruly mob, helping bring about the circumstances that both produced the threat of lethal violence and caused the officer to fire, then the camera's gaze becomes part of what it captures. The many cameras seen within his frame also allude to how participants perhaps were in some ways performing their actions for or with the camera. As Ariella Azoulay maintains, "the act of photography constitutes a *subject-hostage*" who "commands space, documents it, and, in fact, from the moment he wields the camera becomes a captive to the camera's activity."[25] The impunity with which many rioters photographed, recorded, and live-streamed their participation speaks to this transformation. Sullivan's financial motivations for capturing such footage verges into the ethically ambiguous territory of what Sobchack dubs the "professional" gaze,[26] as determined by algorithms and a clickbait economy.

Much like its purported lack of indexicality, theories of digital media also often claim it is placeless and untethered, though more recent scholarship demonstrates that the digital is very much part of increasingly specific, surgical, and multilayered productions of place.[27] Silvana Mandolessi contends that digital memory practices partake in a layered "performance" of place, meaning digital media "construct spatial assemblages" of data, turn place into an "event," and "do something" beyond description.[28] The sheer density of information afforded by digital technologies on January 6th allows both certain actions and actors to be placed "at the scene of the crime" and actively performs place in different ways.

Cameras captured events from multiple angles, and geotags and cell phone pings located participants with incredible accuracy, even allowing researchers to conclude that participants were both not local and politically isolated.[29] A digital animation created for *The New York Times* shows the movement of protesters from the park outside the White House to the Capitol building using cell phone data.[30] Overlaid onto a grayscale satellite image of the National Mall, a swarm of green dots darts from left to right in a GIF that visually resembles the digital animations of data overlapping space in the film *The Matrix* (1999). Using a massive cache of data, the GIF attempts to provide a singular, coherent visual image unavailable otherwise due to Washington, D.C.'s strict proscription against helicopters and drones.[31] In this way, the same technologies that are often charged with fracturing time and space produced the only spatial and temporal visualizations that staged place as an event.

Research collective Forensic Architecture similarly seeks to construct memory from digital fragments, but by turning to the built environment as a witness itself. Founded in 2010 and headed by Eyal Weizman, Forensic Architecture (also the name of the field they coined) researches human rights violations and environmental crimes by mobilizing crowdsourced digital evidence and the affordances of digital technologies, including simulation, data visualization, and mapping. Their work has been exhibited at art museums and biennials all over the world, bridging the spheres of art and social justice. For Weizman, forensic architecture "conceives of spaces/events as material and temporal hybrids distributed throughout the entire architectural field" and "is inclined towards complex, sometimes unstable and even contradictory accounts of events."[32] The digital animation of cell phone pings points to this manner of staging place as an event, as does a 40-minute documentary released by *The New York Times* that synchronizes and maps events based on a six-month investigation of thousands of hours of video footage and police radio.[33] Certainly more projects like this will emerge with time, but what would it mean to look to the built environment itself for evidence in the Capitol Riot? To engage with the "sometimes unstable and even contradictory accounts" that emerge? And how might such a turn to the spatiality of events uncover not just the riot itself but its origins and causes?

Postproduction

Columnist Margaret Sullivan, when attempting to describe why the impeachment montage was so terrifying, wrote "Now, we could finally see context. We could see cause and effect...Set down in a straightforward timeline, the cellphone clips began to form something understandable, if not remotely sensible."[34] Editing provided a kind of cinematic suture to bring temporal and spatial coherence to a series of fragments. Opening with Trump's rally, handheld cameras follow groups from the Ellipse, down Constitution Avenue, to the barriers outside the Capitol, and into its inner chambers. This spatial progression is cross-cut with footage of debate and procedure within the Capitol, captured with the familiar, sleepy mise-en-scene of C-SPAN. Shot from the balcony, the high angle long shots of the C-SPAN coverage of the Electoral College certification have an aesthetic of visual, institutional, and spatial stability as well as a soundscape that is clear, intelligible, and textured with the echo of the grand space. The footage of the crowd, on the other hand, is shaky, crowded, and often inaudible. At times the audio bleeds across the cut and stitches the places together, such as when Trump's words regarding Vice President Mike Pence continue to play as the video cuts from his podium on the Ellipse to C-SPAN footage of a Pence (wearing a mask in the midst of the COVID-19 pandemic) in the House Chamber. Audio similarly plays over the black intertitles, which narrate events and provide sobering visual pauses. Despite the video's lack of explanatory voiceover, it still makes use of documentary and narrative conventions of intertitles and cross-cutting to make the danger palpable.

The montage also bears the traces of its fragmented source material. Aspect ratio and image resolution vary widely, and much of the footage appears with textual watermarks that overlay video's space of witness with the flatness of the digital brand. Online sources like "JAYDEN X" and "ABQ RAW" (a self-described "Run and Gun Web, Video Guerrilla Documentary Filmmaking/News channel" based in Albuquerque, New Mexico)[35] mingle with Instagram handles of citizen journalists and logos for *The New Yorker*, *The Washington Post*, and *C-SPAN*. Residing on the surface of the screen, these brands, along with the black panels that pop up when aspect ratio shifts to the vertical smartphone, disrupt the space within the frame and assert the plane of the screen. The motley sources both point to how cameras of different types blanket public space at events like the Capitol Riot and mimic how we encounter such events on screens and from a variety of independent, mainstream, and even questionable sources.

This is not to suggest in any way that the footage is suspect, as Trump's defense team tried to claim of the video's editing. Instead, I seek to point to traces of the same digital and televisual mediascape that helped produce Trumpism within the impeachment montage. The search for "high-octane" footage follows in the footsteps of reality-tv programming, specifically shows like *Cops* (Fox, 1989–2013, various networks until 2020).[36] As Anita Biressi and Heather Nunn maintain,

> [Shows like *Cops*] constitute a new spectacle of criminality in which it is not the punishment but the act of crime itself presented in the public sphere. Here criminality is visible, often dramatic and unprovoked, yet it can be rewound, replayed, and slowed down for viewers as if it were a sports program…each component, video clip, interview, still image, and so forth—variously sourced and infinitely reproducible—has become a unit of exchange, a small piece of an electronic televisual assemblage.[37]

The "electronic televisual assemblage" of *Cops* is, of course, always bracketed by the law's sovereignty, something that is largely absent in the riot footage.[38] Furthermore, at the time of writing, the criminality captured with the video was even called "legitimate political discourse" by Republican party leadership.[39]

In her influential 2009 essay *In Defense of the Poor Image*, German filmmaker and artist Hito Steyerl examines how the accelerated circulation of digital videos (and their subsequent compression and remixing) create new networks and economies. Ripped, downloaded, and shared, poor images "testify to the violent dislocation, transferals, and displacement of images" just as they challenge the primacy of resolution.[40] In so doing, poor images both point to the emancipatory potential of alternative cinemas and image economies and become battlegrounds for nation, capital, and hate in new ways. Twelve years later, the compression and blur of "poor images" is less pronounced, even as the speeds of their transmission and mutation have increased. In the impeachment montage, some poor images shot on cell phones and uploaded to social media are nearly as rich with resolution as videos from official channels and television. Their trajectory from social media post to television clip to legal exhibit reverses the movements of piracy and sharing discussed by Steyerl, though resolution remains an instrument of power.

Arthur Jafa's recent work demonstrates other ways of producing narratives and potentialities between ripped digital fragments, working across their various resolutions, watermarks, and ethically dubious gazes. *Love Is the Message, the Message Is Death* (2016), Jafa's much-celebrated seven-minute video collage has become one of the defining statements in American contemporary art of the Trump era (though somewhat accidentally, as the work debuted before the 2016 election).

Jafa stitches together snippets of Black expression and experience, from the exuberant to the abject, scored with Kanye West's gospel-inspired song "Ultralight Beam." For his material, the artist culled the vast archive of the poor image, frequently bearing the traces of its low resolution or copyrighted watermark. Recalling the corporeal violence of the brand, "getty images" sits atop black and white news footage of Martin Luther King, Jr. and the burning of a Black church, for instance. "What emerges is not some stonily virtuous monument to Black history but instead a staccato commentary on the power of capital to link the pleasures of the spectacle to the terror of race," in the words of Tobi Haslett.[41] As Christina Knight contends, the work also structures modes of Black community building and being in the world through the formal evocation of Black vocal intonation and the theme of falling.[42] Jafa calls his process of selection and editing one of "affective proximity," a term inspired by the work of filmmaker John Akomfrah and first explored in the Jafa's collage books.

The affective proximity of the clips in Jafa's more recent and much longer piece *The White Album* (2018) deliberately creates a sense of unease and space to confront some of the societal truths behind the Capitol Riot in its 40-minute loop. *The White Album* again turns primarily to online sources only this time to interrogate whiteness as pathology, stitching together music videos, film clips, viral videos of pranks and racist online rants, and grainy surveillance footage of drone strikes and the moments before racial violence. Intercut with this digital collage are high-definition shots of Jafa's white friends, such as gallerist Gavin Brown, where the camera lingers on faces and skin. Unlike in his earlier montage of Black pain and expression, where clips are mere seconds and deny the viewer's gaze a sense of ownership or control, the fragments in *The White Album* linger, forcing viewers to sit with uncomfortable truths in the dark space of projection and absent of the emotional swell of West's music. In some ways, the work tugs at the threads that stitch together the evidentiary narrative of the impeachment montage—not to expose it as mere fabrication but to reveal how simultaneously interwoven the most violent and troubling myths of whiteness are to the entire American project.

Conclusion

Strictly speaking, the impeachment video failed as evidence. The second impeachment of Trump, the first ever against a president who had left office, did not result in a Senate conviction. The video montage and wealth of evidence were no match for the entrenched partisan divide and the block of Trump loyalists in the legislature. The video is also, of course, not a work of art, and we should not expect it to engage the same themes as art or make the same kind of space for uncertainty and contradiction. Nevertheless, the collage of images screened as evidence synthesizes more than just the timeline of January 6th. The medley of video sources through which we collectively experienced the terrifying events circulate and move with the speed of the "poor image," but with place-bound metadata and increased resolution. Their aggregation into a widely viewed 13-minute video churned stomachs and forced averted gazes when screened to a still-traumatized audience at the site of its profilmic event, but for all its power as witness and evidence, the video's embedded data and particular aesthetics also point to a public sphere fractured by conspiracy and fabrication. Contemporary artworks that dwell in these spaces of instability—in the gaps in the data, in the flutter of aspect ratios, and along the scrim of the watermark—offer a way through the murky waters of the post-truth age, and perhaps toward new ways of constructing a public sphere.

Notes

1 Margaret Sullivan, "Perspective | The Jan. 6 Images Were Already Disturbing. The Impeachment-Trial Video Makes Them Terrifying.," *The Washington Post*, February 10, 2021, https://www.washingtonpost.com/lifestyle/media/impeachment-insurrection-video/2021/02/09/85463eb0-6b1f-11eb-ba56-d7e2c8defa31_story.html.

2 Timothy Snyder, "The American Abyss," *The New York Times*, January 9, 2021, sec. Magazine, https://www.nytimes.com/2021/01/09/magazine/trump-coup.html.

3 Reinhold Martin, "Exit, Stage Right," *Places Journal*, May 4, 2021, https://placesjournal.org/article/the-white-nationalist-crusade-for-neoclassical-architecture/.

4 Martin.

5 Martin.

6 Wendy Bellion and Anna O. Marley, "Art and Politics in the US Capitol: Introduction," *Panorama: Journal of the Association of Historians of American Art* 7, no. 1 (Spring 2021), https://editions.lib.umn.edu/panorama/article/art-and-politics-in-the-us-capitol/. From a special section "Art and Politics in the US Capitol."

7 Sven Lütticken, "Divergent States of Emergence: Remarks on Potential Possibilities, Against All Odds," *E-Flux* 115 (February 2021), https://www.e-flux.com/journal/115/374499/divergent-states-of-emergence-remarks-on-potential-possibilities-against-all-odds/.

8 Claire Bishop, *Artificial Hells: Participatory Art and the Politics of Spectatorship* (London: Verso Books, 2012), 45–47.

9 Bishop, 46–47.

10 Luke Mogelson, "Among the Insurrectionists," *The New Yorker*, January 15, 2021, https://www.newyorker.com/magazine/2021/01/25/among-the-insurrectionists.

11 Jonathan M. Metzl, *Dying of Whiteness: How the Politics of Racial Resentment Is Killing America's Heartland* (New York: Basic Books, 2019).

12 Martin, "Exit, Stage Right."

13 Importantly, these live-stream videos were not those included in the opening impeachment montage, though, as I examine in the next section, close scrutiny of specific video sources used by impeachment managers reveals an ethically complicated network of sources.

14 Lütticken, "Divergent States of Emergence."

15 Ellen Gillooly-Kress, "#HEWILLNOTDIVIDEUS: Weaponizing Performance of Identity from the Digital to the Physical," *The Journal of American Drama and Theatre (JADT)* 30, no. 2 (Spring 2018), https://jadtjournal.org/2018/05/29/hewillnotdivideus/.

16 I analyzed the work's participation more fully by coding one minute out of every hour in Annie Dell'Aria, "From Rallying Cry to Dysfunctional Site: Surveying Participation in HEWILLNOTDIVIDE.US," *International Journal of Performance Arts and Digital Media* 15, no. 1 (January 2, 2019): 84–103.

17 Lisa Saltzman, *Making Memory Matter: Strategies of Remembrance in Contemporary Art* (Chicago: University of Chicago Press, 2006), 29.

18 Saltzman, 30.
19 Abram Zapruder recorded the assassination of John F. Kennedy in Dallas in 1963, Holliday taped the beating of Rodney King by Los Angeles police in 1991 from his balcony, and Darnella Frazier courageously turned her phone on to capture the murder of George Floyd by Minneapolis police officer Derek Chauvin in 2020.
20 Jennifer Malkowski, *Dying in Full Detail: Mortality and Digital Documentary* (Durham: Duke University Press, 2017), 8.
21 Jon Swaine et al., "Video Shows Fatal Shooting of Ashli Babbitt in the Capitol," *The Washington Post*, January 8, 2021, https://www.washingtonpost.com/investigations/2021/01/08/ashli-babbitt-shooting-video-capitol/.
22 Vivian Sobchack, "Inscribing Ethical Space: Ten Propositions on Death, Representation, and Documentary," *Quarterly Review of Film Studies* 9, no. 4 (Fall 1984): 294–295.
23 This does not, however, stop rightwing media outlets from using his presence to support conspiracy theories that violence was actually perpetuated by left-wing persons posing as Trump supporters. Clark McCauley, "Introduction to the Special Issue: Putting the Capitol Breach in Context," *Dynamics of Asymmetric Conflict* 14, no. 2 (May 4, 2021): 98, https://doi.org/10.1080/17467586.2021.1925136.
24 Swaine et al., "Video Shows Fatal Shooting of Ashli Babbitt in the Capitol"; Tom Jackman, Marissa J. Lang, and Jon Swaine, "Man Who Shot Video of Fatal Capitol Shooting Is Arrested, Remains Focus of Political Storm," *The Washington Post*, January 16, 2021, https://www.washingtonpost.com/nation/2021/01/16/sullivan-video-arrested/.
25 Ariella Azoulay, *Death's Showcase: The Power of Image in Contemporary Democracy* (Cambridge: MIT Press, 2001), 92.
26 Sobchack, "Inscribing Ethical Space," 295.
27 See Germaine R. Halegoua, *The Digital City: Media and the Social Production of Place* (New York: NYU Press, 2020).
28 Silvana Mandolessi, "Challenging the Placeless Imaginary in Digital Memories: The Performance of Place in the Work of Forensic Architecture," *Memory Studies* 14, no. 3 (June 1, 2021): 622–633, https://doi.org/10.1177/17506980211010922.
29 David Van Dijcke and Austin L. Wright, "Profiling Insurrection: Characterizing Collective Action Using Mobile Device Data," SSRN Scholarly Paper (Rochester, NY: Social Science Research Network, January 31, 2021), https://doi.org/10.2139/ssrn.3776854.
30 Charlie Warzel and Stuart A. Thompson, "Opinion | They Stormed the Capitol. Their Apps Tracked Them.," *The New York Times*, February 5, 2021, sec. Opinion, https://www.nytimes.com/2021/02/05/opinion/capitol-attack-cellphone-data.html.
31 Steve Doig, "It Is Difficult, If Not Impossible, to Estimate the Size of the Crowd That Stormed Capitol Hill," *The Conversation*, January 8, 2021, http://theconversation.com/it-is-difficult-if-not-impossible-to-estimate-the-size-of-the-crowd-that-stormed-capitol-hill-152889.
32 Eyal Weizman et al., "Forensic Architecture," *Architectural Design* 80, no. 5 (2010): 62–63, https://doi.org/10.1002/ad.1134.
33 The New York Times, "Inside the Capitol Riot: An Exclusive Video Investigation," *The New York Times*, June 30, 2021, sec. U.S., https://www.nytimes.com/2021/06/30/us/jan-6-capitol-attack-takeaways.html.
34 Sullivan, "Perspective | The Jan. 6 Images Were Already Disturbing. The Impeachment-Trial Video Makes Them Terrifying."
35 Like Sullivan, ABQ RAW appears to be an independent video source that seeks out sensational content. Their top viewed clips on YouTube include a conspiracy theory video claiming to have spotted deceased sex offender Jeffrey Epstein, raising questions about their journalistic motives and integrity. "ABQ RAW - YouTube," accessed June 27, 2021, https://www.youtube.com/c/Abqraw/videos?view=0&sort=p&flow=grid.

36 This is the term used by RMG Media, an independent video outlet based in Los Angeles that captured footage of the shooting of Ashli Babbitt used in conjunction with Sullivan's by *The Washington Post*. According to their website, they sell "adrenaline-fueled breaking news footage" captured while "armed with video cameras, a $100 police scanner, and a map" to mainstream news outlets. "About Us," RMG News, accessed June 26, 2021, http://rmgnews.com/wp/?page_id=2035.
37 Anita Biressi and Heather Nunn, "Video Justice: Crimes of Violence in Social/Media Space," *Space and Culture* 6, no. 3 (August 2003): 278–279, https://doi.org/10.1177/1206331203251659.
38 Biressi and Nunn, 287–288. *Cops* was finally cancelled in 2020 in the wake of world-wide protests against police brutality, and it and shows like it faced decades of criticism for the heroization of police, demonization of largely poor and nonwhite offenders, and unethical tactics for capturing arrests on tape.
39 Jonathan Weisman and Reid J. Epstein, "G.O.P. Declares Jan. 6 Attack 'Legitimate Political Discourse,'" *The New York Times*, February 4, 2022, sec. U.S., https://www.nytimes.com/2022/02/04/us/politics/republicans-jan-6-cheney-censure.html.
40 Hito Steyerl, "In Defense of the Poor Image," *E-Flux* 10 (November 2009), http://www.e-flux.com/journal/10/61362/in-defense-of-the-poor-image/.
41 Tobi Haslett, "Tobi Haslett on Arthur Jafa's Love Is the Message, the Message Is Death," *Artforum*, December 9, 2016, https://www.artforum.com/film/tobi-haslett-on-arthur-jafa-s-love-is-the-message-the-message-is-death-65183.
42 Christina Knight, "Feeling and Falling in Arthur Jafa's Love Is the Message, the Message Is Death," *The Black Scholar* 49, no. 3 (July 3, 2019): 36–47, https://doi.org/10.1080/00064246.2019.1619120.

Bibliography

"ABQ RAW - YouTube." Accessed June 27, 2021. https://www.youtube.com/c/Abqraw/videos?view=0&sort=p&flow=grid.

Azoulay, Ariella. *Death's Showcase: The Power of Image in Contemporary Democracy*. Cambridge: MIT Press, 2001.

Bellion, Wendy, and Anna O. Marley. "Art and Politics in the US Capitol: Introduction." *Panorama: Journal of the Association of Historians of American Art* 7, no. 1 (Spring 2021). https://editions.lib.umn.edu/panorama/article/art-and-politics-in-the-us-capitol/.

Biressi, Anita, and Heather Nunn. "Video Justice: Crimes of Violence in Social/Media Space." *Space and Culture* 6, no. 3 (August 2003): 276–291. https://doi.org/10.1177/1206331203251659.

Bishop, Claire. *Artificial Hells: Participatory Art and the Politics of Spectatorship*. London: Verso Books, 2012.

Dell'Aria, Annie. "From Rallying Cry to Dysfunctional Site: Surveying Participation in HEWILLNOTDIVIDE.US." *International Journal of Performance Arts and Digital Media* 15, no. 1 (January 2, 2019): 84–103.

Doig, Steve. "It Is Difficult, If Not Impossible, to Estimate the Size of the Crowd That Stormed Capitol Hill." *The Conversation*, January 8, 2021. http://theconversation.com/it-is-difficult-if-not-impossible-to-estimate-the-size-of-the-crowd-that-stormed-capitol-hill-152889.

Gillooly-Kress, Ellen. "#HEWILLNOTDIVIDEUS: Weaponizing Performance of Identity from the Digital to the Physical." *The Journal of American Drama and Theatre (JADT)* 30, no. 2 (Spring 2018). https://jadtjournal.org/2018/05/29/hewillnotdivideus/.

Halegoua, Germaine R. *The Digital City: Media and the Social Production of Place*. New York: NYU Press, 2020.

Haslett, Tobi. "Tobi Haslett on Arthur Jafa's Love Is the Message, the Message Is Death." *Artforum*, December 9, 2016. https://www.artforum.com/film/tobi-haslett-on-arthur-jafa-s-love-is-the-message-the-message-is-death-65183.

Jackman, Tom, Marissa J. Lang, and Jon Swaine. "Man Who Shot Video of Fatal Capitol Shooting Is Arrested, Remains Focus of Political Storm." *The Washington Post*, January 16, 2021. https://www.washingtonpost.com/nation/2021/01/16/sullivan-video-arrested/.

Knight, Christina. "Feeling and Falling in Arthur Jafa's Love Is the Message, the Message Is Death." *The Black Scholar* 49, no. 3 (July 3, 2019): 36–47. https://doi.org/10.1080/00064246.2019.1619120.

Lütticken, Sven. "Divergent States of Emergence: Remarks on Potential Possibilities, Against All Odds." *E-Flux* 115 (February 2021). https://www.e-flux.com/journal/115/374499/divergent-states-of-emergence-remarks-on-potential-possibilities-against-all-odds/.

Malkowski, Jennifer. *Dying in Full Detail: Mortality and Digital Documentary*. Durham: Duke University Press, 2017.

Mandolessi, Silvana. "Challenging the Placeless Imaginary in Digital Memories: The Performance of Place in the Work of Forensic Architecture." *Memory Studies* 14, no. 3 (June 1, 2021): 622–633. https://doi.org/10.1177/17506980211010922.

Martin, Reinhold. "Exit, Stage Right." *Places Journal*, May 4, 2021. https://placesjournal.org/article/the-white-nationalist-crusade-for-neoclassical-architecture/.

McCauley, Clark. "Introduction to the Special Issue: Putting the Capitol Breach in Context." *Dynamics of Asymmetric Conflict* 14, no. 2 (May 4, 2021): 94–109. https://doi.org/10.1080/17467586.2021.1925136.

Metzl, Jonathan M. *Dying of Whiteness: How the Politics of Racial Resentment Is Killing America's Heartland*. New York: Basic Books, 2019.

Mogelson, Luke. "Among the Insurrectionists." *The New Yorker*, January 15, 2021. https://www.newyorker.com/magazine/2021/01/25/among-the-insurrectionists.

RMG News. "About Us." Accessed June 26, 2021. http://rmgnews.com/wp/?page_id=2035.

Saltzman, Lisa. *Making Memory Matter: Strategies of Remembrance in Contemporary Art*. Chicago: University of Chicago Press, 2006.

Snyder, Timothy. "The American Abyss." *The New York Times*, January 9, 2021, sec. Magazine. https://www.nytimes.com/2021/01/09/magazine/trump-coup.html.

Sobchack, Vivian. "Inscribing Ethical Space: Ten Propositions on Death, Representation, and Documentary." *Quarterly Review of Film Studies* 9, no. 4 (Fall 1984): 283–300.

Steyerl, Hito. "In Defense of the Poor Image." *E-Flux* 10 (November 2009). http://www.e-flux.com/journal/10/61362/in-defense-of-the-poor-image/.

Sullivan, Margaret. "Perspective | The Jan. 6 Images Were Already Disturbing. The Impeachment-Trial Video Makes Them Terrifying." *The Washington Post*, February 10, 2021. https://www.washingtonpost.com/lifestyle/media/impeachment-insurrection-video/2021/02/09/85463eb0-6b1f-11eb-ba56-d7e2c8defa31_story.html.

Swaine, Jon, Dalton Bennett, Joyce Sohyun Lee, and Meg Kelly. "Video Shows Fatal Shooting of Ashli Babbitt in the Capitol." *The Washington Post*, January 8, 2021. https://www.washingtonpost.com/investigations/2021/01/08/ashli-babbitt-shooting-video-capitol/.

Times, The New York. "Inside the Capitol Riot: An Exclusive Video Investigation." *The New York Times*, June 30, 2021, sec. U.S. https://www.nytimes.com/2021/06/30/us/jan-6-capitol-attack-takeaways.html.

Van Dijcke, David, and Austin L. Wright. "Profiling Insurrection: Characterizing Collective Action Using Mobile Device Data." SSRN Scholarly Paper. Rochester, NY: Social Science Research Network, January 31, 2021. https://doi.org/10.2139/ssrn.3776854.

Warzel, Charlie, and Stuart A. Thompson. "Opinion | They Stormed the Capitol. Their Apps Tracked Them." *The New York Times*, February 5, 2021, sec. Opinion. https://www.nytimes.com/2021/02/05/opinion/capitol-attack-cellphone-data.html.

Weisman, Jonathan, and Reid J. Epstein. "G.O.P. Declares Jan. 6 Attack 'Legitimate Political Discourse.'" *The New York Times*, February 4, 2022, sec. U.S. https://www.nytimes.com/2022/02/04/us/politics/republicans-jan-6-cheney-censure.html.

Weizman, Eyal, Paulo Tavares, Susan Schuppli, and Situ Studio. "Forensic Architecture." *Architectural Design* 80, no. 5 (2010): 58–63. https://doi.org/10.1002/ad.1134.

2

HOUSING POPULISM

Constructing the "Little Man's" House, Deconstructing the "Queer"[1] Home

Malcolm Rio

From the Bundy standoffs in Nevada (2014) and Oregon (2016)[2] to the gun-toting McCloskeys standing on their St. Louis mansion's front yard in 2020,[3] images of "ordinary," "real Americans" defending their right to own against the imposition of established and elitist interest groups are easily made legible within the dominant tropes of contemporary media coverage.[4] Threading together these acts of armed resistance are the scenes and mythologies of property ownership, the home, and homesteading as spatial sites for politicized conflict. These acts echo in their ethos some of the founding "principles" of American democracy and later the American frontier which illustrates a specific form of political participation in the U.S. that asserts the triumph of certain rights over others; that is, private property over wildlife conservation in the case of the Bundys, or a racial outcry for justice and civil rights in the case of the McCloskeys. Paralleling the armed resistance of the Bundys and the McCloskeys, the January 6th storming of the U.S. Capitol, also commonly known as the "People's House," deployed rhetorics of the home, ownership, and property to legitimize the voting power of "real Americans" over those *Others* viewed as usurping and replacing an authority of whiteness and land tenure that was once definitive of the right to political participation. The U.S. Capitol not only provided an architectural setting to deploy such rhetorics but also, through its physical occupation, was used to embody efforts to reassert what kind of American can claim ownership over the nation.

Yet, the question remains how private property, the protection of the home, and even the normative constructions of the American family have come to be presented as the assumed baseline of public discourse while also serving as the organizing metaphors for populist contumacy. How, then, has populism been mapped onto the symbolic imaginary of home, family, and private property while making some groups fully legible and others illegible or reduced to extreme cases or routine statistics in popular discourse and media?

DOI: 10.4324/9781003272076-4

The main difficulty in writing about the relationship between architecture and populism is properly defining what "populism" and "a populist" are and what they exactly reference. Despite their ubiquity in contemporary political discourse, the terms "populism" and "populist" are quite elusive with disparate meanings for different political camps, in which the terms muddy the boundaries of seemingly contradictory political ideologies. According to a contemporary thesaurus, their close synonyms include such politically varied concepts as "Socialist," "democratic," "constitutional," and "autonomous."[5] The frequency of the use of populism and populist surged, especially across the West and in particular within American English, in the mid-2010s at a time when most Western democracies were embarking on political elections that exhibited high degrees of partisan factionalization.[6] The combination of this degree of use with the lack of precise reference results in a feedback loop in which these terms come to signify a panoply of political positions that are used in service of rhetorical sophistry rather than sincere and specific policy platforms.[7] Thus, both U.S. presidential candidate Bernie Sanders and former U.S. President Donald J. Trump could easily be labeled as "populists" in popular media despite lacking any authentically similar policies: "If everyone is a populist in one way or another, then nobody is not a populist […] It explains absolutely everything, and therefore it explains nothing."[8]

Despite the distant and capacious uses of the terms "populism" and "populist" there is a series of shared genre-defining tropes linking these uses that prioritize a normatively imagined social body—"ordinary people"—set against corrupt, immoral, and most importantly illegitimate elites or "outsiders." This normatively imagined social body mythologized as a collection of "little men" from whom the power of liberal democracy is supposed to originate is simultaneously figured as being besieged by big, abstract, and often urban/global forces determined to disrupt the very reproduction of the normative status quo.[9] Caught up in this mythology are the material and legal factors that underwrite the construction of group identities and their corresponding political coalitions; most saliently private property and homeownership. These factors have been historically, at least within western Europe and more specifically within the U.S., the foundation of the right to political representation, the threshold at which macro and microeconomic forces meet, and the setting in which the heteronormative family as both the essential social and economic unit of a nation is constructed.[10]

At their core, voting rights in the U.S. have always privileged white landholding heterosexual men. Despite the slow and recently threatened expansions of suffrage to women and racial minorities, the constitutional investment in first land and later property ownership, both instruments of white heteropatriarchy, have been maintained up through contemporary policy and rhetoric.[11] From George W. Bush's "Ownership Society" to senior presidential strategist Steve Bannon's recent suggestion that the U.S. return to a pre-Jacksonian voting regime, homeownership tied to the financial mechanism of government-backed mortgages has persistently been treated as an arbiter of acceptance of and in the body-politic of the U.S.[12] Homeownership has been made a condition of membership in the imagined community of "ordinary people" that is the constructed target and outcome of populist appeals. Those structurally excluded from homeownership or who do not conform to white heteronormative models of the nuclear family associated with it therefore find themselves coded as deviant and actively threatening to the property investments or rights of "ordinary people," the perpetuation of society, and the stability of the nation as a whole.[13]

In this setting, if the home is a mechanism of subjective interpellation with particular populist potency, race, gender, and sexuality as they are pathologized through the home as a social, State, and market formation trouble its foundations as a universal ideological hailing apparatus.[14] Historicizing the home as a mechanism for filtering "little men" and their "Others," Lawrence Glickman interprets the early 20th-century working-class ideology of the "American Standard of Living" as produced by and reinscribing of racial, gender, and sexual hierarchies rationalized through consumption, wages, and homeownership. This ideology not only provided an enduring standard by which white men could connect their citizenship with wage-earning economics but as such also provided a populist platform through which an outside group could be constructed around material markers of cultural identity. Negatively characterizing the economic exploitation and conditions many Chinese immigrant laborers encounter in the U.S., an 1880 article in the *Journal of United Labor* claimed:

> They come here more as slaves than anything else... robbing their fellow man of his just heritage, -the right to live in a decent manner, and the to raise his children to become useful citizens of this republic [... they] take out of circulation daily the sum of seventy-five thousand dollars... They trade and traffic entirely with themselves. They spend none of the money they earn with the white merchants of the city. They import most of the articles they use.[15]

By 1905, a clear racialized distinction of living standards between whites, Blacks, and immigrant workers from China and Japan had become entrenched in the American labor movement as well as patterns of consumption that were productive of the "American" home.[16] Part-and-parcel of the American labor critique of the emerging industrial capitalist order and industrial "elites" including John D. Rockefeller, Leland Stanford, and Cornelius Vanderbilt was the villainization of a racially imagined underclass of illegitimate or alien workers recruited by these "elites," whose racialized differences in standards of living supposedly threatened those of white workers.[17] These racialized differences in standards of living were compounded by sexual, religious, and civilizational stereotypes which situated white worker masculinity in the form of the "breadwinner" for his nuclear family at home and against which other racial groups were set.[18]

Thus, Glickman reveals that the American home is not solely the site of moral consumption but simultaneously provides a means of constructing and identifying ideological deviance. Following Glickman's interpretations, Chandan C. Reddy notes that the home serves as a site of constitutive and ongoing violence that marks some, especially queer people of color, as deviant due to their structural and material inability to "properly" respond to or identify with the hailing demands made of them.[19] However, the nuclear-family home that now serves as the standard trope of American domesticity and political participation was decidedly not the norm, even for white Americans, until the postwar period and the attendant massive interventions of the federal government to construct a consumer society. Prior to the 1950s, the majority of Americans were not homeowners, especially within urban and industrialized areas.[20] With the aid of government policies including the creation of the Federal Housing Administration (FHA) in 1934 and the Servicemen's Readjustment Act of 1944 (commonly referred to as the G.I. Bill) combined with efforts to redirect wartime industrial production toward domestic markets, the home—specifically, the single-family detached home on non-agricultural lands—was made a means of economic and evermore symbolic advancement for the individual and the nation.[21]

The G.I. Bill and the homeownership it helped spur are also widely accepted as having contributed to post-war booms in matrimony and fertility as the government invested in and propagandized a peacetime return to normalcy. The Office of War Information, for instance, glorified "apple-pie" values through multiple media that called for the building up of the American population.[22] The subsidizing of these normative values reinforced the home as a material and social Ideological Apparatus for the reproduction of the state and the "little men" from which it drew its authority. As a result, over the next decade and a half a cult around the white nuclear family formed such that "healthy people" were understood to stem from two-parent heterosexual households whereas unmarried people were pathologized as "sick," "immoral," or "neurotic."[23]

The positive and democratizing effects the G.I. Bill and the FHA had on property ownership for the nation as a whole, however, were not democratically experienced across racial, gender, and sexual lines. Although the G.I. Bill afforded the same entitlements to Black and female veterans, both found it extremely difficult to collect their benefits due to longstanding and engrained racial and gender biases. White Americans were largely apathetic to Black military service or the skills Black veterans acquired during the war and maintained an association between Black labor and menial low-paying jobs. If Black veterans refused to accept employment with wages below subsistence levels, the Veteran's Administration (VA) withheld or terminated their unemployment benefits under the guise of noncompliance.[24] Even when benefits were accessed, Black veterans risked retaliatory violence, as occurred in 1946 and 1947 when two Black veterans, in Georgia and Louisiana, were lynched as a form of economic retaliation toward the men for having used their military benefits to build profitable farms.[25]

Political historian Margot Canaday has further analyzed the inaccessibility of state welfare benefits as a structural form of homophobia, while others have noted the inability of women to access financial and governmental services without the approval of a husband.[26] A 1945 ruling by the VA denied G.I. benefits for vet-erans "with an undesirable discharge 'issued because of homosexual acts or ten-dencies,'" making it the first federal policy to explicitly deny economic welfare to homosexual citizens.[27] In her essay, *Building a Straight State: Sexuality and Social Citizenship under the 1944 G.I. Bill*, Canaday argues that the G.I. Bill ensured the institutions of marriage, heteronormativity, and the patriarchal family by priv-ileging men as the automatic accessors of state benefits that forced veterans into specific social-domestic relations in order receive their entitlements:

> The G.I. Bill did more than just create a closet, then. It also institutional-ized heterosexuality by channeling resources to men so that-at a moment when women had made significant gains in the workplace-the economic incentives for women to marry remained firmly in place. The institution-alization of heterosexuality in federal policy was a two-part process that required the state to provide economic support for marriage (through male breadwinners) while it stigmatized homosexuality [...] but also simultane-ously relied on those who differed from the normative to reveal the most deserving strata of the citizenry.[28]

These barriers in accessing welfare benefits for Blacks, women, and homosexual men critically limited not only their ability to receive mortgages, home loans, or other mechanisms of private property ownership but also education and other forms of ordinariness and economic advancement.

Existing segregationist housing policies and a caveat in the VA mortgage in-surance program that required veterans to qualify for mortgages with private banks and loan services vastly limited Black opportunity for homeownership. Additionally, the FHA's notorious practice of redlining reinforced geographic inequality by financially formalizing racist associations of minority families with poverty, crime, and decay, consequently figuring them as poor financial investment opportunities.[29] The combination of these practices and the racially and economically homogeneous suburban communities—such as the various Levittowns—effectively maintained racial segregation and limited financial and physical mobility of non-white and non-heteronormative individuals. At the same time, these communities reified a symbolic imaginary of American or-dinariness embodied in the white, heterosexual, Christian "little man" and his family.

While not directly illustrative of the sexism and homophobia in American housing policy and popular rhetoric, it was the racial division animating the life of Levittowns that brought the populist foundations of American democracy predicated on homeownership most clearly into relief.[30] In an attempt to ac-commodate and take advantage of the marriage and baby boom tied to postwar prosperity, the real-estate development company Levitt and Sons sought to apply Fordist methods and emerging marketing techniques to housing construction and sales. Beginning with the transformation of 400 hectares of potato fields in

Long Island in 1947, Levitt and Sons helped naturalize ownership of a single-detached home, previously unimaginable for most middle- and working-class Americans, as the moral model of American community. In part by removing basement foundations and maintaining monotonous floor plans that allowed for a rapid 27-step construction process that greatly reduced timely and costly skilled labor, Levitt and Sons was able to build what would become one of the nation's largest private housing projects, Levittown, New York, such that even homes on large lots with 750 square feet of interior space were comparatively cheaper than renting an apartment in New York City;[31] the average per-month cost for a long-term, fixed-rate, FHA-insured mortgage was two to three times lower than paying monthly rent in the city.[32] The success of Levittown, NY spurred Levitt and Sons to build seven more Levittowns outside major urban-industrial centers in Pennsylvania (1952), New Jersey (1958), Maryland (1963, 1964, 1970), Virginia (1968), and Puerto Rico (1963).

A central characteristic of the Levittowns was their social and material homo-geneity; comprised mostly of World War II veterans and their families, household adults were identical in terms of age and income group. This social uniformity was architecturally mirrored by the multitude of "little boxes" whose replicable spatial geometry not only made domestic/private life materially homogenous both locally and nationally, but also greatly affected each household's family size.[33] As one Levittown newsletter put it, "our lives are held closely together because most of us are within the same age bracket, in similar income groups, live in almost identical houses and have *common problems*."[34] Scholars of race, American, and white studies, including George Lipsitz, Douglas Massey, and Nancy Denton, have argued that this social and material homogeneity provided "ethnic whites"—Italian, Irish, Greek, Jewish, Catholic, and other European Americans—the means to "invest" in and acquire "whiteness;"[35] or in other words, to eschew the ethnicness that had marked them as non-ordinary. This investment, though, had to be continually preformed through compliance with prescriptive codes of normative conduct. For example, homeowner's manu-als and community rulebooks specified the appropriate times residents could hang laundry outdoors, the allowable number of pets each household could own (limited to cats and dogs only), and the prohibitions on fencing materials and home color choices.[36]

Further, this admission also relied upon the maintenance of racial segrega-tion.[37] Early leases for the Levittowns in NY, PA, and NJ contained a clause that prohibited selling and renting Levittown property to non-whites: "No dwelling shall be used or occupied by members of other than the Caucasian race, but the employment and maintenance of other than Caucasian domestic servants shall be permitted."[38] Even when this clause was removed following the 1948 Supreme Court *Shelley v. Kraemer* decision, its segregationist effects were pre-served through the structural racism of existing financial policies and institutions surrounding home mortgages and real estate. Among the numerous unsubstan-tiated anxieties about desegregation were fears of (forced) intermarriage, the loss of racial status, a rise in crime, neighborhood decline, and an eventual ethnic replacement. But, the major concern, supported by FHA insurance policies against promoting "undesirable community effects," was that non-white residents, specifically Black residents, would greatly depreciate Levittowns' property value.[39]

The continued segregation of the Levittowns attracted the attention of local and national Black activists and organizations including Reverend Ralph Abernathy and the NAACP, as well as white integrationists mainly of Jewish and Quaker background (Figure 2.1).[40] After several years of campaigning for suburban integration and the application of character tests to potential Black "pioneer" families willing to cross Levittowns' color line/bar, this attention came to a head on August 13, 1957: an "ordinary" middle-class family, the Myerses, was selected and approved by multiple Quaker groups to purchase a recently listed home in the Dogwood Hollow section of Levittown, PA.[41] This approval was contingent on several grilling interviews, which Daisy Myers characterized as "stupid" and to the "third degree," but which were deemed necessary to prove the "ordinariness" of the Myers family in ways not expected of white families:[42]

> I finally said that we were only ordinary people [...] we had not invented anything or created sensations or been in any trouble. They pried into our

FIGURE 2.1 Police officer clears crowd outside of Myers' home.

lives so extensively that one would wonder if they were going to give us a house instead of us having to buy it.[43]

With stable and respectable jobs, a military background, an "ideal" family size, and a history of suburban living, the Myerses fit the Levittown's desire for homogeneity, save for their race. Despite this, the initial arrival of the Myers family in Levittown was met with hostility and protest, including a quickly circulated petition objecting to the Myerses presence.[44] This hostility only increased throughout the day, with little police intervention to manage the growing crowds loitering outside their home causing the Myerses to fear for their lives, leave their Levittown home that night, and delay their move by one week.[45]

During this time, community residents lead by a former head of the local Veterans of Foreign Wars post formed the Levittown Betterment Committee as a means "to secure for their community the former status of limitations by *peaceful* means."[46] This meant working to evict the Myerses to prevent perceived future diminishment of the community's property value and future "encroachment upon [white residents'] rights as a limited community."[47] While the committee claimed its motives were not rooted in racism and its methods were non-violent, committee members nonetheless purchased a home directly adjacent to the Myerses' which was dubbed the "Confederate House." This home was adorned with the Confederate flag and repeatedly broadcasted a variation of Daniel Decatur Emmett's "Dixie," while another committee member who had named their dog "Nigger" would publicly call his dog's name while walking past the Myerses' home. Other provocations more directly conflated racist rhetoric and populist appeals to democratic self-determination and property rights. Ku Klux Klan (KKK) activities increased in the community. Burning crosses and painted "KKK" tags appeared in the yards of Myerses' supporters and posters advocating Klan membership featuring the phrase "Save Our Land. Join the Klan" were circulated.[48] These acts of psychological terrorism were accompanied by physical attacks on property throughout the summer that included white residents smashing the Myerses' home's windows, exploding gas bombs, and vandalizing the vehicles of service workers who agreed to do business with the Myerses.[49]

Ultimately, committee members argued it was *their* right and moral obligation to protect the property value of *their* homes and therefore to determine who did and did not belong in *their* community. Blacks were perceived as an "uncivilized race" whose mere presence brought with it crime, violence, and potential sexual degeneracy in the forms of intermarriage and miscegenation that threatened the definition of the "ordinary" in America.[50] Further, the support of the Myerses by government officials and public interest groups were rationalized by white Levittowners as an almost conspiratorial impingement on their lives by elitists determined to transform the social geometry of the nation.[51] Like the white working-class anxieties around racial Standards of Living at the close of the 19th century, if Black families such as the Myerses were able to gain access to homeownership in racially homogenous enclaves like Levittown, then, the imagined value, superiority, and Americanness of these enclaves were suddenly called into question.[52] As if in response to the crisis of populist identity that the presence of a Black family in Levittown raised, white residents performatively reasserted their claim to *their* whiteness, *their* land, *their* homes, and thus to *their* nation by parading in front of the Myerses' home repeatedly chanting "This is America!" and singing "America the Beautiful" (Figure 2.2).[53]

The story of the Myerses and "the [Levittown] that had the riot" is one particularly stark example of how populism and housing have intersected and continue to intersect in the construction of an imagined community of "real Americans" defending their inalienable rights against imposition by established elites.[54] This community is made legible precisely to the extent that it can be contrasted to both these elites and underserving "Others" who are made illegible as hailable subjects or legitimate citizens by the denial of their humanity through their reduction to the stereotypes or statistics that are the fodder of populist rhetorics.[55] The very fragility of this construction, its dependence on abstract boogeymen, and the historical anomaly of mass white working-class

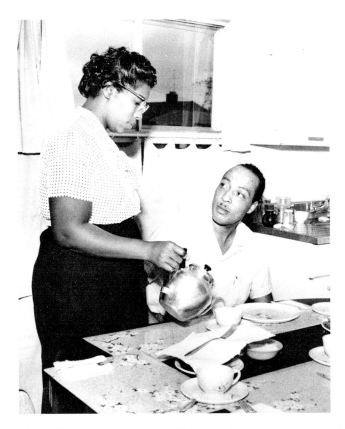

FIGURE 2.2 Mr. William Myers, Jr. and wife Daisy about to eat supper, police stand guard.

heterosexual homeownership, mean that new boogeymen must continually be produced. These figures are often drawn out of those racial, gender, and sexual "deviants" excluded from participation in the home as the nexus of the family, private property, and "ordinary American-ness," as social and economic conditions inevitably change. This is why populist rhetoric often defaults to appeals to an imagined previous state of social and economic harmony (read homogeneity) that has been disrupted or threatened by new formulations, especially of home, house, and property.[56] As sociologist Dan W. Dodson put it, "is there to be no escape from living near negroes. And what of the dream of middle-class respectability? If a negro family can afford what you [a white family] can afford, *how do you justify your feeling of superiority?*[57]

The Levittown example is therefore foundational because the nexus of homeownership, property rights, and populism forged in there and in other spaces of postwar suburbanization set many of the spatial, legal, economic, and cultural terms by which subjects have subsequently been hailed and legitimated, or else ostracized and marked deviant. Yet this nexus too was built from a much longer legacy of property, race, and gender-based populist formations and exclusions that form a broad arc across the history of the U.S. up to the present which has centered white heterosexual Christian property holding men as the assumed normative embodiment of the nation and its ideals. This arc includes not only the treatise of John Locke and its rationalization of the dispossession of indigenous lands through the rhetoric of *moral* property holding on which the antecedents of the U.S. were founded, but also many other moments throughout the development of this ideology in increasingly articulated and all-encompassing manners: the era of Reconstruction when newly freed Blacks were denied "forty acres and a mule" or else had their land expropriated from them and were structurally forced back into sharecropping;[58] Carl Hansberry's purchase of a home in Woodlawn, Illinois and his subsequent U.S. Supreme Court Case, *Hansberry v. Lee*, challenging restrictive convents that elicited violent mob attacks;[59] the razing of Otis Flake, Mattie Flake, and Opal Lee's Fort Worth home on Juneteenth (June 19) 1939 by a mob of whites;[60] the 1985 bombing of MOVE in Philadelphia that destroyed 61 rowhomes and displaced more than 250 citizens, mainly middle-class Blacks;[61] the failure of the U.S. state and market to protect the housing rights of queer and trans people and a broader failure of the normative home that lead to the creation of the house-ballroom subculture and the Street Transvestite Action Revolutionaries (STAR) House in the 1970s and 1980s;[62] the discriminatory housing policies against people with HIV/AIDS;[63] the recent exposure of systemic diminishment of property appraisal values for Black homeowners.[64] Contrasting these examples of populist violence and state indifference to the elevation of the Bundys and McCloskeys into causes célèbres by right-wing, ethno-nationalist, and sovereign citizen movements, the capitol insurrection of January 6, 2021 is not so much an anomaly as a continuation of a longer history of the relation between populism and place.

In a perverse dialectic, certain groups have been constructed through and given preferential access to participation in the symbolic imaginary and material benefits of home, family, property, and nation, all of which are collapsed into each other through populist sophistry. Consequently, those excluded from participation in this symbolic imaginary or its material benefits find themselves hailed, though not as subjects, but rather as the threatening "Other" through which the ordinary and normative subject is produced as such. The deep irony then, is that populism and its rhetorics are underwritten not by ordinariness but by a belief in an inherent extra-ordinariness; a superiority of self, which, when the "little man's" way of life is challenged by new norms, even assimilationist and structurally conservative ones such as gay marriage, it engenders violent denials and performative reassertions of this extra-ordinariness. The "little man," even when he finds himself in the political minority, still imagines himself as possessing supreme rights. Poignantly noting the contradictions at the heart of this irony and the dynamics of ownership and exclusion underwriting populism on display on January 6, 2021, MSNBC News anchor, Joy Reid observed live that:

> The reason […] that these people were so unafraid of the cops […] The reason they could easily and casually, with their cameras on, film themselves throwing things through the walls of our capitol, our property—going inside the capitol, sitting in Speaker Pelosi's office, casually take pictures of themselves, have that played on Fox News—They know that they are not in jeopardy—Because, the cops are taking selfies with them, walking them down the steps to make sure they're not hurt, taking care with their bodies—not like they treated Freddie Gray's body. White Americans aren't afraid of the cops. White Americans are never afraid of the cops, even when they're committing insurrection. Even when they are engaged in attempting to occupy our capitol to steal the votes of people who look like me, because in their minds *they own* this country, *they own* that capitol, *they own* the cops, the cops work for *them*, and people like me have no damn right to try to elect a president, because we don't get to pick the president. *They* get to pick the president. *They own* their president. *They own* the White House. *They own this country.* And so, *when you think you own it, you own the place, you ain't afraid of the police because the police are you*, and the police reflect back to them, "We're with you. You're good. We're not gonna hurt you, 'cause you're not *them*." Guarantee you if that was a Black Lives Matter protest in D.C. there would already be people shackled, arrested, or dead—Shackled, arrested, en masse, or dead.[65]

The insurrection of January 6th was a group of frantic extra-ordinary people desperately trying to perpetuate the myth of their ordinariness, even if it meant seizing control of the "People's House," as they have seized "Others'" so many times before.

Acknowledgment

A thank you to the Special Collections Research Center at Temple University Libraries for providing the images within this chapter gratis. A special thank you to Aaron Tobey for your comments, feedback, and time in drafting this piece. All shortcomings are my own.

Notes

1 Here I use "queer" in both its literal capacious definition as "strange," "odd," and "unusual" as well as to reference homosexuality and non-heteronormativity. While this essay does not always focus on non-normative sexuality, its analysis of the home is deeply inspired from queer and trans studies' vast literature on the subject.

2 The 2014 and 2016 Bundy standoffs were armed confrontations between Nevada rancher Cliven Bundy, his family, and supporters (some of which were armed militia) and the U.S. Bureau of Land Management. The standoff of 2014 came to a head when the U.S. law enforcement began to seize Cliven Bundy's cattle after the BLM claimed Cliven had been illegally grazing his herds on 600,000 acres of federal lands for approximately two decades and which had cost the federal government more than 1 million dollars in his unpaid land use fees. Cliven claimed he was not obligated to pay any land use fees to the federal government because no formal contract existed between himself and the federal government. These standoffs have been framed by Bundy supporters as emblematic of government overreach and abuse of powers. As Cliven put it in an interview with CBS, "The money's not the deal. The cows are not the deal. It's freedom and liberty and access to our land and get [*sic*] rid of this abusive government." In 2016, Ammon Bundy, Cliven Bundy's son, with the support of armed non-government militia and sovereign citizen groups seized the headquarters of the Malheur National Wildlife Refuge in Oregon. Ammon and his supporters protested the conviction of two area ranchers for federal land arson and believed that the federal government was required to relinquish the public lands it managed to individual states. The occupation lasted for 41 days. Similar to the 2014 standoff, the occupation Malheur National Wildlife Refuge was framed by supporters as an act of patriotism against government overreach and abuse of power.

"NV Rancher's Fight with Feds Reaches Boiling Point," 10 WBNS, April 11, 2014, Accessed October 3, 2021, https://www.10tv.com/article/news/nv-ranchers-fight-feds-reaches-boiling-point/530-5917caba-d6dc-4037-8fd5-dd606b3db4b8.

3 In June 2020, approximately 500 participants of Black Lives Matter (BLM) protests over the killing of George Floyd entered into Portland Place, a private gated community in St. Louis, Missouri, in an attempt to gather outside the home of then St. Louis Mayor Lyda Krewson. As the participants walked through the community gate, Mark and Patricia McCloskey came outside their home and went to their front yard armed with a handgun and semi-automatic rifle to yell at the BLM protesters. The McCloskey were recorded via livestream yelling at protestors that their community was "private property" while pointing their weapons at the crowd. The McCloskey's claim that, at the time, they felt they were in imminent danger from the crowd and that they were acting in self-defense to prevent protestors from breaking and entering into their home. Mark McCloskey said in an interview with KSDK, "I really thought it was Storming the Bastille, that we would be dead and the house would be burned and there was nothing we could do about it."

Azi Paybarah, "St. Louis Couple Who Aimed Guns at Protesters Plead Guilty to Misdemeanors," *New York Times,* August 3, 2021, Accessed October 3, 2021, https://www.nytimes.com/2021/06/17/us/mark-patricia-mccloskey-st-louis-couple-protesters.html?smid=url-share.

4 The 2014 and 2016 Bundy standoffs were armed confrontations between Nevada rancher Cliven Bundy, his family, and supporters (some of which were armed militia) and the U.S. Bureau of Land Management. The standoff of 2014 came to a head when the U.S. law enforcement began to seize Cliven Bundy's cattle after the BLM claimed Cliven had been illegally grazing his herds on 600,000 acres of federal lands

for approximately two decades and which had cost the federal government more than 1 million dollars in his unpaid land use fees. Cliven claimed he was not obligated to pay any land use fees to the federal government because no formal contract existed between himself and the federal government. These standoffs have been framed by Bundy supporters as emblematic of government overreach and abuse of powers. As Cliven put it in an interview with CBS, "The money's not the deal. The cows are not the deal. It's freedom and liberty and access to our land and get [sic] rid of this abusive government." In 2016, Ammon Bundy, Cliven Bundy's son, with the support of armed nongovernment militia and sovereign citizen groups seized the headquarters of the Malheur National Wildlife Refuge in Oregon. Ammon and his supporters protested the conviction of two area ranchers for federal land arson and believed that the federal government was required to relinquish the public lands it managed to individual states. The occupation lasted for 41 days. Similar to the 2014 standoff, the occupation Malheur National Wildlife Refuge was framed by supporters as an act of patriotism against government overreach and abuse of power.

"NV Rancher's Fight with Feds Reaches Boiling Point," 10 WBNS, April 11, 2014, Accessed October 3, 2021, https://www.10tv.com/article/news/nv-ranchers-fight-feds-reaches-boiling-point/530-5917caba-d6dc-4037-8fd5-dd606b3db4b8.

5 Philip Lief Group, "Populist," in *Roget's 21st Century Thesaurus, Third Edition*, Accessed June 6, 2021, https://www.thesaurus.com/browse/populist.

6 Using Google's Ngram Viewer, "populism" and "populist" returned graphs which showed marked increases within English (2019), American English (2019), British English (2019), French (2019), German (2019), Italian (2019), and Spanish (2019) corpuses. The Russian (2019) corpus reflects a notable range of peaks and valleys in use. The frequency of within the English Fiction (2019) corpus reflect a significant decrease between 1990 and 2019. Not data was available for Chinese (simplified) (2019) and the Hebrew (2019) corpuses.

Jean-Baptiste Michel et al., "Quantitative Analysis of Culture Using Millions of Digitized Book," *Science* 331, No. 6014 (2011): 176–182.

7 Hamilton Nolan, "Words That Mean Nothing," *In These Times*, June 1, 2021, https://inthesetimes.com/article/politics-woke-cancel-culture-socialism-critical-race-theory.

8 University of Reading Professor of Comparative European Politics Daphne Halikiopoulou as quoted in: Yasmeen Serhan, "*Populism* Is Meaningless," *The Atlantic*, Mach 14, 2020, https://www.theatlantic.com/international/archive/2020/03/what-is-populism/607600.

9 Illustrative of the mythology of the "little man" is Winston Churchill's 1944 speech on the foundation of all democracy. Catherine Fieschi, *Populocracy: The Tyranny of Authenticity and the Rise of Populism* (Newcastle upon Tyne: Agenda Publishing, 2019), 13, 15, 17; "The Churchill Spirit—In His Own Words," *New York Times,* August 2, 1964, https://www.nytimes.com/1964/08/02/archives/the-churchill-spiritin-his-own-words.html.

10 Ben W. Ansell, "The Politics of Housing," *Annual Reviews of Political Science* 22 (2019): 168–169.

11 Neoclassical economists such a John Bates Clark elide the distinction between land and capital that classical economists such as David Ricardo, Adam Smith, and Thomas Malthus maintained. As a consequence, 20th-century economic theory treats land and other forms of property as interchangeable forms of capital that could therefore be "incorporated in the simple two-factor view of production and growth" (Ansell, 169). For more on the relationship between private property and whiteness see Harris. For more on the relationship between private property and heterosexuality see Reddy. For more on contemporary restrictions on voting, especially for people of color, in the U.S. See Fandos and Epstein and Corasaniti.

Ansell, "The Politics of Housing," 169; Cheryl I. Harris, "Whiteness as Property," *Harvard Law Review* 106, No. 8 (1993): 1707–1791; Chandan C. Reddy, "Home,

House, Nonidentity: *Paris Is Burning*," in *Burning Down the House: Recycling Domesticity*, edited by George Rosemary (Boulder: Westview, 1997), 355–379; Nicholas Fandos, "As Biden Vows to 'Fight Like Heck,' Voting Overhaul Falters in Congress," *New York Times*, June 1, 2021, https://www.nytimes.com/2021/06/01/us/politics/-voting-rights-congress.html; Reid J. Epstein and Nick Corasaniti, "Inside Democrats' Scramble to Repel the G.O.P. Voting Push," *New York Times*, June 1, 2021, https://www.nytimes.com/2021/05/07/us/politics/democrats-republican-voting-rights.html.

12 As part of a 2003 effort to promote home ownership in the U.S. framed around claims that it promoted independence and choice, president George W. Bush stated "It is in our national interest that more people own their own home. After all, if you own your own home you have a vital stake in the future of the country."

George W. Bush, President of the U.S., "Remarks on Signing the American Dream Downpayment Act," *The American Presidency Project*, December 16, 2003, https://www.presidency.ucsb.edu/documents/remarks-signing-the-american-dream-downpayment-act; Philip Bump, "Steve Bannon Once Suggested Only Property Owners Should Vote. What Would That Look Like?," *Washington Post*, November 28, 2016, https://www.washingtonpost.com/news/the-fix/wp/2016/11/28/steve-bannon-once-suggested-only-property-owners-should-vote-what-would-that-look-like.

13 Benedict Anderson connects in his 1983 *Imagined Communities* the rise of nationalist sentiments on which populism draws to the enumeration and classification of subjects made legible through the language of private property.

Reddy, "Home, House, Nonidentity," 372–373; Benedict Anderson, *Imagined Communities: Reflections on the Origin and Spread of Nationalism* (London: Verso, 1983), 68, 113.

14 An Ideological State Apparatus (ISA) is a theory developed by Marxist philosopher Louis Althusser. In contrast to (repressive) state apparatuses, which function by means of both physical and nonphysical violence or coercion predominately within the public/political domain, ISAs are a plurality of distinctive and specialized institutions that's are a part of civil/private society and thus are seemingly social and apolitical. Examples of ISAs included institutions of religion, education, law, employment, culture, entertainment, and family.

Reddy, "Home, House, Nonidentity," 355; Lisa Lowe, "Unfaithful to the Original: The Subject of *Dictée*," in *Immigrant Acts: On Asian American Cultural Politics* (Durham, NC: Duke University Press, 1996), 145–146; Louis Althusser, "Ideology and Ideological State Apparatuses (Notes Towards and Investigation)," in *Lenin and Philosophy and Other Essays* (New York: Monthly Review Press, 1971), 142–144.

15 *Journal of United Labor* as quoted in Lawrence Glickman, "Inventing the 'American Standard of Living': Gender, Race and Working-Class Identity, 1880–1925," *Labor History* 34, No. 2–3 (1993): 231–232.

16 Glickman, 231.

17 An 1885 article in *John Swinton's Paper* compared the Chinese standard of living with that of vermin that made it impossible to for American (white) workers to maintain their higher standard of living.
Glickman, 231.

18 W. W. Stone, labor leader in San Francisco, claimed that Chinese immigrant-workers had no nuclear family of their own and were "content with a fractional interest in the body of a female slave" that created stark divide between their immoral licentiousness and the Christian uprightness of white breadwinning men.

W. W. Stone, "The Chinese Labor Problem," in *The Labor Movement: The Problem of Today*, George McNeill (Boston: A.M. Bridgman and Co, 1887), 433–434.

19 Reddy, "Home, House, Nonidentity," 355–356.

20 "Historical Census of Housing Tables: Homeownership," *U.S. Census Bureau*, Accessed June 11, 2021, https://www.census.gov/data/tables/time-series/dec/coh-owner.html; Lizabeth Cohen, *A Consumers' Republic: The Politics of Mass Consumption*

in Postwar America (New York: Vintage Books, 2003), Kindle Edition, kindle location 2255–2259.

21 David Moteyne, "Framing the American Dream," *Journal of Architectural Education* 58 (2004): 30; Peter G. Rowe, *Making a Middle Landscape* (Cambridge, MA: The MIT Press, 1991), 44–54; See also: Cohen, *A Consumer's Republic.*

22 Norman Rockwell's "Freedom from Want" poster is an iconic illustration of these postwar "apple pie" values. The illustration was a part of a series of four oil paintings inspired by U.S. President Franklin D. Roosevelt's 1941 State of the Union Address.
   Norman Rockwell (artist), *Ours to Fight For: Freedom from Want*, oil painting, 1943, Washington, D.C.: U.S. Government Printing Office.

23 David Brooks, "The Nuclear Family Was a Mistake," *The Atlantic*, Accessed May 11, 2020, https://www.theatlantic.com/magazine/archive/2020/03/the-nuclear-family-was-a-mistake/605536.

24 Hilary Herbold, "Never a Level Playing Field: Blacks and the GI Bill," *The Journal of Blacks in Higher Education* 6 (Winter 1994–1995): 105.

25 Herbold, 105.

26 Margot Canaday, *The Straight State: Sexuality and Citizenship in Twentieth-Century America* (Princeton, NJ: Princeton University Press, 2009); Nancy F. Cott, *Public Vows: A History of Marriage and the Nation* (Cambridge, MA: Harvard University Press, 2000).

27 Margot Canady, "Building a Straight State: Sexuality and Social Citizenship under the 1944 G.I. Bill," *The Journal of American History* 90, No. 3 (December 2003): 935; Allan Bérubé, *Coming Out Under Fire: The History of Gay Men and Women in World War II* (Chapel Hill: University of North Carolina Press, 1990).

28 Canady, "Building a Straight State," 957.

29 Cohen, *A Consumers' Republic*, kindle location 3181–3188; For more on redlining, see: Richard Rothstein, *The Color of Law: A Forgotten History of How Our Government Segregated America* (New York: Liveright, 2017).

30 While the history of the Myerses may not directly reveal the sexism and homophobia present in postwar suburbia, several scholars have written about the sexual and gender politics of Levittown and other postwar suburban communities, particularly as manifest in the physical layout of the home and yard. See: Dianne Harris, *Little White Houses: How the Postwar Home Constructed Race in America* (Princeton, NJ: Princeton University Press, 2011).

31 Kenneth T. Jackson, *Crabgrass Frontier: The Suburbanization of the United States* (New York: Oxford University Press, 1985), 234–235.

32 Jackson, 206.

33 David-Olivier Gougelet and Ellen K. Feder, "Genealogies of Race and Gender," in *A Companion to Foucault*, ed. Christopher Falzon, Timothy O'Leary, and Jana Sawicki (Malden, MA: Wiley-Blackwell, 2013), 478.

34 Emphasis added. As quoted in Gougelet and Feder, 477.

35 Gougelet and Feder, 478–479; George Lipsitz, "The Possessive Investment in Whiteness: Racialized Social Democracy and the 'White' Problem in American Studies," *American Quarterly* 47, No. 3 (1995): 369–387; Douglas Massey and Nancy Denton, *American Apartheid: Segregation and the Making of the Underclass* (Cambridge, MA: Harvard University Press, 1993); Harris, "Whiteness as Property."

36 Gougelet and Feder, 479.

37 George Lipsitz argues that during the postwar period ethnic differences became less of a social concern than racial difference. Simultaneously, ethnic whites were encouraged to abandoned their urban ethnic enclaves and integrate with the broader racial identity of American whiteness that was being formed in the suburbs.
   Lipsitz, "The Possessive Investment in Whiteness," 373–374.

38 Commonly referred to as "Clause 25." As quoted in Gougelet and Feder, "Genealogies of Race and Gender," 479.

39 James Wolfinger, "'The American Dream—For All American': Race, Politics, and the Campaign to Desegregate Levittown," *Journal of Urban History* 38, No. 3 (2012): 434.

40 Historically, Quakers were leading abolitionist figures in the U.S. However, the subtext of much of their advocacy was rooted in racial eugenics and a white savior mentality, most notable in Frederick Winslow Taylor's writing.
    Bill Cook, "The Denial of Slavery in Management Studies," *Journal of Management Studies* 40, No. 8 (December 2003): 1906; Dorothy Anderson, "Politicians Leading Campaign to Chase Myers Out Levittown," *Philadelphia Tribune* (Philadelphia, PA), September 7, 1957, 1–2.

41 "Pioneers" is a term some scholars use to describe those who are the first to transgress the color line in America. Among these Quaker groups were the Bucks County Human Relations Council and the American Friends Service Committee. Although I do not go into the entire history of the Myerses' integration into Levittown, PA in this article, a more complete overview can be found in: Wolfinger, "'The American Dream—For All Americans,'" 439–440.

42 Wolfinger, 439–440.

43 Wolfinger, 439.

44 Wolfinger, 440.

45 The efforts of the police to control and deter mob violence has been interpreted by the Myerses, their supporters, and scholars as "weak at best and tacitly supporting the mob at worst."
    Wolfinger, 441.

46 Emphasis added. The Levittown Betterment Committee quoted in Wolfinger, 440.

47 The Levittown Betterment Committee quoted in Wolfinger, 440.

48 Wolfinger, 441.

49 Wolfinger, 441; Anderson, "Politicians Leading Campaign to Chase Myers Out Levittown," 1–2; Dorothy Anderson, "Levittown a Disgrace to America," *Philadelphia Tribune* (Philadelphia, PA), August 17, 1957, 1, 4; "Five Arrested in Levittown Disorder," *Levittown Times* (Lowe Bucks County, PA), August 14, 1957, 1, 3; "Council Lauds Calm Levittowner Stand," *Levittown Times* (Lowe Bucks County, PA), August 14, 1957, 1, 3; "Protest Over Negro Family Ends Meetings," *Levittown Times* (Lowe Bucks County, PA), August 15, 1957, 1, 3; "Anti-Negro Group Seeks Legal Bolster," *Levittown Times* (Lowe Bucks County, PA), August 16, 1957, 1; "Legal Means Sought to Force Negroes to Leave Levittown," *Levittown Times* (Lowe Bucks County, PA), August 16, 1957, 3; "Troopers Break Up Crown; Man Arrested," *Levittown Times* (Lowe Bucks County, PA), August 20, 1957, 1, 3; "Crowds Stay Away from Dogwood," *Levittown Times* (Lowe Bucks County, PA), August 22, 1957, 1, 3.

50 Wolfinger, "The American Dream—For All Americans," 441.

51 Rather than accepting the reality that a Black family could afford a house in Levittown, some white residents developed and circulated rumors that the Myerses were secretly receiving financial support from integrationist organization or that they had moved into white communities before Levittown as part of a broader conspiracy to desegregate the nation. The integration of Little Rock, Alabama schools, which was swiftly at the center of national media, bleed into these conspiracies. See testimonies in: PeriscopeFilm, "1957 Race Relations Documentary 'Crisis in Levittown,' Pennsylvania 47664."

52 The Myerses were even offered $15,000 to sell their Levittown home in attempts to convince them to leave; the offer was almost $3,000 more than they initially paid ($12,150). The Myerses turned down the offer and in a press conference William E. Myers, Jr. expressed that they were there to stay.
    "Crowds Stay Away from Dogwood," 1.

53 Wolfinger, "The American Dream—For All Americans,'" 442.

54 Sociologist Herbert J. Gans notes that the riots over the Myerses move into Levittown, PA gave it a worldwide reputation as "a riot-torn community." Residents in

newer Levittowns distinguished themselves from the older Levittowns by their notorious reputation. For literature on the connection between homeownership, property value, and populist politics mainly within European democracies but applicable to America nonetheless, see: David Adler and Ben Ansell, "Housing and Populism," *West European Politics* 43, No. 2 (2020): 344–365; Ansell, "The Politics of Housing"; Herbert J. Gans, *The Levittowners: Ways of Life and Politics in New Suburban Community* (New York: Vintage Books, 1967), 375–376.

55 Cornel West has bluntly and rightfully called out this dynamic as "niggerization," which seeks to abstract diverse groups of peoples into monolithic boogeymen.

Cornel West, "Niggerization," *The Atlantic*, November 2007, Accessed June 18, 2021, https://www.theatlantic.com/magazine/archive/2007/11/niggerization/306285.

56 Reddy calls the important distinction between house and home as ideological constructs and sites of subjectivation or its denial, especially for queer and trans people of color. Thus, a house never replace a home, but rather serves as its "nonidentical supplement," operating as a marker of loss or wounding that may still take on positive dimensions.

Reddy, "Home, Houses, Nonidentity," 372.

57 Emphasis mine. Transcribed by the author. "Crisis in Levittown, PA" is 1957 documentary by Lee Bobker and Lester Becker. The short film is a part of "A series on Changing Neighborhoods" in the U.S. produced and planned by Dynamic Films, Inc.

PeriscopeFilm, "1957 Race Relations Documentary 'Crisis in Levittown,' Pennsylvania 47664," YouTube Video, 31:44, November 6, 2016, https://www.youtube.com/watch?v=oIPos4YYXnk&t=461s.

58 For more on the failures of Reconstruction and the specific anti-Blackness underlying this failure, see: W. E. B. Du Bois, *Black Reconstruction in America, 1860–1880* (Washington, DC: Free Press, 1998)

59 Carl Hansberry was the father of playwright and activist Lorraine Hansberry. Her most renowned work, *A Raisin in the Sun* was inspired by her experience of these events. The play itself serves as an illustration of the myths of the American Dream and populist inclusion via homeownership for Blacks through the perpetual denials and hardships it dramatizes.

Allen R. Kamp, "The History Behind *Hansberry v. Lee*," *U.C. Davis Law Review* 20, No. 3 (1987): 481–499; Lorraine Hansberry, *To Be Young, Gifted, and Black* (New York: Signet, 2011); Lorraine Hansberry, *A Raisin in the Sun* (New York: Vintage, 2004).

60 "Opal Lee." in *Newsmakers Online*, Accessed June 19, 2021, https://link.gale.com/apps/doc/K1618007130/BIC?u=columbiau&sid=summon&xid=885d64d2.

61 Gene Demby, "I'm From Philly. 30 Years Later I'm Still Trying to Make Sense of the MOVE Bombing," *NPR*, May 13, 2015, https://www.npr.org/sections/codeswitch/2015/05/13/406243272/im-from-philly-30-years-later-im-still-trying-to-make-sense-of-the-move-bombing; Heather Ann Thompson, "Saying Her Name," *The New Yorker*, May 16, 2021, https://www.newyorker.com/news/essay/saying-her-name.

62 Reddy, "Home, Houses, Nonidentity;" Malcolm Rio, "Architecture Is Burning," *Thresholds* 48 (2020): 122–132; Iván López Munuera, "Lands of Contagion," *E-flux*, November 30, 2020, https://www.e-flux.com/architecture/sick-architecture/363717/lands-of-contagion.

63 Christina B. Hanhardt, *Safe Space: Gay Neighborhood History and the Politics of Violence* (Durham, NC: Duke University Press, 2013), 110; Randy Shilts, *And the Band Played On: Politics, People, and the AIDS Epidemic* (London: Viking, 1988).

64 Debra Kamin, "Black Homeowners Face Discrimination in Appraisals," *New York Times*, August 27, 2020, https://www.nytimes.com/2020/08/25/realestate/blacks-minorities-appraisals-discrimination.html.

65 Emphases added. Joy Reid transcribed by the author. MSNBC, "Reid: If This Was a BLM Protest, 'There Would Already Be People Shackled, Arrested or Dead,' MSNBC," YouTube video, January 6, 2021, https://youtu.be/TWgQ1vKCeEo.

Bibliography

Adler, David, and Ben Ansell. "Housing and Populism." *West European Politics* 43, No. 2 (2020): 344–365.

Althusser, Louis. "Ideology and Ideological State Apparatuses (Notes Towards and Investigation)." In *Lenin and Philosophy and Other Essays*. New York: Monthly Review Press, 1971.

Anderson, Benedict. *Imagined Communities: Reflections on the Origin and Spread of Nationalism*. London: Verso, 1983.

Anderson, Dorothy. "Levittown a Disgrace to America." *Philadelphia Tribune* (Philadelphia, PA), August 17, 1957.

Anderson, Dorothy. "Politicians Leading Campaign to Chase Myers Out Levittown," *Philadelphia Tribune* (Philadelphia, PA), September 7, 1957.

Ansell, Ben W. "The Politics of Housing." *Annual Reviews of Political Science* 22 (2019): 165–185.

Bérubé, Allan. *Coming Out Under Fire: The History of Gay Men and Women in World War II*. Chapel Hill: University of North Carolina Press, 1990.

Brooks, David. "The Nuclear Family Was a Mistake." *The Atlantic*, March 2020. https://www.theatlantic.com/magazine/archive/2020/03/the-nuclear-family-was-a-mistake/605536.

Bump, Philip. "Steve Bannon Once Suggested Only Property Owners Should Vote. What Would That Look Like?" *Washington Post*, November 28, 2016. https://www.washingtonpost.com/news/the-fix/wp/2016/11/28/steve-bannon-once-suggested-only-property-owners-should-vote-what-would-that-look-like.

Bush, George W. "Remarks on Signing the American Dream Downpayment Act." *The American Presidency Project*, December 16, 2003. https://www.presidency.ucsb.edu/documents/remarks-signing-the-american-dream-downpayment-act.

Canady, Margot. "Building a Straight State: Sexuality and Social Citizenship under the 1944 G.I. Bill." *The Journal of American History* 90, No. 3 (December 2003): 935–957.

Canaday, Margot. *The Straight State: Sexuality and Citizenship in Twentieth-Century America*. Princeton, NJ: Princeton University Press, 2009.

Cohen, Lizabeth. *A Consumers' Republic: The Politics of Mass Consumption in Postwar America*. New York: Vintage Books, 2003.

Cook, Bill. "The Denial of Slavery in Management Studies." *Journal of Management Studies* 40, No. 8 (December 2003): 1895–1918.

Cott, Nancy F. *Public Vows: A History of Marriage and the Nation*. Cambridge, MA: Harvard University Press, 2000.

Demby, Gene. "I'm From Philly. 30 Years Later I'm Still Trying to Make Sense of the MOVE Bombing." *NPR*, May 13, 2015. https://www.npr.org/sections/codeswitch/2015/05/13/406243272/im-from-philly-30-years-later-im-still-trying-to-make-sense-of-the-move-bombing.

Du Bois, W. E. B. *Black Reconstruction in America, 1860–1880*. Washington, DC: Free Press, 1998.

Epstein, Reid J., and Corasaniti, Nick. "Inside Democrats' Scramble to Repel the G.O.P. Voting Push." *New York Times*, June 1, 2021. https://www.nytimes.com/2021/05/07/us/politics/democrats-republican-voting-rights.html.

Fandos, Nicholas. "As Biden Vows to 'Fight Like Heck,' Voting Overhaul Falters in Congress." *New York Times*, June 1, 2021. https://www.nytimes.com/2021/06/01/us/politics/voting-rights-congress.html.

Fieschi, Catherine. *Populocracy: The Tyranny of Authenticity and the Rise of Populism.* Newcastle upon Tyne: Agenda Publishing, 2019.

Gans, Herbert J. *The Levittowners: Ways of Life and Politics in New Suburban Community.* New York: Vintage Books, 1967.

Glickman, Lawrence. "Inventing the 'American Standard of Living': Gender, Race and Working-Class Identity, 1880–1925." *Labor History* 34, No. 2–3 (1993): 221–235.

Gougelet, David-Olivier, and Feder, Ellen K. "Genealogies of Race and Gender." In *A Companion to Foucault,* edited by Christopher Falzon, Timothy O'Leary, and Jana Sawicki, 472–489. Malden, MA: Wiley-Blackwell, 2013.

Hanhardt, Christina B. *Safe Space: Gay Neighborhood History and the Politics of Violence.* Durham, NC: Duke University Press, 2013.

Hansberry, Lorraine. *A Raisin in the Sun.* New York: Vintage, 2004.

Hansberry, Lorraine. *To Be Young, Gifted, and Black.* New York: Signet, 2011.

Harris, Cheryl I. "Whiteness as Property." *Harvard Law Review* 106, No. 8 (1993): 1707–1791.

Harris, Dianne. *Little White Houses: How the Postwar Home Constructed Race in America.* Princeton, NJ: Princeton University Press, 2011.

Herbold, Hilary. "Never a Level Playing Field: Blacks and the GI Bill." *The Journal of Blacks in Higher Education* 6 (Winter 1994–1995): 104–108.

Jackson, Kenneth T. *Crabgrass Frontier: The Suburbanization of the United States.* New York: Oxford University Press, 1985.

Kamin, Debra. "Black Homeowners Face Discrimination in Appraisals." *New York Times,* August 27, 2020. https://www.nytimes.com/2020/08/25/realestate/blacks-minorities-appraisals-discrimination.html.

Kamp, Allen R. "The History Behind *Hansberry v. Lee.*" *U.C. Davis Law Review* 20, No. 3 (1987): 481–499.

Levittown Times (Lowe Bucks County, PA). "Anti-Negro Group Seeks Legal Bolster." August 16, 1957.

Levittown Times (Lowe Bucks County, PA). "Council Lauds Calm Levittowner Stand." August 14, 1957.

Levittown Times (Lowe Bucks County, PA). "Crowds Stay Away from Dogwood." August 22, 1957.

Levittown Times (Lowe Bucks County, PA). "Five Arrested in Levittown Disorder." August 14, 1957.

Levittown Times (Lowe Bucks County, PA). "Legal Means Sought to Force Negroes to Leave Levittown." August 16, 1957.

Levittown Times (Lowe Bucks County, PA). "Protest Over Negro Family Ends Meetings." August 15, 1957.

Levittown Times (Lowe Bucks County, PA). "Troopers Break Up Crown; Man Arrested." August 20, 1957.

Lipsitz, George. "The Possessive Investment in Whiteness: Racialized Social Democracy and the 'White' Problem in American Studies." *American Quarterly* 47, No. 3 (1995): 369–387.

Lowe, Lisa. "Unfaithful to the Original: The Subject of *Dictée.*" In *Immigrant Acts: On Asian American Cultural Politics,* 128–153. Durham, NC: Duke University Press, 1996.

Massey, Douglas, and Denton, Nancy. *American Apartheid: Segregation and the Making of the Underclass.* Cambridge, MA: Harvard University Press, 1993.

Michel, Jean-Baptiste, et al. "Quantitative Analysis of Culture Using Millions of Digitized Book." *Science* 331, No. 6014 (2011): 176–182.

Moteyne, David. "Framing the American Dream." *Journal of Architectural Education* 58 (2004): 24–33.

MSNBC. "Reid: If This Was A BLM Protest, 'There Would Already Be People Shackled, Arrested Or Dead,' MSNBC." YouTube Video. 04:52. January 6, 2021. https://youtu.be/TWgQ1vKCeEo.

Munuera, Iván López. "Lands of Contagion," *E-flux*, November 30, 2020. https://www.e-flux.com/architecture/sick-architecture/363717/lands-of-contagion.

Newsmakers Online. "Opal Lee." *Gale.* Accessed June 19, 2021, https://link.gale.com/apps/doc/K1618007130/BIC?u=columbiau&sid=summon&xid=885d64d2.

New York Times. "The Churchill Spirit—In His Own Words." August 2, 1964. https://www.nytimes.com/1964/08/02/archives/the-churchill-spiritin-his-own-words.html.

Nolan, Hamilton. "Words That Mean Nothing." *In These Times*, June 1, 2021. https://inthesetimes.com/article/politics-woke-cancel-culture-socialism-critical-race-theory.

PeriscopeFilm. "1957 Race Relations Documentary 'Crisis in Levittown,' Pennsylvania 47664." YouTube Video. 31:44. November 6, 2016. https://www.youtube.com/watch?v=oIPos4YYXnk&t=461s.

Philip Lief Group. "Populist." In *Roget's 21st Century Thesaurus, Third Edition.* Accessed June 6, 2021. https://www.thesaurus.com/browse/populist.

Reddy, Chandan C. "Home, House, Nonidentity: *Paris Is Burning.*" In *Burning Down the House: Recycling Domesticity*, edited by George Rosemary, 355–379. Boulder: Westview, 1997.

Rio, Malcolm. "Architecture Is Burning." *Thresholds* 48 (2020): 122–132.

Rockwell, Norman (artist). *Ours to Fight For: Freedom from Want.* Oil painting. 1943. Washington, DC: U.S. Government Printing Office.

Rothstein, Richard. *The Color of Law: A Forgotten History of How Our Government Segregated America.* New York: Liveright, 2017.

Rowe, Peter G. *Making a Middle Landscape.* Cambridge, MA: The MIT Press, 1991.

Serhan, Yasmeen. "*Populism* Is Meaningless." *The Atlantic*, Mach 14, 2020. https://www.theatlantic.com/international/archive/2020/03/what-is-populism/607600.

Shilts, Randy. *And the Band Played On: Politics, People, and the AIDS Epidemic.* London: Viking, 1988.

Stone, W. W. "The Chinese Labor Problem." In *The Labor Movement: The Problem of Today*, edited by George McNeill, 429–453. Boston: A.M. Bridgman and Co, 1887.

Thompson, Heather Ann. "Saying Her Name." *The New Yorker*, May 16, 2021. https://www.newyorker.com/news/essay/saying-her-name.

U.S. Census Bureau. "Historical Census of Housing Tables: Homeownership." Accessed June 11, 2021. https://www.census.gov/data/tables/time-series/dec/coh-owner.html.

West, Cornel. "Niggerization." *The Atlantic*, November 2007. https://www.theatlantic.com/magazine/archive/2007/11/niggerization/306285;

Wolfinger, James. "'The American Dream—For All American': Race, Politics, and the Campaign to Desegregate Levittown." *Journal of Urban History* 38, No. 3 (2012): 430–451.

3

REPRESENTATION AND REFUSAL

From State Architecture to Highway Protests

Jeffrey Kruth

Introduction

Donald Trump, perhaps more so than any other presidential candidate and US political figure in recent years, deployed the media landscape to his political advantage through social media. Similarly, John F. Kennedy famously excelled in the first televised presidential debate, fostering a media presence furthering his ability to defeat Richard Nixon. Franklin D. Roosevelt (FDR) similarly used radio addresses to combat rumors and directly address the American public. As FDR's press secretary Stephen Early said of the value of the radio, "It cannot misrepresent or misquote. It is far reaching and simultaneous in releasing messages given it for transmission to the nation or for international consumption."[1] Although seemingly odd presidential comparisons given their eras of influence, Trump and FDR both understood an emerging media landscape and both deployed architecture as political media and shaped sensibilities of what was possible in their given eras.

For Trump, it meant a return to a vague notion of architectural neo-classicism and preferred relationship with architectural types like churches and state government buildings. As both real estate developer and media personality, Trump's relationship to images of power is conscious, and at times even staged. His decision to forcibly remove peaceful protesters from outside the White House to walk to St. John's Episcopal Church in Washington, D.C. to promote his "law and order" agenda in the wake of protests against the murder of George Floyd in June 2020 is one of the most obvious examples. Using the backdrop of the St. John's parish house with Bible in hand, Trump sought to use his bully pulpit to dominate the media coverage of the protests and his administration's response to them, while also linking himself to a particular lineage of American religious symbolism. This event and its intended imagery of control, domination,

DOI: 10.4324/9781003272076-5

and order would contrast the violence at the Capitol on January 6, 2021 where images of Trump-supporting rioters and insurrectionists overtaking the Capitol building received extensive media coverage.

Much of the media produced at the Capitol on January 6th suggests a relaxed and touristic occupation of the building as the crowd casually strolled through it. Occupiers of the building casually paused for photos while illegally occupying the building, and in some instances taking property from the offices of elected officials. Some footage shows security forces simply allowing Trump protestors to walk into the building. The images of touristic strolling contrast with some of the more violent and forceful images from that day. Taken together, however, these images point a nuanced portrait of how certain audiences align themselves with both media and state architecture. For Trump and his supporters, images in front of St. John's Cathedral, the Capitol occupation, and even Trump's own announcement of his presidential campaign with the backdrop of Trump Tower, suggest a reflexive relationship between existing institutions of power and the audiences they intend to serve. Trump and his supporters intentionally build mediatic relationships with existing institutions of the church, the state, and the corporation to suggest they are sources from which they derive their power.

In contrast to a reflexive media relationship between institution and audience, recent protests at infrastructural sites such as highways in the wake of the police murder of George Floyd, or Indigenous activists at Standing Rock suggest a different tactic and mediatic relationship for the representation of population. Infrastructure, in contrast to state buildings, is more ubiquitous and anonymous. Its primary functions are often circulation and flow of goods and information. It holds a more direct relationship to economic flows, and the multiple overlapping disparities inherent in much of the American built environment. Some thinkers like Keller Easterling suggest that infrastructure space is not only the hard materials of pipes and bridges and cables, but also the development protocols and patterns that spur the repetitive, homogenizing effects of the developer's pro forma. Infrastructure and the many megaprojects that characterize United States land use patterns are rooted in both explicit and implicit discrimination. Dianne Harris refers to these as "racialized landscapes" that "not only reflect, but reinforce and even create racially based practices of exclusion, oppression, minoritization, and privilege."[2] They normalize racial identities of places and people. Therefore, protests at infrastructural sites offer a unique vantage point to think about disruption, use, and representation.

In this chapter, I seek to understand three things. First, I unpack the reflexive binary relationship between right-wing and white supremacist protests and their occupation of state architecture and public space. Second, I attempt to show that the frameworks of universal representation stemming from the modern project and infused in architectural and technological thinking are not always desirable, and reinforce existing power dynamics. They are both an incomplete promise and tend to subsume other narratives in favor of a totalizing hegemonic paradigm. Third, I offer that infrastructural occupation, as demonstrated by Black

Lives Matter protestors, climate activists, and Indigenous rights activists offers an opportunity to think beyond state architecture as a unique site of representation.

Architectures of Representation & Networks of Control

Similar to the occupation of the Capitol in Washington DC, in late April of 2020, militia groups and armed right-wing protesters overtook the State Capitol Building in Lansing, Michigan. They first occupied the steps in front of the Capitol in protest of Democratic Governor Gretchen Whitmer's stay-at-home order in relation to the COVID-19 pandemic spreading through the state. The protest was labeled the "American Patriot Rally," and organized by Michigan United for Liberty. In Michigan, it is legal to carry firearms into state-owned buildings where protesters eventually occupied the lobby and gallery of the state Senate's deliberating chambers to disrupt the legislative body. Media photographers captured the event with two prominently circulated images. The first showed an unmasked man in the lobby yelling past security guards in surgical masks. The second was an image of six armed white men wearing tactical gear and armed with assault rifles as part of a militia group posing for a photo. Military shemaghs cover their faces, partly obscuring their identity, and presumably used as a way to prevent the spread of the coronavirus to one another. This image in particular suggests street-ready combatant insurgents in stark contrast to the ornate detail of their backdrop in the State Capitol; typically a space of decorum. These and similar occupations across the country appeared to foreshadow the events at the January of 2021 occupation of the federal Capitol Building in Washington, D.C. by Trump supporters. Images from the occupation included insurrectionists with flex cuffs intended to kidnap politicians, and in contrast, images circulated of those who casually posed for media photographs such as Adam Johnson, seen taking Speaker of the House Nancy Pelosi's podium or Richard Barnett who broke into the Speaker's office and famously posed with his feet up on her desk.

For Trump and his supporters, they are enacting the visual aesthetics of what Jacques Ranciere refers to as "consensus."[3] Their relationship to architecture is one that inherently recognizes their hierarchical relationship to the existing order. Right-wing movements foreground their relationship to architectures of the state in order to reinforce their existing relationship with state power as a form of reifying consensus. They do so through two primary means: first, by visually resembling state power through military-style garb, and second through the relative display of comfort with which they occupy state buildings. They enact and reinforce Ranciere's notion that, "Consensus as a mode of government says: It is perfectly fine for people to have different interests, values, and aspirations, nevertheless there is one unique reality to which everything must be related…"[4] That is to say, there is no alternative to the consensus hierarchical order of the state, and its relationship to socio-cultural or economic policy.

These two aesthetics are at first seemingly at odds; one of intimidation through the display of heavy tactical gear, assault rifles, and military-style fatigues, and the other of touristic relaxation. Taken together, they display the aesthetic link to consensus and Ranciere's notion of the "distribution of the sensible," which reveals who can have a share in what is common to the community through institutions like police forces.[5] The state itself is seen to belong to right wing-demonstrators, and by extension suggests the inheritance of racial and gendered hierarchies within a capitalistic framework as the most sensible political framework. This aesthetic representation is perhaps best captured by the Boogaloo Movement, a loosely organized coalition with sympathies toward white supremacists, neo-Nazis, and other libertarian sentiments. They have links to domestic acts of terrorism and plotted to kidnap Michigan Governor Gretchen Whitmer. They are noticeable in that their aesthetic combines the casual wear of colorfully patterned aloha shirts, coupled with military fatigues and other combat apparel. This suggests a level of comfort with their presence in public amid street demonstrations. They un-abashedly make their bodies present in the street as both an act of identity and intimidation. With their tactical military gear, they blend in with the existing state apparatus, reifying their supposed identity as defenders of the state (Figure 3.1).

Much of the organizing of the Boogaloo Movement and others occurs online, outside the confines of locally defined geographies to foster identity and solidarity. Indeed, the origins of the Boogaloo Movement wearing aloha shirts stems from online discussions with members seeking to start a race war. The origins of aloha shirt itself are colonial in nature, as the colorful patterns were intended for American audiences who feared the incorporation of the non-white Hawai'ian population into the American nation. The adoption of graphics and popular culture into movements like the Boogaloos is intentional for other reasons, too. Ethan Zuckerman discusses such deployments of popular culture within otherwise authoritarian and dangerous groups as an act that is inherently fruitful

FIGURE 3.1 Members of the Boogaloo Movement at a protest.

because subversive content cannot be easily isolated by authoritarians and digital surveillance.[6] The adoption of the meme "Pepe the Frog" by white nationalists plays into similar forms of obfuscation and intentional subculture by co-opting popular internet graphics to thwart authorities, and to make less explicitly legible their presence in online spaces.

In recent years, these internet subcultures have begun to make their presence known beyond digital space to occupy public space and state buildings. What began as a digital aesthetic emerges in the public realm as both dangerous, but also casual and playful.

Their aesthetic carries over into physical public space, while images of them then circulate back online, blurring the boundaries of digital organizing and the occupation of public space. The fact that they are photographed and these images are then recirculated online further bolsters their presence. As architect John May suggests, "Images are data and all imaging is, knowingly or not, an act of data processing."[7] The reproduction of these images online further drives data consumption and thus representation in both digital and physical space.

Representation, then, is a more complex term to consider within the networked infrastructure of today's contours of power. Representation also entails surveillance, tracking, and embedded systems of power in a networked society. This becomes apparent when looking at the Black Lives Matter Movement. Representation within both digital and physical space is complicated, as it brings inherent risks of both being erased through choosing not to represent, but also the threat of violence and surveillance through participation. As Data for Black Lives co-founder Yeshimabeit Milner offers, "[t]he decision to make every Black life count as three-fifths of a person was embedded in the electoral college, an algorithm that continues to be the basis of our current democracy."[8] All representations are not equal, and simply suggesting representation of marginalized populations as an end goal in itself brings with it a host of assumptions that the existing systems and networks of technology can accommodate such ideas. To destabilize such a notion asks that we change how we see, not just augment what we already see through additional data sets. In discussing surveillance and data collection on Black bodies, Simone Browne's observes "the incommensurability of lived realities between people who are monitored and those who do the monitoring, and the paradoxical ways in which someone can be surveilled and yet still be rendered invisible."[9] Browne offers a counter representation as "dark sousveillance" which are "the tactics employed to render one's self out of sight… Dark sousveillance is a site of critique, as it speaks to black epistemologies of contending with antiblack surveillance."[10]

In contrast to ideas of a "control society" to which Browne and others respond might be a diversity of tactics seemingly offers possibilities, rooted in how social movements and populations choose to represent themselves.

Networked technologies also allow new ways of interaction, as a two-way communication that Brecht and Benjamin hoped for in technologies like the radio. In a dispersed and interactive media network, power might ultimately be restructured. As media scholar Tung-Hui Hu suggests, the idea of a central-ized source of authority seemingly "disappears with the advent of borderless decentralized computer networks that confound a sovereign's ability to rule over subjects within his or her borders."[11] However, as Hu points out, this decentral-ized notion of power reforms into a new form of sovereignty resulting in real violence from NSA counterterrorism, but ultimately wields power "less through brute force than through detecting and flagging financial operations."[12] In this way, power exerts itself as part of the control society through the everyday log-ics of computation, where the operating system shapes what we think of as the computer "user." Similarly, Tarleton Gillespie suggests that software not only confines or restricts a user's behavior, but also "install(s) a world view by which behaviors they encourage or erase."[13] Networked technologies obscure their politics, and present a vision of decentralized neutrality, while simultaneously forming new sovereignties. A networked or global user is thus imagined as part of the smooth flows of networked economies. This echoes Stephen Graham's studies of satellites and bunkers as contemporary sites of control and visioning. He suggests that such systems and forms of imaging offered by technologies like satellites do not offer "an absolute form of imperial vision" but rather, "satellite imaging (is) a highly biased form of visualizing…rather than some objective or apolitical transmission of its 'truth.'"[14] Thus, power is both networked, but not omniscient, suggesting the ability to counter its worst impacts.

Refusal as Representation

In contrast to the perception of smooth flows and the perceived freedoms offered by networked technology, it is worthwhile to consider how contemporary social movements represent themselves in relation to such forms of surveillance and the architectures that discipline everyday life to both reinforce existing representa-tions, and disrupt the material sites of networked production. Here, I'd like to suggest that contemporary movements associated with the left in the United States differ in aesthetic representation in comparison to recent spatial and me-diatic occupations by the right. Spatial occupations of state buildings and the media produced in relation to them by right-wing movements reinforce ideas about the sovereign state as a symbolic relationship to architecture. In contrast, social movements of the left intentionally obstruct infrastructures of the state associated with historic forms of dispossession as a form of representation. For example, protests at Standing Rock by indigenous populations and others con-fronted the Dakota Access Pipeline, while others confronted the Keystone XL pipeline. Standing Rock Sioux sued the Army Corps of Engineers for threaten-ing "environmental and economic well-being, and would damage and destroy sites of great historic, religious, and cultural significance."[15] Their ongoing ef-forts ultimately stopped the progression of the Keystone XL pipeline in 2021.

In late summer of 2014 in Ferguson, Missouri, on the outskirts of St. Louis, protesters gathered to seek justice after 18-year-old Michael Brown was shot and killed by police. Brown's death as an African American highlighted long-standing tensions between police and local communities of color. Occupying Interstate 70, protesters disrupted traffic, prompting police in riot gear and the arrest of 35 people. Similarly, in June of 2020, protesters marched between the State Capitol in St. Paul Minnesota to Minneapolis, blocking the I-94 highway in response to the murder of George Floyd by Minneapolis police officer Derek Chauvin. Multiple other highways saw similar occupations including I-630 in Little Rock, I-40 in Memphis, and I-75 in Cincinnati. More than 1500 protesters blocked highways into downtown Atlanta.

The US highway system is recognized as a long-standing symbol of dispossession and displacement for Black Americans. When highways were constructed, their paths largely traversed long-standing Black communities, who were already subjected to segregation through policy tools like redlining, restrictive covenants, and physical racial barriers. While a symbol for displacement and segregation, the highway also stands as a perpetual network of exclusion from many of the monetary benefits associated with suburban sprawl, such as increased real estate prices and school funding structures that benefit existing wealth through their tax structure. While it is an infrastructural site of control for those who have access to it, as Deleuze suggests, it also excludes and reifies existing patterns of segregation. The highway multiplies its effects, proliferating both suburban culture as well as the abstract financial logics that increase property values and financial opportunities in the suburbs.[16] It is not surprising, then, to see the highway as a site of protest, occupation, and contestation. The protests are a struggle for justice against the desires of smooth economic flows. The highway as an artery of economic logistical infrastructure is an important component to disrupt the politics of consensus (Figure 3.2).

Visually, protestors assemble as an anonymous collective in such protests. Protesters often intentionally wear black to these protests. In contrast to the bright militaristic aesthetics of the Boogaloo Movement, Black Lives Matter protesters often wear black. Black clothing can be inexpensive and is widely available. Black clothing can also make it more difficult for police to identify any one specific individual to arrest. Together, the aesthetics of anonymity brought about by black clothing, and the choice of sites for protests allow for a disruption of the sensible. The sensible is disrupted as the anonymous crowd becomes both too large and too mobile to be contained by police power. The power balance is shifted. Occupation of more open space allows for the quick convergence and dispersal of the crowd. It is horizontally organized. It allows for what Hannah Arendt refers to as the "space of appearance." For Arendt, all political action requires a space of appearance. It is a space "where men [sic] exist not merely as others appear to me, where men exist not merely like other living or inanimate things, but make their appearance explicitly."[17] This space is not specifically tied to any one location, and it is a space that is only created "between people," thus allowing it to mutate, disperse, and emerge when possible or necessary. This alliance between people brings about its own location. The alliance that emerges is spatial as well as networked, while allowing anonymity and quick dispersal.

FIGURE 3.2 Black Lives Matter protestors block a highway in downtown Miami, Florida.

Through occupying highways, they occupy the networked logistics of the system of dispossession, rather than the direct symbolic architecture of state architecture which is more static and representational. They disrupt the flows of the networked infrastructure that has historically dispossessed them of opportunity within the realm of spatial production. Through their anonymity of assembly, they avoid both identification by police forces on the ground, and detection through emerging facial recognition and other smart technologies used in cities like New York. Such technologies tend to amplify racially discriminatory policing and fundamentally threaten the right to protest and are condemned by human rights organizations like Amnesty International.[18] These technologies build from historically problematic "smart" policing strategies, like former New York City Mayor Giuliani's "Compstat" program; an early attempt to computationally and statistically predict crime hot spots which biased policing strategies in communities of color. This ability to map the world through geo-statistical data aligns with the technologies and frameworks of Foucauldian disciplinary control through practices like geodemography.[19] The world of access to more information falsely suggests proximity to objectivity, and this falsity is reinforced by the popular idea that new media is seamless and instantaneous, abstracting the cloud and the network from its material presences and its consequences. As anthropologist David Graeber has argued in his study of debt, there is a complex and long-standing link between capital's demand for abstraction and violence.[20] This echoes Henri Lefebvre's study of the abstraction of space by the state and the tools of visioning deployed by the architect. He states, "Through its control, the state tends to accentuate the homogenous character of space, which is fractured by exchange. This space of state control can also be defined as being optical and visual."[21]

Representations of any assembly of bodies or space are always incomplete and emerging. This is why it is useful to study the tactics of representation deployed by groups like Black Lives Matter. Their space of appearance in protests is both anonymous and temporally fluid in its gatherings and dispersions. It is largely horizontal and self-organized. What can be gleaned from this type of occupation to form spaces of appearance? How might designers aligned with such social movements understand these tactics and their broader implications for representation within designed space, when their disciplinary focus is traditionally aligned with state or privatized interests?

Media theorist B. Coleman offers that in the emerging Smart City, communities of color and the marginalized might consider three trajectories in relation to what she refers to as the "technology of the surround"; the right to resist, to represent, and to disappear.[22] Drawing from Èdouard Glissant's notions of marronage (flight) as freedom and Rahul Mehrotra's concept of "pirate modernity," Coleman suggests the opportunity to opt out of any formal representations by the state, and goes beyond binaries of public and counterpublic into something she refers to as a "stacked existence *in motion*."[23] She offers an "elastic urban condition" avoiding any utopian grand vision, but instead seeks a "grand adjustment."[24]

The more elusive forms of representation of Black bodies in public space stem partially from the inherent dangers for protestors. bell hooks offers that the home has traditionally been a site of Black resistance, as it is a "private space where we do not directly encounter white racist aggression." hooks goes on to say that Black women, in particular, "resisted by making homes where all people could strive to be subjects, not objects...where we could restore to ourselves the dignity denied us on the outside in the public world."[25]

The ability to resist, represent, and disappear allows for a drifting agency which is ultimately useful for a social movement under constant surveillance. Insisting on representation in certain arenas of existing public discourse might be useful as a tactic in particular situations. As geographer Ruth Wilson Gilmore has shown, precarity of life is unequally distributed, making certain populations more prone to injury and early death. Thus, Black Lives Matter is not only a rally against police and state brutality, it is a rallying call against the precariousness of life forged by existing capitalistic frameworks. It is a call against the current distribution of the sensible through representation and resistance. Resistance allows for a space of appearance and the ability to break from existing consensus politics. As Simone Browne suggests in thinking through forms of resistance to surveillance infrastructure, "Talking back, then, is one way of challenging surveillance and its imposition of norms."[26] The right to disappear affords an opting out both from surveillance technologies, but also from existing frameworks of representation. Representation is not always desirable, and in fact, may expose further vulnerabilities to those whose lives are already more precarious and valued differently.

Black Lives Matter protests located on highways also create a form of protest that denies received notions of public space and state architecture. The narrative of public space and a state architecture intended to represent a whole population has always only been partial. As images of the attack on the US Capitol on January 6, 2021 suggest, right-wing movements seek to iconoclastically co-opt existing forms of power through its state architecture, and use it to perpetuate a narrative that they are the true inheritors of the country as suggested by its founders. These images suggest destruction of existing power as plumes of smoke from tear gas canisters and rioters storming the Capitol occupy otherwise iconic framings of the image of the Capitol. At the same time, the image of those same structures reifies a narrative of inheritance that they wish to convey. They largely see themselves as the true patriots and defenders of the nation, which is otherwise corrupted by the existing liberal party. State architecture, and their occupation of it, becomes increasingly important to the projection of their image.

In contrast, the architectural backdrop of state buildings holds less importance for marginalized populations. Architectural historian Mabel Wilson offers that Black knowledge and history are largely erased from the received narratives of institutional buildings, and that this is part of a larger Enlightenment project. She says, "[T]he Western episteme…becomes universal. That's its trick. It absorbs all other bodies of knowledge and posits that there's only one body of knowledge and one way of being in the world."[27] This extends to architecture and the audiences it represents. This partially offers an explanation of why those movements aligned with White supremacy and its ideologies seek to occupy existing government buildings, and why images from the January 6th occupation of the Capitol showed an occupant carrying the battle flag of the Confederacy. Such imagery links White supremacist ideologies with the architecture of the state.

The Universal, the User, and an Imagined Commons

If full representation within state architecture and public space has always been elusive for large segments of the population, then the occupation of infrastructural sites offers the potential of redefining notions of the public. Indeed, as Mabel Wilson suggests, much of the universalizing project of modernity tends to subsume entire narratives of populations in favor of a flattened ideology of unification. Within many disciplines including architecture, recuperation of those lost narratives is an ongoing research project. The impacts of a universalizing narrative, however, can be traced through much of the modern architectural project. Within the last generation, the architectural media project of designers Ray and Charles Eames' *Powers of Ten* offers an example of such a narrative. Initially conceived in 1968, the final version of the film was released in 1977. The film optimistically envisions seamless universal connectivity and implies a role for designers in such a framework.

In December of 1972, the crew of the Apollo 17 spacecraft took an image of the earth, widely circulated as the "Big Blue Marble." In 1973, the U.S.

Defense Advanced Research Projects Agency (DARPA) began research to investigate techniques for interlinking networks resulting in what would become the Internet. The individuals and countries within the "Blue Marble" seen from outer space could soon be networked through communication to share information and fundamentally re-shape political possibilities. The world beyond the nation-state could be imagined as a networked collective in various forms of a "multitude" as political theorists Michael Hardt and Antonio Negri have argued. New ways of visualizing, observing, and analyzing could seemingly offer new possibilities for organizations. These new global communities could be analyzed from above, opening new sites of occupation and observation Geographer Stephen Graham notes in emphasizing vertical observational technologies inherent in satellites and underground data centers that after centuries of colonization, "the horizontal and global extent of the earth's surface was both fully explored and fully claimed."[28] Observation from above could solidify new communities (Figure 3.3).

FIGURE 3.3 Big Blue Marble. NASA. 1972.

This global connectedness was famously visualized by Ray and Charles Eames in their *Powers of Ten* film from 1977. Their video begins at the human scale with individuals enjoying public space in Chicago's Burnham Park, and through narration and animation incrementally zooms to the scale of the galaxy, and back to the scale of the microscopic. The video suggests interconnectedness through seamless transitions of scale, which could be empirically observed. Planners, scientists, and geographers could now photographically and geographically visualize data in real time. Connections between the scale of the global and the microscopic could be considered to be on the same continuum, codified today through empirical processes in GIS and geodemographic analytics.

Beyond more optimistic visions of global connectedness, much of the postwar landscape continued to be shaped by Cold War politics. As emerging frameworks for empirical analysis and global visioning gained favor in the post-war era, the theoretical basis for emerging research into what would become the internet took influence from post-war military strategy applied to built environments. Sophisticated work on "queuing theory" by the RAND Corporation and others offered the ability to think through moving large amounts of population on the still emerging Interstate Highway System, as well as in the grocery store, and assembly lines. This ability to think through large numbers of population ultimately influenced the theoretical frameworks for the Internet and its ability to scale up millions of switching nodes without seriously impacting performance.[29] The postwar Interstate Highway System influenced dispersal and suburban growth away from the blast range of a Soviet atomic bomb. Dispersal as a federal defensive strategy atomized the politics of urban population, prompting new ways of trying to understand a dispersed population as a political body, fitting well with emerging technologies of observation and analysis of large-scale populations.

Working at this enlarged scale, methods such as Ian McHarg's "layered cake" emerged as a way to think about territory tied to demographics and natural systems. Architects at the building scale opted to understand population through the lens of "user." Eschewing terms like "occupants" or "client," the term user was thought to be more inclusive of those beyond who might be financing a particular building.[30] The concept of "user" emerged as a political prospect for architects by thinkers like Henri Lefebvre in *The Production of Space* first published in 1974. The search for a return to use value over exchange value in Lefebvre's work highlighted a consistent tension in architecture between buildings as commodities, and the social uses those same spaces accommodate. Lefebvre offers that, "The user's space is *lived*—not represented (or conceived.)"[31] In contrast to the broad universalism deployed by early modernists, the architectural profession by the post-war period sought to go beyond the reductive qualities of modernism by incorporating user studies. Parallel to Lefebvre's thinking, though less politically, radical, sociologists like William H. Whyte, in turn, began to study existing behaviors of public users through his 1970 Street Life Project, and codified in Whyte's seminal work, *The Social Life of Small Urban Spaces* in 1980.

Frameworks offered by Whyte and others seemed to offer a redemptive potential for the modernist project, while seemingly being both bottom-up and scientific in their approach. However, as historian Adrian Forty argues, the seamless connection between the architect's deployment of the term "user" and its outcomes were rarely a successful endeavor. Noting the work of Herman Hertzberger as a possible exception, Forty offers three shortcomings of such a search by architects in their search for successfully incorporating observations of the user into their practices. First was the false assumption that attention to people's activities would lead to non-traditional architectural forms. Second, Forty sees it as an expansion of the functionalist paradigm through incorporating user studies and interviews to justify existing functionalist programs. Third, the user sustained architects' belief-system that they were designing for a society of equals through the post-war welfare state; convincing architects that the client was in fact the end user, as opposed to those who commissioned their work, like local bureaucracies or, more recently, private interests acting on behalf of the state in neoliberal frameworks.[32]

Taken together, the expanded tools for observation and the broad, incomplete application of the "user," produced a post-war subject that led to easy quantification and the gaze of the expert observer. The user, while potentially liberating in its possibilities to dispel notions of territory and sovereignty, instead becomes part and parcel of emerging socio-technical frameworks and the land use patterns influenced by their infrastructure. These frameworks evolved toward notions of the quantified self through data metrics and demographics still prevalent in architectural and planning camps today.

Ultimately, the vision of the user as a universal subject flattens the nuances of design production and cultural differences. The optimistic and universal vision of the Eames' *Powers of Ten* is replaced with a seamless gaze of globalized surveillance, which impacts communities differently. Not all seek to be represented within a system at all times. They do not inherently seek to be the user of a media system designed for the universal, and yet deployed by existing power structures to further marginalize through surveillance. Thus, the occupation of infrastructure and direct engagement with the systems of urban dispossession usurp the intended and seemingly abstracted user. Indeed, infrastructure abstracts the user in favor of supposed universal access. Yet infrastructural systems like American highways are paid for by public resources, but require a privatized vehicle to access them. Despite the perception that infrastructure exists in the background of everyday life as an uninterrupted, secure, and efficient system of connections it is decidedly more nuanced. Indeed, as recent protests by Black Lives Matter and others show, it is occupiable, disruptive, and subject to alternative repurposing.

How else might representation function in the spaces of infrastructure, and what might it mean for public life? Infrastructural spaces offer different opportunities than the representations of state architecture favored by right-wing demonstrators and insurrectionists. In an era of continued austerity, both infrastructure and public space are often sold off and privatized to balance ever-decreasing public budgets. Shrinking cities like Detroit, Cleveland, and Flint are key examples of such austerity, as well as the numerous small towns across the country. While people reclaim small pieces of vacancy and public space, these are largely seen as placeholder forms for a commons to come. Lauren Berlant in their discussion on infrastructural commons, asks "Will the state's abandonment of its publics lead to abandonment of the state, or an intensification of the demand for a sovereign?"[33] Seemingly, in the case of Trump, such calls from his supporters for a more powerful and less accountable executive suggest the latter. Alternatively, Berlant suggests a process for unlearning the expectations of sovereignty as the alignment of the citizen and worker, and the imagination of society as a space for expansion of the rich life and perpetual growth.

If the occupation of the Capitol by Trump supporters insists on reproducing the image of the citizen in a reflexive relationship to state architecture, then the occupation and representation offered in infrastructural spaces allow for a more diffractive and diffuse form of representation. In a similar way, the notion of a universal user collapses narratives to the point of erasure of specific community narratives. More specific and yet fluid practices and communities are possible within infrastructural space. Practices in such spaces might insist on obligations to specific communities, kinship networks, and the recuperation of narratives subject to erasure by contemporary media practice. In offering such alternative forms of representation new forms and practices of agency may emerge.

Notes

1 George E Reedy, "FDR and the News Media," *The Review of Politics*, (1992): 152–155, https://www.jstor.org/stable/1407932.
2 D. Harris, "Race, Space, and the Destabilization of Practice," *Landscape Journal* 26, no. 1 (January 2007): 1–9, https://doi.org/10.3368/lj.26.1.1.
3 Jacques Rancière, *Dissensus: On Politics and Aesthetics*, ed. Steven Corcoran (London: Continuum International Publishing Group, 2010).
4 Ranciere, *Dissensus*, 144.
5 Ranciere, *Dissensus*, 95.
6 Metahaven, *Can Jokes Bring Down Governments?: Memes, Design and Politics* (Moscow: Strelka Press, 2014), 27.
7 John May, *Signal. Image. Architecture: (Everything Is Already an Image)* (New York: Columbia books on architecture and the city, 2019), 47.
8 Ruha Benjamin, *Race after Technology Abolitionist Tools for the New Jim Code* (Cambridge: Polity, 2020), 10.
9 Jessica Lingel, *Catalyst: Feminism, Theory, Technoscience*, (2016): 1–5, https://doi.org/10.28968/cftt.v2i2.76.g191.
10 Simone Browne, *Dark Matters: on the Surveillance of Blackness* (Durham, NC: Duke University Press, 2015), 21.
11 Tung-Hui Hu, *A Prehistory of the Cloud* (Cambridge, MA: The MIT Press, 2016), 94.
12 Hu, *Prehistory of the Cloud*, 95.
13 Anna Everett, John Thornton Caldwell, and Tarleton Gillespie, "The Stories Digital Tools Tell," in *New Media: Theories and Practices of Digitextuality* (New York: Routledge, 2003), 114.
14 Stephen Graham, *Vertical*, 46.

15 Complaint for Declaratory and Injunctive Relief (US District for the District of Montana Great Falls Division July 27, 2016).
16 Keller Easterling, *Organization Space: Landscapes, Highways, and Houses in America* (Cambridge, MA: The MIT Press, 2001), 79–84.
17 Hannah Arendt, *The Human Condition* (Chicago, IL: University of Chicago Press, 1958), 198.
18 "Ban the Scan," *Amnesty International* (May 4, 2021), https://banthescan.amnesty.org/.
19 McLain Clutter, "Radical Railbanking and Scenarios for Detroit," *Journal of Architectural Education* 68, no. 1 (February 2014): 104–114, https://doi.org/10.1080/10464883.2014.865971.
20 David Graeber, *Debt: the First 5,000 Years* (New York: Random House Inc., 2012).
21 Henri Lefebvre, "Space and the State," in *State/Space: A Reader*, ed. N. Brenner, B. Jessop, M. Jones, and G. Macleod (Malden, MA: Blackwell, 2003), 84–88.
22 B. Coleman, "Right to the Smart City: How to Represent, Resist, or Disappear," in *Ways of Knowing Cities*, ed. Laura Kurgan and Dare Brawley (New York: Columbia Books on Architecture and the City, 2019), 147.
23 B. Coleman, "Right to the Smart City," 155.
24 B. Coleman, "Right to the Smart City," 155.
25 bell hooks, "Homeplace (a Site of Resistance)," in *Yearning: Race, Gender, and Cultural Politics* (New York: Routledge, Taylor & Francis Group, 2015), 384, 388.
26 Simone Browne, *Dark Matters: on the Surveillance of Blackness* (Durham, NC: Duke University Press, 2015), 62.
27 Mabel Wilson, "Radical Repair," *Log*, no. 48 (2020), 22.
28 Stephen Graham, *Vertical: The City from Satellites to Bunkers* (London: Verso, 2018), 19.
29 Paul E. Ceruzzi, *Internet Alley: High Technology in Tysons Corner, 1945–2005* (Cambridge, MA: MIT Press, 2011), 24–51.
30 Adrian Forty, *Words and Buildings: A Vocabulary of Modern Architecture* (London: Thames & Hudson, 2019), 315.
31 Henri Lefebvre, *The Production of Space* (Malden: Blackwell, 2016), 362.
32 Forty, *Words and Buildings*, 314.
33 Lauren Berlant, "The Commons: Infrastructures for Troubling Times," *Environment and Planning D: Society and Space* 34, no. 3 (2016): 393–419, https://doi.org/10.1177/0263775816645989.

Bibliography

Alderman, Derek H., and Robert N. Brown. "When a New Deal Is Actually an Old Deal: The Role of TVA in Engineering a Jim Crow Racialized Landscape." *Engineering Earth*, 2010, 1901–1916. https://doi.org/10.1007/978-90-481-9920-4_105.
Amnesty International. "Ban the Scan." *Amnesty International*, May 4, 2021. https://banthescan.amnesty.org/.
Arendt, Hannah. *The Human Condition*. Chicago: University of Chicago Press, 1958.
Benjamin, Ruha. *Race after Technology Abolitionist Tools for the New Jim Code*. Cambridge: Polity, 2020.
Bertolt Brecht. "The Radio as an Apparatus of Communication." In *New Media: Theories and Practices of Digitextuality*, edited by Anna Everett and John T. Caldwell. New York and London: Routledge, 2003.
Browne, Simone. *Dark Matters: on the Surveillance of Blackness*. Durham, NC: Duke Univ. Press, 2015.
Coleman, B. "Right to the Smart City: How to Represent, Resist, or Disappear," In *Ways of Knowing Cities*, edited by Laura Kurgan and Dare Brawley. New York: Columbia Books on Architecture and the City, 2019.

Complaint for Declaratory and Injunctive Relief (US District for the District of Montana Great Falls Division July 27, 2016).

Deleuze, Gilles. *Two Regimes of Madness: Texts and Interviews 1975–1995*. Edited by David Lapoujade. Translated by Ames Hodges and Mike Taormina. New York: Semiotext, 2007.

Easterling, Keller. *Organization Space: Landscapes, Highways, and Houses in America*. Cambridge, MA: The MIT Press, 2001.

Forty, Adrian. *Words and Buildings: A Vocabulary of Modern Architecture*. London: Thames & Hudson, 2019.

Gandy, Matthew. "The Paris Sewers and the Rationalization of Urban Space." Essay. In *The Fabric of Space: Water, Modernity, and the Urban Imagination*. Cambridge, MA: The MIT Press, 2017.

Gillespie, Tarleton. *New Media: Theories and Practices of Digitextuality*. Edited by Anna Everett and John Thornton Caldwell. New York: Routledge, 2003.

Graeber, David. *Debt: the First 5,000 Years*. New York: Random House Inc., 2012.

Graham, Stephen. *Vertical: The City from Satellites to Bunkers*. London: Verso, 2018.

Harney, Stefano, and Fred Moten. *The Undercommons: Fugitive Planning and Black Study*. Wivenhoe: Minor Compositions, 2013.

Harris, Dianne. "Race, Space, and the Destabilization of Practice." *Landscape Journal* 26, no. 1 (2007): 2. https://doi.org/10.3368/lj.26.1.1.

Laski, Harold J. "The Roosevelt Experiment." *The Atlantic*, February 1934. https://www.theatlantic.com/magazine/archive/1934/02/the-roosevelt-experiment/307116/?single_page=true.

Lefebvre, Henri. *The Production of Space*. Malden: Blackwell, 2016.

Lefebvre, Henri. "Space and the State." In *State/Space: A Reader*, edited by N. Brenner, B. Jessop, M. Jones, and G. Macleod. Malden, MA: Blackwell, 2003.

Lipsitz, George. "The Racialization of Space and the Spatialization of Race: Theorizing the Hidden Architecture of Landscape." *Landscape Journal* 26, no. 1 (2007): 10–23. https://doi.org/10.3368/lj.26.1.10.

May, John. *Signal. Image. Architecture: (Everything Is Already an Image)*. New York, NY: Columbia Books on Architecture and the City, 2019.

Metahaven. *Can Jokes Bring down Governments?: Memes, Design and Politics*. Moscow: Strekla Press, 2014.

Petti, Alessandro, Sandi Hilal, and Eyal Weizman. *Architecture after Revolution: Decolonizing Architecture Art Residency*. Berlin: Sternberg Press, 2013.

Rancière, Jacques. *Dissensus: on Politics and Aesthetics*. Edited by Steven Corcoran. London: Continuum International Publishing Group, 2010.

Reedy, George E. "The First Great Communicator" Review of FDR and the News Media, *The Review of Politics*, (1992): 152–155. https://www.jstor.org/stable/1407932.

Weinberg, Alvin M. "Can Technology Replace Social Engineering?" In *Technology and the Future*, edited by Albert H. Teich. Belmont, CA: Thomson/Wadsworth, 2003.

4

ARCHITECTURE AND DISCIPLINARY KNOWLEDGE

A Case Study of Hong Kong's Heritage and Politics

Isaac Leung

Introduction

The starting point of this book is the unrest at the Capitol Building in the United States on January 6, 2021. Beyond the mediated representation of that unrest, and the most obvious speculations about the symbolic role of the site itself, it seeks to extrapolate some of the more complex and nuanced factors at play behind the cultural, social and political readings of architecture and public space more broadly. In that sense, it can be seen as part of broader debates about architecture and how, apart from serving both utilitarian and aesthetic ends, it is often deeply intertwined with politics.[1] From monumental structures to housing and commercial developments, architecture orchestrates spatial boundaries, carving out situations, imaginations and activities that encourage and yet prohibit certain social interactions.[2] The power of physical space embodied in architecture is capable of shaping, forming and representing dominant values and ideological parameters, thus shaping social norms.

In Hong Kong, architecture resonating political power—especially the very transition from the past to the present—can be consistently seen everywhere. During the colonial period, buildings such as the Central Government Offices, the Former French Mission Building and the Old Supreme Court all created a profound symbolic function ensuing effective administration under the British colonial rule.[3] St John's Cathedral was built in 1849 on Government Hill, a prime location where the residence of the colonial governor and the former government headquarters was located.[4] It was constructed to set forth specific doctrines and moral values related to ways of living during the colonial period. After the transfer of sovereignty of Hong Kong to China in 1997, the new Central Government Complex was constructed. It is a square-shaped building with a hollow middle facing Victoria Harbour, characterised by the metaphor of 'door

DOI: 10.4324/9781003272076-6

always open'.[5] It is intended to present a sense of openness and transparency in governance symbolising the unleashing of the city from its colonial past and ushering it into the new era. Next to it is the People's Liberation Army Hong Kong Building illuminated by a neon-lit five-pointed red star. Together with flags of China and Hong Kong lit by LED lights across many government and commercial buildings by the harbour, the architecture of this site serves as a vital tool in addressing certain political goals, creating a unique sense of place and national identity.

Within this tapestry of politically symbolic buildings is Tai Kwun (a colloquial name literally meaning 'big police station'),[6] which was first established by the British in 1864 and later revitalised as one of the largest cultural districts in Hong Kong.[7] Located in a site of unrest itself in 2019, the transformation of the former Central Police Station into a series of contemporary art galleries not only follows the narrative of the Hong Kong Government's vision to position the city as a cultural centre but also underscores how the preservation and revitalisation of colonial heritage have been adopted as a tool to make certain part of the past continues to animate in the present.[8] Since Tai Kwun's revitalisation in 2018, the premise has become one of the most popular places for leisure and entertainment. In examining the building and the stories around it, this chapter asks what role does the former police station play in the larger public realm? It does so in two parts. The first revisits the exhibition 'Tai Kwun 101', which took place against the backdrop of political unrest in the city in 2019. The second draws on observations at the site. By studying the architecture, exhibitions and cultural consumption of Tai Kwun, the chapter explores how a symbol of law and order, the former police station, has been re-articulated in recent times into narratives that fit a wider political agenda, encapsulated in increasingly complex urban, political and media landscapes.

A Brief History of the Central Police Station Compound

The former Central Police Station witnessed the establishment of law and order in Hong Kong. After the British troops landed on Hong Kong Island and following the end of the First Opium War in 1842, Captain William Caine became the first chief magistrate of the city.[9] In the early years of the colonial period, Caine was responsible for setting up the Hong Kong Police Force and overseeing the construction of the first magistracy and prison in the city.[10] During that time, Governor Alexander Robert Johnston focused on maintaining law and order. The Legislative Council was established in 1843, followed by the Colonial Police Force and the Supreme Court a year later.[11]

In 1860, the Second Opium War ended.[12] The British Empire acquired Kowloon, along with the New Territories being leased for 99 years from 1898.[13] Later on, the Colonial Police Force expanded. The earliest Central Police Station was then moved from Wellington Street to the current site of Tai Kwun,[14] following a plan to form an integrated law enforcement system in which the police station, the magistracy and the prison were situated within the same compound. Thereafter, an array of buildings was designed to provide facilities for the police force, including living quarters, offices, stables and holding cells.[15] The number of buildings at the compound continued to grow in the late 19th century: an expanded prison and the Central Magistracy were constructed later on, in 1897 and 1914, respectively.[16] The Central Police Station was responsible for maintaining public order, including detection of crime, cleanliness and arresting illegal immigrants. Despite being criticised for being harsh in enforcing the law, the very notion of law and order began to take root.

In December 1941, the compound suffered severe bomb damage due to the Imperial Japanese military's invasion of China. The compound's buildings were used by the Japanese military until the end of World War II. After Japan surrendered on 15 August 1945, the Central Magistracy and the Victoria Prison were subsequently reopened.

By the end of the 1970s, the Central Magistracy was decommissioned. The building was then turned into the Supreme Court and the Immigration Department later on. During the 1980s, offenders' rehabilitation was increasingly emphasised, and the Prisons Department was officially renamed the Correctional Services Department in 1982. For that reason, The Bauhinia House, which served as a watchtower in the 19th century, was turned into a halfway house for female inmates in 1984.

In 1995, under the Antiquities and Monuments Ordinance, the Central Police Station Compound was listed as a Declared Monument. Following the decommissioning of the station and prison in 2004 and 2006, respectively, a plan was initiated by the government and The Hong Kong Jockey Club to revitalise the compound, making it the single largest heritage project throughout the history of the city. After that, a non-governmental organisation was established to oversee the revitalised site. Architecture firm Purcell, together with Herzog & de Meuron and Rocco Design Architects, began to revitalise 16 heritage buildings and design two new buildings within the compound.[17] In May 2018, Tai Kwun opened to the public.[18]

The Power of Display: Tai Kwun 101 under the Backdrop of Protests

In 2019, a year after Tai Kwun opened, Hong Kong witnessed a series of protests due to the government's proposal concerning the Fugitive Offenders Amendment Bill on Extradition.[19] These protests began in March, with sit-ins at the government headquarters, followed by a demonstration in June 2019, with 2 million people participating.[20] Concurrent to the protests in the city, Tai Kwun launched its first-anniversary exhibition on 25 May, 'Tai Kwun 101', showcasing the history of the buildings within the compound over time. In this section, I discuss the rallies that occurred on Pedder Street, which is approximately seven minutes' walk from Tai Kwun. By examining how these events were visually presented through various media channels, I consider how narratives are reinforced by the depiction of the symbolism of the street. This section also describes the exhibition that was concurrently shown at Tai Kwun during the rallies. If the former Central Police Station served as an agency of discipline that was part of the colonial state apparatus, how is the current Tai Kwun juxtaposed to or aligned with the rallies and political unrest?

The Chaotic Scenes on Pedder Street

During the protests over 2019 and 2020, several rallies took place on Pedder Street. The street runs from Queen's Road Central and ends at Connaught Road Central. The street established itself as the centre of commerce in the early colonial days. It was home to the Supreme Court and the offices of Dent & Co, one of the biggest opium trading houses, which later became the wealthiest British merchant firms.[21] The street is now filled with commercial buildings and architectural landmarks, including Wheelock House, a steel-framed structure that resembles many international-style buildings. Opposite Wheelock House is the Landmark, a commercial complex and shopping mall that houses headquarters of global firms and top-tier luxury brands. The only historical building left on the street is the Pedder Building, a Beaux-Arts-style pre–World War II structure that currently houses Gagosian, one of the world's leading commercial galleries, on its top floors. The ground floor used to house the Hong Kong flagship store of Abercrombie and Fitch, which cost over HK$7 million in rent per month back in 2012.[22] The street epitomises prosperity and is one of the busiest areas in Hong Kong.

On 27 May, two days after the opening of Tai Kwun 101, hundreds of people, including activists and office workers, gathered on Pedder Street. By 1 pm, protesters had filled Pedder Street.[23] The event ended with riot police firing pepper pellets and many protesters and pedestrians dispersing to nearby shopping malls and office buildings. The event on 27 May was not the only rally on Pedder Street. In 2019 and 2020, several major rallies took place at the same site, including a few flash mob protests in October 2019[24] and a massive protest alongside a citywide strike on 11 November.[25] As a result, some participants of these rallies were prosecuted, including a securities brokerage clerk charged with participating in riots and sentenced to 30 months in prison.[26]

Many of these rallies took place in an impromptu manner, sometimes over a few days in a row, other times once a week. The prolonged protests during 2019 and 2020 were guerrilla style. Known as the 'Lunch With You' rally, the demonstrations on Pedder Street attracted office workers during their lunch breaks. The tactic was not to occupy particular sites but to show up in one place and re-emerge in another, a principle inspired by Bruce Lee's words: to be 'formless, shapeless, like water'.[27] Unlike many protests where participants want to make a point through highlighting particular buildings (e.g., the series of protests outside Trump International Hotels across many cities in the United States and supporters of Trump gathering at the Capitol building to riot on January 6, 2021), the prolonged protests in Hong Kong aimed to claim urban spaces sporadically and temporarily without much consideration of the architectural symbolism as a backdrop. These rallies gathered together different communities, including office workers, interweaving the everyday life of the city with the movement.

Despite the participants of the series of rallies not targeting any particular building, the backdrop on Pedder Street portrayed in the media highlights the important influence of architecture on society. Indeed, the visual narrative presented through the media revealed entirely different perspectives.

For example, a *Time* article titled 'Lawyers and Bankers Join Radicals at the Barricades as Hong Kong's Protests Rock the City's Financial District' includes a photo of people standing and protesting in front of a glass facade with 'Louis Vuitton' spelled out across it.[28] In front of the flagship luxury store designed by Japanese architect Jun Aoki is a well-groomed businesswoman wearing a lace dress. Beside her are two young girls wearing backpacks on their front. Another article published in *Time* had the same glass facade as the backdrop, portraying 'officer workers and pro-democracy protesters form[ing] a human chain to pass bricks during a demonstration'.[29] The high-end flagship store is a symbol of prosperity, and these photos portray the 'central district elite' joining the rallies with young people, who are considered to have 'no stake in society'.[30] People in these photos are always grouped together, demonstrating an empathetic view of those participating in the movement.

Photos of buildings with luxury shops were frequently published by the media during the protests. Apart from the photos symbolising civil liberties, many photos depict police and protesters clashing in front of shops. On 12 November 2019, the *South China Morning Post* featured a photo of office workers holding umbrellas and attempting to flee from tear gas in the air. In the backdrop of the photo is a typical footbridge adjoining commercial buildings; next to it is the flagship store of Audemars Piguet, a luxury watch shop, in front of which masses of pedestrians are running away.[31]

There was some media focus on the lawlessness and violence occurring during the events. For example, local newspaper *Shing Tao Headlines* published an image of Pedder Street with damaged traffic lights and littered with bricks. In the backdrop of the chaotic street is a store facade with the logo of Emporio Armani. In front of it is an ex-pat carrying a briefcase and trying to cross the street.[32] This image created a clear message that the rallies disrupted economic activity and dragged Hong Kong into chaos. These photos focus on examples of criminality, reinforcing that the movement was illicit and, thus, challenging the core value of the city—the rule of law. During the month-long protest, many pro-government media outlets framed the photos of the rallies through this lens.

Images of the buildings on Pedder Street, together with the luxury shop storefronts, were frequently published by the media during the protests. They symbolise prosperity yet offer a visual narrative that depicts and reinforces distinct perspectives concerning the rallies. Despite the protestors not purposefully using architectural symbolism as a backdrop, architecture still plays a key role in shaping visual narratives of certain political ends in various media publications.

Ultimately, the protests between 2019 and 2020 resulted in a radical change in law enforcement and policing. The Hong Kong Government maintained that the social movement was undermining the rule of law, but how does this reconcile with Tai Kwun 101, a few minutes' walk from the chaotic scene, portraying the law enforcement from the past? How does the symbol of the former colonial police headquarters being revamped align with the deepening distrust of institutions and the media, no matter where one sits within the political spectrum?

'Objects Through Time': An Inception of a Disciplinary Turn

Tai Kwun 101 was divided into three parts: 'Objects Through Time', 'Lost and Found' and 'Objects that Speak to Us'. The exhibition included 101 objects found on the site, aiming to provide a historical perspective on the criminal justice system over time.

Beginning with 'Objects Through Time', the exhibition presented audiences with a chronological history of the compound between 1841 and 2006. Inside the exhibition space, visitors stepped into an abundant collection of historical contents stretched over three walls. The timeline revealed an interpretive sensibility, an effort not just to illustrate a chronology of past events but to situate the compound in the context of time. For example, the very first line of the exhibition read: 'British troops land in Hong Kong. Captain William Caine is appointed Chief Magistrate with the power of arrest and detain criminals according to the law'.[33] The story of Caine was followed by Ordinance 12 announced in 1844, explaining how the police force was established with respect to the inception of law within the colonial society. Law-abiding governance has played an important role in Hong Kong's success story. The historical buildings within the compound are not only structures with roofs and walls standing on the site: the functional qualities and social attributes associated with these buildings can be used to understand society and its institutions. The timeline made sure that visitors were reminded explicitly that the establishment of the compound was derived from a system of institutional procedure that abode by the law, which legitimately conferred the power of the police force. The timeline, apart from offering visitors a chronological record of events, became a tool in which to engage its viewer in thought about the principle of the judicial system.

'Lost and Found': No One Could Escape from the Rule the Game Had in Place

The second part of the exhibition, 'Lost and Found', explored various stakeholders of the compound. The exhibition was divided into five sections, each differentiated by wall panels and installations. The first installation sitting on the floor on the opposite side of the gallery space represented prisoners of the past. Decorated with brightly coloured prison cell bars, the audience could sit on a stool and take a selfie. Next to the prison cell bars were lines of text affixed to a wall panel in vinyl, illustrating in what way an individual would be found guilty and deprived of their liberty: the verdict of a jury or the decision of a judge were authoritative in determining the criminal guilt of a person. The myriad of writing on the wall suggested that a reform of the criminal justice system was inevitable. Despite harsh punishments often being inflicted at the compound during the early British colonisation of Hong Kong,[34] the exhibition's designers hoped to show that changes happen in all eras of history: the past is only an inevitable moment in history, waiting for a progression towards ever greater liberty. Indeed, cranking, short-drilling and walking on a treadwheel, which were widely adopted punishments in the 1850s, were replaced by new principles of correction.[35] The compound, including police, the courtroom and the prison from the past, was portrayed as a progression towards a fairer system up to now.

Exhibition as an Instrument of Social Governance

In *Discipline and Punish*, Michel Foucault conceptualises that power has shifted from a top-down fashion, in which punishment is manifested through physical coercion and public spectacle, to a more ubiquitous form of social surveillance, evident in terms of a 'humane' punishment of prison sentences.[36] In this respect, the establishment of the compound, together with the judicial system, could be viewed as an effective 'technique' deployed by the colonial government to actively 'create governable subjects'.[37] If the compound during the colonial era served as a means to regulate individuals' behaviour, the same rules of conduct could be found in Tai Kwun.

In 'Objects Through Time', the historical timeline played a prominent visual and thematic role in projecting a 'straightforward narrative' that is 'stable' and 'irreversible'.[38] Distinct events were grouped and made relevant to the present. The compound made visible in the exhibition was an 'indestructible system', justified by and grounded in the newly invented law during the colonial time.[39] The exhibition served as a reminder of the past yet was intended to maintain the impression of the continuity of moral policing to the present. 'Lost and Found' illustrated how individuals were regulated in a systematic process within and outside the compound. By presenting the objects from the past, the exhibition demonstrated how police officers, prisoners and the public were constructed as governable subjects, due to the 'dispersed locus of power' mediated by the newly invented institutional form.[40]

The compound, structured as an instrument of punishment, was transformed into another institutional form, distinguished by exhibition programming. The Tai Kwun exhibition was capable of carrying forward the legacy of the system of prisons, police and legal hierarchies yet neutralising conflict and struggle—emphasising things that fit into the current agenda of society and rendering things society does not wish to remember absent. Despite the former police station, courtroom and prison having been substituted by an exhibition, the representations of the past—exhibition strategies creating meanings from the order of things—hold a currency of 'truth', bringing into play political rationality and presenting a logic that entertainment and consumption are inevitably a source of knowledge, in the light of the new logic of a market-driven cultural economy.[41]

In contrast to the social conflict reflected in the chaotic scenes on Pedder Street, Tai Kwun 101 reinforces the legitimacy of law and order as the foundation of stability and prosperity. The exhibition aligns with the government discourse concerning the rule of law in Hong Kong, a concept applied during the British colonial rule as a tool for governance, which is perpetually legitimised as a dominant grand narrative to safeguard the city by rightfully enforcing the law and punishing those who violate it. As such, the former site of power—Tai Kwun—has been redeveloped as a discursive site characterised by stability and continuity, reaffirming the power of law and order. In the meantime, the current site of conflict—Pedder Street—is a place characterised by temporal togetherness, where the notion of law and order is contested, negotiated and represented in a situational manner. One way or the other, the discourse of law and order is ubiquitous; no one can escape from the rules the game has in place.

New Reality of a Constructed Space: Guided Tour of the Revamped Architecture

Since Tai Kwun's opening in 2019, the compound has been revitalised into a museum, together with restaurants and bars housed inside 14 buildings constructed between 1864 and 1925.[42] Within the compound dotted with colonial buildings, two new buildings, named JC Contemporary and JC Cube, were built alongside the prison yard, where an old-meets-new juxtaposition is evident. Tai Kwun attracted more than 3.4 million visitors within its first year of operation.[43] It has, no doubt, become one of the most popular attractions in Hong Kong.

To capture how Tai Kwun represents the past, I joined a guided tour offered by the heritage team in May 2021, to examine how the organisation of space, time and people's activity played a role in representing history and shaping the audience's identity through retellings of stories from the past. The texts below are based on my participation in the guided tour and my observations of the various buildings within the compound. The field experience allowed me to cross the paths of other visitors and ambassadors of Tai Kwun. By observing the visitors' body language and probing questions to the ambassadors and studying every detail of the spatial arrangement and invisible structures of different spaces within the compound, I aimed to make sense of the contingent relational aspects of the compound in the context of the site's present and past.

The Barrack Block: Architecture as a Powerful Testimony of the Colonial Past

On a sunny day at 1 pm, I had set aside an hour before my appointment for a guided tour so I could snoop around the compound. During the busy lunch hour, one could easily find people gathering in small groups outside every corner of the restaurants, shops and sightseeing spots. It took me no time to find the visitor centre, which is located at the Barrack Block. The building was designed by Surveyor General Charles Cleverly, a renowned architect during the colonial period who also designed the St John's Cathedral of Hong Kong in 1849.[44] The building was part of the first construction phase of the compound, and it was one of the first buildings on the site.[45] Similar to many British military barracks, the neo-classical building consists of a roof supported by columns at regular intervals, finished with stone quoins adjoining the walls of the building. The archways on the ground floor and verandas on the upper floors are the epitome of early colonial design.[46] The building played a major functional role in the past, where public offices, such as the report room, were housed.[47]

The first place I found myself in the building was a souvenir shop, which was located at the entrance. Visitors must pass the souvenir shop either when they enter or leave the visitor centre. At the shop, a variety of products were quietly fighting for attention on layers of wall-mounted shop shelves. Among all the products, one that caught my attention was the book *Hong Kong Past & Present*, written by journalist Sherry Lee. The cover of the book displayed two images of the Cenotaph War Memorial: a waving Union Jack on the left and a Five-star Red Flag on the right. Above the book were a few plush pillows designed by Japanese pop artist Takashi Murakami, featuring the iconic symbol of the artist's smiling flowers. Despite the book and the artist-designed merchandise being seemingly unrelated, the contrast between the concepts behind these objects fitted well into the mission of Tai Kwun: an explicit link between history and cultural consumption is simultaneously engineered everywhere at the site.

Change is a constant at heritage sites: incorporating new uses and reinserting them to cope with evolving expectations is essential in making heritage buildings sustainable. Inside the building, the former offices are replaced by restaurants, a tailor shop and studios for bonsais and ceramics. Besides the exterior of the building being graced with elaborate decoration in colonial style, the interiors of the restaurants and shops also possess patterns similar to the building façade. Indeed, many businesses in the building are colonial themed, aiming to mimic an authentic 18th-century experience for diners and shoppers. For example, Madame Fù, a restaurant named after an imaginary persona from Shanghai, is located on the top floor of the building. According to the restaurant's website, after Fù moved from Shanghai to Paris, she received generous sponsorship from a wealthy admirer for her education there. After that, she became active in the dazzling salons and was a well-known socialite.[48] The vision of femininity in the statement represents a typical colonial stereotype of a passive Asian woman being rescued by Western society, which has continued to manifest itself at Tai Kwun. For many people, colonial nostalgia is equivalent to problematic stereotypes. Those having lunch at the restaurant decorated with both Chinese lantern lamps and Western antiques appeared oblivious to the contradiction. The restaurant was jam-packed with expatriates for the lunch service. For a second, I thought I was travelling back in time when the boundary between colonial bourgeoisie and local working class was sharply divided. Architecture is a powerful testimony of old Hong Kong.

Exactly ten minutes before the tour started, I found myself at the visitor centre with five other visitors waiting in line to pick up a wireless headset for the guided tour. The visitors standing next to me appeared excited to find out more about the compound. After a short exchange of greetings, a docent dressed in a white tee-shirt began discussing the history and aesthetic style of the compound court-yard, where police officers' typical daytime patrol took place in the past. Pointing at the Barrack Block, the docent addressed the group:

> Look at the chimney on the roof of the Barrack Block, which is an unusual design for Chinese's architecture. In Hong Kong, people don't need to burn coal to warm interior spaces, as we all know the city is located at the tropical zone. Without any actual function, this chimney well-exemplifies the British's desire to reproduce the same aesthetic in architecture of home-land in the colonial outpost. ... The Barrack Block was built 20 years after Captain Charles Elliot established a police force in Hong Kong in 1841.

The docent was forced to stop abruptly due to an interruption by one of the par-ticipants. 'Hong Kong was ceded to the British in 1842'. Her face squinted as she asked: 'How come the police force was established before that?'

The docent awkwardly idled for a second before replying:

> The British knew that Hong Kong was a strategic location politically and economically and they wanted this piece of land for a long time. That's why they took control of Hong Kong Island and planned ahead the estab-lishment of the police force even back in 1841, before the Qing Dynasty agreed to cede the Hong Kong Island to the British.[49]

In recent years, Hong Kong has witnessed a heightened sensitivity concerning its colonial legacy. From old post boxes from the colonial era to street names that reference its British past, there has been a great deal of heated debate about whether objects and symbols rooted in colonialism are politically incorrect.[50] Tai Kwun, a project that was initiated by the government, seems to be exempt from the phenomenon of political correctness currently taking place in the city. Particularly in the case of Madame Fù, one may wonder, does it make the repackaging of the 'shameful past' associated with colonial power and geared to the promotion of the tourism economy right? Despite that the cultural enunciation of the colonial era represented in Tai Kwun's buildings seemed to be unquestionably accepted everywhere within the compound, it was not surprising that the docent showed full awareness of the sensitivity of the issue involved.

The Police Headquarters Block: A 'Heterotopia' Reinforced through a Bricolage of Things

A few minutes later, the other participants and I were in front of the Police Headquarters Block. The building was completed in 1919. The south façade of the building faces the parade ground, while the north façade fronts the main entrance from Hollywood Road, a major road connecting downtown and the surrounding neighbourhoods. Finished in classical style, the façade of the building is covered with Canton red brick on the south side and cement plaster on the north side.[51]

Standing at the entrance, one can observe two high-rise buildings sitting behind the headquarters. The gigantic proportion of these two buildings compared to the compound creates a stark contrast, intruding on the incredible view of the cluster of colonial buildings. Looking up the building from the parade ground of Tai Kwun, I could feel the massiveness of the buildings' façade: one wrapped with a gigantic advertisement, presenting a Chanel 55.55-carat diamond necklace, and another covered with stickers along its façade, with the words 'Fitted Offices. Flexible Terms' displayed. The apparent incompatibility of things—art, heritage and businesses from all times and styles—is cramped into one single place similar to what Foucault called a 'heterotopia' (Frew 2016). For a second, the imagined dystopian metropolis portrayed in *Blade Runner* was evoked, and gigantic billboards blanketing a city were no longer something set in the future, proving that the imaginary city is here and now. Once we entered the building, the docent addressed the group:

> The principle of revitalising this compound is to rescue the existing materials as much as possible. When this building was decommissioned in 2004, many floor tiles were already damaged. We have collected many of the usable tiles and replaced the damaged one with tailor-made tiles ordered from the original factory.[52]

The balustrade of the staircase inside the building was upgraded to meet the present standard requirements for stair railing height, while maintaining the integrity of the original design. From preserving the floor tiles to strengthening the staircase balustrade, Tai Kwun has demonstrated a respectful preservation in regard to the historical values of the built environment. The symbolic and aesthetic importance of classical colonial iconography of the floor tiles and staircase balustrade, on the one hand, present a utopian feature in which the design, including form and function, are resting on a belief in the perfectibility of colonialism, keeping the remnants as utopic (Foucault 2010). On the other hand, the add-ons—the modern stair railing made with metal and of appropriate height and the tailor-made flooring next to the remnant floor tiles—provided the visitors an experience of a place where the past is simultaneously intersecting with the culture of the present.

The Courtroom: Remaining the Same Way from One Era to the Next

The docent then gave us a tour of the courtroom. The typical grandiose colonial-style interior of the room—the orderly setting of walls, barriers and partitions—immediately offered the visitors a sense of authority and power. Despite the solemn atmosphere, many visitors had their smartphones ready, striking poses in front of the judge's bench and taking selfies at the public spectator seating area. Behind the public spectator seating area, a few interactive booths captioned 'High-profile Court Cases', presented a plethora of cases heard through the history of the Central Magistracy. Peter Fitzroy Godber, a British police chief superintendent who was once a respected policeman confronting rioters in 1967, was accused of corruption in 1973. The case marked an important milestone for the colonial government in fighting against corruption, particularly due to the identity of Godber as a high-ranked expatriate. The docent addressed the group:

> The former Central Police Station, Central Magistracy and Victoria Prison formed a one-stop approach for law and order. This courtroom is where justice being delivered in the past. The law and order in Hong Kong has been maintained continually to the present.[53]

Behind the judge's bench, an animation was presented, illustrating the case of a European being charged for not paying a Chinese rickshaw 'coolie' and assaulting a police constable. Despite the polarising racial tensions between the defendant and the witness, the ending presented the visitors with a sense of justice, at the same time as revealing problems such as elitism and racism. Even though the contents selected in the courtroom clearly made the past and the present two separate entities, the juxtaposed differences between the colonial era and the present persuasively conveyed to the visitors the unchanged truth—that the established system is reinforced while the law remains a standard to measure and shape who we are here and now.

The Victoria Prison: A Great Leap Forward in Progress Between the Past and the Present

The last stop of the tour was the former Victoria Prison, known as the B Hall. Entering the prison cell, one immediately had an agonising feeling, as if going to a torture museum that aims to reveal a dark time when justice could only be manifested with the aid of sticks and spikes.

The B Hall looked like a typical prison with a corridor in the middle and cells on both sides. On the left-hand side, the first cell was covered with a panel, captioned 'Harsh Punishment as a Deterrent'. It illustrated how the application of harsh punishment was considered the best way to maintain law and order during the colonial period. The idea of harsh punishment was followed by texts which read:

> The 1877 Gaol Committee suggested making the lives of prisoners, especially Chinese inmates, as distasteful as possible through imprisonment in basic conditions plus harsh punishment.[54]

The cells are redesigned in a way to offer visitors an emotionally engaging experience of the stories of imprisonment in the past. On the screen next to the wall panel, an interactive game was presented, portraying various means of corporal punishment adopted in the past. The descriptions in the game highlighted how racism and coloniality were ingrained in the penitentiary system.

Behind the limestone walls was another eerie room covered in projections of silhouettes, presenting a chained prisoner being spanked by a uniformed police officer. During the 19th century, prisoners were subject to cruel punishments. Public flogging was regarded as public entertainment. Before Governor John Pope Hennessy's arrival in 1877, approximately 200 public floggings took place annually in Hong Kong.[55] Before the abolishment of the death penalty in 1993, execution was carried out inside the prison. The underlying logic of the colonial governance is exemplified in one of the quotes by Hennessy presented on a panel in the prison cell:

> In every part of the British Empire, Her Majesty's Government have laid down what they believe to be sound principle … a due mixture of severe punishment with some attempt at reformation.[56]

At the far end of the corridor, one could see that the prison had been transformed in line with a new mode of management, to correct the barbarity of a previous time and to focus on rehabilitation in the late 19th century. In one of the last cells leading to the corridor exit, a projection of a silhouetted prisoner mopping a floor was presented, marking an end to the time when physical torture was lawfully executed in the prison.

'Colonial prisons were overcrowded. Do you know how many prisoners were held in a cell when the prison reached a peak?' asked the docent.

'Four', answered one of the participants passionately.

'Seven prisoners crammed into these tiny cells! We have no idea how they did it. I suppose they were sitting one behind the other while they were sleeping', said the docent, expressing at once doubt and confusion.

'What about now? Are the current prisons available for us to visit?' continued the participant.

'I'm not sure whether the current prisons are available for the public to visit. But I'm sure the conditions of the prisons now are much better', replied the docent affirmatively.[57]

At the end of the tour, I found myself at the centre of the open space in the prison yard with the other participants. Behind us was a century-old prison wall and in front of us was JC Contemporary, designed by Jacques Herzog and

Pierre de Meuron. Looking up at the buildings enveloped by a precast alumin-
ium façade that resembles the surrounding buildings' granite blocks from the
past, I suddenly felt like I was taking a surreal leap into another world—a place
where old and new are confronting each other, reflecting the past and the future.
Herzog and de Meuron once said they wanted to transform the forbidding prison
yard into a new open public space.[58] Despite chains and whips being replaced
with contemporary art in this space, the deep indentations of the façade of the
two new buildings inevitably give one the impression of a prison, as if punishments still exist but are no longer taking place behind the locked doors.

New Mode of Spatial Configuration:
Continuity and Change in History

I have illustrated my experience during a guided tour of Tai Kwun. The evolving
and complex relationships among architecture, visitors and the ambassadors suggest
the reinvention of the former police station, court and prison into a new place capable
of creating unique experiences. The preservation of the existing buildings, together
with the newly added restaurants, shops and events, were utilised to communicate
various cultural meanings, thus sketching a sense of continuity from the past.

Despite the heightened sensitivity about the city's colonial legacy in which
symbols rooted in colonialism are found to be politically incorrect, under the
guise of heritage and creative industry, Tai Kwun presents itself as a space capable of testifying the city's colonial past. At the Barrack Block and the Police
Headquarters Block, the architectural fragments, alongside the colonial-themed
restaurants, the newly installed floor tiles and handrails and the surrounding skyscrapers, constructed a landscape that is fragmented and contradictory: reflecting
the distinctions between past and present, commercial and cultural, and colonial
and post-colonial aspects. These buildings juxtapose axes of time and space, offering a heterotopic vision that is mediated by a hybridity of sensitivities. In *Of
Other Spaces: Utopias and* Heterotopias, Foucault explains the concept of heterotopia as 'worlds within worlds'[59]; it has a 'function in relation to all the space
that remains', and it is simultaneously illusive and perfect.[60] The heterotopic
setting of these buildings at Tai Kwun offers an opportunity for visitors to see
the unseen, providing an engagement that 'contrast[s] with the everyday and the
mundane'.[61] The otherness of these spaces allows visitors to gaze upon fragments
of time and to internalise this experience through the contradiction between
imagination and lived experience. On the one hand, these buildings represent
the colonial past, capable of offering a 'perfect' visual and cultural experience
away from current Hong Kong society. On the other hand, visitors' experience is
framed by an 'illusion' characterised by the idea of a cultural economy—the past
is conceptualised as an ideal representation, only encapsulated within consumption at the site. No wonder Foucault interprets gaze as something 'not bound
by the narrow grid of structure', which allows 'variations' and 'tiny anomalies'
to take place.[62] The 'abnormality' of the colonial past manifests itself through a

'socially organised and systematised gaze',[63] which is integral to systems of power mediated by the newly built cultural complex.

In the courtroom and the Victoria Prison, architecture is a thematic representation of the judicial and penal system. They serve as evidence of the compound's history, as much as offering a 'unified worldview' of the colonial past.[64] The courtroom reaffirms the legal instruments and criminal proceedings established during the colonial period. The stories portrayed in the courtroom suggest to visitors, despite problems such as elitism and racism during the colonial period, that the authority of the court remained an effective means to offer justice in society. The history portrayed in the courtroom not only portrays the significance of the judicial system in the past to visitors but also positions them in specific relations of power 'necessarily ordered by the present state of knowledge'.[65] By inviting visitors to immerse themselves in the former courtroom, the building reaffirms the city's commitment to the rule of law and offers visitors a sense of identity as citizens here and now. Victoria Prison is presented as transforming from a position of embracing harsh punishments to an approach of addressing correction and rehabilitation. Indeed, the apparent progression also suggests a continuity of the penal system's 'disciplinary power'. Even the prison is no longer serving its original purpose—the concept of prison as a disciplinary institution has changed.[66] The former prison has been transformed, with a new spatial configuration permitting the retelling of the stories of the past. It marked a sense of 'liberation' and yet induces new forms of disciplinary knowledge, in tandem with the wider public's interest in heritage and cultural industries.

Conclusion

In the above, I have presented detailed descriptions of the exhibition Tai Kwun 101, followed by my observations of the built spaces, the surrounding neighbourhood and the activities in a guided tour. The new spatial configurations of the former police station compound show that architecture is now a means by which the government strives to build a cultural profile of the city yet with heritage remaining a tool for articulating the past in support of the present agenda. Architecture and politics are engineered in a new reality: upholding the functionality of certain things in the past, manifested in social life as a commodity and through the legitimacy of the law, and containing other aspects as artefacts of present-oriented cultural experience. Architecture plays a key role in sustaining disciplinary knowledge, characterised by consumer culture. The newly invented space and stylistic experiences of Tai Kwun provide both pleasure and discipline within ever-expanding boundaries of architecture and governance.

Notes

1 Petra Čeferin, 'The Architectural Object', in *The Resistant Object of Architecture: A Lacanian Perspective*, ed. Čeferin Petra, 104 (Abingdon: Routledge, 2021).
2 Juhani Pallasmaa, 'Body, Mind, and Imagination: The Mental Essence of Architecture', in *Mind in Architecture: Neuroscience, Embodiment, and the Future of Design*, ed. Juhani Pallasmaa and Sarah Robinson (London: MIT Press, 2015).

3 Tris Y-C. Kee and Wah Sang Wong, eds., *Architecture in Hong Kong: Teaching Kit for the Appreciation of Architecture in Secondary School Curriculum*, vol. 1–4 (Hong Kong: Hong Kong Institute of Architects, 2012).

4 Kee and Wong, *Architecture in Hong Kong*.

5 Cristian Aguila, 'HKSAR Government Headquarters/Rocco Design Architects', *ArchDaily*, accessed 28 February 2014, https://www.archdaily.com/481237/hksar-government-headquarters-rocco-design-architects.

6 Tiffany Tang, 'Between the Skyscrapers; Hong Kong Hidden Heritage Gems Come Alive', *iDiscover*, accessed 6 August 2019, https://i-discoverasia.com/hk-hidden-heritage/.

7 Enid Tsui, 'Hong Kong Central Police Station Restoration: How City's Most Ambitious Heritage Project Overcame the Odds', *South China Morning Post*, 15 June 2018, https://www.scmp.com/lifestyle/article/2150710/hong-kong-central-police-station-restoration-how-citys-most-ambitious.

8 Michel Foucault, 'Nietzsche, Genealogy, History', in *The Foucault Reader*, ed. Paul Rabinow (London: Penguin Classics, 2020), 81.

9 William Travis Hanes and Frank Sanello, *The Opium Wars: The Addiction of One Empire and the Corruption of Another* (Naperville, IL: Sourcebooks, 2007), 149–162; Christopher Munn, *Anglo-China: Chinese People and British Rule in Hong Kong, 1841–1880* (Aberdeen, Hong Kong: Hong Kong University Press, 2009), 109–255.

10 Tai Kwun, 'Brief History of the Central Police Station Compound', Heritage Conservation, Historical Timeline, accessed 19 July 2021, https://www.taikwun.hk/en/taikwun/heritage_conservation/historical_timeline.

11 Ambrose Yeo-Chi King and Rance Pui-leung Lee, 'Emphasis', in *Social Life and Development in Hong Kong*, ed. Ambrose Yeo-Chi King and Pui-leung Lee Rance (Hong Kong: Chinese University Press, 1988); Lawrence K. K. Ho and Yiu Kong Chu, 'Opening of Chaos: The Birth of Police Force on the Island', in *Policing Hong Kong 1842–1969: Insiders' Stories*, ed. Lawrence K. K. Ho and Yiu Kong Chu (Hong Kong: City University of Hong Kong Press, 2012); Anton Cooray, 'General Introduction', in *Constitutional Law in Hong Kong* (Alphen aan den Rijn: Wolters Kluwer, 2020).

12 Kathryn Meyer, 'Deadly Dreams: Opium and the Arrow Wars (1856–1860) in China. J. Y. Wong'. *The China Journal* 48 (2002).

13 Andrew Lynch, 'The "Glocolization" of Spanish in Asia', in *The Routledge Handbook of Spanish in the Global City*, ed. Andrew Lynch (New York: Routledge, 2021).

14 Kwun, 'Brief History of the Central Police Station Compound'.

15 May Holdsworth and Christopher Munn, 'Barrack Block and Headquarters Block', in *Crime, Justice and Punishment in Colonial Hong Kong Central Police Station, Central Magistracy and Victoria Gaol*, ed. May Holdsworth and Christopher Munn (Hong Kong: Hong Kong University Press, 2020).

16 Kwun, 'Brief History of the Central Police Station Compound'.

17 British Council, 'Tai Kwun Tour with Purcell Heritage Architects', SPARK: The Science and Art of Creativity, accessed 16 July 2021, https://www.britishcouncil.hk/en/spark/festival-programme/tai-kwun-tour.

18 The Hong Kong Jockey Club, 'Phased-Opening of Tai Kwun to Mark a Major Milestone for Heritage Revitalisation in Hong Kong', *Corporate News. About HKJC*, 9 May 2018, https://corporate.hkjc.com/corporate/corporate-news/english/2018-05/news_2018050902057.aspx.

19 Tony Cheung, 'What Is Behind Hong Kong's Anti-Extradition Protests?', South China Morning Post, 13 June 2019, https://www.scmp.com/news/hong-kong/politics/article/3014261/what-behind-hong-kongs-anti-extradition-protests.

20 Martin Purbrick, 'A Report of the 2019 Hong Kong Protests', *Asian Affairs* 50, no. 4 (2019). Civil Human Rights Front's estimate. The police estimated that there were 338,000 demonstrators.

21 Solomon Bard, '1895', *Voices from the Past: Hong Kong, 1842–1918* (Hong Kong: Hong Kong University Press), 141; Dezső Bozóky, 'Pedder Street, Central District',

DigitalRepository@HKUL, image, 1908, https://digitalrepository.lib.hku.hk/catalog/0r967532s#?c=&m=&s=&cv=&xywh=-2750%2C-38%2C9099%2C4034.

22 Nikki Sun and Laura He, 'Abercrombie & Fitch to Shut Down Hong Kong Store in Wake of Economic Downturn', *South China Morning Post*, 19 November 2016, https://www.scmp.com/news/hong-kong/economy/article/2047586/abercrombie-fitch-shut-hong-kong-store-wake-economic-downturn.

23 Claire Hung, 'Hong Kong Police Fire Pepper Pellets as Hundreds Rally, Li Ka Shing Defends New Security Law', *The Straits Times*, 28 May 2020, https://www.straitstimes.com/asia/east-asia/hong-kong-police-protesters-lock-horns-over-national-anthem-bill-new-security-law.

24 Martin Choi, Kathleen Magramo and Kanis Leung, 'Halloween Protests in Hong Kong: Police Fire Tear Gas in Mong Kok, Central and Sheung Wan as People Denounce Alleged Force Brutality and March against Mask Ban', *South China Morning Post*, 31 October 2019, https://www.scmp.com/news/hong-kong/politics/article/3035804/tear-gas-fired-hong-kong-protesters-gather-mong-kok.

25 Kris Cheng, 'Hong Kong Police Fire Tear Gas in Central against Protesting Crowds', *Hong Kong Free Press*, 11 November 2019, https://hongkongfp.com/2019/11/11/hong-kong-police-fire-tear-gas-central-protesting-crowds/.

26 Liu Anqi, 'Securities Brokerage Clerk in Central for Participating in Riots Sentenced to 30 Months in Prison', *Bastille Post*, 2 July 2021, https://www.bastillepost.com/hongkong/article/8723609-%E3%80%90%E5%92%8C%E4%BD%A0lunch%E3%80%91%E8%AD%89%E5%88%B8%E8%A1%8C%E6%96%87%E5%93%A1%E4%B8%AD%E7%92%B0%E5%8F%83%E8%88%87%E6%9A%B4%E5%8B%95-%E5%88%A4%E5%9B%9A30%E6%9C%88.

27 Independent Police Complaints Council, *A Thematic Study by the IPCC on the Public Order Events Arising From the Fugitive Offenders Bill Since June 2019 and the Police Actions in Response* (Hong Kong: Independent Police Complaints Council, 2020), 75, https://www.ipcc.gov.hk/en/public_communications/ipcc_thematic_study_report.html; Mary Hui, 'Bruce Lee's 'Be Water' Philosophy works for Hong Kong Protests – Can It Work for Trail Runners?', *South China Morning Post*, 28 August 2019, https://www.scmp.com/sport/outdoor/trail-running/article/3024649/bruce-lees-be-water-philosophy-works-hong-kong-protests.

28 Amy Gunia, 'Lawyers and Bankers Join Radicals at the Barricades as Hong Kong's Protests Rock the City's Financial District', *Time*, 15 November 2019, https://time.com/5727880/hong-kong-bankers-lawyers-protests/.

29 Amy Gunia, 'More Chaos in Hong Kong as Protesters Make a Fresh Attempt to Enforce a Territory-Wide Strike', *Time*, 11 November 2019, image caption, https://time.com/5724726/hong-kong-strike-protests-chaos/

30 Hong Kong Special Administrative Region, 'Transcript of Remarks by CE at Media Session', 9 August 2019, Hong Kong Special Administrative Region Press Releases, transcript, https://www.info.gov.hk/gia/general/201908/09/P2019080900869.htm.

31 Peter Forsythe, 'Hong Kong Protests: Why There's No Sense in Blaming 'Both Sides', *South China Morning Post*, Letters, 12 November 2019, https://www.scmp.com/comment/letters/article/3037205/hong-kong-protests-why-theres-no-sense-blaming-both-sides.

32 Liu Anqi, '[Lunch with You] Securities Broker Zhonghuan Participated in the Riot and Sentenced to 30 Months in Prison', *Hong Kong News*, 2 July 2021, https://hd.stheadline.com/news/realtime/hk/2118702/%E5%8D%B3%E6%99%82-%E6%B8%AF%E8%81%9E-%E5%92%8C%E4%BD%A0lunch-%E8%AD%89%E5%88%B8%E8%A1%8C%E6%96%87%E5%93%A1%E4%B8%AD%E7%92%B0%E5%8F%83%E8%88%87%E6%9A%B4%E5%8B%95-%E5%88%A4%E5%9B%9A30%E6%9C%88.

33 Fieldnotes, Tai Kwun, Hong Kong, May 2021.

34 Purcell Miller Tritton, *The Old Central Police & Victoria Prison Hong Kong. Conservation Management Plan* (Purcell Miller Tritton, June 2008), https://www.heritage.gov.hk/en/online/press2008/cmp.pdf, 18.

35 Purcell Miller Tritton, *The Old Central Police & Victoria Prison Hong Kong*, 18.
36 Débora de Carvalho Figueiredo, 'Discipline and Punishment in the Discourse of Legal Decisions on Rape Trial', in *Language in the Legal Process*, ed. Janet Cotterill (Basingstoke: Palgrave Macmillan, 2007), 260–274; Foucault, 'Nietzsche, Genealogy, History', 81.
37 John Morrissey, 'Foucault and the Colonial Subject: Emergent Forms of Colonial Governmentality in Early Modern Ireland', in *At the Anvil: Essays in Honour of William J. Smyth*, ed. Patrick J. Duffy and William Nolan (Geography Publications: Dublin, 2012).
38 Dino Franco Felluga, 'Archaeology (Archaeological)', in *Critical Theory the Key Concepts*, ed. Dino Franco Felluga (London: Routledge, 2015), 17.
39 Felluga, 'Archaeology (Archaeological)'.
40 Breda Gray, 'Governing Integration', in *Globalization, Migration and Social Transformation: Ireland in Europe and the World*, eds. Bryan Fanning and Ronaldo Munck (Burlington, VT: Ashgate, 2011), 93–106.
41 Leonie Sandercock and Peter Lyssiotis. 'Who Knows? Exploring Planning's Knowledges', in *Cosmopolis II: Mongrel Cities of the 21st Century* (London: Continuum, 2003).
42 Tsui, 'Hong Kong Central Police Station Restoration'.
43 HG Masters, 'New Director for Tai Kwun', *Art Asia Pacific*, 9 April 2020, http://artasiapacific.com/News/NewDirectorForTaiKwun.
44 Holdsworth and Munn, 'Barrack Block and Headquarters Block'; Purcell, *Conservation Management Plan and Heritage Impact Assessment* (Hong Kong: Purcell, 2015), https://www.amo.gov.hk/form/HIA_Report_CGOWW.pdf.
45 Purcell Miller Tritton, *The Old Central Police & Victoria Prison Hong Kong*, 83; Munn, 'Crime and Justice'.
46 Munn, 'Crime and Justice'.
47 Purcell Miller Tritton, *The Old Central Police & Victoria Prison Hong Kong*, 83.
48 Madame Fù, 'Grand Café Chinois: Hong Kong: Chinese Cuisine', Madame Fù, accessed 17 July 2021, https://www.madamefu.com.hk/about-us.
49 Fieldnotes, Tai Kwun, Hong Kong, May 2021.
50 John Carney, 'Hong Kong's Vintage Colonial Postboxes to Be Preserved', *South China Morning Post*, 23 September 2012, https://www.scmp.com/lifestyle/article/1043342/hong-kongs-vintage-colonial-postboxes-be-preserved.
51 Purcell Miller Tritton, *The Old Central Police & Victoria Prison Hong Kong*, 37
52 Fieldnotes, Tai Kwun, Hong Kong, May 2021.
53 Fieldnotes.
54 Fieldnotes.
55 Fieldnotes.
56 Fieldnotes.
57 Fieldnotes.
58 Herzog & De Meuron, '296 Tai Kwun, Centre for Heritage & Arts', Herzog & De Meuron Projects, accessed 17 July 2021, https://www.herzogdemeuron.com/index/projects/complete-works/276-300/296-tai-kwun.html.
59 Swetlana Stefanova, 'Waterways and Ships as Heterotopia', in *Negotiating Waters: Seas, Oceans, and Passageways in the Colonial and Postcolonial Anglophone World*, eds. André Dodeman and Nancy Pedri (Delaware: Vernon Press, 2019), 119–134.
60 Michel Foucault, 'Of Other Spaces', *Architecture/Mouvement/Continuité* 5 (1984): 46–59, trans. Jay Miskowiec, https://web.mit.edu/allanmc/www/foucault1.pdf, 8.
61 Jonas Larsen and John Urry, *The Tourist Gaze, 3* (London: Sage Publications UK, 2011).
62 Larsen and Urry, *The Tourist Gaze*, 1.
63 Larsen and Urry, *The Tourist Gaze*, 1.
64 Suzanne Gearhart, 'The Taming of Michel Foucault: New Historicism, Psychoanalysis, and the Subversion of Power', *New Literary History* 28, no. 3 (1997), https://doi.org/10.1353/nlh.1997.0032.

65 Michel Foucault, 'Introduction', in *Archaeology of Knowledge* (London: Psychology Press, 2002).
66 John S. Ransom, 'Foucault's Discipline', in *Foucault's Discipline: The Politics of Subjectivity*, ed. John S. Ransom (Durham, NC: Duke University Press, 1997).

Bibliography

Aguilar, Cristian. 'HKSAR Government Headquarters/Rocco Design Architects'. *ArchDaily*. Accessed 28 February 2014. https://www.archdaily.com/481237/hksar-government-headquarters-rocco-design-architects.

British Council. 'Tai Kwun Tour with Purcell Heritage Architects'. SPARK: The Science and Art of Creativity. Accessed 16 July 2021. https://www.britishcouncil.hk/en/spark/festival-programme/tai-kwun-tour.

Carney, John. 'Hong Kong's Vintage Colonial Postboxes to Be Preserved'. *South China Morning Post*, 23 September 2012. https://www.scmp.com/lifestyle/article/1043342/-hong-kongs-vintage-colonial-postboxes-be-preserved.

Čeferin, Petra. 'The Architectural Object'. In *The Resistant Object of Architecture: A Lacanian Perspective*, edited by Čeferin Petra, 104. Abingdon, Oxon, Oxfordshire: Routledge, 2021.

Cheung, Tony. 'What Is Behind Hong Kong's Anti-Extradition Protests?'. *South China Morning Post*, 13 June 2019. https://www.scmp.com/news/hong-kong/politics/article/3014261/what-behind-hong-kongs-anti-extradition-protests.

Cooray, Anton. 'General Introduction'. In *Constitutional Law in Hong Kong*, 17. Alphen aan den Rijn: Wolters Kluwer, 2020.

Dikötter, Frank. 'Open Borders'. In *The Age of Openness: China Before Mao*, edited by Dikötter Frank, 37. Berkeley: University of California Press, 2009.

Felluga, Dino Franco. 'Archaeology (Archaeological)'. In *Critical Theory the Key Concepts*, edited by Dino Franco Felluga, 93–106. London: Routledge, 2015.

Figueiredo, Débora de Carvalho. 'Discipline and Punishment in the Discourse of Legal Decisions on Rape Trial'. In *Language in the Legal Process*, edited by Janet Cotterill, 260–274. Basingstoke: Palgrave Macmillan, 2007.

Foucault, Michel. 'Introduction'. In *The Archaeology of Knowledge*, edited by Michel Foucault, 5. London: Tavistock Publications, 1972.

Foucault, Michel. 'Of Other Spaces'. *Architecture/Mouvement/Continuité* October 5 (1984): 46–59. Translated by Jay Miskowiec. https://web.mit.edu/allanmc/www/foucault1.pdf.

Foucault, Michel. 'Labour, Life, Language'. In *The Order of Things: An Archaeology of the Human Sciences*, 285–285. London: Routledge, 2010.

Foucault, Michel. 'Nietzsche, Genealogy, History'. In *The Foucault Reader*, edited by Paul Rabinow, 81. London: Penguin Classics, 2020.

Frew, Elspeth. 'The Père-Lachaise Cemetery'. In *Dark Tourism and Place Identity: Managing and Interpreting Dark Places*, edited by Leanne White and Elspeth Frew, 15. London: Routledge, 2016.

Gearhart, Suzanne. 'The Taming of Michel Foucault: New Historicism, Psychoanalysis, and the Subversion of Power'. *New Literary History* 28, no. 3 (1997): 457–480. https://doi.org/10.1353/nlh.1997.0032.

Gray, Breda. 'Governing Integration'. In *Globalization, Migration and Social Transformation: Ireland in Europe and the World*, edited by Bryan Fanning and Ronaldo Munck, 93–106. Burlington, VT: Ashgate, 2011.

Hanes, William Travis and Frank Sanello. *The Opium Wars: The Addiction of One Empire and the Corruption of Another*. Naperville, IL: Sourcebooks, 2007.

Herzog & De Meuron. '296 Tai Kwun, Centre for Heritage & Arts'. Herzog & De Meuron Projects. Accessed 17 July, 2021. https://www.herzogdemeuron.com/index/projects/complete-works/276-300/296-tai-kwun.html.

HKedcity. 'Architecture in Hong Kong: Teaching Kit for the Appreciation of Architecture in Secondary School Curriculum. Topic 09. VISIT: Central — Architectural Forms in Different Time Periods'. Updated 2021. http://minisite.proj.hkedcity.net/hkiakit/eng/Arts/lesson_9.html.

Ho, Lawrence K. K. and Yiu Kong Chu. 'Opening of Chaos: The Birth of Police Force on the Island'. In *Policing Hong Kong 1842–1969: Insiders' Stories*, edited by Lawrence K. K. Ho and Yiu Kong Chu, 132–134. Hong Kong: City University of Hong Kong Press, 2012.

Holdsworth, May and Christopher Munn. 'Barrack Block and Headquarters Block'. In *Crime, Justice and Punishment in Colonial Hong Kong Central Police Station, Central Magistracy and Victoria Gaol*, edited by May Holdsworth and Christopher Munn, 24. Hong Kong: Hong Kong University Press, 2020.

Kee, Tris Y-C. and Wah Sang Wong, editors. *Architecture in Hong Kong: Teaching Kit for the Appreciation of Architecture in Secondary School Curriculum*, vol. 1–4. Hong Kong: Hong Kong Institute of Architects, 2012.

King, Ambrose Yeo-Chi and Rance Pui-leung Lee. 'Emphasis'. In *Social Life and Development in Hong Kong*, edited by Ambrose Yeo-Chi King and Pui-leung Lee Rance, 131–131. Hong Kong: Chinese University Press, 1988.

Larsen, Jonas and John Urry. *The Tourist Gaze*. London: Sage Publications UK, 2011.

Lim, Patricia. 'How Early Hong Kong Arranged Itself'. In *Forgotten Souls: A Social History of the Hong Kong Cemetery*, edited by Patricia Lim, 76–76. Hong Kong: Hong Kong University Press, 2011.

Lynch, Andrew. 'The "Glocolization" of Spanish in Asia'. In *The Routledge Handbook of Spanish in the Global City*, edited by Andrew Lynch, 18. New York: Routledge, 2021.

Masters, HG. 'New Director for Tai Kwun'. *Art Asia Pacific*, 9 April 2020. http://artasiapacific.com/News/NewDirectorForTaiKwun.

Meyer, Kathryn. 'Deadly Dreams: Opium and the Arrow Wars (1856–1860) in China. J. Y. Wong'. *The China Journal* 48 (2002): 264–265. https://doi.org/10.2307/3182493.

Morrissey, John. 'Foucault and the Colonial Subject: Emergent Forms of Colonial Governmentality in Early Modern Ireland'. In *At the Anvil: Essays in Honour of William J. Smyth*, edited by Patrick J. Duffy and William Nolan. Dublin: Geography Publications, 2012.

Munn, Christopher. *Anglo-China: Chinese People and British Rule in Hong Kong, 1841–1880*. Aberdeen, Hong Kong: Hong Kong University Press, 2009.

Pallasmaa, Juhani. 'Body, Mind, and Imagination: The Mental Essence of Architecture'. In *Mind in Architecture: Neuroscience, Embodiment, and the Future of Design*, edited by Juhani Pallasmaa and Sarah Robinson, 51–74. London: MIT Press, 2015.

Purbrick, Martin. 'A Report of the 2019 Hong Kong Protests'. *Asian Affairs* 50, no. 4 (2019): 465–487. https://doi.org/10.1080/03068374.2019.1672397.

Purcell. *Conservation Management Plan and Heritage Impact Assessment*. Hong Kong: Purcell, 2015. https://www.amo.gov.hk/form/HIA_Report_CGOWW.pdf.

Purcell Miller Tritton. *The Old Central Police & Victoria Prison Hong Kong. Conservation Management Plan*. Purcell Miller Tritton, June 2008. https://www.heritage.gov.hk/en/online/press2008/cmp.pdf.

Ransom, John S. 'Foucault's Discipline'. In *Foucault's Discipline: The Politics of Subjectivity*, edited by John S. Ransom, 18. Durham, NC: Duke University Press, 1997.

Sandercock, Leonie and Peter Lyssiotis. 'Who Knows? Exploring Planning's Knowledges'. In *Cosmopolis II: Mongrel Cities of the 21st Century*, 58–82. London: Continuum, 2003.

Stefanova, Swetlana. 'Waterways and Ships as Heterotopia'. In *Negotiating Waters: Seas, Oceans, and Passageways in the Colonial and Postcolonial Anglophone World*, edited by André Dodeman and Nancy Pedri, 119–134. Delaware: Vernon Press, 2019.

Tai Kwun. 'Brief History of the Central Police Station Compound'. *Heritage Conservation*, Historical Timeline. Accessed 19 July 2021. https://www.taikwun.hk/en/taikwun/heritage_conservation/historical_timeline.

Tang, Tiffany. 'Between the Skyscrapers; Hong Kong Hidden Heritage Gems Come Alive'. *iDiscover*. Accessed 6 August 2019. https://i-discoverasia.com/hk-hidden-heritage/.

The Hong Kong Jockey Club. 'Phased-Opening of Tai Kwun to Mark a Major Milestone for Heritage Revitalisation in Hong Kong'. *Corporate News. About HKJC*, 9 May 2018. https://corporate.hkjc.com/corporate/corporate-news/english/2018-05/news_2018050902057.aspx.

Tsui, Enid. 'Hong Kong Central Police Station Restoration: How City's Most Ambitious Heritage Project Overcame the Odds'. *South China Morning Post*, 15 June 2018. https://www.scmp.com/lifestyle/article/2150710/hong-kong-central-police-station-restoration-how-citys-most-ambitious.

Zhu, Yujie. 'Lifestyle Mobility: Shifting Conception of Home in Modern China'. *International Journal of Tourism Anthropology* 6, no. 4 (2018): 357–374.

Zhu, Yujie. *Heritage Tourism: From Problems to Possibilities*. Cambridge: Cambridge University Press, 2021. https://doi.org/10.1017/9781108914024.

5

MEDIATING CONSENSUS AND ENACTING DISSENSUS

Contested Space, Architecture and the Limits of Representation

Joern Langhorst

The images of a crowd violently gaining access to the Capitol building in Washington, DC on January 6, 2021 made an impact far beyond the United States. Triggering instant concerns over immediate threats to a political and constitutional system that had been considered eminently stable, the event and its rapidly proliferating visuals were quickly absorbed into larger concerns and debates about the future and viability of liberal democracy and the Western political systems that became a model for political order in the aftermath of the Second World War. The rise of populist movements threatening these post-war representative and liberal democracies – whether in Hungary, Poland, Brazil or the United States, but also emergent in populist and nationalist movements in many other places – were (and are) on most commentators' minds.[1]

The reception of events of January 6th, as one of the most visible expressions of populist and right-wing movements, occurred vis-à-vis that of contemporary and past democratic protest movements challenging "the privileges and power of governing elites:",[2] such as Black Lives Matter (BLM), the Arab Spring, the Occupy movements, and the 2013 protests in Rio de Janeiro.

This essay, using the Capitol events and the 2013 protests in Rio de Janeiro as bookends to the spectrum of political and politicized, spatial and spatialized acts, attempts to investigate and explain how architecture and its spatial/material manifestation in (public) space influence and are affected by political and politicized acts of protest. How do architecture and space contribute to the construction of political realities? Looking at politics as the interplay of consensus and dissensus, the essay lays out a framework that explores the roles of space as *immediate* tool and medium (space is being directly shaped or occupied) or as *indirect* tool and mediated (space as represented/visualized through other media). Both roles are "played" simultaneously in protest movements and acts. Torraca's[3] notion

DOI: 10.4324/9781003272076-7

of "cornered democracy" foregrounds the need to understand these entangled interplays and interdependencies and to look at both the physical–material dimension of architecture and space, but also at their visual–aesthetic dimension in political and politicized actions that invariably operate in the tension between producing consensus and/or dissensus.[4] The following is an attempt to contextualize this central issue in a range of relevant discourses across numerous disciplines and fields, expanding classic critiques by the more contemporary emphasis on dissensus in assemblage theory and agonistic pluralism, and on the meaningful and effective enactment of democracy relying on the continuous producing and reproducing of difference – and ultimately of contestation and conflict.

Past and current successful mass-mobilizations of democratic and populist protest movements worldwide demonstrate the importance of challenging established orders that are seen as unjust as well as the ability of seemingly broad and disparate movements to contest long-standing power structures. I argue that the complex and specific contexts – political opportunities, uneven capacities to organize, horizontal and democratic modes of political action (what Hardt and Negri refer to as "leaderless movements")[5] and the overall complex, convoluted and contradictory assemblages of different interests, ideologies and agendas within such movements reveal the central role of space and spatial relations (and, by extension, of architecture). Streets and public squares became not just the locations of protest, but the "vortices through which radically different groups connected and assembled to protest against, or wrest control from, those holding the reins of power."[6]

This kind of assembling of large numbers of diverse individuals and groups with distinctive and often non-aligned ideologies and political imaginaries is not just relying on and occurring in public space, but evidences very sophisticated and successful spatial strategies and tactics. "Taking to the streets" has certainly been a long tradition in many societies, as a last (and often the only) resort to voice dissent with the powers that are. Public space has emerged as another battleground – or another medium – for the discourse over ideologies, agendas, policy and politics – and ultimately as that of a battle over identity, participation, and inclusion, about who "belongs" to society and who gets to participate in the decisions about its future.[7]

The central question is the role of space and architecture in the making and unmaking of different versions and visions of democracy – what kind of tool architecture and space might be, who wields it, and to what ends, focusing on public space and the architecture(s) that set it up. This question cannot be addressed without understanding consensus and dissensus as key dimensions of political action.

Established ideas of liberal democracy foreground the building of consensus as a central process in the resolution of conflicts and interests, whether themselves spatial in nature or not. The production of architecture is often consensus-driven as well, in particular if public in nature or occurring in public space. Beyond, it is a means to generate, spatialize, reify and enforce consensus.

Conversely, the way populist movements, the insurrection at the US Capitol on January 6, 2021, the protests of the Black Lives Matter Movement and of the Arab Spring as well as the Occupy movement use public space suggest that public space and architecture itself may also play a central role in the articulation and enactment of dissent.

While critical concepts such as Chantal Mouffe's "pluralistic agonism"[8] embrace conflict as central and ongoing, and suggest that compromise and consensus as the end goal of political deliberation are inherently problematic and often unjust, prevailing critiques of the roles of public space and architecture in the enactment of dissent or manufacturing of consent have often been limited to its representational agency, in particular as potent symbols of hegemonic political and economic orders, or its qualities to act as a medium and ground through and upon which different claims and interests are negotiated. This essay presents a new framework that significantly expands extant critiques and foregrounds architecture and space as a central agent in the processes of "exposing, proposing, and politicizing"[9] the mechanisms and machinations of representative democracy and neoliberal capitalism. Based on a new interpretation of the concepts of "spatial strategies" and "spatial tactics",[10] it interrogates the capacities of space to operate as a *medium* for enacting discourse, conflict, and dissent – and to *mediate* society, culture and people in their relationships to each other and then world around them, with a particular view toward empowering excluded and marginalized communities and interests, and enacting a "right to the city" and a right to be seen, heard and included in the deliberative processes that make up civilized society.

Grounding Politics: Liquid Modernity, Solid Buildings and the Role of Space and Place

It could be argued that at the core of the current protest movements – even of those diametrically opposed, such as Black Lives Matter and the Capitol insurrection – lies a fear of loss of identity, a fear of not being a part of the society and places one lives in. It is hardly surprising that such fear is perceived as existential, and easily makes acceptable even radical forms of action.

For many, society and place, as once stable constructs and foundations for individual and collective identity, have been superseded by a world that is rapidly changing, liquid, interconnected, globalized, and whose inherent uncertainty creates "an atmosphere of ambient fear".

Zygmunt Bauman describes that

> the dominant sentiment is the feeling of uncertainty – about the future shape of the world, about the right way of living in it, and about the criteria by which to judge the rights and wrongs of one's way of living. Uncertainty is not exactly a newcomer in the modern world, with its past. What is new, however, is that it is no longer seen as a mere temporary nuisance

which, with due effort may be either mitigated or completely overcome. The postmodern world is bracing itself for life under a condition of uncertainty which is permanent and irreducible.[11]

His concept of "liquid modernity"[12] describes our current "liquid society" as characterized by instability and ambiguity and by the erosion or altogether disappearance of what appeared to be stable or solid categories of identity. This liquidity affects the very concepts and practices of territoriality and belonging, and their spatializations. Rapid change is operating at a speed and scale that social patterns and institutions no longer have time to respond to and provide solid and meaningful bases of human identity and collective action.[13] Even systems of power are perceived as less stable and often elusive when one tries to engage them. As Manuel Castells suggested, "the flows of power generate the power of flows, whose material reality imposes itself as a natural phenomenon that cannot be controlled or predicted… People live in places, power rules through flows".[14] While power has concentrated in elusive and largely inaccessible global networks ("spaces of flows"), the actions of people and groups that are not closely associated with hegemonic power are increasingly circumscribed in localities (spaces of places).[15]

Bauman sharpens this point by stating that "power rules because it flows, because it is able (beware ever forgetting it!) to flow – to flow away".[16]

Speaking truth to power, holding hegemonic and elusive systems accountable or counteracting their policies and actions then needs to return power "to its foundations in substantive landscapes, and (…) that the political is practiced in places, counteracting the capacity of power to disengage from place and people and generate fear and uncertainty."[17] While arguably this is exactly what movements such as Black Lives Matter are attempting to do, they are simultaneously combating and playing into liquid fear. Liquid fear is generated by endemic uncertainty and severely impacts our ability to engage in meaningful social action to produce a viable future. Liquid fear is without obvious source, derivative and based on an internalization of "a vision of the world that includes insecurity and vulnerability.[18]

Liquid fear has been used by state actors and other hegemonic elites to ensure compliance and social passivity from its citizens, as the state is not able to deliver on its promise to protect people. The social stability on which the state's claims rely has been worn away by the uncertainties of global capitalism, and the inherent inequities of this system have generated a milieu of physical threats to personal safety, for example "in the form of so-called terrorist violence."[19]

Hannah Arendt famously stated that "Work and its product, the human artifact, bestow a measure of permanence and durability upon the futility of mortal life and the fleeting character of human time."[20] Buildings, and spaces conceived and created by humans in general, have always played a central role in making safe and secure places to dwell in, to keep the threatening forces of change outside. Buildings are maybe the most potent of all human artifacts – they epitomize solidity and permanence. Their materiality and tectonic (set in stone)[21] as well as their power as a signifier of larger cosmologies (e.g., churches, temples and palaces) appear to be immutable and stable against the onslaught of the tides of change – solid buildings in and against liquid fear, liquid power and liquid modernity. It might indeed – and this argument will be picked up in the conclusion – be exactly here that the truly disturbing quality and impact of January 6, 2021 lies – that a building representing the stability, permanence and solidity of a political system and culture which was considered inviolate – was successfully breached. The fact that the Capitol was not just the symbol of legislative power and constitutional order, but the actual location where the processes at the core of a liberal democracy take place, adds considerable impact.

The emplacement of meaningful political action may form a potent counter to the elusive liquidity of power. Without attempting to disentangle the complexities of the concept of "place"[22] it is central in understanding the roles space and architecture play in the practices of democracy and everyday life.

David Harvey[23] proposes two modalities of place: "Place in itself" describes the place-based relations which form the essential building blocks for "assembling scattered individuals into a cohesive force for social and political change. Conversely, "place for itself" centers on the geographic defense of places and territories against all considered outsiders, undermining the ability to connect to distant others and present a unified front in the face of new geometries of capitalist power.[24]

Place and space play a central role in enabling or disabling social movements. John Agnew describes places as sites where economic and political processes are played out (locations), social and organizational relations develop to mediate micro responses to macro-level processes (locale), and spatial imaginaries form to give people a sense of meaning in their particular worlds (sense of place)[25] These qualities of place are entangled, overlapping within one another and form the contexts through which people experience and live in their everyday worlds.[26] He argues that general social processes (e.g., formation of class, gender, race) intersect with one another in concrete places,

> serving as fields through which ongoing processes become inscribed into social habitus, identities, relations of trust and belonging, and political dispositions. People do not become familiar with their social positions by situating their locations in abstract structures, but through everyday interactions with other people, things and images that make up their locale.[27]

Harvey and Agnew's writings, much in the tradition of DeCertau, Lefebvre and others suggest that place is not just a result of cultural production or a passive ground upon which human activity "takes place", but that place and its material qualities and dimensions in turn influences and impacts human thought and action. This dialogic quality of place then becomes critical in the kind of political action that takes place in public space

Medium and Mediation: Reframing Architecture and Public Space

What kind of tool is architecture and space in the practices of politics and of democracy? How does it operate, and who is using it to what ends?

Cities, the most dominant Western cultural formation,[28] have been variously described as dynamic, full of contradictions and diversity. Mainstream architectural and urban planning and design discourses, following Habermas' ideas about democracy,[29] foreground the building of consensus in the resolution of conflicts and interests, whether themselves spatial in nature or not. However, the building of consensus, inherent in different approaches to "participation", might be problematic and camouflage hegemonial agendas. Beyond, it can serve as a means of control and a way to depoliticize planning and design processes. In these contexts, space becomes very much the place of and a tool for the ordering of difference(s).

This is not only germane to any meaningful analysis of the works of architecture that "make" cities and urban space, but also to conclusions about who can use urban space – and how. Famous architects and planners, such as Ebenezer Howard, Le Corbusier, and Frank Lloyd Wright, did not set out to solve space, or even the city, as a problem.[30] Their aim was to address issues like public health (the mental and physical impacts of industrialization), the consequences of income and class inequality, disenfranchisement from social and political life, and, above all, the domination of life by the imperatives of a capitalist economic and social order. Landscape, space and architecture were used as fundamental devices to propose solutions to these problems; space and architecture playing *the* central role in their political imagination. Their proposed spaces and architecture not only provided pragmatic solutions to the problems they intended to solve – but in each case their designs presented a particular political imagination to their preconceived inhabitants. These political imaginaries very much paralleled those of their designers.[31] Their proposed spaces were arranged to not only organize the pragmatic requirements of everyday life, but also to be "read,"[32] for their underlying political imaginary, social order and cosmology to be deciphered and followed. A prominent example is the "City Beautiful" movement of the late 19th and early 20th centuries in the United States. "Beauty," as presented by neoclassical architecture for its public spaces and buildings was not only produced for its own sake, but to create moral and civic virtue among urban populations.[33] Advocates of this philosophy argued that this "beautification" should promote a harmonious social order that would increase the quality of life by reducing conflict – a position heavily criticized by many – including Jane Jacobs, who considered it an "architectural design cult".[34]

Such overt social engineering is still pervasive in many of the utopian grand schemes that contemporary architects propose – New Urbanism (which owes a lot to the City Beautiful movement) as well as the "Green New Deal" and its resilient cities, public spaces and dwellings all assume (or construct) a particular kind of inhabitant with a particular set of values and a particular behavioral code.

It is strange that the dynamic, heterogeneous, diverse character of cities and of its public spaces is fetishized by architects and planners; yet the design of almost all public space is homogenous and homogenizing. "Public space," as Diana Fernandez stated in a recent talk about "Heterogeneous Futures," "is not common."[35] Whilst "the other" is being celebrated in rhetoric, it is similarly excluded in the spatial-material configurations, or policed by other means. Contemporary public space as the space of encounter is really an encounter with the mirror image of neoliberal capitalism and its hegemonic leitkultur. Henri Lefebvre's, David Harvey's and Don Mitchell's "right to the city" is a right that is unevenly distributed and mediated, and manipulated and suppressed under the guise of "consensus".

If designed public space has both agency and instrumentality in the making and unmaking of contemporary versions and visions of "democracy", "resilience", "sustainability" and formations of the "urban" and "urbanity" – and of society in general this agency and instrumentality needs to be interrogated.

I propose an alternative approach, based on agonism and assemblage as theoretical and conceptual frameworks[36] to realize the "right to the city" and to counteract the post-political erosion of the urban public sphere associated with austerity and neoliberal governmentality.

As stated earlier, urban public space, in the context of rapid and pervasive global urbanization, and the high level of conflict and contestation inherent in past and contemporary urban conditions, is a central location where the dynamic relationships between spatial conditions, socio-cultural processes, and the attendant geometries of power are played out. The history of democracy in general (at least in the West) is predominantly urban, and most theoretical perspectives on the relationship between the spatio-material and the "democratic" (with its socio-cultural-economic and behavioral dimensions) foreground the highly diverse, contested, and "uneven" urban processes of production and reproduction, recent scholarship being concerned that the various processes of neoliberal restructuring are threatening democracy.[37]

Versions of the Same Scene: Four Lenses

Four lenses can be used to organize selected key contemporary and historical-theoretical approaches and perspectives on architecture and public space, outlining their proposed relationships between space and social/cultural/economic/ecological processes. These reveal how actions of intentional spatial change and occupation may operate to enable or disable democratic, inclusive and discursive actions and practices that are socially and environmentally just.

The *first lens* interrogates notions of "the public" and "the public sphere", starting with Hannah Arendt's definition of the public sphere as "the space of appearances", Habermas' understanding of the (bourgeois) public sphere as a mediation of relations between state and society in capitalism, and Nancy Fraser's critiques of the exclusivity of the public sphere, identifying multiple subaltern and counter-publics.

The *second lens* investigates public space in the context of hegemonic and counterhegemonic/marginal/transgressive practices on the background of Harvey's (1973, 2008) and Smith's (1984) concepts of "uneven development" and "accumulation by dispossession", rooted in a materialist critique of (urban) development and redevelopment. Lefebvre's (1996) "Right to the City", DeCerteau's (1984) "spatial strategies" and "spatial tactics" expand this critique by arguing that the right to the city is not just about material access to urban space, but a renewed right to urban life. The "right to the city," wrote Lefebvre:

> should modify, concretize and make more practical the rights of the citizen as an urban dweller and user of multiple services. It would affirm, on the one hand, the right of the user to make known their ideas on the space and time of their activities in the urban area; it would also cover the right to the use (…).[38]

Lefebvre's "Right to the City" and DeCertau's "spatial tactics" and "spatial strategies" in particular provide insights into the ways space is utilized by different movements. In simplified terms, spatial strategies require the ability to set a "lieu propre",[39] a strategic territory with considerable power to shape relations and environments. They are associated with actors that control the means of spatial production, whether economic, political or material, for example, the kind of hegemonic power that shapes the built environment. Baron Hausmann's "renovation" of Paris, one of the most ambitious public works to improve public health, but to also improve the spatial conditions for a military response to uprisings such as the February 1848 revolution is a historic example, while contemporary, often overtly benevolent projects, such as parks (e.g., New York's High Line) are frequently just as double-edged as Hausmann's.[40]

Conversely, spatial tactics are deployed by those who do not control the means of spatial production and are frequently associated with acts of resistance. Both De Certeau and Lefebvre count quotidian actions such as walking down a sidewalk among those tactics. Temporary occupation, demonstrations and graffiti are all spatial tactics – they are opportunistic, flexible, temporary and impermanent, and allow for quick evasion. De Certeau makes an important observation associating spatial strategies with a "victory of space over time", while spatial tactics "depend on time"[41] and make no permanent claims, arguing essentially that spatial tactics are a subversion of the way space is "fixed", and ultimately of space as a permanent construct.

The *third lens* dissects the roles of public space within a Foucaultian continuum of utopian-dystopian-heterotopian, investigating concepts of space based on the relationships between multiple simultaneous and competing ordering systems.[42]

The role of architecture in presenting and reifying utopian worlds and societies is arguably as old as architecture itself – there are few ideologies that have not relied on architecture to create a stage for their vision of the future to unfold on, and to construct the spatial conditions for their proposed social order. Buildings' overt roles as visible symbols of a new order and alleged better world frequently rely on the impact of immediate experience: The use of scale to present the maxim of the collective being everything and the individual being nothing in the architecture of fascist regimes in Italy or Germany, or Stalin's grand architectural visions of Soviet cities make individuals feel dwarfed and insignificant against a towering and overwhelming architectural massing.[43] The same kind of architecture then frequently serves to denote the dystopian consequences of the failures of utopian schemes – and they seem to inevitably fail, both in science fiction and in the real world – spectacularly framed by the dramatic implosion of housing schemes such as Pruitt Igoe in St. Louis, the slow decline and demise of Cabrini Green in Chicago, or the everyday dystopias of the 1950s and 1960s tower blocks in Great Britain. All these were built based on assumptions their designers made about the kind of people who were going to inhabit them, and about how they were to be appropriately inhabited.[44] The notion of heterotopia as a space that contains multiple and competing ordering systems[45] seems particularly potent if conflict occurs overtly and visibly in architectural space. The apparent disorder of a crowd storming the Capitol Building, the chaos of the encampments of the Occupy movement, and the crowds in Egypt's Tahir Square or in the Black Lives Matter protests are set against an apparent architectural order that represents and reifies the very political order that is being challenged. Graffiti that appeared on State Capitol buildings after Black Lives Matter demonstrations are another powerful and visible expression of heterotopian and heterogeneous claims to space.

The *fourth lens* applies a situationist critique of urban space as both "spectacle"[46] and "hyperreality,"[47] investigating underlying representational systems and practices that govern possible meanings and interactions of and with such space. This representational agency of public space is particularly critical and insidious as it is less obvious and frequently serves to camouflage or naturalize power relations. Any architectural or intentionally designed space reifies ideas about order, occupation, use and behavior – whether the designers are conscious of those or not. Economic or political power elites, the people and organizations De Certeau associates with spatial strategies "make" those spaces, or at least heavily influence their designs, performances and appearances – while others have to live with and in such spaces,[48] with implicit or explicit rules they are expected to follow. The representation of the spatial strategists' values runs the gamut of overt to covert – from spectacle to invisible. Buildings that have an overtly representational function – such as the US Capitol, but also other kinds of buildings of an architecture that is intentionally "spectacular"[49] – operate very much as signifiers, and often are a catalyst in the ways the conflicts that are at the core of society play out in public space.

The Aesthetics of Constructing Realities and Truth: Space, Architecture and Their Representational Roles

The representational role of architecture and space in cultural and political contexts – their ability to communicate meaning and values – is twofold: first, architecture and space is itself a representation of cultural and political agendas, and as a medium it directly communicates or evokes those. Second, it becomes an object in other forms of representation and (visual) media, and is subject to being "framed" and manipulated.[50]

Gillian Rose's incisive analysis of the workings of visual media discerns between the "site of production", the "site of the image" itself, and the "site of audiencing".[51] The ability to critique and understand imagery is dependent on discerning those three sites and their relationships which determine how and to what effect an object or situation "appears" in visual media. Helphand[52] discerns four different "roles" of architecture and space in films: That of *setting* (where something "takes place"), that of *subject* (what it is), that of *symbol* (what it stands for) and that of *character*. It is the last two that are most potent in their ability to communicate and insinuate meaning and evoke emotions. The symbolic dimension and agency of landscape and designed space in the making of collective social, political and epistemic identities have been described in detail by Denis Cosgrove.[53] The appearance of space and architecture as character is likely less familiar – but the ability of architecture to carry a significant part of a narrative and act as a kind of mirror for and of human emotions and attitudes is something historically used to great effect in film[54] and repeated in the media imagery of events like January 6th, the BLM protests, or in the Rio de Janeiro protests of 2013.

Aesthetics then becomes a central dimension of political discourse as it plays out (or is played out), mediated and takes place in public space,[55] and architecture's operation, impact and agency might lie in this dimension at least as much as in its actual material-spatial ability to directly manipulate or influence human behavior. The role of constructed aesthetics of architecture and space in the mediating of consensus and dissensus, of often diametrically opposed interests, values and agendas, warrants a closer look, expanding extant and extensive critiques of visual materials, media[56] and the role of the visual in general.[57]

The 2013 demonstrations in Rio de Janeiro provide one of the most interesting cases to explore these dynamics. Mass demonstrations followed a 20-cent increase in bus fare. A quickly emergent movement called the "Free Pass Movement" (MPL) called for protest that "set the Brazilian streets on fire"[58] – coinciding with the eve of the 2013 FIFA Confederations Cup, and in response to the planning and administrative actions preceding the 2014 World Cup and the 2016 Summer Olympic and Paralympic Games. The expression "more than twenty cents" came to quickly represent the heterogeneity of the protesters and the "polyphony of the streets",[59] and it equally quickly shook the "hegemony of the Brazilian mainstream media that had always controlled the construction of (...) reality".[60] The reaction by state actors was harsh and militarized: the UPP

(Units of Pacification Police), which had previously been operating in the slums of Rio de Janeiro now operated throughout the city, and expanded what Giorgio Agamben calls "a permanent state of exception"[61] far beyond the favelas. The social division that characterized the daily lives of the inhabitants of the city and fueled the complex and heterogeneous interests underlying the riots exposed the "distance between the democracy of the asphalt (i.e. formal neighborhoods) and the bare life of the slum (the non-urbanized and informally occupied land) – a distance that has been potentiated by the interference of the hegemonic media."[62]

It is this role of the media, and the use and appearance of space and architecture as a medium of consensus and dissensus that makes what Torraca calls "cornered democracy" so revelatory of the entanglements and dependencies between aesthetics, space, architecture, politics and media. Underlying these entanglements is the interdependence of neoliberal capitalism, neoliberal democracy and consumer society. Whether labeled "liquid fear,"[63] "anthropophagic democracy"[64] or "cornered democracy",[65] the current state of (neoliberal) democracies is reliant on a projection of division and difference: In the case of Rio de Janeiro and the 2013 demonstrations between "a democracy of privilege for those who live in the asphalt, and its absence for those who suffer in the slums."[66] These crises are transformed into spectacles by the mainstream media: Coverage from the Occupy protests in New York City, the protests against the G7 conferences in Genoa or Seattle, the 2013 demonstrations in Rio de Janeiro, the Black Lives Matter protests, or the violent breach of the US Capitol propagated and constructed an aesthetic of violence and a narrative of "peace by war". While public space, for maybe the first time in a while became truly "public" again in Hannah Arendt's sense as a space of encounter between different people with different values, interests, agendas and privileges, the mainstream media presentation was almost uniformly constructing the "spectacle of the real" that visualized and aestheticized an "us vs. them". The proliferation of cell phone video, of digital media easily accessible by bystanders and activists picked up by many alternative media made audiences see how a large part of mainstream media engages in the construction of reality as truth. Alternative points of view (literally and figuratively) and their dissemination quickly became a form of resistance against the hegemony of the single perspective, the unison voice and a uniform view of "the facts"[67] – against the most powerful tool in the manufacturing of consensus.

The four lenses presented above enable a multidimensional "read" of public space that reveals underlying, camouflaged or suppressed heterogeneities and simultaneous contested hybridities. A key finding is that, although different communities and people are occupying the same space at the same time, their lived experiences and resultant life worlds are radically different – of which the Black Lives Matter movement has raised much needed awareness. The demonstrative occupation of public space and public buildings, including the Capitol, is exceedingly successful in calling attention to the disjoints and disconnects that appear in the very space that is considered "public" and "common", revealing the diverse and conflicting claims and counterclaims that are habitually rendered invisible by ways of consensus-oriented political and design/planning cultures.

Assembling Architecture, Politics and Space: Consensus and Dissensus

Assemblage, as a comparatively new concept[68] has the potential to provide a meta-perspective that can meaningfully relate the four lenses to each other, but also significantly expands the discourses on public space, architecture, and politics.[69] Deleuze and Parnet[70] suggest that urban actors, forms or processes are defined less by a pre-given property and more by the assemblages they enter and reconstitute. Assemblage is "a double emphasis: on the material, actual and assembled, but also on the emergent, the processual and the multiple."[71] Focusing on process and emergence, the assemblage approach is not describing a spatial category, output or resultant formation, but a process of doing, practices and events produced through different temporalizations and contingencies.[72]

Public space then is "assembled", and the intentional design operates within these fluid environments, emphasizing the need to understand both this "assemblage" and the ways by which possible actions and practices intersect and interact with it.

Consequentially, the need to build – or, since this process tends to give different weight to different actors, to manufacture – consensus about intentional place change will have to be interrogated and replaced with approaches that foreground conflict and contestation,[73] such as Chantal Mouffe's[74] and Ernesto Laclau's[75] concept of "agonism."

Agonism provides a way to think about democracy

> that is different from the traditional liberal conception of democracy as a negotiation among interests (…) that the aim of the democratic society is the creation of a consensus (….). However, while we desire an end to conflict, if we want people to be free we must always allow for the possibility that conflict may appear and to provide an arena where differences can be confronted. The democratic process should supply that arena.[76]

Agonism is not simply the undifferentiated celebration of antagonism, but implies a deep respect and concern for the other and their positions. Agonism, and agonistic pluralism endeavor "to affirm the perpetuity of the contest". Their goal "is not to celebrate a world without points of stabilisation; it is to affirm the reality of perpetual contest, even within an ordered setting, and to identify the affirmative dimension of contestation."[77] Agonistic pluralism substantively and procedurally challenges consensual conceptions of democracy. Honig argues that every political settlement engenders remainders to which it cannot fully do justice. Agonistic pluralism brings out the emancipatory potential of political contestation and of the disruption of settled practices. Conversely, she recognizes that politics also involves the imposition of order and stability.

Politics then can neither be reduced to consensus, nor to pure contestation, but both are essential dimensions of politics – and consequentially of public spaces and their design.

Spatializing Dissensus: Toward an Architecture of Dialog, Diversity and Inclusion

Spatial design and planning professions, unless they are an exercise of autocratic power,[78] have relied on the manufacturing of consensus as both foundation and goal, in particular if the project has a public dimension or involved public space. There are many problematic assumptions – the aforementioned issue that many needs and wants of many constituencies and communities cannot be accommodated and that benefits and burdens will invariably be unevenly distributed, perpetuating, increasing or introducing patterns of spatial and environmental injustice. Equally problematic is the (generally unacknowledged) assumption that space and the ways it is used are stable over long periods of time, and the resultant desire to avoid any kind of contestation of established uses and meanings.

In line with DeCertau, Lefebvre, Mouffe and Laclau I argue that contestation is not just a permanent and unavoidable condition of (public) space and politics, but in fact, the very quality that creates it – space is the location where one encounters difference and "the other". Such encounters continuously reshape space itself, but also how it is perceived and conceived, and how diverse people make sense of it or assign meaning to it.[79] A dimension of this process is the imposition of an ordering system, whether manifested physically, or by some other means of representation or visualization. Any such ordering system will immediately invite or cause transgression, challenges or contestations against itself, leading to the presence of multiple simultaneous and competing ordering systems.[80]

Only few of these multiple, simultaneous and competing ordering systems, meanings, rituals of use, etc. are overt and visible – most are covert, hidden, invisible or unseen. One reason is their suppression by systems of hegemonic power: spatial form is – at least on the outset – determined by those who can deploy spatial strategies, and most spatial tactics do not permanently or significantly change the spatial-material form but leave less material, permanent and obvious impacts. Such invisibility, and the invisibility of the communities who rely on spatial tactics, ultimately excludes them from participating in the democratic processes.

The geographer Maria Kaika suggests that:

> (...) despite a conceptual shift in what cities are (...), when it comes to the how of making cities 'safe, resilient, sustainable and inclusive' appear already to have been hijacked by the same research agendas and the same policy and methodological frameworks of the past. (...) What if, alongside

changing the conceptual framework within which we understand cities, we also changed our research questions, our methodological tools and our institutional frameworks? But in order to change tools, methods and questions, we need to change interlocutors. We need to focus on who has been silenced in the design and delivery of past sustainable development agendas and goals, and why.[81]

Attempts to create inclusivity and "get everybody on board" by ways of established participatory processes – so typical of architectural projects that are "public" or have a public impact – are fraught with suppression and can in fact be seen as working in the traditions of colonialism: for example, residents in New Orleans that participated in the public planning processes after hurricane Katrina

> (…) realized that this only legitimized the injustice of existing practices and reproduced fixed roles and power positions. When invited to be "included", there was already a clear role assigned to them: not that of the equal co-decision maker in setting development goals and allocating resources, but that of the subordinate subject, who is only allowed to choose from a set menu of monetary or other compensatory practices in return for the destruction of her/his livelihood and environment.[82]

Following Mitchell's postulate "to be effective, politics must be made visible in public space",[83] the role of more critical, dialogic and inclusive practices in architecture, landscape architecture and planning would be to make existing differences visible as a first step to the inclusion of any and all people, actors, agendas, values and interests instead of prioritizing stakeholders defined and established *a priori* by the powers that are and the processes they prescribe. Agonism and assemblage theory may offer some productive frameworks and approaches to manage ways to identify and engage diversity and dissent, and decolonize spatial planning and design.[84] Truly critical spatial design and planning practices then will need to engage in "exposing, proposing, and politicizing" such processes and actors, and make these steps a critical and central component of the design (or other constructions) of space that are democratic and public in the very sense of these words.

Kaika's suggestion of a radical shift from "the building of consensus" to the "monitoring of dissensus"[85] – to discover new "contentious internal liminalities"[86] and "focus on where, how, why, and by whom conflict and disagreement are generated"[87] might facilitate the design of space that is affirmative for communities that are different from Euro-Anglo normative assumptions. Lefebvre's right to the city and its multiple dimensions and extensions, far from being a static legalistic construct, involves a knitting together of subjects, materials, and traces in a multivocal, dissonant revelation of rights characterized by "simultaneity and encounter."[88] The meaningful and effective enactment of rights then occurs along a persisting continuity of producing and reproducing difference – and ultimately of contestation and conflict. Instead of building consensus, the fostering of dissent and contention might focus on "agonistic space", spatializing the concept of agonistic pluralism. The enactment of rights to place, the city, and landscape might have to rely on conflict and contestation as a catalyst, a driving force, to increase and differentiate participation in the making and remaking of space, place, and, ultimately of society itself.

This then begs the question of what kind of architecture will create public spaces that make politics visible. What are spaces, shapes, forms and material qualities that will not just allow and accommodate, but encourage the non-violent enacting of discourse, conflict and dissent, that are a product of and location for the encounter of spatial strategies and tactics? How can the capacity of architecture and space mediate society, culture and people in their relationships to each other and then world around them? To understand architecture and the spaces it designs and creates as an instrument to make politics visible might be a first step. To think of it not so much as a tool to homogenize difference, to manufacture consensus by ways of exclusion, privilege and oppression, but of making visible differences and provide an arena for the appearance and negotiation of difference would render it a powerful means to enact and enable the right to the city, the right to participate in the democratic processes for all people – and create space that is truly public.

The architecture of public space matters. It matters a great deal, but not in the way most architects and planners think. While they are – as a victim of a tradition of inventing and masterplanning new (and allegedly better) worlds – concerned with, so to speak, designing the stage, writing the play and casting the actors – the utopian grand scheme or the pragmatic master plan – a truly public space needs to be a stage that invites everyone to enact, or at least make visible, their own stories, ideas, values and identities. In a heterogeneous society, this might be the hardest thing to do.

Looking at the rise of democratic movements in the early 21st century and at the populist movements that are ultimately antidemocratic, it becomes clear that "physical space is not the only requirement for dissent. Space, in fact, will become only indispensable if its democratic functions and uses are restored."[89]

This requires nothing less than to develop a language and invent a common culture that can sustain an open dialogue in public spaces. As long as that language and culture does not exist, the shape, form, materiality and aesthetic expression are secondary, and so is the role of architecture. It is a tempting assumption, and a valid question, if architecture can help to create this new language and culture. It can only do so if it understands the limits of the role of space – and its pitfalls. Peter Marcuse's rejection of the fetishization of space, written in the aftermath of the police raid on the Occupy Wall Street movement's encampment in Zuccotti Park lays out the dangers of focusing too much on the physical locations of protest, and provides a set of principles that could guide for how space might become a centerpiece in the enactment of dissensus, and ultimately, of democracy itself. Marcuse lays out seven functions of the Occupy movement: (1) the *confrontation function* ("taking the struggle to the enemy's territory confronting and potentially disrupting the operations at the center of the problem"); (2) a *symbolic function* which registers a collective, unified by discontent with current conditions; (3) an *educational function,* "provoking questioning, exploration, juxtaposition of differing viewpoints and issues, seeking clarification and sources of communality within difference"; (4) a *glue function* "creating a community of trust and commitment in the pursuit of common goals"; (5) an *umbrella function,* "creating a space (…) in which quite disparate groups can work together in pursuit of (…) mutually reinforcing goals"; (6) an *activation function,* "inspiring others to (…) sharper focus on common goals (…) providing space for cross discussions among supporting groups and interests"; and (7) a *model function,* "showing by its internal organization and methods of proceeding that an alternative form of democracy is possible".[90]

Designing spaces that can accommodate and, even more so, *invite* such actions and functions might be the best service architecture and anyone who is involved in the design of spaces that are public can provide to stabilizing democracy and empowering a truly democratic and inclusive society. Many movements, communities and individuals will use public space in different ways, pursuing different interests and agendas, using a variety of tactics. Ideas of a homogenous society, and the use of space to manufacture consensus is antithetical to this. Architects and planners, beware: Utopias, after all, can be dangerous things.

Notes

1 For an overview see Valur Ingimundarson and Sveinn Jóhannesson (eds.), *Liberal Disorder, States of Exception, and Populist Politics* (Abingdon: Routledge, 2021). See also Mark Purcell, *Recapturing Democracy: Neoliberalization and the Struggle for Alternative Urban Futures* (Abingdon: Routledge, 2008).

2 Walter Nicholls et al., "Conceptualizing the Spatialities of Social Movements," in *Spaces of Contention: Spatialities and Social Movements*, ed. Byron Miller and Walter Nicholls (Abingdon: Taylor & Francis 2013), 1.

3 Liz Torraca, "A Cornered Democracy: The Echo of the 2013 Demonstrations in Rio de Janeiro and the Architecture of Crisis," in *Urban Public Spaces. From Planned Policies to Everyday Politics,* ed. Luciana Capanema Alvarez and Jorge Luiz Barbosa, The Urban Book Series (Cham: Springer, 2018), 57–72.

4 See e.g. Chantal Mouffe, *On the Political* (New York: Taylor & Francis, 2005); Chantal Mouffe, *Dimensions of Radical Democracy: Pluralism, Citizenship, Community* (London: Verso, 1992); and Maria Kaika, "'Don't call me Resilient Again!' The New Urban Agenda as Immunology … or What Happens When Communities Refuse to be Vaccinated with 'smart cities' and Indicators," *Environment & Urbanization*, vol. 29, no. 1 (2017): 89–102.

5 Michael Hardt and Antonio Negri. *Assembly* (Oxford: Oxford University Press, 2017).

6 Nicholls et al., *Conceptualizing the Spatialities of Social Movements*, 1.

7 For a critical approach to the relationship between space, place, territory, belonging, participation and identity see Joern Langhorst, "Situating Landscape Citizenships: Borders, Margins, Hybridity, and the Uncanny," in *Landscape Citizenships,* ed. Tim Waterman, Jane Wolff and Ed Wall (Abingdon: Routledge, 2021), 109–129.

8 Chantal Mouffe, "Deliberative Democracy or Agonistic Pluralism," *Political Science Series*, vol. 72 (2000). Institute for Advanced Studies, Vienna.

9 Peter Marcuse, "From Critical Urbanism to Right to the City," *City*, vol. 13 (2009): 185–197.

10 Michel DeCerteau, *The Practice of Everyday Life* (Berkeley: University of California, 1984).

11 Zygmunt Bauman *Cultural Identities and the Politics of Anti- Racism*, ed. Prina Werbner and Tariq Modood (London: Zed Books, 1997), 50–51.

12 See Zygmunt Bauman *Liquid Modernity* (Cambridge, MA: Polity Press, 2000).

13 For a detailed analysis of the relationships between space, place, belonging and identity see Langhorst, "Situating Landscape Citizenships," in *Landscape Citizenships*, ed. Tim Waterman, Jane Wolf and Ed Wall (Abingdon: Routledge, 2021), 109-129).

14 Castells, Manuel, *The Informational City: Information, Technology, Economic Restructuring and the Urban Regional Process* (Oxford: Blackwell, 1989), 349.

15 Manuel Castells (*The Power of Identity*. Oxford: Blackwell, 1997) adds that localizing state discourses and strategies, under conditions of advanced globalization, have intensified the disjuncture between global elites and local activists.

16 Zygmunt Bauman, "City of Fears, City of Hopes," *Critical Urban Studies: Occasional Papers* (2003), 14.

17 Langhorst, "Situating Landscape Citizenships", 116.

18 Langhorst, 116–117.

19 Zygmunt Bauman, *Liquid Fear* (Cambridge, MA: Polity Press, 2006), 3.

20 Hannah Arendt*, Human Condition* (Chicago and London: University of Chicago Press, 1958), 8.

21 See Richard Sennett, "Reflections on the Public Realm. The Body and the City in Western *Civilization*," in *The New Blackwell Companion to Cities*, ed. Gary Bridge and Sophie Watson (Hoboken: Wiley – Blackwell, 2012), 390–397 and *Flesh and Stone* (New York and London: W.W. Norton & Co, 1994).

22 See e.g. Yi-Fu Tuan, *Space and Place* (Minneapolis: University of Minnesota Press, 1977); Tim Ingold, *The Perception of Environment* (London: Routledge, 2000); Tim Creswell, *In Place/Out of Place* (Minneapolis: University of Minnesota Press, 1996).

23 See David Harvey, "Militant Particularism and Global Ambition: The Conceptual Politics of Place, Space, and Environment in the Work of Raymond Williams," in *Spaces of Capital: Towards a Critical Geography*, by David Harvey (Edinburgh: Edinburgh University Press, 2001), 158–187.

24 See also Nicholls et al., *Conceptualizing the Spatialities*, 6.

25 John Agnew, *Place and Politics, Place and Politics: The Geographical Mediation of State and Society* (Boston: Allen and Unwin, 1987), 28.

26 See also Michel DeCertau, *The Practice of Everyday Life* and Henri Lefebvre, *The Critique of Everyday Life, Volume 1* (London: Verso. 1991).

27 Nicholls et al., *Conceptualizing Spatialities*, 4.

28 Raymond Williams, *The Country and the City* (New York: Oxford University Press, 1973).

29 See Juergen Habermas, *The Structural Transformation of the Public Sphere: An Inquiry into a Category of Bourgeois Society* (Cambridge, MA: The MIT Press, 1989). Habermas understands the (bourgeois) public sphere as a mediation of relations between state and society in capitalism.

30 Jane Jacobs famously titled a chapter in her book *Death and Life of Great American Cities* (New York: Random House, 1961) "The Kind of Problem a City is".

31 The role of political and other imaginaries in avant-garde and utopian design is extensively discussed in the forthcoming Beck, Jody. *Landscape and Utopia,* (Abington: Routledge).

32 see John Dixon Hunt, *Site, Sight, Insight. Site, Sight, Insight: Essays on Landscape Architecture* (Philadelphia: Pennsylvania, 2016).

33 See Daniel M. Bluestone, "Detroit's City Beautiful and the Problem of Commerce," *Journal of the Society of Architectural Historians*, vol. XLVII, no. 3 (1988): 245–262.
34 Jacobs, *Life and Death of Great American Cities*, 375. See also Pablo Sendra and Richard Sennet, *Designing Disorder: Experiments and Disruptions in the City* (London: Verso, 2020).
35 Diana Fernandez, "Heterogeneous Futures: Design Thinking Alternatives for Anthropologically and Ecologically Diverse Landscapes."
36 For a more detailed description of this framework see Joern Langhorst, *Enacting Landscape Democracy: Assembling Public Open Space and Asserting the Right to the City* (Cheltenham: Edward Elgar, 2018), 106–118.
37 See Mark Purcell, "Excavating Lefebvre: The Right to the City and its Urban Politics of the Inhabitant," *GeoJournal, 'Social Transformation, Citizenship, and the Right to the City,'* vol. 58, no. 2/3 (2002): 99–108.
38 Henri Lefebvre, "Right to the City," in *Writings on Cities* (Oxford: Basil Blackwell, 1996), 3.
39 DeCertau, *The Practice of Everyday Life*, XXI.
40 See e.g. the phenomenon of "green gentrification". An excellent introduction is Isabelle Anguelovski et al., "New Scholarly Pathways on Green Gentrification: What Does the Urban 'Green Turn' Mean and Where Is It Going?" *Progress in Human Geography*, vol. 43, no. 6 (Dec. 2019): 1064–1086. and Sendra and Sennett's *Designing Disorder.*
41 DeCertau, *The Practice of Everyday Life*, XXI.
42 Kevin Hetherington, *Badlands of Modernity: Heterotopia and Social Ordering* (London: Routledge, 2007).
43 The aforementioned City Beautiful movement could – and arguably should – also be considered in this context.
44 J.G. Ballard's novel *High Rise* (1975) and its film adaptation of the same name (2015, directed by Ben Wheatley) vis-à-vis a classic film, such as Fritz Lang's *Metropolis* (1927) show the power and role of architecture in the making, unmaking, ordering and disordering of society. Terry Gilliam's *Brazil* shows a masterful use of architecture and landscape in illustrating the utopia/dystopia/heterotopia complex.
45 I am following here the definition Hetherington put forward in *Badlands of Modernity*. Foucault's heteroptopia is a considerably broader and more sophisticated construct, but applying it in this context without oversimplifying it would be beyond the scope of this essay.
46 Guy Debord, *The Society of the Spectacle (La Société du Spectacle)* (Paris: Buchet-Chastel, 1967).
47 Jean Baudrillard, *Simulations* (New York: Semiotexte, 1983).
48 They are literally 'put in their place'.
49 These include, but are not limited to, corporate headquarters, or those that are about the ostentatious display of wealth, such as the Burj al Arab in Dubai.
50 The way film represents a particular building or space and the suggested reading of this cinematic locus (with its attached "genius") influences the reading of the "real" place, thus precluding or constituting particular conceptions of existing places. The inverse is equally true – the meaning of existing spaces and buildings may heavily influence the meaning they communicate in film or other media.
51 Gillian Rose, *Visual Methodologies. An Introduction to the Interpretation of Visual Materials* (London: Sage Publications. 2007).
52 See Kenneth Helphand, "Landscape Films," *Landscape Journal*, vol. 5, no. 1 (1986): 1–8.
53 Denis Cosgrove argues in (*Social Formation and Symbolic Landscape* (Madison: University of Wisconsin Press, 1998), XIV) that "landscape constitutes a discourse, through which identifiable social groups historically have framed themselves and their relations with both the land and with other human groups, and that this discourse is closely related epistemically and technically to ways of seeing."

54 This has been most convincingly argued by Bela Balazs, considered one of the fathers of film theory: Balazs wrote that the cinema as art is unique in its ability to anthropomorphize objects, and in that role has a gnostic function, revealing relationships between humans and landscape that previously had been hidden. See Bela Balazs, *Early Film Theory: Visible Man and the Spirit of Film* (Berghahn Books, 2011, originally 1924/1930).

55 See Jim Josefson, *Hannah Arendt's Aesthetic Politics* (New York: Palgrave Macmillan, 2019), in particular the chapter on "Res Publica".

56 A key text is Rose, *Visual Methodologies*.

57 E.g. Debord, *The Society of the Spectacle* and Andreas Huyssen, *"In the Shadow of McLuhan" Twilight Memories: Marking Time in a Culture of Amnesia* (New York: Routledge, 1995).

58 Torraca, "A Cornered Democracy," 58.

59 Torraca, 59.

60 Torraca, 59.

61 Giorgio Agamben, "State of Exception," in *Homo Sacer: Sovereign Power and Bare Life*, ed. Giorgio Agamben (Stanford, CA: Stanford University Press, 1998).

62 Agamben, 59.

63 Bauman, 2006.

64 Torraca, *Democracia Encurralada*.

65 Torraca, "A Cornered Democracy."

66 Torraca, 59.

67 See Mikhail Bakhtin's concept of "monoglossia" in *The Dialogic Imagination. Four Essays* (Austin: University of Texas Press, 1981), also Rose, *Visual Methodologies*; and Langhorst, *Landscape Citizenships*.

68 See e.g. Manuel DeLanda, *A New Philosophy of Society: Assemblage Theory and Social Complexity* (London: Continuum Press, 2006).

69 A key problem with many of the "classic" approaches, perspectives and frameworks referenced here is that they are inherently analytical and interpretive, but provide little to no guidance how space might be designed to enable democratic processes. Purcell (2002, 99) exemplifies this in his critique of Lefebvre's "right to the city" as "more radical, more problematic, and more indeterminate".

70 Gilles Deleuze and Claire Parnet, *Dialogues II* (New York: Columbia University Press, 1977 [2007]), 52.

71 Ignacio Farías, "Introduction: Decentering the Object of Urban Studies," in *Urban Assemblages: How Actor-Network Theory Changes Urban Studies*, ed. Ignacio Farías and Thomas Bender (London: Routledge, 2009), 15.

72 See T. Murray Li, "Practices of Assemblage and Community Forest Management," *Economy and Society*, vol. 36, no. 2 (2007): 263–293.

73 See Kaika, "Don't Call Me Resilient."

74 See Mouffe "Deliberative Democracy or Agonistic Pluralism" and *Dimensions of Radical Democracy*.

75 See Ernesto Laclau, *Emancipation(s)* (London: Verso, 1996) and also Dave Castle, "Hearts, Minds and Radical Democracy: Interview with Ernesto Laclau and Chantal Mouffe," https://www.redpepper.org.uk/hearts-minds-and-radical-democracy/, 1998, accessed May 31, 2020.

76 Castle, "Hearts, Minds and Radical Democracy."

77 Bonnie Honig, *Political Theory and the Displacement of Politics* (Ithaca, NY: Cornell University Press, 1993), 15.

78 Those disciplines have a long history and tradition of – intentionally or inadvertently – serving as instruments of systems of political and economic power, with disregard for its legitimacy: "For nearly every injustice in the world, there is an architecture that has been planned and designed to perpetuate it." Bryan Lee Jr. Bloomberg City Lab, June 3, 2020, Bloomberg.com, accessed March 27, 2021

79 There are intriguing parallels between the ways language and rhetoric is shaped and the ways space is used and "inscribed". De Certeau, in *The Practice of Everyday Life* compares acts of spatial use to speech acts. Bakhtin's work on the dialogic construction of language, discourse and meaning provides important insights for architecture and the design of public space. See Joern Langhorst, "Grounding Landscape Citizenships" and Mikhail Bakhtin, *The Dialogic Imagination.*
80 The kind of "heterotopia" Hetherington presents in *Badlands of Modernity.*
81 Kaika, "Don't Call Me Resilient," 94.
82 Veliçu and Kaika, cited in Kaika, "Don't Call Me Resilient," 96
83 Don Mitchell, *The Right to the City: Social Justice and the Fight for Public Space* (New York: Guilford Press, 2003), 211.
84 See e.g. Bruno Latour, *Reassembling the Social: An Introduction to Actor-Network Theory* (Oxford: Clarendon, 2005); Nicholas Tampio, "Assemblages and the Multitude: Deleuze, Hardt, Negri, and the Postmodern Left," *European Journal of Political Theory*, vol. 8 (2009): 383–400 and Colin McFarlane, "Assemblage and Critical Urbanism," *City*, vol. 15, no. 2 (2011): 204–224.
85 Kaika, "Don't Call Me Resilient," 94.
86 Homi Bhabha, "DissemiNation: Time, Narrative, and the Margins of the Modern," in *Nation and Narration* by Homi Bhabha (London: Routledge, 1990), 291–322.
87 Kaika, "Don't Call Me Resilient," 94
88 Lefebvre, *The Right to the City*, 148
89 Henry Giroux, *Youth in Revolt. Reclaiming a Democratic Future* (Boulder and London: Paradigm Publishers, 2013), 107.
90 Peter Marcuse, "The Purpose of the Occupy Movement and the Dangers of Fetishizing Space," https://pmarcuse.wordpress.com/2011/11/15/the-purpose-of-the-occupation-movement-and-the-danger-of-fetishizing-space/November 15, 2011, accessed June 8, 2021.

Bibliography

Agamben. Giorgio. "State of Exception." In Giorgio Agamben. *Homo Sacer: Sovereign Power and Bare Life.* Stanford: Stanford University Press, 1998.
Agnew, John. *Place and Politics: The Geographical Mediation of State and Society.* Boston: Allen and Unwin, 1987.
Anguelovski, Isabelle, James JT Connolly et al. "New Scholarly Pathways on Green Gentrification: What Does the Urban 'Green Turn' Mean and Where Is It Going?" *Progress in Human Geography*, vol. 43, no. 6 (Dec. 2019), 1064–1086, doi:10.1177/0309132518803799.
Arendt, Hannah. *The Human Condition.* 2nd ed. Chicago and London: University of Chicago Press, 1958.
Bakhtin, Mikhail M. *The Dialogic Imagination. Four Essays.* Ed. Michael Holquist. Austin: University of Texas Press, 1981 [1934–1941].
Balazs, Bela. *Bela Balazs' Early Film Theory: Visible Man and the Spirit of Film* (R. Livingstone, Trans.). Berghann Books, 2011, originally 1924/1930).
Baudrillard, Jean. *Simulations.* New York: Semiotexte, 1983.
Bauman, Zygmunt. City of Fears, City of Hopes (Critical Urban Studies: Occasional Papers), 2003. Available at: www.gold.ac.uk/media/documents-by-section/departments/.../city.pdf (Accessed 23 April 2018).
Bauman, Zygmunt. *Liquid Fear.* Cambridge, MA: Polity Press, 2006.
Bauman, Zygmunt. *Liquid Modernity.* Cambridge, MA: Polity Press, 2000.
Bauman, Zygmunt. "The Making and Unmaking of Strangers." In *Debating Cultural Hybridity: Multi-Cultural Identities and the Politics of Anti-Racism*, edited by Prina Werbner and Tariq Modood, 46–47. London: Zed Books, 1997.
Beck, Jody. *Landscape and Utopia*, (Abington: Routledge, in press).

Bhabha, Homi K. "DissemiNation: Time, Narrative, and the Margins of the Modern." In Homi Bhabha. *Nation and Narration*, 291–322. London: Routledge, 1990.

Bluestone, Daniel. "Detroit's City Beautiful and the Problem of Commerce." *Journal of the Society of Architectural Historians*, vol. XLVII, no. 3 (September 1988), 245–262.

Castells, Manuel. *The Informational City: Information, Technology, Economic Restructuring and the Urban-Regional Process*. Oxford: Blackwell, 1989.

Castells, Manuel. *The Power of Identity*. Oxford: Blackwell, 1997.

Castle, Dave. Hearts, Minds and Radical Democracy: Interview with Ernesto Laclau and Chantal Mouffe by Dave Castle, 1998. https://www.redpepper.org.uk/hearts-minds-and-radical-democracy/ accessed May 31, 2020.

Cosgrove, Denis. *Social Formation and Symbolic Landscape*. Madison: University of Wisconsin Press, 1998.

Cresswell, Tim. *In Place/Out of Place: Geography, Ideology and Transgression*. Minneapolis: University of Minnesota Press, 1996.

Debord, Guy. *La société du spectacle*. Paris: Buchet-Chastel, 1967.

De Certeau, Michel. *The Practice of Everyday Life*. Berkeley: University of California, 1984.

DeLanda, Manuel. *A New Philosophy of Society: Assemblage Theory and Social Complexity*. London: Continuum Press, 2006.

Deleuze, Gilles and Claire Parnet. *Dialogues II,* New York: Columbia University Press, 1977 [2007].

Diana Fernandez. "Heterogeneous Futures: Design Thinking Alternatives for Anthropologically and Ecologically Diverse Landscapes." Presentation at the 2020 Landscape Architecture Foundations (LAF) Innovation + Leadership Symposium, June 16, 2020.

Dixon-Hunt, John. *Site, Sight, Insight: Essays on Landscape Architecture*. Philadelphia: Pennsylvania, 2016.

Farías, Ignacio. "Introduction: Decentering the Object of Urban Studies." In *Urban Assemblages: How Actor-Network Theory Changes Urban Studies,* edited by Ignacio Farías and Thomas Bender, 1–24. London: Routledge, 2009.

Fraser, Nancy. "Rethinking the Public Sphere: A Contribution to the Critique of Actually Existing Democracy." *Social Text*, vol. 25/26 (1990), 56–80.

Giroux, Henry. *Youth in Revolt. Reclaiming a Democratic Future*. Boulder and London: Paradigm Publishers, 2013.

Habermas, Juergen. *The Structural Transformation of the Public Sphere: An Inquiry into a Category of Bourgeois Society*, Cambridge, MA: The MIT Press, 1989.

Hardt, Michael and Antonio Negri. *Assembly*. Oxford: Oxford University Press, 2017.

Harvey, David. "Militant Particularism and Global Ambition: The Conceptual Politics of Place, Space, and Environment in the Work of Raymond Williams." In *Spaces of Capital: Towards a Critical Geography*, by David Harvey, 158–187. Edinburgh: Edinburgh University Press, 2001.

Harvey, David. "The Right to the City." *New Left Review*, vol. 53 (2008), 23–40.

Harvey, David. *Social Justice and the City*. London: Edward Arnold, 1973.

Helphand, Kenneth. Landscape Films. *Landscape Journal*, vol. 5, no. 1 (1986), 1–8.

Hetherington, Kevin. *Badlands of Modernity: Heterotopia and Social Ordering,* London: Routledge, 2007.

Holl, Steven. *Parallax*. Princeton: Princeton Architectural Press, 2000.

Honig, Bonnie. *Political Theory and the Displacement of Politics*. Ithaca, NY: Cornell University Press, 1993.

Huyssen, Andreas. *In the Shadow of McLuhan. Twilight Memories: Marking Time in a Culture of Amnesia*. New York: Routledge, 1995.

Huyssen, Andreas. *Present Pasts: Urban Palimpsests and the Politics of Memory*. Palo Alto: Stanford University Press, 2003.

Ingimundarson, Valur and Sveinn M. Jóhannesson (eds.), *Liberal Disorder, States of Exception, and Populist Politics*. Abingdon: Routledge, 2021.

Ingold, Tim. *Being Alive: Essays on Movement, Knowledge and Description*. London: Routledge, 2011.

Ingold, Tim. *The Perception of the Environment: Essays on Livelihood, Dwelling and Skill*. London: Routledge, 2000.

Ingold, Tim. "The Temporality of Landscape." In *The Perception of the Environment. Essays on Livelihood, Dwelling and Skill*, edited by Tim Ingold, 189–208. London: Routledge, 2011.

Jacobs, Jane. *Death and Life of Great American Cities*. New York: Random House, 1961

Josefson, Jim. *Hannah Arendt's Aesthetic Politics: Freedom and the Beautiful*. New York: Palgrave Macmillan, 2019.

Kaika, Maria. "'Don't call me Resilient Again!' The New Urban Agenda as Immunology … or What Happens When Communities Refuse To Be Vaccinated with 'Smart Cities' and Indicators." *Environment & Urbanization*, vol. 29, no. 1 (2017), 89–102.

Laclau, Ernesto. *Emancipation(s)*. London: Verso, 1996.

Langhorst, Joern. "Enacting Landscape Democracy: Assembling Public Open Space and Asserting the Right to the City." In *Defining Landscape Democracy*, edited by Shelley Egoz, Tim Richardson, Deni Ruggeri and Karsten Jørgensen, 106–118. Cheltenham: Edward Elgar, 2018.

Langhorst, Joern. "Re-branding the Neoliberal City: Urban Nature as Spectacle, Medium and Agency." *Architecture_MPS: A Journal of Architecture, Media, Politics Society*, vol. 6, no. 4 (2015). Retrieved from http://architecturemps.com.

Langhorst, Joern. "Situating Landscape Citizenships: Borders, Margins, Hybridity, and the Uncanny." In *Landscape Citizenships*, edited by Tim Waterman, Jane Wolff and Ed Wall, 109–129. Abingdon: Routledge, 2021.

Latour, Bruno. *Reassembling the Social: An Introduction to Actor-network Theory*. Oxford: Clarendon, 2005.

Lefebvre, Henri. *The Critique of Everyday Life, Volume 1* (John Moore trans.), London: Verso. 1991. (Originally published 1947).

Lefebvre, Henri. "Right to the City." In *Writings on Cities*, edited and translated by E. Kofman and E. Lebas, 63–177. Oxford: Basil Blackwell, 1996.

Li, T. Murray. "Practices of Assemblage and Community Forest Management." *Economy and Society*, vol. 36, no. 2 (2007), 263–293.

Lumann, Niklas. *The Reality of the Mass Media*. Stanford, CA: Stanford University Press, 2000.

Marcuse, Peter. "From Critical Urbanism to Right to the City." *City*, vol. 13 (2009), 185–197.

Marcuse, Peter. "The Purpose of the Occupation Movement and the Dangers of Fetishizing Space." https://pmarcuse.wordpress.com/2011/11/15/the-purpose-of-the-occupation-movement-and-the-danger-of-fetishizing-space/November 15, 2011, accessed June 8, 2021.

McFarlane, Colin. "Assemblage and Critical Urbanism." *City*, vol. 15, no. 2 (2011), 204–224.

Miller, Byron and Walter Nicholls (eds.). *Spaces of Contention: Spatialities and Social Movements*. Abingdon: Taylor & Francis Group, 2013.

Mitchell, Don. *The Right to the City: Social Justice and the Fight for Public Space*. New York: Guilford Press, 2003.

Mouffe, Chantal. "Deliberative Democracy or Agonistic Pluralism," *Political Science Series*, vol. 72. Vienna: Institute for Advanced Studies, 2000.

Mouffe, Chantal. *Dimensions of Radical Democracy: Pluralism, Citizenship, Community.* London: Verso, 1992.

Mouffe, Chantal. *On the Political.* New York: Taylor & Francis, 2005.

Nicholls, Walter, Byron Miller, and Justin Beaumont. "Conceptualizing the Spatialities of Social Movements." In *Spaces of Contention: Spatialities and Social Movements,* edited by Byron Miller and Walter Nicholls, 1–24. Abingdon: Taylor & Francis Group, 2013.

Purcell, Mark. "Excavating Lefebvre: The Right to the City and its Urban Politics of the Inhabitant." *GeoJournal, 'Social Transformation, Citizenship, and the Right to the City,'* vol. 58, no. 2/3 (2002), 99–108.

Purcell, Mark. *Recapturing Democracy: Neoliberalization and the Struggle for Alternative Urban Futures.* Abingdon: Routledge, 2008.

Ranciere, Jacques. *Dissensus. On Politics and Aesthetics.* London and New York: Continuum, 2010.

Rose, Gillian. *Visual Methodologies. An Introduction to the Interpretation of Visual Materials.* London: Sage Publications. 2007.

Sendra, Pablo and Richard Sennet. *Designing Disorder: Experiments and Disruptions in the City.* London: Verso, 2020.

Sennet, Richard. *Flesh and Stone. The Body and the City in Western Civilization.* New York and London: W.W. Norton & Co., 1994.

Sennet, Richard. "Reflections on the Public Realm." In *The New Blackwell Companion to Cities,* edited by Gary Bridge and Sophie Watson, 390–397. Hoboken: Wiley – Blackwell, 2012.

Slater, Tom. *The Resilience of Neoliberal Urbanism.* Retrieved February 2, 2014 from http://www.opendemocracy.net/opensecurity/tom-slater/resilience-of-neoliberal-urbanism.

Smith, Neil. *Uneven Development: Nature, Capital and the Production of Space.* Oxford: Blackwell, 1984.

Tampio, Nicholas. "Assemblages and the Multitude: Deleuze, Hardt, Negri, and the Postmodern Left." *European Journal of Political Theory,* vol. 8 (2009), 383–400.

Torraca, Liz Beatriz Texiera. "A Cornered Democracy: The Echo of the 2013 Demonstrations in Rio de Janeiro and the Architecture of Crisis." In *Urban Public Spaces. From Planned Policies to Everyday Politics,* edited by Luciana Capanema Alvarez and Jorge Luiz Barbosa, 57–72. The Urban Book Series. Cham: Springer, 2018.

Torraca, Liz Beatriz Texiera. *Democracia Encurralada. Os reflexos da manifestações de 2013 no Rio de Janeiro.* Lumen Juris: Rio de Janeiro, 2016.

Tuan, Yi-Fu. *Space and Place: The Perspective of Experience.* Minneapolis: University of Minnesota Press, 1977.

Vidler, Anthony. "The Explosion of Space: Architecture and the Filmic Imaginary." *Assemblage Vol. 2.* Cambridge, MA: MIT Press, 1993.

Williams, Raymond. *The Country and the City.* New York: Oxford University Press, 1973.

Intersection

6

ARCHITECTURE JOURNALISM AND THE PROTO-POLITICAL[1]

Peggy Deamer and Ian Volner

The ransacking of the Capitol Building on January 6th, just like the attack on the World Trade Center in 2001, offered a chance for the media to foreground architecture-cum-symbol—a symbol of American economic hegemony on the one hand, and American democracy on the other. The collective imaginary that this "news" played into is a deeply confounded one. On the one hand, it is political: a building, as the public has already been primed to believe, could seemingly both shape and be shaped by its economic and governmental programs. On the other hand, what was also revealed in January was a commonly held, *apolitical* understanding of architecture: first because the nature of American political power is virtually never challenged so directly (let alone analyzed in the media) and second because, in non-crisis times, the media offers up buildings that—while toney, expensive, formally dexterous, and generally in white neighborhoods—refuse to acknowledge their elitist economic circumstances. The public, as a result, is presented with an image of architecture that is not political per se, but proto-political, preconfiguring a political attitude that shapes what is and is not asked of design. Courtesy of this mediated image of the discipline, the public has come to expect an architecture that is fabulous without being controversial, publicly charming but privately developed, humane but profit-driven.

In considering the operation of the print and online media in this context, one needs to distinguish between articles authored by architecture critics and those authored by non-architecture journalists—general commentators who emerge at these architecturally pregnant times, those writing in the real estate section, and those that bandy about the term "architecture" in non-architectural contexts. This chapter will concentrate on architectural criticism, but the contributions of lay journalists are highly suggestive. In particular, the role that the metaphorical "architect" plays in the proto-political domain of public opinion is pervasive: Karl Rove was invariably referred to as "the architect" of George W. Bush's

DOI: 10.4324/9781003272076-9

presidency; Steve Bannon received the same moniker on occasion in reference to Trumpism; every general manager in baseball, if they are at all successful, gets the "architect" treatment. If anything subliminally shapes the public mind as to what architects are, it may be this constant repetition of the word *architect* outside its proper context, suffusing the profession with a mysterious omnipotence and turning the image of the practitioner into something between a James Bond villain and a mad scientist, with overtones of the Wizard of Oz.[2]

Likewise, the symbolic charge of architecture—its perception as an essential and essentially non-political good—is rooted, at least in part, in an ideology that can only be called "Builderism." The appearance of new buildings, new infrastructure, new architecture of any description is almost always looked on as a net positive, at least in the abstract; even if the overall popular impression of the building in question is negative (i.e., it is ugly), there's little doubt mooted in the media that something needed to be built: never a question of *if*, only *what*. Illustrative of this phenomenon was the debacle late last year surrounding the Trump executive order on classical architecture. Following the mandate's appearance in December of 2020, article after article appeared in the press as to whether the government should build this way or that, with both industry and general-interest media staging a mini revival of the stylistic debates of the 1980s (modernism vs. postmodernism, white vs. grey, blob vs. box, etc.). Little of the debate focused on whether massive building programs were required to begin with: nothing about whether construction as such is environmentally sound; or whether more government buildings might only magnify the scope of state control; or whether there might be alternatives to the myth that the economy must grow at all costs, with development as a major driver of that growth.

While relying on the same assumptions, real estate journalism tends to be far more direct regarding the reality of development, making blunt assessments about the finances that motivate a building project, the political negotiations that determine its program and its height, and the users (rarely contiguous with the developer) who occupy it. A cursory examination of recent headlines in industry tabloid *The Real Deal* shows an emphasis on dollar amounts ("Nightingale, Wafra Secure $500M Loan Package To Revamp 111 Wall Street," "Mack-Cali Offloads Red Bank Office Complex for $84M"), as well as political maneuvering (Landlords Urge Biden To Let Eviction Ban Expire). But even here, one of two things tends to occur. On the one hand, articles such as the recent "New Buildings Lure Tenants With Free Rent"—a C.J. Hughes piece in *The New York Times* about the appeal of recently built developments—go into considerable depth about multiple projects, without once mentioning the name of a single architect, as though the buildings had simply appeared out of nowhere. Alternatively, and in peculiar contradiction to the above, there is journalism such as *The New York Times's* "The Hangover: Cantilevered Buildings of New York" by Robin Finn—an article describing how cantilevered floor designs allow increased square footage—that foreground the architects who employ such structural tricks as if they, not the developers, were masters of financial legerdemain.[3]

True, the architects quoted in an article like Finn's are complicit in the misrepresentation of power and responsibility, and that is part of the tragedy. But such coverage in real estate media only compounds the confusion as to what architects actually do and how.

Not that things are necessarily made that much clearer by those nominally closer to the profession. Turning to look at architecture journalism properly, it quickly becomes evident how inadequate most design journalism has become to the task of deep reflection—an inadequacy made all the more glaring in light of the Covid epidemic, a crisis every bit as revealing as January 6th.

Perhaps the most egregious example: the "Virtual Walking Tours in NYC" that *The New York Times* architecture critic, Michael Kimmelman, offered New York readers during the height of the pandemic.[4] New Yorkers, Kimmelman assumed, could vicariously visit places that the lockdown physically denied them. The result was creepy in its nostalgia. As Mary Woods has said,

> I kept hearing George Gershwin's 'Rhapsody in Blue,' and then Woody Allen's voice over from his film *Manhattan*: 'He adored New York City. He idolized it all out of proportion.' Both Allen and Kimmelman are writing valentines to a battered city in 1979 and now 2020. And more than four decades later New York is still a city for and about white privilege.[5]

While the readership could remain charmed by these 17 walks (only three of which were in anyway "ethnic"), the subliminal message was three-fold. First, the series offered up "histories"—all implicitly describing colonization and environmental abuse—that resolve into an ideal present; the city, for all the contextualization that the experts leading the walking tours provided, comes across as simply waiting for its looking-glass moment. Second is the implication that the critic's role is merely to sooth or to serve; this conception (the critic as "architectural barista… brewing up steaming cups of truth," in Michael Sorkin's mocking formulation) infantilizes the reader while evacuating the critical profession of any power to change practice or improve the urban prospect. And third is the implication that Kimmelman's readers represent "the public." Not only are those who lead these tours an inside crowd—architects, planners, historians— but they presume a readership divorced from rent debt, homelessness, crime, or environmental destruction.

The roots of this superficial*, bien pensant*-ist response to the Covid disaster are embedded in a general reluctance, endemic among critics, to touch the *how* of architectural production rather than simply the *what* (i.e., buildings). Architectural work, as critics rarely scruple to tell their audiences, is precarious, dependent on the developer's phone call and on the meager fees that are offered when the call finally comes; indeed, the known axiom among developers is that the cost of architectural design is the most easily negotiated and reduced. Compared to US doctors, whose mean average salary is $313,000, and US lawyers, whose mean average salary is $168,550, architects on average make a mere $80,750 per year. And those in the field know that architectural employees are in an entirely different labor class than firm owners. Employees' jobs, no less than the jobs of their bosses, are dependent on paid projects—but their plight is compounded by the lower wages and often illegal labor practices to which they are regularly subject, including being deprived of overtime pay. These deplorable conditions were exacerbated still further during the pandemic when projects were put on hold: as documented by James Russell in a spring 2020 article for *Architectural Record*, New York City's public works programs were halted almost immediately, with architectural offices reportedly "stunned" to receive official stop-work orders and many smaller practices left in financial peril as a result. Thrown back on private-sector clients, many studios were obliged to focus on completing projects already in the office, and were therefore at the mercy of developers' demands that work carry on lest income-producing buildings get stalled. Firm principals were caught between a rock and a hard place—the need to increase the pace of work while staff were supposed to avoid coming into the office—but most employers chose to insist on extra work at home and/or, after the strict lockdown was over, coming into the office in unsafe conditions.

To some extent, this is hardly surprising: all businesses were affected by lockdown. But in view that other *Times* cultural critics were busily documenting the effect of Covid on other aspects of creative work—the toll on art museums and their staff, the tragedy of musicians with few performance options and cut pay, the actors out of work, the chefs with closed restaurants[6]—Kimmelman's silence in this regard seems fairly stunning. Even as a stream of articles appeared under his byline concerning the design of test sites and the overall texture of the city during Covid, there was scarcely a word from the country's most prominent architecture critic regarding how the architecture profession itself, and the people who make it work, were faring amidst the chaos. The reader could only infer that Kimmelman does not think of architects as creative workers, or that architecture just makes itself.[7]

The *Times* was hardly alone in manifesting this blinkered view of the field, though some of its peer publications did at least marginally better. There are of course fairly few other journalists occupying Kimmelman's privileged perch as a masthead architecture critic at a major metropolitan daily. Indeed the Covid-era honor roll is now appallingly short, comprising (in no particular order) John King of the *San Francisco Chronicle*; Blair Kamin of the *Chicago Tribune* (who retired during the pandemic); Philip Kennicot of *The Washington Post*; Robert Campbell of *The Boston Globe*; Robert Behre of *The Post and Carrier*; Steven Litt of *The Plain Dealer*; Mark Lamster of *The Dallas Morning News*; Mary Louise Schumacher of *The Milwaukee Journal Sentinel*; Michael J. Lewis of *The Wall Street Journal*; and Inga Saffron of *The Philadelphia Inquirer*. From these emerged an array of pandemic responses, ranging from virtual silence (Kamin, Campbell, Behre, Lewis) to discussions about the fate of the local art museum and galleries (Kennicot, Behre, Litt) to emerging post-pandemic programs (John King) to those who were obliged by Covid to accept buyouts and leave their paper altogether (Schumacher). But whatever the particular merits or demerits of each approach—and despite the fact that nothing could be more manifestly spatial than an emergency that literally mandated people keep their distance from each other—most of those who chose to write about the situation failed to tease out its deeper implications. Among the few who attempted more searching critiques were Mark Lamster (who wrote about the economic and personal changes that come with virtuality, as well as some insightful observations on the Black Lives Matter protests) and Inga Saffron (who penned numerous articles demonstrating a host of cultural shifts caused by the virus, including the intensified city versus suburb debate, the end of office work, and the history of Philadelphia surviving previous plagues). Otherwise, the remaining on-staff newspaper critics tended to fall back on a what-over-how, Builderist mentality, focusing on what new sorts of structures and interiors might be necessary to respond to the pandemic and what kinds of design trends might emerge in its wake.

In all of this, there is a stark contrast between the current, often bland fare from America's newspaper writers and that proffered by such bygone luminaries as Ada Louise Huxtable, the first to hold the official critic post at the *Times*, and Michael Sorkin, the long-time in-house architecture writer at *The Village Voice*. Both not only addressed urban/architectural crises head on, but dug them out from underneath our complacent noses. Huxtable, writing for *The New York Times* from 1963 to 1982, called out the challenges of urban flight, the misunderstood importance of streets, and the missteps planners made regarding public engagement; in bringing the plight of modern urban dwellers to public attention, she remains the best counterexample to the ills of today's architecture criticism. Sorkin—both in the ten years he wrote for Voice in the 1980s and (until his untimely death from Covid-19 in March 2020) for *The New York Times*, *Metropolis*, *The Wall Street Journal*, and other trade magazines—relentlessly attacked the zoning rules, building codes, and economic forces that thwarted the democratic public domain and the misguided governmental policies that exacerbated environmental destruction.[8] Their employment at major news organizations did not deter either writer from taking the broadest possible view. Their readership was the richer for it.

Of course, given the limited number of dedicated newspaper critics remaining, most self-described design writers nowadays are of the freelance description. Among this cohort Covid coverage was also a mixed bag: for *Elle Décor*, the co-author of the present chapter wrote a decidedly trivial (if somewhat tongue-in-cheek) story on the unlikelihood of serious post-Covid change for *Elle Décor*; for *Architect*, Karrie Jacobs conducted a thoughtful interview with authors Geoff Manaugh and Nicola Twilley who have researched quarantine since well before the current pandemic (naturally the piece reflected their thinking rather than hers); Eva Hagberg, writing as ever from a personal perspective, produced 70 Virtual Memory Covid-19 Sessions, podcast interviews with friends and wrote about long-distance friendships; Zach Mortice, writing for *Bloomberg News* and other publications, wrote about a more socially equitable post-pandemic built environment; and Mimi Zeiger, writing for *Metropolis,* expanded the concept of "refuge" from environmental-crisis discourse to apply to the Covid-crisis, charging architects with imagining a sci-fi future refuge. Kate Wagner—technically on staff at the *New Republic,* but also freelancing for other journals—made the daring move, very much to her credit, of aiming her critique at other publications, pointing specifically at online vertical *Dezeen* and all but demanding that the blog stop posting architectural projects that used the pandemic to showcase self-promoting architectural imaginaries. Notably, Wagner's anti-"coronagrifting" piece appeared on her personal website McMansion Hell, which thanks to her canny internet presence has grown into a highly influential source of online criticism. But the fact that the piece did not appear in a published journal is significant: in looking at the above list, the primary determinant of the character and quality of any given freelancer-written article is the venue for which the freelancer happens to be writing. This is hardly a coincidence, since unlike their fully employed counterparts, these writers work under a specific set of constraints, and are subject to a precarity analogous to many of their junior colleagues in architecture. This is a direct function of the publishing marketplace—of which more to follow.

But there is one additional group of architecture critics who bear consideration. These are the critics who are cultural generalists, whose beat isn't architecture per se but have it under their purview. Certainly, various species of "outsider" critic have appeared in architecture before—the *Times*'s first regular design contributor, late-19th-century author Montgomery Schuyler, started his career as a music critic; both Kimmelman and his opposite number at *New York Magazine,* Justin Davidson, began in art and music respectively—but as the number of full-time design critics has continued to decline, there has been a corresponding boomlet in generalist writers occasionally dabbling in design. *The New Yorker,* for example, no longer has its own critic, but tends to rely on writers with a more varied background; the magazine's most prominent contribution to Covid architecture journalism came from Kyle Chayka, a media critic by trade whose June 2020 account of Covid-era design was more thorough than most, but mostly amounted to a review of other designers' and thinkers' ideas on the topic (most of them fairly Builder-ish). Robin Pogrebin, also of *The New York Times,* enjoys a very broad remit as a Culture writer that regularly involves architecture writing, though her Covid reportage looked almost exclusively at the art market. Interpretive pieces by such non-architectural intellectuals have definite advantages: as writers from outside the field, they are notionally less susceptible to architecture's most endemic discursive bugbears (jargonism, the tendency to overvalue the discipline's social potential, etc.). But the reliance on writers of this stripe also guarantees a blind spot as to the actual mechanics of design *qua* material process. At a minimum there should be a place within the design mediasphere for voices who have actually participated in the activity they now speak for, who can be candid regarding the position they now occupy (advocacy or reporting? reporting or opinion-shaping?

criticism or celebration?), as well as to their own politics (cultural elitism or rank-and-file?).

The question of training and background is key; yet it points to still more vexing problems of critical identity in a field where, for all the prominent women critics mentioned here, most of those who write for major publications are men, and most of those men are white. Since Ada Louise Huxtable's retirement from the *Times* in 1982, all of her successors (Goldberger, Herbert Muschamp, Nicolai Ourosoff, Kimmelman) have been white men. The perils of this situation were on full display in 2018, when a media panel during Yale's "Rebuilding Architecture" symposium (convened by the primary author of this chapter) featuring Kimmelman and moderated by journalist (and the chapter's other author) Ian Volner became the occasion for an audience-prompted discussion of the #MeToo movement's implications for architecture. During the Q&A session, female attendees asked pointed questions about the *Times*'s occasionally slow and spotty reporting on the topic, questions to which the *Times* critic proved somewhat ill-equipped to respond (to say nothing of the moderator). Coloring what gets reported, when and from what perspective, the relative racial and gender uniformity of the senior architectural press corps has at least a potential spill-over effect on practice, reinforcing the analogous homogeneity of the design profession. As Mimi Zeiger has written,

> This perception of scarcity… reinforces structural inequity in architecture. Only a few individuals—white and often male—hold architecture critic positions. Their entrenchment, for a decade or three, at the top of the food chain systemically restricts a plurality of voices from reaching the widest of audiences, from benefiting from networks of power, and from economic solidity.[9]

At the same time, a more diverse field would still suffer from structural issues that place the entire critical enterprise on shaky ground. Ostensibly, the present moment would seem rife with opportunity: the conventional model of design writing—the standalone building review written by the card-carrying architecture critic, the mainstay of the profession since Lewis Mumford's "Sky Line" column for *The New Yorker* in the 1930s—is now in full rout. Yet the emergence of a more engaging, more engaged mode of popular criticism faces a host of obstacles, all of them products of the 21st-century publishing marketplace and the demands of 21st-century capital. These obstacles touch every critic or would-be critic now writing, though they pose a special challenge to the freelance writers who now account for the better part of architectural criticism appearing in newspapers, magazines, and online media in the United States and abroad.

For one, the financial bottom-line pressures of journals, especially print journals, are at all times paramount. The very fact that so many critics now work freelance is a product of this economic crunch: in LA, Chicago, and Providence, newspapers have eliminated their full-time architecture critics with no replacement. And once cast into the freelance fold, the pay for journalists is notoriously bad. For all the news accounts of unions being formed by writers and editors in prestigious news organizations like *The New Yorker*, no such labor protections are likely to reach contract writers in the near term.[10] The bad pay ensures that journalism and criticism are open only to those who can afford them; as Mimi Zeiger has written,

> If newspapers, magazines, and online publications want to support a more diverse set of writers, they first need to take a hard look at how much they pay and recognize that low rates contribute to unsustainable and inequitable practices. Not everyone, especially historically marginalised groups, can afford to make criticism a hobby or side gig.

The freelancer's marginalized position produces many dilemmas, but not the least of them is the problem of travel: absent regular newspaper employment, journalists cannot typically afford to finance travel themselves; in order to write about buildings, the buildings have to be seen (to review a project otherwise is little different than reviewing a book you haven't read) and so the freelancer must accept whatever funding comes their way. This often means taking a paid junket, with transit, food, and accommodations financed either by the architects, the developers or, in the case of an exhibition or other event, the organizers. The architecture journalist is therefore in an ethical pickle from the very moment they arrive, beholden to the very people they're meant to be critiquing.[11]

More insidious is the fact that journalists writing for the public at large, not for the trade, are caught in a double bind. Tasked with educating their readers while "representing" the discipline, they are also expected to contribute to their publication's commercial well-being, wedding them to a status quo definition of what the public "wants." The journalist is therefore forever torn between the job's *occupational* and *vocational* aspects: in one's occupation, as a reporter, the writer must state clearly and accurately when the project was completed, what the billionaire who financed it said, how much it cost; in one's vocation, as a critic, one must call the project ugly, corrupt and overpriced. There are areas of overlap, and occasional opportunities to convey, however subtly, a critical insight even while writing a seemingly "objective" piece of reportage. But the hat-switching is hardly easy, and the economics of journalism make it harder still. The financial pressure on journals means they must cater to the popular, meaning that critics must also cater to the popular, all but guaranteeing that content will be attractive to look at and easy to digest. For all the talk in recent years of "the death of the starchitect" and the fall of "iconic architecture," the public consciousness is still fixated on architecture as image.

Once again, the recent history of *The New York Times* shows the trajectory. In 2008, the paper created "Home and Garden" as one of its special sections; it lasted only seven years. In 2015, its subjects were scattered over sections for Real Estate, Styles, Travel, Food and then *The Times*'s Sunday magazine and *T*

Magazine, the latter described as coverage of the "luxury lifestyle." Criticism of architecture and profiles of architects continued in the Arts section. The special sections in which architecture had a presence have steadily devolved into PR releases for upcoming films, plays, fashion, furniture, and decoration, all with an eye to attracting niche advertisers. The pattern is undeniable: when architecture is given attention, it is almost exclusively as aesthetic spectacle. And for that reason, we should not be at all surprised that architects themselves continue to feed the aesthetic craving.

Consciously or otherwise, designers create work with the express objective of producing sensational images for media consumption. The process did not begin with the advent of websites like *Dezeen*; indeed, over the last century, architecture's prevailing formal strategies can be seem to change as the means of representation change—Modernism looks best in the black and white images of Ezra Stoller and his contemporaries; Postmodernism was perfectly suited to the glossy color magazines and music videos of the 1980s; and the internet is an ideal medium for Gehry-esque. "iconic" design. But the last decade has seen an intensification of this process of mediation: witness, among other things, the young designers whose booths at commercial fairs (Salone del Mobile, ICFF, Design Miami) are specifically engineered in content and arrangement to attract notice on social media, with every table, every chair, every object precisely placed to fit within Instagram's equilateral square frame. Visuality of this sort is the stock and trade of architects today, who must operate in the same media environment as the influencer, the fashion designer, the hip restaurateur. It is not that architects are innocent victims in this process, forcibly marginalized into makers of pretty images, but the chicken-and-egg relationship between design and the media corrupts both in a cycle that has been enabled by both, and that is accelerated, as ever, by capital.

In one sense, the decline of architecture criticism seems shocking. How could such an essential thing as the built environment, which shapes our bodies' connections to other bodies and thereby structures our identity, be so ignored and trivialized in public discourse? What could be more important and worthy of serious comment?

But then we shouldn't really be so surprised. There are those who recognized the problem long in advance—not the least being Walter Benjamin, in his landmark treatment of modern media "The Work of Art in the Age of Mechanical Reproduction." In the text, Benjamin observes that architecture, unlike other arts, possesses an *intrinsically* proto-political aspect, one only exacerbated by the process of mediation witnessed in our time. As he writes:

> Architecture has always offered the prototype of an artwork that is received in a state of distraction and through the collective. The laws of architecture's reception are highly instructive... Buildings are received in a twofold manner: by use and by perception. Or, better: tactilely and optically. Such reception cannot be understood in terms of the concentrated attention of a

traveller before a famous building. On the tactile side, there is no counter-part to what contemplation is on the optical side. Tactile reception comes about not so much by way of attention as by way of habit. The latter largely determines even the optical reception of architecture, which spontaneously takes the form of casual noticing, rather than attentive observation.[12]

According to this argument, architecture is not consciously received because it is so pervasive; it resides in our subconscious, a subconscious that apprehends the power our built environment has over in ways that our conscious understanding cannot grasp. And because this prototypicality is in architecture's very nature, the media can hardly dispel it. In the moment the critics describe a building's appearance, its effect on the mind and on the body, they have already enfolded a building's proto-politics into their critique.

Perhaps, given the public's pre-ordained indifference, journalists would be best advised to concentrate their own analyses on the various ways—different in each stylistic era—the real power dynamics at play in the production of our phys-ical space are obfuscated. Still, it seems sad to think that architectural journalism can't do heavier lifting. In doing so, it needn't abandon aesthetic appraisal, or even Builderism; rather, it would merely acknowledge that Builderism operates in a network of labor (both design and construction), a system of finance (private, national, global), and complex structures of governance. These are all things that journalists in the other arts have long ago come to grips with and exposed. It can be difficult to analyze what is right in front of our faces, yet this is exactly where psychotherapy is most needed. Architectural journalists have such impor-tant work to do, if they could see it.

It was only unfortunate that so few saw it in time for the events of January 6th. Having neglected, despite the rare opportunity afforded by the Covid ep-idemic, to convey the "how" of architectural economics, design media and the media in general robbed the American public of the intellectual tools required to properly understand the symbolic pantomime of the Capitol Riot, allowing the agents of the attack to more effectively prey on the proto-political subconscious. What could have proofed the American mind against such theatrics? One sug-gestion (and the central hypothesis of this chapter): a more sensitive, more com-prehensive project of research and exposure of architectural production. Such a project could lay the groundwork for a thorough power mapping of various architectural developments, a map that would surely show the link between the powers that build monuments and the oligarchs who exert such outsized influence over our floundering democracy and our decaying environment. Just as promisingly, from the perspective of practice, such power maps could help locate and multiply locations within the built environment for the staging of *real* political acts—rather than vain and violent dumb shows—capable of fostering community and furthering social equity. Some architectural theorists are already at work on this crucial mapping, but their results need to reach the public, and we must rely on journalists to make that happen. Once again, what we don't know can only hurt us.

Notes

1 The origins of this chapter was an article written by Peggy Deamer and Mary Woods for *Platform*, itself motivated by our joint dismay of the Virtual Architectural Walks written by *New York Times'* architecture critic, Michael Kimmelman, during Covid lockdown. The authors here want to acknowledge our debt to Woods' contribution to this theme and the material in this chapter. That article is here: https://www.platformspace.net/home/covid-19-architectural-journalism-a-conversation.

2 Billionaire Barry Diller actually referred to Heatherwick as the "wizard of Oz" in a piece Ian Volner wrote for *New York Magazine* published May 20, 2021, *Barry Diller is Ready to Show Off his Big Beautiful Baby, Little Island*. He was pilloried, among other things, for supposedly amplifying the incredible claims about Heatherwick's (indeed very dubious) genius. Guilty perhaps but there is an important lesson here.

3 Robin Finn, "The Hangover: Cantilevered Buildings of New York," *The New York Times*, January 10, 2014, https://www.nytimes.com/2014/01/12/realestate/-cantilevered-buildings-of-new-york.html?searchResultPosition=1

4 Michael Kimmelman, "Virtual Walking Tours in NYC," *The New York Times*, https://www.nytimes.com/interactive/2020/12/02/arts/design/new-york-city-walking-tours.html

5 Mary Woods' comment was in a draft for the above cited *Platform* article draft but was excised in the final version.

6 The following are links to articles in *The New York Times* that covered the effects of the first year and a half of the pandemic on various cultural disciplines and institutions. Again, architecture is not among them:

https://www.nytimes.com/2020/03/31/arts/design/museums-coronavirus-pandemic-artifacts.html?searchResultPosition=1; https://www.nytimes.com/2021/02/10/us/covid-los-angeles-museums.html?searchResultPosition=10; https://www.nytimes.com/2020/09/16/arts/design/brooklyn-museum-sale-christies-coronavirus.html; https://www.nytimes.com/2020/06/03/arts/design/museums-arts-leadership-coronavirus-protests.html;https://www.nytimes.com/2020/05/28/arts/design/elizabeth-diller-architecture-virus.html; https://www.nytimes.com/2020/03/18/arts/design/met-museum-coronavirus-closure.html;https://www.nytimes.com/2020/12/07/arts/music/-new-york-philharmonic-pay-cuts.html?searchResultPosition=1;https://www.nytimes.com/2020/09/08/arts/music/jazz-clubs-coronavirus.html?searchResultPosition=4; https://www.nytimes.com/2021/03/15/arts/music/metropolitan-opera-pandemic.html?searchResultPosition=10;https://www.nytimes.com/2021/03/18/arts/music/met-opera-nezet-seguin.html?searchResultPosition=16; https://www.nytimes.com/2020/04/23/magazine/closing-prune-restaurant-covid.html

7 Kimmelman has indicated in various conversations with Deamer between 2018 and 2020 that he feels the public isn't interested in the "how" of architectural production, only the what. But how is the public to know that there is a relationship between what architects produce and the economic conditions that determine how they are able to produce?

8 In the original article written by Deamer and Woods for *Platform*, Woods, comparing Kimmelman's walks to those she wanted to hear from Sorkin writes,

> I want to hear him re-create his twenty-minute walk from his apartment on Waverly Place to his Tribeca office in covid's wake in which he would bring to the surface social, political, and economic stores. Surely he would talk about the further implosion of independently owned stores and shops and restaurants, threats to cultural institutions like the IFC and Film Forum, and the loss of jobs in design, graphic, and IT firms in Tribeca, and how working from home will further accelerate our cities' collapse into ghettoes for transnational oligarchs and then the homeless and impoverished.

https://www.platformspace.net/home/covid-19-architectural-journalism-a-conversation

9 Mimi Zeiger, "It's Time to Abolish the Architecture Critic," *Dezeen*, March 1, 2021, https://www.dezeen.com/2021/03/01/abolish-architecture-critics-newspaper-mimi-zeiger/

10 Katie Robertson and Rachel Abrams, "New Yorker Employees Stage Protest Outside Anna Wintour's Townhouse," *The New York Times*, June 8, 2021, https://www.nytimes.com/2021/06/08/business/media/new-yorker-union-anna-wintour.html?searchResultPosition=1

11 As an attendant anecdote to the above, Blair Kamin, lately of *The Chicago Tribune*, criticized his colleagues in 2019 for coming to his city's biennial by such paid-for arrangements (Volner was among them), questioning whether their objectivity had been thereby compromised. He was right to do so; but he was also speaking from a position of privilege as one of the few staff critics left. Notably he is no longer in the post; nor has he been replaced.

12 "The Work of Art in the Age of Mechanical Reproduction," *Illuminations* (New York: Schocken Books, 1969), 239–240.

Bibliography

Abend, Lisa. "Museums Scramble to Document the Pandemic, Even as It Unfolds." *The New York Times*, March 31, 2020. https://www.nytimes.com/2020/03/31/arts/design/museums-coronavirus-pandemic-artifacts.html?searchResultPosition=1

Benjamin, Walter. "The Work of Art in the Age of Mechanical Reproduction." *Illuminations*. New York: Schocken Books, 1969, 239–240.

Cavanaugh, Suzannah. "Dear Mr. President: Landlords Urge Biden to Let Eviction Ban Expire." The *Real Deal*, June 14, 2021.

Cowan, Jill and Robin Pogrebin. "The Pandemic's Toll on Los Angeles Museums." *The New York Times*, February 10. https://www.nytimes.com/2021/02/10/us/covid-los-angeles-museums.html?searchResultPosition=10

Deamer, Peggy and Mary Woods. "Covid-19 Architectural Journalism: A Conversation." *Platform*, July 27, 2021. https://www.platformspace.net/home/covid-19-architectural-journalism-a-conversation

Finn, Robin. "The Hangover: Cantilevered Buildings of New York." *The New York Times*, January 10, 2014. https://www.nytimes.com/2014/01/12/realestate/cantilevered-buildings-of-new-york.html?searchResultPosition=1

Hagberg, Eva, "Virtual Memory Covid-19 Sessions: How to Be Loved - A Memoir of Lifesaving Friendship." https://www.youtube.com/watch?v=UvftcsljYKY

Hamilton, Gabrielle. "My Restaurant Was My Life for 20 Years. Does the World Need It Anymore?" *The New York Times*, April 23, 2020. https://www.nytimes.com/2020/04/23/magazine/closing-prune-restaurant-covid.html

Hughes, C.J. "New Buildings Lure Tenants With Free Rent." *The New York Times*, June 9, 2021.

Jacobs, Julia. "The Met Opera's Musicians, Unpaid Since April, Are Struggling." *The New York Times*, March 15, 2021. https://www.nytimes.com/2021/03/15/arts/music/metropolitan-opera-pandemic.html?searchResultPosition=10

Jacobs, Julia. "Met Opera's Music Director Decries Musicians' Unpaid Furlough." *The New York Times*, March 18, 2021. https://www.nytimes.com/2021/03/18/arts/music/met-opera-nezet-seguin.html?searchResultPosition=16

Jacobs, Julia. "New York Philharmonic Musicians Agree to Years of Pandemic Pay Cuts." *The New York Times*, December 7, 2020. https://www.nytimes.com/2020/12/07/arts/music/new-york-philharmonic-pay-cuts.html?searchResultPosition=1

Kamin, Blair. "Can You Trust Journalists on a Junket? Chicago's Architecture Biennial Pays Travel Expenses of Some Who Cover it." *Chicago Tribune*, September 16, 2019.

Kimmelman, Michael. "Join the Times Architecture Critic Michael Kimmelman for Virtual Walking Tours Throughout New York City." *The New York Times*. https://www.nytimes.com/interactive/2020/12/02/arts/design/new-york-city-walking-tours.html

Matsudo, Akiko. "Mack-Cali Offloads Red Bank Office Complex for $84M." *The Real Deal*, January 14, 2021.

Pogrebin, Robin. "Brooklyn Museum to Sell 12 Works as Pandemic Changes the Rules." *The New York Times*, September 16, 2020. https://www.nytimes.com/2020/09/16/arts/design/brooklyn-museum-sale-christies-coronavirus.html

Pogrebin, Robin. "Could There Be a More Difficult Time to Become an Arts Leader?" *The New York Times*, June 3, 2020. https://www.nytimes.com/2020/06/03/arts/design/museums-arts-leadership-coronavirus-protests.html

Pogrebin, Robin. "Met Museum Prepares for $100 Million Loss and Closure Till July." *The New York Times*, March 18, 2020. https://www.nytimes.com/2020/03/18/arts/design/met-museum-coronavirus-closure.html

Pogrebin, Robin. "Practicing Architecture in a Pandemic." *The New York Times*, May 28, 2020. https://www.nytimes.com/2020/05/28/arts/design/elizabeth-diller-architecture-virus.html

Robertson, Katie and Rachel Abrams. "New Yorker Employees Stage Protest Outside Anna Wintour's Townhouse." *The New York Times*, June 8, 2021. https://www.nytimes.com/2021/06/08/business/media/new-yorker-union-anna-wintour.html?searchResultPosition=1

Russell, James. "Exclusive: New York City Halts Public Design Work." *Architectural Record*, April 6, 2020. https://www.architecturalrecord.com/articles/14559-exclusive-new-york-city-halts-public-design-work

Sisario, Ben and Giovanni Russonello. "Jazz Lives in Clubs. The Pandemic Is Threatening Its Future." *The New York Times*, September 8, 2020. https://www.nytimes.com/2020/09/08/arts/music/jazz-clubs-coronavirus.html?searchResultPosition=4

Sorkin, Michael. *Twenty Minutes in Manhattan*. New York: North Point Press, 2009.

Staff. "Nightingale, Wafra Secure $500M Loan Package To Revamp 111 Wall Street." *The Real Deal*, June 14, 2021. https://therealdeal.com/2021/06/14/nightingale-wafra-secure-500m-loan-package-to-revamp-111-wall/

Volner, Ian. "Barry Diller Is Ready To Show Off His Big Beautiful Baby, Little Island." *Curbed*, May 20, 2021. https://www.curbed.com/2021/05/barry-diller-shows-off-his-big-beautiful-baby-little-island.html

Zeiger, Mimi. "It Is Time to Abolish the Architecture Critic." *Dezeen*, March 1, 2021. https://www.dezeen.com/2021/03/01/abolish-architecture-critics-newspaper-mimi-zeiger/

PART TWO

7

THE PRESS PHOTOGRAPHY OF 'RED VIENNA', 1929–1938

Eva Branscome

The storming of the Capitol in Washington, DC on a late afternoon in midwinter 2021 was broadcast to a global audience as evidence of the acts of violence taking place to prevent the ratification 46th American president who had been democratically elected. The film footage and images that flooded the media dissemination of this event, focused on the oversized classical white dome that had until then been understood as the quintessential icon of the 'free world'. On this fateful day, the west front of the building was in the process of being set up for the peaceful transition of power with the inaugural platform and a media tower already in place for the imminent media spectacle. But what happened on the 6th of January was not a celebration, and the images show a restless horde breaching security barriers amidst American flags and smoke flares. Above this turbulence, the rotunda is seen lit up from within like a lantern as if washed in gold. The feathered Statue of Freedom at the very top of the building appears oblivious to the ongoings.

The architecture of what is known as the 'Nation's Stage' of the USA became rebranded at this moment to subvert the eternal ideas of a unified democracy that the building and its photography had until then represented. As the relationship of the photographic image to architecture within a politicised framework remains one in flux, only time will be able to tell if the meaning of the Capitol has been forever tainted. As scholars have observed, images serve to reproduce culture and society, and as such cannot ever be treated simply as 'illustrations'. Instead, images either build or challenge realities – and in doing so, they help create specific memories and stories. Given this observation, photographs as a medium must always be understood as social constructions, whether they be from recent events in the USA or examples produced and reproduced at other times and in other parts of the world like those we will discuss in this chapter from Europe in the 1920s and 1930s.[1]

DOI: 10.4324/9781003272076-11

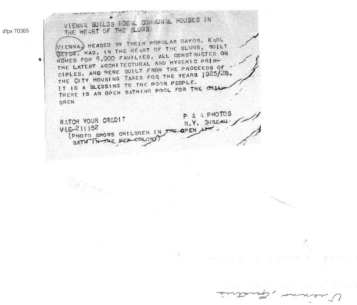

FIGURE 7.1   This photograph (front and back) shows the Rabenhof social housing block opened in Vienna in 1927, and the version sent to the USA in 1929. The typical courtyard setting provided a sheltered environment for the children of the estate to play, while balconies and loggias allowed fresh air to be part of the private living spaces. The flats themselves were very small and ranged in size from 38 to 57 m^2.

Vienna in Transition

At the back of my filing cabinet is a collection of journalistic photographs of inter-war Viennese housing estates, including celebrated examples like the Karl-Marx-Hof. Yet these are not the typical images used in architectural history: instead, they are prints of official municipal photographs used as US press photographs that I have purchased over the years through internet sites. Altogether I have now collected around 32 of these photographs, creating my own small archive. What this chapter will do is to scrutinise a selection of these images to reflect upon the slippery relationship between architecture, politics and media, with the dramatic – and often brutal – events of Austria in the 1920s and 1930s providing the frame.

The inter-war photographs discussed in this chapter feature the vast social housing estates in Vienna, bold new additions to a city that had been for centuries up until the First World War the shimmering capital of the Austro-Hungarian Empire. The selected images are those specifically used by the American press, and which form a key part of the media background in their documentation of three dramatic political scenarios which took place within a time span of less than a decade.

The first scenario, in the period from 1923 to 1934, was when Vienna was run as a democratic municipality by the Social Democrat Party. During this time some 200,000 poverty-stricken people were rehoused in new publicly funded apartment blocks – the icons of what is known as 'Red Vienna'. The second scenario arose from the Austrian Civil War in February 1934, a brief period in which those same buildings were used as fortresses of resistance against the right-wing populist aggression of the Dollfuss dictatorship, speedily leading Austria towards fascism. The last scenario is encapsulated by a photograph taken just after the *Anschluss* (Connection) of 1938 whereby Austria was forcibly made a part of the Pan-German Reich – that is, subsumed by Nazi Germany. The backdrop for the three different scenarios was always the same Viennese social housing blocks, and the dramatic events over those ten years prove that neither architecture nor photography can ever be politically or historically innocent.

In this sense, the press photos being analysed here arguably illustrate and document more clearly than any other media the implicit linkage of buildings to historical events, politics and culture. It would be erroneous however to view these photographs as coincidental or neutral representations: rather, they were consciously created as visual narratives for events taking place, thus becoming cultural objects that speak instantly of their location, action and time. Media as history. Media as a spectacle and event. Media that also set the stage for architecture.

Thus, the best-known housing estates of 'Red Vienna' – the Karl-Marx-Hof, the Rabenhof, the George-Washington-Hof and others – became important arenas for political struggle, with the press photographs offering direct testimony unmasking the subversive media strategies of the right-wing populist government in early-1930s Austria, and then the imposition of Nazi ideology thereafter. The distinctive technology of these photographs, made evident in their materiality and their attached press releases, can be seen as a mediatory device that reveals the instability of the word-image relationship.

The impetus for my research into the vast photographic archive documenting the architecture of 'Red Vienna'[2] is hence essentially about photography as a kind of historical evidence and record. More specifically, this chapter seeks to ask: what is the relationship between photography, architecture, and the city as a cultural process? What it will suggest is that there is a constant slippage between image and reality that puts into question the neutrality of this medium that so many of us still take for granted.

The story about this particular set of photographs is temporally and geographically located in Austria on the cusp of becoming absorbed into the Greater Germanic Reich. As a consequence of the First World War, in 1918 Austria had lost a multi-cultural empire of almost 52 million people, who between them spoke more than twelve languages. The remaining rump of the Austrian nation-state in the 1920s became concerned that it was unviable in the modern world, with now just 6.5 million people speaking mainly one language: German, albeit with their distinctive accent. Vienna also suddenly took on even greater importance since its population remained at around 2 million, thus amounting to nearly a third of all Austrian citizens.[3]

The German-American journalist John Gunther, who initially worked for the *Chicago Daily News* and then for the *Daily News* in London, reported from Vienna between 1930 and 1935 as a foreign correspondent for Europe, the Balkans and the Middle East. To set the scene for American readers, he compared the whole of Austria to the size of states like Maine and South Carolina, while also noting that the city of New York numbered twice as many people. Gunther described vividly the rapidly unravelling situation in the fourth edition of his bestselling book, *Inside Europe*, where the vast demographic imbalance was central:

> The capital, Vienna, like the swollen head atop a dwarfed and shrunken body, contains more than one-third of the country's inhabitants, and this acute disproportion has been a chief economic problem since 1918. The country has to import more than it exports; it does not raise enough to feed itself; therefore it is very poor. Vienna, a gaping maw, swallows more than the mountainously beautiful but economically almost useless hinterland can produce. The chief crop of provincial Austria is – scenery.[4]

Gunther went on to explain the political polarization of Austria's populace that was split across this urban/rural divide:

> Vienna was socialist, anti-clerical, and as a municipality, fairly rich. The hinterland was poor, backward, conservative, Roman Catholic, and jealous of Vienna's higher standard of living. The socialists, to defend themselves in what they thought was their impregnable citadel, founded a private army

of young workmen and intellectuals, the Schutzbund. The countryside promptly countered with a similar army – but recruited from primitive and hungry peasant lads, in leather breeches and green hats – the Heimwehr. The struggle between these two forces resulted in the civil war of February, 1934.[5]

It is useful to note that Gunther was reporting during the 1930s – just when photography was emerging as an important component in news reportage. While by the 1920s photographs had already become an integral component of the tabloid press, it was precisely the populist feel of their immediacy that initially caused resistance among journalists who viewed this ubiquitous analogue media as a threat to their own profession as writers.[6] For the three scenarios discussed in this chapter, the press photographs sent from Vienna to the USA showed the architecture of 'Red Vienna' as a sequence of storyboards, omnipresent, in your face, but then forgotten and replaced by other images of the same places. They were in effect flashbulbs of history. Therefore, this chapter exposes a curious intersection between a country like Austria in the 1930s, riven with right-wing populist politics, and the emergence of new ways to document and disseminate architectural ideas that involved globalized systems of media transference. At that specific juncture, politics, architecture and photographic images coalesced to allow participants to forcibly visualise how history was actually happening.

Architecture for the Masses (1923–1934)

In Austria, faced in the 1920s with an urgency to address the trauma of a defeated and depleted population, the capital city in wake of imperial collapse reinvented itself through an ambitious programme for 'Red Vienna' – promoted architecturally through the socially minded provision of its baths, schools, kindergartens, gymnasia and health clinics, but most importantly via its extensive social housing programme that very soon was drawing international attention.[7]

Figure 7.1 shows both sides of a printed photograph of the Rabenhof in Vienna sent to the USA in 1929 with the image on the front along with the accompanying press release on its back. Designed by Heinrich Schmid and Hermann Aichinger in 1927, this social housing complex provided more than 1,000 apartments in courtyard arrangements and included many other social facilities. It is interesting to note that due to the changing political climate of that era, the estate was then renamed several times. Figure 7.2 is of the same housing estate again at the time of its opening sent to the USA a year later in 1930.

Both press photographs are not only about the images themselves. Pasted to their backs are typical press releases attached by foreign correspondents based in Vienna who were sending these composite pieces of information back to the USA. They were published in various American newspapers to explain the massive efforts of Vienna's provision of social housing for the poorest citizens following the empire's collapse, which had triggered the mass migration of displaced ethnic German speakers from the territories to the capital city. In documenting a

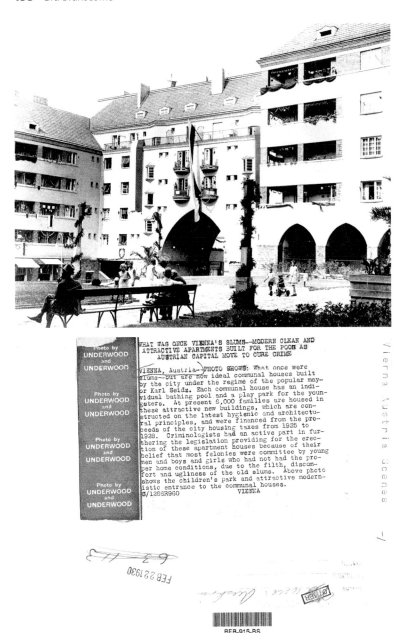

FIGURE 7.2 Another photograph (front and back) illustrating the same event of the opening of the Rabenhof, again used by the press in the USA to tell the story of the new Viennese social housing. The blocks were mainly five floors high and in harmony with the urban scale of existing Viennese tenement blocks. The back of the photograph documents its use by a press agency, Underwood and Underwood, in 1930 for a readership in the USA.

fixed relationship between the written words and the photographed subject, they thereby suggest a rigid meaning for this particular historical event in relation to the lived practices of Vienna at that time.

The first photograph (Figure 7.1) discussed here is date-stamped 1 October 1929 and the attached press release reads in English:

Vienna Builds Ideal Communal Houses in the Heart of the Slums

Vienna, headed by their popular mayor, Karl Seidz [sic], has, in the heart of the slums, built homes for 6,000 families, all constructed on the latest architectural and hygienic principles, and were built from the proceeds of the city housing taxes for the years 1925/28. It is a blessing to the poor people. There is an open bathing pool for the children.

(Photo shows children in the open air bath in the new colony)[8]

In this quote, it is pertinent to draw attention to the use of the word 'colony' by the US journalist involved.

The second photograph (Figure 7.2) under discussion arrived at the US newspaper office on 22 February 1930. It explained more explicitly, in a utopian sense, that architecture should be understood as a kind of scientific remedy to social ills and depravity – one that, of course, if applied methodically could result in specific parameters of form, space and light:

What was Once Vienna's Slums – Modern Clean and Attractive Apartments Built for the Poor as Austrian Capital move to Cure Crime

Vienna, Austria — Photograph Shows: What once were slums — but are now ideal communal houses built by the city under the regime of the popular mayor Karl Seidz [sic]. Each communal house has an individual bathing pool and a play park for the youngsters. At present 6,000 families are housed in these attractive new buildings, which are constructed on the latest hygienic and architectural principles, and were financed from the proceeds of the city housing taxes from 1925 to 1928. Criminologists had an active part in furthering the legislation providing for the erection of these apartment houses because of their belief that most felonies were committed by young men and boys and girls who had not had the proper home conditions, due to the filth, discomfort and ugliness of the old slums. Above photo shows the children's park and attractive modernistic entrance to the communal houses.[9]

But these Viennese municipal housing blocks were even more than what was described in these press releases. They were literally urban villages. Or more accurately, they functioned more like cities within cities. Self-contained they were capable of sustaining artificially transplanted communities of several thousand people each, in the example of the most celebrated of these social housing estates – the Karl–Marx–Hof – the scheme afforded living space for 5,000 citizens. There were not just sunny courtyards with paddling pools, colourful facades (often in muted shades of red), airy balconies and billowing flags in the Viennese colours, but were also plentiful kindergartens, communal gardens, laundry facilities, shops including pharmacies and doctors' surgeries, community spaces, cinemas and theatres, as well as access to public transport.[10]

For the new residents in the 'Red Vienna' estates, this was no dislocation of a poverty-stricken community into a ghetto devoid of services that might render the cohesion of these transplanted individuals as unviable and dangerous. Arguably, England only finally reached a similar ambition in its urban planning by the late-1960s with the Barbican Estate just north of the City of London. Yet that London housing project, while statistically comparable to the Karl–Marx–Hof in its size and scope, was not created as a social housing programme. It indeed

FIGURE 7.3 These photographs by Martin Gerlach Jr produced for the Vienna Planning Department show two of the Rabenhof, one of the Sandleitenhof and one of the Matteottihof. They are strikingly similar to those sent by foreign correspondents in Vienna to the USA for publication in newspapers there. The architecture of 'Red Vienna' was contemporary, devoid of surface ornamentation and cubic in composition but avoided the avant-garde use of materials and design experimentation. While the large estates were mostly located beyond the Ringstrasse they were well-connected to the inner city by public transport.

was the near-opposite, being intended as a post-war infusion of a well-educated, middle-class reinvented City of London that wished to be ready for international commerce. Conditions in 'Red Vienna' were so utterly different.

The media campaign to record and publicise the architecture of 'Red Vienna' on a local, national and international scale utilized photography profusely in its many prospectuses,[11] books,[12] exhibitions[13] and postcard collections.[14] Many of these images were commissioned by the Wiener Stadtbauamt, Vienna's town planning department, who had contracted several photographers – Martin Gerlach Jr, Fritz Sauer, Karl Zapletal and Bruno Reiffenstein – to document their vast social housing projects and other building activities. Whereas the exact provenance of the press photographs discussed in this chapter remains unresolved, the two images depicting the Rabenhof, and also those of the Sandleitenhof and the Matteottihof that will be considered in the next situated historic scenario, are clearly professional studio-quality. Gerlach alone took some 4,000 photographs for the Viennese municipality, and a comparison of the press photographs that I have been able to amass shows strong similarities both in terms of viewpoints and their modern-yet-moderate compositions (Figure 7.3).[15] The preference for street-level perspectives in the photographs allows the viewer to identify more personally with the architecture at a human scale, rather than focusing upon the size and monumentality of these new estates. Most of Gerlach's photographs show unpeopled scenes, thus foregrounding the architecture – although children form a notable exception, and as such frequently enliven the built environments in his shots, playing, laughing and often scampering around the urban scenography.[16]

Same Architecture, Different Story (1934–1938)

While the glossy images of these iconic social housing blocks appealed to me profoundly when I discovered them during my research into 20th-century architecture in Austria, more intriguing are the accompanying texts that describe historical events, as if frozen in time, for an American audience. Often showing exactly the same views as documented in the earlier municipal photographs of the architecture of 'Red Vienna', the press photographs[17] that started to be disseminated in the USA after the 1934 coup became dramatic illustrations of a city in a spiralling process of reinterpretation and reappropriation by politically opposed populist agendas (Figures 7.4 and 7.5).

This time around, the near-identical set of photographs 'illustrate' a far more sinister story of power in action: a story of desperation, chaos and invariably disaster. Housing blocks in a Vienna that was no longer 'red' were again providing a key backdrop to the political stage.[18] In 1933, the Austrian Chancellor Engelbert Dollfuss decided to assume dictatorial powers as a response to twin pressures: from the political right, National Socialists were pushing for a unification with Nazi Germany following Adolf Hitler's appointment as Chancellor in January that year, and from the political left, actual Social Democrats were reminding people that they had the support of more than half the population.

FIGURE 7.4 These photographs of 'Red Vienna' sent to the USA in 1934 communicated very different news that was no longer about the architecture of the housing blocks and their social facilities. The top left photograph of the Reumannhof is the only one in fact taken at the time of the civil war – albeit from a safe distance – and the only one that visually corresponds to its message.

Dollfuss, while staunchly right wing, was more of an admirer of Benito Mussolini's Italian fascism whom he wanted to emulate by imposing an authoritarian 'Austrofascism'.

In reality, Austria had existed in a political crisis ever since the end of the First World War and the dissolution of the large, multicultural Austro-Hungarian Empire. Left somewhat arbitrarily with its German-speaking nucleus of around 6.5 million, it could not sustain itself in terms of food or industrial production: the core areas for each had been located in Hungary and Czechoslovakia respectively. From the early-1920s, Austria was plunged into a crisis of starvation, literally. And from that condition arose the idea by some that letting itself be absorbed by Germany would not necessarily be a bad thing for Austria – even if this meant sacrificing its own highly unique culture as expressed linguistically, artistically and through its famously multicultural cuisine.[19]

The autonomy of this new 'German Austria' as a state was also critical to a constellation of newly established countries and re-emergent independent nations that had been part of the old empire or else held some of their territories within

FIGURE 7.5   The captions on the back of the press photographs explain the rapid progression of a civil war in which many of Vienna's social housing estates were used as fortresses of resistance.

it: Hungary, Czechoslovakia, part of the Second Polish Republic, the regions inhabited by Slovenes, Croats and Serbs that were now absorbed into Yugoslavia, as well as Bukovina, Transylvania and large parts of Banat subsumed into Romania. Within such a volatile region, Vienna was thus seen as a potential trigger for a domino effect that could lead to great disaster for Europe at large. The city's inherent instability made it a node of political interest, locally and globally. This explains why Vienna became such an important international news centre from the late-1920s, as reflected in the copious press coverage in the USA among other countries. It was also the reason for discussing now a further set of press photographs.

First, it is worth sketching in a bit more of the political background. Greatly stunted in growth, Engelbert Dollfuss had been born in 1892 in a village in rural Lower Austria as the illegitimate son of a peasant woman. The young Dolfuss did well at school and attended university in Vienna, where he studied law. As a member of the Christian Social Party, he was staunchly Catholic and politically conservative. Becoming president of the Federal Railways just before his 38th birthday, he was given the role of Federal Minister of Agriculture and Forestry only five months later. His rise seemed unstoppable. By 10 May 1932 Dollfuss was made Chancellor of Austria and he subsequently assumed dictatorial powers within less than a year due to the aforementioned pressures.[20]

Austrian political complexities at the time are not easy to summarise. The situation in Vienna was particularly fraught because the city itself was headed by a mayor representing the Social Democratic Workers Party, whereas the national government headed by Dollfuss was deeply conservative.[21] There were various private militias affiliated to these political parties. The Heimwehr acted as an auxiliary army for the Dollfuss regime, while the Schutzbund was founded to protect the Social Democrats.[22] These names say a lot about their respective agendas. 'Heimwehr' literally means 'home defence force', implying sentiments of domestic security usually associated with childhood, family and nation within a specific geographical location. In contrast, 'Schutzbund' translates as 'protection alliance' and as such feels less emotionally laden.

Despite the bitter tensions between the ideologies of the Social Democrats and the conservative government, the Dollfuss regime's biggest threat came from the far-right. By the early-1930s the National Socialists were not merely a menacing force beyond the border to the north, but also very active locally. Italy considered Austria as a buffer zone to Nazi Germany, and therefore the Heimwehr was partially financed by Mussolini. It was the latter who pushed Dollfuss to move brutally against the socialists in 1934 in an attempt to eliminate once and for all a group that Italian fascists perceived to be a threat to Austrian autonomy. The Heimwehr duly advanced against the Schutzbund and civil war broke out. Vienna was torn apart by these two adversary populist movements, and its new social housing complexes were soon implicated in this struggle.[23]

The top left photo is dated 12 February 1934, the day the civil war started, and the press release on the back explains:

Vienna Tenements turned into Forts.

Vienna, Austria – The centres of the socialist resistance against the government forces in the present fighting are hugh [sic] municipal dwelling blocks, constructed by the socialist regime and inhabited mostly by organized Social Democrats. Photo shows a block in the Reumannhof, occupied by more than a thousand tenants, which became a stronghold of resistance.[24]

On this very day, as part of the purge of left-wingers, Karl Seitz, Vienna's popular Social Democratic mayor, was incarcerated, only eventually afforded amnesty at the end of 1936. The fighting ended as a victory for the Dollfuss dictatorship, the Social Democratic Party was outlawed and all activities associated with socialism were banned.[25]

The bottom left photo shows the Sandleitenhof, an estate that provided homes for 5,000 people. This meant that it was in fact even larger than the Karl-Marx-Hof. Its design was based on Camillo Sitte's town planning ideas about what made urban space feel warm and welcoming in a picturesque sense. The Sandleiten was spared the more geometrical rigour of most other Viennese housing estates: instead, there were small piazzas, curved streets, green spaces and varied block sizes and it was not conceived in terms of closed structures configured around a courtyard, or 'Hof'. While the photograph showed undoubtedly modern architecture bathed in sunshine, and with little girls dancing ring-around-the-rosie, the press release from 13 February 1934 tells a jarringly different story. This was the second day of fighting and so the caption reads:

Bombarded as Austrian Government Fights Revolt.

The Sandeleiten [sic] Apartments housing 1,300 [families], one of Vienna's finest achievements in social charity, which was under heavy machine gun and howitzer fire by local troops as the government endeavoured to quell the bloody socialist revolution, between 400 and 500 are dead, including women and children, as the fighting spread throughout the country.[26]

Here the disjunction between image and word could not be more blatant or disturbing.

The top right photo went on to describe the rapidly unravelling situation on 14 February 1934:

Vienna's modern apartments become fortresses.

The Matteottihof, another of the modern municipal apartment houses built in recent years in Vienna, is pictured here. Structures like these became fortresses in the fighting between socialists and government troops.[27]

Originally this housing estate had been named to commemorate Giacomo Matteotti as a sign of solidarity with Italy's fight against fascism, but after the socialist uprising was quashed, the Dollfuss regime renamed it as Giordanihof after the leading Italian fascist, Giulio Giordani, as a sign of respect for Mussolini. Later, following the end of the Second World War, the estate's original name was again reinstated.

The bottom right photo also elaborated on the events of 14 February 1934:

The George Washington Hof (above) in Vienna was the scene of bloody fighting between the socialists who had taken up a position there and the governmental Heimwehr forces trying to dislodge them. The Hof is one of the magnificent municipal apartment houses in Vienna. It was named after George Washington and dedicated with impressive ceremonies. Photo shows the building at the time of the dedication.[28]

This last photo was the only one to acknowledge that it had not been taken at the time of the political action being described within the press release.

FIGURE 7.6 In the image on the left a couple stands gazing at a map of Great Germany while in the wire photo on the right the city celebrates the annexation of Austria in front of the Bundeskanzleramt in Vienna: These
photographs dating from 1938 were heavily retouched to enhance their
messages ready for reproduction in newsprint.

From Frying Pan to Fire (1938–1945)

Once the socialists were defeated, rather than bolstering Dollfuss's position,
the National Socialists thrived in the power vacuum. Hence the outcome was
exactly the opposite of what Mussolini, and Dollfuss as his puppet, had been
hoping to achieve. A relentless far-right terrorist campaign was launched,
sponsored by Hitler's Germany. When an assassination attempt on Dollfuss
failed on 3 October 1933, the National Socialist Party was outlawed in Austria. But these Nazis then simply fled across the border to Germany so that
they could reconsolidate there and prepare for the forthcoming *Anschluss*. A
virulent propaganda battle commenced with anti-Dollfuss flyers dropping
from planes out of the sky and Nazi radio broadcasts filling the airwaves from
Munich.[29]

On 25 July 1934, just five months after the civil war against the socialists,
Nazis still active on Austrian soil surreptitiously stormed the Federal Chancellery
in Vienna. This contingency of conspirators mostly consisted of military servicemen and police officers, and when they attacked, they disguised themselves
by wearing *Deutschmeister* uniforms.[30] John Gunther evocatively recounted this
unfolding event offset by ornate Viennese architecture:

The Bundeskanzleramt, or Federal Chancellery, is the old Metternich palace where the Congress of Vienna met in 1815. Certainly from that day to this it can have witnessed no more dramatic and agitated a situation. A stately baroque building, its cream-colored façade opens on the Ballhausplatz. Grilled balconies of graceful iron project twenty feet over the sidewalk. Directly opposite is a post-office built into the heavy walls of the Hofburg, the former imperial palace, and on the west side a high gate leads to the green meadow of the Burg garden.

The hundred and forty-four Nazis from Siebensterngasse, sweeping into the courtyard, had seized those members of the government within, Dollfuss, Fey and Fey's assistant Karwinsky, and about one hundred and fifty members of the staff, civil servants, clerks, and so on. The guards of the building, sixty strong, suspected nothing or at least put up no resistance and were disarmed and arrested. The police plotters knew well the corridors and rooms of the complicated building (some of them, indeed, had previously been posted there on duty), and the occupation was quick and thorough. The analogy for America would be the seizure of the White House, since the Bundeskanzleramt is the central ganglion of government in Austria.[31]

His description of this drama all too eerily echoes the storming of the Capitol in Washington, DC in January 2021. Rabble-roused by the electorally defeated Donald Trump as a last stand to keep hold of his expiring presidency, many observers regarded this as no less than an attempted coup.

As part of this putsch, however, Engelbert Dollfuss was callously murdered. A former army corporal called Otto Planetta shot him twice just before 1 pm and then allowed him to slowly bleed out. This all was happening unbeknownst while negotiations to achieve the safe passage of the hostages were being conducted from the balcony with Odo Neustädter-Stürmer − the ideological pillar of the Heimwehr − down in the street below who was accompanied by his militia, and with a growing crowd of journalists, policemen and general onlookers. Neither a doctor nor priest was allowed to attend to Dollfuss. His blood overflowed a basin that had been placed under the Louis XV divan on which the Chancellor lay dying, pooling on the floor. By 3.45 pm, he had expired.[32]

The other hostages were eventually released in the early evening on the express condition that the small band of National Socialist rebels would be transited unharmed to the German border. But when the Nazis came out of the building, believing that they were about to be given safe passage to the Reich, they were swiftly dispatched into detention at the nearby Marokkaner police barracks. In the end, and despite Dollfuss's death, the putsch failed because the Austrian army did not mutiny in the way that had been expected. And so, as a consequence, the Nazi sympathizers that were estimated to form 50–60% of the Austrian population, did not rise up across the land. Even more crucially, the Nazi German agitators who had been inciting unrest in Austria since 1933 did not march across the border to support the rebels. The so-called 'Austrian Legion' stayed put in Germany, whereas the Italian army was already mobilized to advance across the Brenner Pass to deflect any strategically planned takeover by Hitler's Reich. After a fateful and turbulent afternoon, Dr Kurt von Schuschnigg, who had been minister of justice and a loyal supporter of Dollfuss, was made the Austrian Chancellor and a regular government was reinstated. Thirteen rebels were subsequently hanged for treason, of which four were policemen.[33]

During this period, elections were generally avoided in Austria because of the fear that they would allow the National Socialists to seize control, as had happened in Germany. The leader of both the Heimwehr and Fatherland Front militias, Prince Ernst Rüdiger von Starhemberg was appointed Schuschnigg's vice-chancellor. Of noble lineage that was descended from the Holy Roman Empire, von Starhemberg owned fourteen castles. Having embarked on a military career aged seventeen, he came to know Hitler while in Bavaria as a soldier of fortune for the Freikorps Oberland. He was also part of Hitler's Beer Hall Putsch in 1923, returning to Austria disenchanted to commence on a political career. And thus, the Schuschnigg-Starhemberg government resumed the image of an 'Austrofascist' dictatorship sandwiched between those of Mussolini and Hitler. Meanwhile, Franz von Papen, who had hitherto led the National Socialist campaign within Austria, now dialled down the volume of his rhetoric, and, after being appointed as the German ambassador to Austria, set about establishing more subtle tactics to ensure an Austrian merger with Nazi Germany.[34]

On 12 March 1938, the Nazis were finally successful in their strategy: it was the day of the *Anschluss*, when Austria 'joined' the Third Reich. The swastika was duly raised from the Chancellery's balcony (Figure 7.6). And thus, the last scenario in this discussion of press photography and its manipulation of the buildings of 'Red Vienna' are from this final period of inter-war Austria. The caption of this photograph (Figure 7.7) reads:

(March 29) Vienna – Nazis Bring Bread:

In front of the once socialist Karl Marx tenement house, these soldiers of the German army are shown as they distributed food to Vienna's poor. It was in 1934 that the late Chancellor Engelbert Dollfuss ordered troops to fire on socialists barricaded in the Karl Marx. German field kitchens have been busy continuously since the occupation distributing food.[35]

Cynically, in this press photograph of my final set, the Karl-Marx-Hof becomes the knowing backdrop for a Nazi propaganda drive by depicting a feeding station in which the desperate residents of that celebrated estate are struggling to obtain food for their starving families. The icon of Social Democracy has been deliberately reappropriated to suit the purposes of National Socialism.

FIGURE 7.7   By 1938, the Karl-Marx-Hof was used as the backdrop for a Nazi propaganda drive. Its iconic façade subverted to convey a message of fascist
superiority. The technology of the wire photograph made it possible for
the breaking news event to reach its distant audience across the ocean
almost instantly.

These three very distinct scenarios reveal how photographs of the architecture
of 'Red Vienna' could be used to express three completely different ideologies
and stories, whether the opening of these social housing estates up to 1934, their
roles as fortresses of resistance during the 1934 civil war, and then their annexation by the Nazi agenda after the 1938 *Anschluss*.

The Foreign Correspondents and Questions of Authorship

Viewed against this historical backdrop, these press photographs serve to highlight architecture's role as a political stage – and furthermore, in doing so, they
raise the question of authorship. It is notable that to illustrate the first two historical scenarios, with just one exception as already explained, the photographs
used by the press were the original ones taken at the time these estates were
constructed. Yet in the slippage between image and text, the meaning of the
photographs was altered completely. This then raises the question who were the
foreign journalists that were using these images in this manner, literally attaching
narratives to denote different interpretations of crucial events?

An understanding of the culture of these foreign reporters is crucial. For instance, the fact that the accompanying press releases were written in perfect
English is perplexing within the inter-war Austrian condition. The actors that

situated and contextualized these press photographs constitute an intriguing process of cultural transfer. This was an Austrian story being told for an American audience, and the photographs were part of a parallel exchange of newspaper images at the time. What is clearly evident when considering these objects today is that our thinking about the inter-war political situation in Austria, and indeed in Central Europe, was greatly influenced by the overseas newspaper reporters stationed in Vienna. They need to be understood as part of the history-making process helping to forge a common sentiment that triggered an Allied reaction once the Second World War broke out. Their reportage was not passive.

Interestingly, the English-speaking foreign correspondents in Vienna organised themselves in 1930 into the Anglo-American Press Association, the initiative of an American journalist named Robert Best who worked for the United Press.[36] They constituted a curious crowd ranging from political activists to hybrid individuals working on the thresholds of international diplomacy and espionage – as indeed did Robert Best. Many of these men and women later wrote histories of this era, factual and fictional, including Gunther's respected sequence of *Inside Europe* books that were aimed at a populist audience. Quickly becoming bestsellers in multiple editions seemingly added to every year during the mid-1930s, they described the deteriorating political situation in Europe as a process that was leapfrogging Gunther's books as soon as he published them.[37] For this chapter, I have therefore drawn heavily on his writing – as well as those of M.W. Fodor[38], Friedrich Scheu[39] and G.E.R. Gedye[40] – since they were so directly embroiled in the historical tale I am examining. The active presence of the foreign reporters in the events of 1930s Vienna offers us a very different view to that found in conventional architectural history. It reminds of the time when Charles Jencks explained to me his own methodological approach:

> [Y]ou can write history on the battlefield and you get one kind of history. You can write it retrospectively and you get another kind. Recollected in tranquillity. But if you're writing it on the battlefield that has the virtue of being vivid and a report. If you are writing it in retrospection after it's dead, you know, it's a different kind of history. It's the usual history. Anyway, so [my approach] is kind of midway between the two kinds of writing. It's got the perspective of looking backwards but it has the immediacy of journalism and relevance, because you know you were there.[41]

Indeed, it is interesting today to read the accounts of English-language reporters in 1930s Vienna as people who were there when events were taking place and that would prove to become so critical to Europe and the world at large. These journalists faced numerous challenges in sending their copy back to newspapers waiting in Britain and the USA. The infrastructures available included the postal system, which relied on trains and ships, as well as homing pigeons and sight signals for a quicker local relaying of messages, and of course the key technologies of the telegram, telephone and radio. While the journalists were based in Vienna, using these infrastructures they could cover a vast territory reaching all the way to Bucharest, and even beyond to Athens.[42]

Back in the USA, which is the location to which my selected set of photographs were sent, the mass production of the daily news of the moment acted as a great social leveller. As both a product and driver of modernity, news was facilitated by technological advances like the telegraph (1850s), telephone (1880s) and typewriter (1880s). Such innovations allowed news to become a form of communication that was transferred at a steadily increasing pace, while at the same time the mechanization and speed of the printing press meant that newspapers were cheaper to produce and buy. Speed was the very essence. Described as a 'perishable commodity', the saying goes that old news has very little value.[43]

Because of this demand, the foreign correspondents in Vienna decided to form the cartel of the Anglo-American Press Association so that they could share their news with one another, given that it was often too difficult to get information first-hand or on one's own. Sponsored as government information organs, Austrian newspapers were in no way reliable sources of news, and instead functioned as propaganda devices. John Gunther explained:

> Give a man complete power over the written word in any country and half the job is done. Thus in Austria you find every paper faithfully reflecting the point of view of the clerical, quasi-Fascist regime. News which the government doesn't like simply doesn't appear in print.[44]

Gathering news in Vienna was thus a complicated and convoluted steeplechase of activities, all of which centred mainly on the Café Louvre as that was where the foreign correspondents could set up a *Stammtisch* – this term, meaning a 'reserved table'. The Café Louvre became the place where news was traded and exchanged like in a stock market.[45]

And so, Gunther described his own routine as follows:

> Every day at about eleven I walk downtown and spend a half hour or so at the Café Imperial, on the broad flank of Schwarzenbergplatz. The coffee house is, of course, the inner soul of Vienna, the essential embodiment of the spirit of the town. It is, as everyone knows, much more than just a place to drink coffee in. Coffee you may have, in literally forty different varieties, but you have also literature, conversation, and peace of soul and mind. And in the Café Imperial, in the morning, and the more modest Café Louvre, in the afternoon, you get journalism, Viennese-brand.[46]

Hence, the Café Imperial was where the journalists went first. It stocked 20 local and between 40 and 50 international newspapers. You could go there and drink a cup of coffee and read for as long as you wished. Yet, it was the smaller and far more modest Café Louvre that served as actual place where information was exchanged and traded. It lay directly between the main radio building (Radio

Verkehrs AG, or RAVAG) and the telegraph building (K.K. Telegraphen An-stalt): the two key locations from which information could be relayed. All four destinations – two cafes and two communications posts – were in central Vienna and geographically situated, practically in one line. Yet what was even more im-portant was that the Café Louvre had a telephone that the foreign correspondents were allowed to use. The telephone had increasingly become their technology of choice because it was so instant, relatively cheap and also more immune to censorship. While the individual newspapers in Britain and the USA were in fierce competition with one another, the journalists on the ground in Vienna had formed a pact of mutual collaboration. No one missed out on an important story, even though the territory they were covering was vast and the political conditions of the time were volatile, highly complex and interwoven.[47]

This method was not only very efficient, but it also had the advantage that the news reports endorsed and validated each other – thereby corroborating and legitimising the story. Back home this sequencing elevated the journalist of the breaking news as the champion.[48] The era of the Café Louvre that effectively started in 1929 and ended in 1938 thus coincides with my selection of press photographs that manipulated the architecture of 'Red Vienna' to explain three distinct political scenarios to a global audience. But as soon as Austria became consolidated into Nazi Germany, now called the 'Ostmark', the foreign corre-spondents left Vienna one after the other and Austria's function as an interna-tional hub for Central European news was over.[49]

The Press Photograph Emerges

The activities of the foreign correspondents in the Café Louvre seem enchant-ing, even romantic, today, but in this final section of the chapter, I would like to return to my starting point – press photographs as cultural objects. Photography had of course from its start been used to document evidence. Yet up until the 1930s, the fields of photography and journalism were still quite distinct, not least because it was very expensive to reproduce photographic images in mass print runs. Change however was afoot. By the 1920s, with cinematic films in Hollywood and elsewhere becoming longer, and telling more elaborate stories, public interest in visual culture soon meant that photographs were increasingly used by tabloid newspapers to help convey sensationalist stories. This change in public attitudes towards photography happened particularly in the USA, and in doing so pushed forward the development of printing technology that made it far less costly to reproduce photographs in newspapers. There were of course also other major technological advances, with cameras becoming more compact and easier to use. By 1930, Leica started producing small hand-held cameras with exchangeable lenses. Photographic film also improved and was now able to deal with more movement. Both this and the invention of flashbulbs meant that tripods were no longer necessary. Photography thus moved out of the studio and into the streets, enabling it to record events as they happened and becoming increasingly relevant to news reportage. Curiously for us today, there was some degree of opposition from within the profession, with journalists insisting upon the pre-eminence of the written word over the analogue photograph.[50]

One reality was that it was also very costly for the newspapers to maintain their own photographers and all the expensive equipment required. It is estimated that in 1935 there were 2,100 newspapers in the USA, of which only 300 had their own in-house photographers. The vast majority therefore relied on the photographic agencies. Thus, the backs of the press photos discussed here are evidence of this trade in images, negotiating the exchange of photographs between the independent photographers and the newspapers as commodities in the hands of the big American players: Underwood and Underwood, ACME Newspictures, Keystone Press Agency and Associated Press.[51]

The profession of the press photographer first emerged around 1890 when photographs started to appear in newspapers, gradually replacing the drawings and engravings that had been commonly used during the 19th century. The earliest agency selling photographs to newspapers was founded in 1895 by the American photographer, George Grantham Bain. Anton Holzer's fascinating analysis of press photography in Austria offers a great deal of insight into this long-overlooked field of study, perhaps neglected academically due to its all-too-common intersections with popular culture. The press photograph was considered an inferior type of image also because of its mass reproduction in newspapers while the difference to studio photography often resided in its news value. Thus, rather than focusing on aesthetic composition, qualities of lighting and texture, the press photograph was far more important as a visual record of reality that could be traded as a commodity for the information it depicted. A further layer of complexity in terms of socio-political impact came from the juxtaposition of photographic images with the accompanying news text within mass media.[52]

What also becomes clear from Holzer's investigation is that the Austrian press was generally slower than the press in Britain or the USA to integrate photographic images into their publications – probably because Austria was technologically less advanced, but also potentially because they maintained an even more traditionally conservative attitude towards the use of illustrations. Thus, while the daily newspapers in Britain and the USA initially resisted the use of press photographs, the right-wing Dollfuss dictatorship was actively determined to inhibit the development of photojournalism in Austria – with the *Anschluss* in 1938 then marking the end of free press culture altogether. Holzer explains that most of the original photographs that were reproduced in newsprint no longer exist because so many German-language press archives from before the Second World War have either been lost or disposed of, hence the rarity of the set of photographs being discussed in this chapter. They have survived as complex cultural objects of information only because they were sent outside Austria for publication.[53]

The global circulation of press photographs as a mass medium has arguably had a profound influence on the historical events they documented, and thus the processes involved in sending the images from Austria to the USA also deserve some attention. The last photograph I have discussed from my set – that in which the Karl-Marx-Hof became the backdrop for the distribution of food by Nazi German soldiers – is somewhat fuzzy and so was heavily retouched (Figure 7.6). Time was clearly of the essence due to the fierce competition between papers to break the story. As physical objects, printed press photographs until the 1930s had to be transported on express trains and ships, and even sometimes on chartered airplanes. For shorter journeys, couriers on motorcycles were used as were carrier pigeons. From the 1920s, however, new technology developed in the USA made it possible to transmit images by telephone wire from one place to another, almost instantly. By 1935, it was possible to do this on a widespread basis using existing telegraph and telephone lines. Finally, reporters were able to send press photographs and their associated texts around the world to be published simultaneously as headline news. The Associated Press was the first to use this new medium, famously in covering major conflicts like the Spanish Civil War of 1936–1939. But the quality of the wire photograph reproductions lacked clarity when printed in newspapers, and so many journalists avoided them.[54]

Once these wire photos had been printed out by the newspaper or photo agency back in the USA, the images were often retouched manually. The process of improving the photographs in this way allowed the meaning of the image to be heightened, often focusing viewers' eyes on a detail that might otherwise have gone unnoticed. Sometimes things were added that had simply not been there in the original analogue photograph, as is the small Hitler-style moustache on the man in the middle of the scrum at the Karl-Marx-Hof feeding station. Of course, retouching had long been a practice in newspaper photographs, but this was done onto the print directly either by the original photographer or the agency, and frequently these altered images were then rephotographed prior to sending them on for publication.

On one conventional press photograph depicting Austria as part of Nazi Germany (Figure 7.6 left), it is difficult to tell which part constitutes analogue photography, and what has been retouched and collaged as part of this composite artifice. The text sent as integral to the wire photograph on 12 March 1938 (Figure 7.6 right) explains the ongoing situation it is documenting in the embedded caption:

> Vienna, Mar 12 – NAZI FLAG WAVES – This radiophoto sent to New York from London early today, shows a man on a balcony of the Austrian chancellory [sic] here, waving a Nazi flag to the crowd that assembled after Schuschnigg government fell yesterday and was succeeded by one backed by Nazi Germany.
>
> *(AP Wirephoto) 38*[55]

The previously mentioned wire photo of the Nazi feeding station (Figure 7.7) likewise responded to an event in action and is retouched in a way that makes it intriguingly contrary to the aesthetic intent of the photographs taken of the

Karl-Marx-Hof and other estates in the 'Red Vienna' era – which aimed to demonstrate real pride in the city's accomplishment of rehousing some 200,000 people.[56] The photograph in 1938 suggests instead architecture in crisis.

Photography as an Unstable Witness

As already noted, the ambitious rehousing programme of 'Red Vienna' was accompanied by a media campaign that included exhibitions and lectures which relied heavily on camerawork. A vast pictorial record was hence made of the estates to facilitate mass dissemination, and so these images quickly found their way into the collections of photo agencies and appeared alongside text in many newspaper articles in Austria and internationally.[57]

The second use of these same images was to illustrate the outbreak of civil war in 1934 and to portray the housing estates as fortresses of resistance. At that point, there was a rupture in the image/text relationship, probably because it was simply too dangerous for anyone to take photographs of the actual fighting. For reporters, it was easier to recycle the architectural photographs from the 'Red Vienna' campaign than to source an actual image of the events taking place.

This dichotomy was pointed out by Roland Barthes in an early 1960s essay:

> The press photograph is a message. Considered overall this message is formed by a source of emission, a channel of transmission and a point of reception. The source of emission is the staff of the newspaper, the group of technicians certain of whom take the photo, some of whom choose, compose, and treat it, while others, finally give it a title, a caption, and a commentary. The point of reception is the public which reads the paper.[58]

The press photographs discussed in this chapter were intended for an audience of visual, cultural and political consumers, and the captions added another contextual dimension. The meaning of the photograph was clear because the press release was either glued to it in the actual telex message, or else was part of the wire-photo print. This juxtaposition thus documented, mediated and created an enhanced storyline.

Yet it was the changing relationship between the word and the image that was in flux. By reframing the same analogue architectural photographs of 'Red Vienna', the whole narrative could be altered, exposing the fictions created by the images. Susan Sontag had also observed this slippage created by the juxtaposition of image and text in her final book-length essay on war photography in 2003 explaining that "all photographs wait to be explained or falsified by their captions."[59] Re-reading these press photographs today, we can gain a further layer of understanding about how the narrative of 1930s Austria was constructed and reconstructed for an American newspaper readership. This set of press photographs is thus testimony to history-writing while also evidencing a critical transition in the use of mediated photographs to make international political developments more accessible to diverse audiences. Finally, the technology of the wire photo made near-instant the process of crossing oceans, and of spreading political agendas.

Understanding these images requires interdisciplinary crossovers between architecture, journalism, photography and image technology. What began as a search for 'illustrations' of 'Red Vienna' for a lecture I was giving, became far more complex in terms of reading such representations of architecture. Too often, we treat photographs as equivalents of reality that are fixed through their objectivity, yet this is not the case. What these prints demonstrate is that there is a problem in using architectural photography all too casually. It is necessary to question why a photograph has been taken, and how it is then used. Buildings are not just a coincidental background for political actions, and as such this set of photographs exposes their complicity in the history-making of inter-war Vienna. They were the stage-sets for storytelling in what they depicted physically, and then reused as press photographs to reinterpret meaning.

Before his deposition as mayor, Karl Seitz once stated in a speech about the buildings of 'Red Vienna' somewhat hopefully:

When we are there no longer, then these stones will speak for us.[60]

It seems appropriate to end on this note.

Notes

1 Hanno Hardt and Bonnie Brennen, "Introduction," in *Picturing the Past: Media, History, and Photography*, ed. Bonnie Brennen and Hanno Hardt (Urbana/Chicago: University of Illinois Press, 1999), 2, 5–7, 9–10.
2 Marion Krammer, "Fotografie, Bildpropaganda und visuelle Kommunikation," in *Das Rote Wien 1919–1934: Ideen, Debatten Praxis*, ed. Werner Michael Schwarz, Georg Spitaler and Elke Wikidal (Basel: Birkhäuser Verlag GmbH, 2019), 287–295.
3 M.W. Fodor, "Chapter I: Austria," in *Plot and Counterplot in Central Europe: Conditions South of Hitler* (Boston: Houghton Mifflin Company, 1937), 6–8.
4 John Gunther, "Danube Blues," *Inside Europe* (New York/London: Harper & Brothers, 1936), 270.
5 Gunther, 271.
6 Barbie Zelizer, "Journalism's Last Stand: Wirephoto and the Discourse of Resistance," *Journal of Communication* 45, no. 2 (Spring 1995): 80, 83, 88.
7 Harald R. Stühlinger, "Einleitung," in *Rotes Wien publiziert – Architektur in den Medien und Kampagnen*, ed. Harald R Stühlinger (Vienna/Berlin: Mandelbaum Verlag, 2020), 11.
8 Press photograph of Rabenhof estate date-stamped 1st October 1929 and supplied via the press agency, Pacific & Atlantic Photos (author's personal archive).
9 Press photograph of Rabenhof estate date-stamped 22 February 1930 and supplied via the press agency, Underwood and Underwood (author's personal archive).
10 Elizabeth Denby, "Summary and Conclusions," *Europe Re-housed* (London: George Allen & Unwin, 1938), 253.
11 Harald R. Stühlinger, "Broschüren: Ein Genre der gedruckten Propaganda," in *Rotes Wien publiziert – Architektur in den Medien und Kampagnen*, ed. Harald R. Stühlinger (Vienna/Berlin: Mandelbaum Verlag, 2020), 113–133.

12 Michaela Maier, "Das Neue Wien – Die Neue Stadt: Programmatische Schriften, ein Künstlerbuch und ein voluminöser Leistungsbericht," in *Rotes Wien publiziert – Architektur in den Medien und Kampagnen*, ed. Harald R Stühlinger (Vienna/Berlin: Mandelbaum Verlag, 2020), 141–153.

13 Krammer, *Das Rote Wien 1919–1934*, 290.

14 Anna Stuhlpfarrer, "Sendet Ansichtskarten! Die Fotokarte als Propagandamedium im Roten Wien," in *Rotes Wien publiziert – Architektur in den Medien und Kampagnen*, ed. Harald R. Stühlinger (Vienna/Berlin: Mandelbaum Verlag, 2020), 141–153.

15 Wolfgang Mayer, *Wien im Spiegel des Fotoarchivs Gerlach: Stadtbild und Baugeschehen 1925–1972*, Kleinausstellung des Wiener Stadt- und Landesarchivs, Heft 28 (Wien: Wiener Stadt- und Landesarchivs, 1990).

16 Krammer, *Das Rote Wien 1919–1934*, 288–289.

17 I would like to thank Catalina Mejia Moreno for her insights relating to developments in early photography and press agencies in an earlier iteration of presenting this research material that was presented as part of the exhibition at UCL Art Museum in 2014 as an example of the rare set of Viennese press photographs, I have been collecting over the years.

18 Elizabeth Denby, "Vienna," *Europe Re-housed* (London: George Allen & Unwin, 1938), 148.

19 M.W. Fodor, "Chapter VX: The work of the Social-Democratic Regime in Vienna", "Chapter XVIII: Mussolini adopts Little Dollfuss", and "Chapter XXI. Mussolini Makes a Gesture," *Plot and Counterplot in Central Europe: Conditions South of Hitler* (Boston: Houghton Mifflin, 1937), 142, 171, 196–197.

20 Gunther, *Inside Europe*, 272–275.

21 Gunther, 281.

22 Gunther, 277.

23 M.W. Fodor, "Chapter XXII: Berlin attempts to Balkanize Vienna," and "Chapter XXIII: Fascism and Civil Strife in Vienna," in *Plot and Counterplot in Central Europe: Conditions South of Hitler* (Boston: Houghton Mifflin, 1937), 203, 208, 217, 219–225.

24 This press photograph of Reumannhof estate includes an attached press release dated 12th February 1934 yet without any information on which press agency (author's personal archive).

25 M.W. Fodor, "Chapter VX: The work of the Social-Democratic Regime in Vienna," and "Chapter XXIII: Fascism and Civil Strife in Vienna," in *Plot and Counterplot in Central Europe: Conditions South of Hitler* (Boston: Houghton Mifflin, 1937), 140, 225.

26 This press photograph of Sandleitenhof estate includes an attached press release dated 13 February 1934, although also date-stamped 28 February 1934, and supplied via the press agency, ACME Newspictures Inc (author's personal archive).

27 This press photograph of Matteottihof estate includes an attached press release dated 14 February 1934, although also date-stamped 21 December 1937, when it was received by the *Daily Times* (author's personal archive).

28 This press photograph of the George-Washington-Hof includes an attached press release dated 14 February 1934, and was supplied via the press agency, The Associated Press (author's personal archive).

29 Gunther, *Inside Europe*, 275–277, 289.

30 M.W. Fodor, "Chapter XXIV: The Dollfuss Murder," in *Plot and Counterplot in Central Europe: Conditions South of Hitler* (Boston: Houghton Mifflin, 1937), 229.

31 Gunther, *Inside Europe*, 297.

32 Gunther, 302–303.

33 Gunther, 276, 301, 306.

34 Gunther, 310–313.

35 This press photograph of the Karl-Marx-Hof estate is dated 29 March 1938, when it was supplied via the press agency, AP Wirephoto; it is also date-stamped 29 March 1938, when it was received at the *Daily Times* (author's personal archive).

36 Friedrich Scheu, *Der Weg ins Ungewisse: Österreichs Schicksalkurve 1929–1938* (Vienna/Munich/Zurich: Verlag Fritz Molden, 1972), 23–27.

37 Albin Krebs, "John Gunther Dead: Wrote 'Inside' Books," *The New York Times*, 30th May 1970: 1.

38 Fodor, *Plot and Counterplot*.

39 Scheu, *Der Weg ins Ungewisse*.

40 G.E.R. Gedye, *Betrayal in Central Europe. Austria and Czechoslovakia: The Fallen Bastions* (New York/London: Harper & Brothers, 1939).

41 Interview by the author with Charles Jencks at his home in London on 16 February 2009 as part of the research for another project.

42 J. Emlyn Williams, "Vienna Between Two Wars," *The Christian Science Monitor,* September 23, 1964: 1, 2.

43 Marianne Salcetti, "The Emergence of the Reporter: Mechanization and the Devaluation of Editorial Workers," in *Newsworkers: Towards a History of the Rank and File*, ed. Hanno Hardt and Bonnie Brennen (Minneapolis: University of Minnesota Press, 1995), 49–52.

44 John Gunther, "Dateline Vienna," *Harpers Magazine* 171 (July 1935): 199.

45 Scheu, *Der Weg ins Ungewisse*, 20.

46 Gunther, *Harpers Magazine*, 201.

47 Gunther, 207.

48 Scheu, *Der Weg ins Ungewisse*, 22. Translation from German by Eva Branscome:

> Der Grundsatz bestand darin, daß jeder Journalist, der eine ‚exklusive' Nachricht bekommen hatte, sich selbst ungefähr eine Stunde Vorsprung gewährte. Damit hatte seine Zeitung den Vorteil der Aktualität gegenüber den anderen. Nach einer Stunde rief der Besitzer der ‚exklusiven' Nachricht das Café Louvre an. Dort war immer ein ‚Diensthabender', der bereit war, die Nachricht zu übernehmen und diese dann der Reihe nach an alle anderen telephonisch weiterzugeben.

49 Scheu, 11, 295.

50 Zelizer, *Journal of Communication*, 80, 82–84, 88.

51 Zeynep Devrim Gürsel, "A Short History of Wire Service Photography," *Getting the Picture: Visual Culture in the News*, ed. Jason E. Hill and Vanessa R. Schwartz (London: Bloomsbury, 2015): 206–208.

52 Anton Holzer, *Rasende Reporter: Eine Kulturgeschichte des Fotojournalismus. Fotographie, Presse und Gesellschaft in Österreich 1890 bis 1945* (Darmstadt: Der Primus Verlag, 2014), 7, 8, 10, 11, 21.

53 Holzer, 15, 16, 18.

54 Zelizer, *Journal of Communication*, 78.

55 This press photograph of the National Socialists' takeover of the Austrian Chancellery is dated 12th March 1938, and was supplied via the press agency, AP Wirephoto; it is also date-stamped 13 March 1938 when it was received at the *Daily Times* (author's personal archive).

56 Eve Blau, "Re-Visiting Red Vienna as an Urban Project," The Austrian Embassy in Washington DC, USA, accessed on 11 October 2020, https://www.austria.org/revisiting-red-vienna

57 Eve Blau, "Architecture and Proletariat," *The Architecture of Red Vienna 1919–1934* (Cambridge, MA/London: MIT Press, 1999), 388–393.

58 Roland Barthes, "The Photographic Message" (1961), in *A Barthes Reader*, ed. Susan Sontag (New York: Hill and Wang, 1982), 194.

59 Susan Sontag, *Regarding the Pain of Others* (London: Hamish Hamilton, 2003), 9.

60 Karl Seitz, mayor of Vienna from 1923 to 1934, at the inaugural speech for the Karl-Marx-Hof on 12 October 1930. Quoted in Scheu, *Der Weg ins Ungewisse,* 76. Translation from German by Eva Branscome: „Wenn wir einst nicht mehr sind, werden diese Steine für uns sprechen.

Bibliography

Barthes, Roland. "The Photographic Message" (1961). In *A Barthes Reader*, edited by Susan Sontag, 194–210. New York: Hill and Wang, 1982.

Blau, Eve. "Architecture and Proletariat: The Semantics of Form." In *The Architecture of Red Vienna 1919–1934*, 340–401. Cambridge, Massachusetts/London: MIT Press, 1999.

Blau, Eve. "Re-Visiting Red Vienna as an Urban Project." Austrian Embassy Washington, accessed on 11 October 2020, https://www.austria.org/revisiting-red-vienna.

Brennen, Bonnie and Hanno Hardt, eds. *Picturing the Past: Media, History, and Photography.* Urbana/Chicago: University of Illinois Press, 1999.

Denby, Elizabeth. *Europe Re-housed.* London: George Allen & Unwin Ltd, 1938.

Durning, Dan. "Vienna's Café Louvre in the 1920s & 1930s: Meeting Place for Foreign Correspondents." unpublished (February 2012).

Fodor, M.W. *Plot and Counterplot in Central Europe: Conditions South of Hitler.* Boston: Houghton Mifflin Company, 1937.

Gedye, G.E.R. *Betrayal in Central Europe. Austria and Czechoslovakia: The Fallen Bastions* New York/London: Harper & Brothers, 1939.

Gulick, Charles A. *Austria from Habsburg to Hitler (2 Vols).* Berkeley/Los Angeles/London: University of California Press, 1948.

Gunther, John. "Dateline Vienna." *Harpers Magazine* 171 (July 1935): 198–208.

Gunther, John. *Inside Europe.* New York/London: Harper and Brothers, 1936.

Gürsel, Zeynep Devrim. "A Short History of Wire Service Photography." In *Getting the Picture. Visual Culture in the News*, edited by Jason E Hill and Vanessa R Schwartz, 206–211. London: Bloomsbury, 2015.

Holzer, Anton. *Rasende Reporter: Eine Kulturgeschichte des Fotojournalismus. Fotographie, Presse und Gesellschaft in Österreich 1890 bis 1945.* Darmstadt: Der Primus Verlag, 2014.

Krammer, Marion. "Fotografie, Bildpropaganda und visuelle Kommunikation." In *Das Rote Wien 1919–1934: Ideen, Debatten Praxis,* edited by Werner Michael Schwarz, Georg Spitaler and Elke Wikidal, 286–295. Basel: Birkhäuser Verlag GmbH, 2019.

Lefaivre, Liane. *Rebel Modernists: Architecture in Vienna Since Otto Wagner.* London: Lund Humphries Publishers Ltd, 2017.

Mayer, Wolfgang. *Wien im Spiegel des Fotoarchivs Gerlach: Stadtbild und Baugeschehen 1925–1972.* Kleinausstellung des Wiener Stadt- und Landesarchivs, Heft 28. Wien: Wiener Stadt- und Landesarchivs, 1990.

Salcetti, Marianne. "The Emergence of the Reporter: Mechanization and the Devaluation of Editorial Workers." In *Newsworkers. Towards a History of the Rank and File,* edited by Hanno Hardt and Bonnie Brennen, 48–74. Minneapolis: University of Minnesota Press, 1995.

Scheu, Friedrich. *Der Weg ins Ungewisse: Österreichs Schicksalkurve 1929–1938.* Vienna/Munich/Zurich: Verlag Fritz Molden, 1972.

Sealy, Peter. "After a Photograph, Before Photography (Takes Command)." *The Journal of Architecture* 21, no 6 (September 2016): 911–937.

Stühlinger, Harald. "Archi-Prop! Die Wahl der Mittel im Roten Wien." In *Gedruckte Fotografie: Abbildung, Object und mediales Format,* edited by Irene Ziehe and Ulrich Hägele, 117–132. Münster/New York: Waxmann, 2015.

Stühlinger, Harald, ed. *Rotes Wien publiziert – Architektur in den Medien und Kampagnen.* Vienna/Berlin: Mandelbaum Verlag, 2020.

Susan, Sontag. *Regarding the Pain of Others*. London: Hamish Hamilton, 2003.

Williams, J. Emlyn. "Vienna Between Two Wars." *The Christian Science Monitor*, September 23, 1964: 1–2.

Zelizer, Barbie. "Journalism's Last Stand: Wirephoto and the Discourse of Resistance." *Journal of Communication* 45, no. 2 (Spring 1995): 78–92.

8

DIPLOMACY UNDER SIEGE

Belgium's Diplomatic Patrimony as Political
Target during the Boxer Rebellion (1900) and the
Lumumba Assassination (1961)

Charlotte Rottiers and Bram De Maeyer

Introduction

> Laura and I are watching the scenes of mayhem unfolding at the seat of
> our Nation's government in disbelief and dismay. It is a sickening and
> heart-breaking sight. This is how election results are disputed in a ba-
> nana republic – not our democratic republic ... The violent assault on
> the Capitol – and disruption of a Constitutionally-mandated meeting of
> Congress – was undertaken by people whose passions have been inflamed
> by falsehoods and false hopes. Insurrection could do grave damage to our
> Nation and reputation.[1]

On January 6, 2021, former American President George W. Bush issued this
statement by which he strongly condemned the Capitol attack. As Bush witnessed the media coverage of a mob attacking one of the most important American public buildings to show their political discontent, it indubitably brought
back a lot of memories to a relatable kind of attack that he had condemned during
his presidency. This previous attack on an American public building did, however, not take place in Washington, D.C., but on foreign soil. More specifically,
on February 8, 2006 then President Bush issued a press statement in which he
condemned the string of attacks on American and other Western embassies in
the Muslim world.[2] These attacks were intrinsically linked to the publication of
a series of controversial cartoons satirising the Prophet Muhammad in several
Western newspapers. Considering the cartoons to be blasphemous, popular protests were staged in front of Western embassies in the Muslim world. Being the
most visible symbol representing a state actor abroad, the diplomatic buildings
served as a magnet that attracted thousands of Muslim demonstrators in over a
dozen different capitals. In Damascus, Jakarta and Teheran, Western embassy

DOI: 10.4324/9781003272076-12

premises were turned into sites of vandalism as rioters stormed, ravaged and even set diplomatic buildings ablaze. In a similar fashion to the Capitol insurrection, Muslim protestors resorted to acts of violence against the architecture of the political establishment that they detested. The attacks on Western embassies in 2006 and the Capitol in 2021 serve as recent reminders of the ambiguous relationship between political architecture and the popular masses. Often conceived by state actors as instruments to legitimate the political regime and construct a national identity, government buildings can turn into arenas of contestation and conflict overnight in times of political turmoil, adding a sinister side to their representational function. In the case of literature on diplomatic architecture, this sinister dimension is often only mentioned in passing. Instead, architectural historians have primarily examined how state actors have invested in diplomatic architecture as an instrument of national representation on foreign soil.[3] Within this body of literature, architectural scholars often portray diplomatic buildings as a stately venue for political negotiations and social gatherings. As such, the building's representational function is often interpreted as a positive quality. As the above-mentioned attacks have illustrated, however, diplomatic buildings can also turn into a scene of violent confrontations. Framed as the architectural surrogate of state actors on foreign soil, diplomatic buildings can become high-profile political targets in times of strained bilateral relations. Poised to strike at the very symbol representing a state actor abroad, demonstrators turn diplomatic premises into a site to enter into conflict with a foreign country. This can vary from a demonstration in front of the diplomatic premise to an all-out attack on the building itself.

Attacks on diplomatic missions have largely remained unexplored within the literature on diplomatic architecture. When authors do mention such violent incidents, they mainly discuss the most extreme and thought-out type of attack: terrorist attacks. In addition to addressing just one type of attack, the scope is also fairly limited to terrorist attacks on diplomatic missions of superpowers. Jane Loeffler, for instance, discusses how the devastating Al-Qaeda bombing attacks on the American embassies in Kenya and Tanzania in 1998 turned US embassies into gated communities flanked by military checkpoints and barracks.[4] In his study on British embassies, Mark Bertram paints a similar picture. He indicates that the British Foreign Office has beefed up security since the late 1990s as a response to the rise of global terrorism.[5] Indeed, the impact of terrorism on diplomatic architecture has already been pointed out by Robert Bevan. In his highly acclaimed book *The Destruction of Memory. Architecture at War*, Bevan offers the insight that "… attacks on the buildings – embassies especially – of an oppressor by the oppressed have … become the *lingua franca* of nationalist and regionalist terror groups."[6] As the example of the Mohammed cartoons and subsequent attacks on diplomatic premises have showcased, terrorist attacks are not the only type of attack targeting diplomatic architecture. However, they have not yet been dealt with as extensively as terrorist attacks in academic literature.

Building on this hiatus, this chapter aims to broaden our understanding of attacks on diplomatic premises by shifting the perspective on two different levels. First, it shifts the focus from terrorist to mob attacks on diplomatic premises. Whereas terrorist attacks are meticulously planned and carried out by well-trained individuals, redirection of popular rage can be framed as a less organised type of attack carried out by ordinary citizens. Furthermore, mob action usually follows a very different trajectory than terrorist attacks. Whereas the latter is thought out well in advance and carried out within a short time span, mob attacks are characterised by a certain built-up to the attack itself. Usually, the mob first assembles in front of the diplomatic premise and holds a protest which eventually culminates into a popular outburst of violence. While the demonstrators turn into assailants upon trespassing the diplomatic grounds, the diplomatic premises suddenly transform from a locus of peaceful dialogue and cultural exchange into a warzone as they endure plundering and destruction.

Secondly, this contribution shifts the perspective from great powers to Belgium, a small state actor. Whereas the aforementioned great powers such as the United States and Great Britain are somewhat usual suspects, Belgium does not immediately come to mind in the context of attacks on diplomatic buildings. Founded in 1830, the country initially maintained a neutrality policy imposed by the great European powers at the time. Following the Second World War, Belgium abandoned its neutral doctrine and fully embraced a multilateral diplomatic approach which was exemplified by the country's leading role in the political-economic unification of the European continent.[7] Notwithstanding this non-aligned and later on consensus-driven foreign policy, the Belgian diplomatic patrimony has not been immune to attacks. This chapter discusses two examples: the assaults on the diplomatic premises in China during the Boxer Rebellion of 1900 and the string of violent incidents in front of Belgian embassies in 1961 following the assassination of the first Congolese Prime Minister Patrice Lumumba. While these incidents might not seem directly related, they both have been driven by the growing outrage with King Leopold II's expansionist and colonial policies and its political legacy in the early 1960s.

For each case, the chapter discusses how popular discontent with Belgian foreign policy was redirected towards its diplomatic buildings. First, it examines the underlying mechanisms fuelling this aggression and discusses the severity of the damage inflicted while taking both sides – Belgium and the assailants – of the spectrum into account. Second, special emphasis is given to the role of the media in covering the built-up, the eventual attacks on Belgian diplomatic premises and the political fallout. Third, the chapter sheds light on the unsolicited role of diplomatic architecture as a tool of retaliation and unravels the short- and long-term implications of these attacks on the representational role of Belgium's diplomatic patrimony. In order to frame these attacks on Belgian diplomatic premises on a conceptual level, the chapter uses the term iconoclasm defined by Kristine Kolrud and Marina Prusac as "… the destruction or alteration of images or objects imbued with some kind of symbolic value."[8] Kolrud and Prusac indicate that iconoclastic attacks are often associated with the destruction of holy symbols, but that the term can also be applied to non-religious contexts in which individuals intentionally damage and destroy objects with great symbolic value.[9] Continuing along these lines, this contribution discusses how rioters directed their anti-Belgian sentiments towards the tangible objects – architecture, furniture and artwork – representing Belgium abroad. Therefore, it calls upon a wide variety of source material such as archival material of the Belgian Ministry of Foreign Affairs, parliamentary debates, and press coverage of these outbursts of aggression towards the symbolic architectural settings and their interiors representing the Belgian state abroad.[10]

The Belgian Experience of the Siege of the Legation Quarter: An Eye-Opening Exercise in the Conception of Diplomatic Architecture

The 1900 Boxer Rebellion in China was only one of many waves of violence and xenophobia in China but became a major milestone in Western historiography because of the siege of the Legation Quarter, an unseen attack in scale and aggressiveness towards the diplomatic representatives residing in China. The siege has been the subject of many books, based on the unprecedented number of ego documents and memoranda written in the wake of this uprising. However, the role of the original Legation buildings in Peking as silent witnesses of this episode has not yet been fully uncovered.

The Legation Quarter in Peking is best known in its post-1900 form, as a separate district designed for the international diplomatic corps in China. However, it only acquired its walled, protected status and distinctive European neo-style architectural expression as a direct result of the Boxer Rebellion. In an attempt to chase out and even exterminate the foreign, diplomatic presence from China, the original legation buildings were almost all destroyed in the fighting. The Belgian legation building was the first diplomatic building to be attacked and destroyed in the Siege of the Legations. Its history has often been overlooked as at the time Belgium was a small, neutral state that did not partake in sending a legion of relief forces to China. Notwithstanding the Belgian foreign policy, its legation proved not to be a safe haven for diplomats and would prompt the Belgian Ministry of Affairs to rethink its duty and strategy when housing diplomats abroad. By analysing the siege of the Legation Quarter as a case of architectural iconoclasm, the mechanism becomes apparent of how diplomatic architecture was framed by the Boxers as the symbol for the foreign diplomatic influence in Peking.

The first diplomatic relations between hegemonic China and the international community were enforced in 1861 after the Second Opium War. The signatories of the Treaty of Tianjin (1858) – the UK, USA, France and Russia – for the first time had obtained the right of permanently residing national diplomatic representatives in the Chinese capital.[11] They took up residence in the *Dongjiaomin Xiang* district, the 'Eastern Lane of the Mingling of Peoples' on the inside of the southern Tater Wall.[12] In the eyes of Chinese officials, its history as a customs district with accommodation for foreign tributary vassals from Tibet, Mongolia, Korea or Vietnam, and its association with politically inferior 'barbarians', made it a fitting location for diplomatic residency. The diplomats soon appropriated their assigned location and renamed it 'Legation Street' or 'Rue des Legations', unaware of previous history and connotations behind this location.[13]

From then on, an increasing amount of diplomatic ties were established and many legations opened up on Legation Street or its connected streets. By 1900, 11 diplomatic missions were established in Peking: The United States of America, Germany, France, Great Britain, Holland, Italy, Japan, Austria-Hungary, Russia, Spain and Belgium.[14] While Belgian-Chinese diplomatic ties were already established in 1865, Belgium only in the last decennium of the 19th century became heavily involved in the construction of the railway Peking-Hankow and mining concessions, as part of Leopold II's economic and colonial expansion.[15] The Legation Quarter was not yet a delineated quarter, but rather a district where most of the foreign legations were established, intermixed with the local population, government offices, as well foreign institutions like the Hong Kong and Shanghai Bank, the Imperial Maritime Customs, and commercial functions like the Peking Hotel and stores.[16] The legations themselves were mainly housed in renovated Chinese houses. The new diplomatic function of the district and the presence of foreign representatives were immediately manifested visually: flags were hoisted on top of their rented palaces and became a fixed part of the cityscape.[17]

Unlike the other legations, the Belgian building was not part of the legation district. It was located on the corner of Ha Ta Men street and Changan Avenue, in a 15–20 minutes walking distance from Legation Street.[18] This legation was built in the late 1870s in cooperation with vicar Alphonse Favier (1837–1905) and the Lazarist brothers on a plot of land that was already owned by the religious order, and constructed following Chinese construction principles in a constellation of three courtyards. The trimestrial rent was paid for by the Belgian Ministry of Foreign Affairs, which assumed financial responsibility (Figure 8.1).[19]

From 1898 onwards, various reports of attacks on Chinese Christians reached the legation district, and via the media, Brussels, where questions were raised about the security against a possible attack.[20] The seriousness of these attacks first became apparent to the Belgian envoys in 1899, when a couple of Belgian priests were beheaded in Mongolia.[21] At the same time, minister-resident Baron Charles de Vinckx de Deux Orp (1859–1931) and later on as well the secretary of the legation Baron Emile de Cartier de Marchienne (1871–1946) decide to return to Europe. Cartier de Marchienne is left temporarily in charge until deputy minister-resident Maurice Joostens (1862–1910) arrives in Peking on May 8, 1900. As by then peace seems to have been restored in China, Cartier de Marchienne prepared for the return trip. However, he could not have misjudged the situation any worse: the problems were far from over, but rather were ready to escalate, as Belgium found itself in the eye of the storm.[22]

FIGURE 8.1 View on the former Belgian legation in Beijing, 1889.

The Belgian envoys themselves noticed first-hand the rising tension and un-easiness among the population, as they came across building exteriors that: "… se couvraient d'affiches xenophobes relatant les prétendus méfaits des étrangers. La foule attentive se massait aux carrefours pour les lire et les commenter."[23] On May 28, the legation received the message that there was an attack at Chang-Hsin-Tien, one of the stops on the Belgian-owned railway Peking-Hankow, 20 miles from Peking. Later that day, two Belgian staff members who survived the attack arrived at the legation and reported on the Boxers' attack. More attacks followed and prompted the legations to take precautions. From 30th May on-wards, Peking was militarily taken over by the Imperial troops.[24]

While the Boxers' attacks were not initially aimed at the diplomatic envoys, they would later on target the diplomatic community as well. A first, open attack on the diplomatic community would follow suit at the start of June.[25] As the wave of violence was spreading towards Tientsin and the vicinity of Peking, the staff of the British legation was getting ready, as is their annual custom, to move into summer villas near Fengtai, 15 miles southwest of Peking. Some govern-ments had permanent bases here and in 1897, the UK bought a site to construct their colonial bungalows fitting to the needs of their large staff. By spring 1900, the constructions were completed; Lady MacDonald and her family arrived on June 3 to enjoy the new summer villas for the first time. In Peking, meanwhile, the gravity of the situation dawned on them and an armed escort arrived the very next day to accompany the family back to Peking. This turned out to be a wise decision, as the following week all the brand new bungalows are being burned down by the Boxers.[26] While this was not the official legation building, these summer residences sprawling out over the countryside were inherently linked with and symbolised the foreign presence in China. Although at the time not yet recognised as such, this first incidence of architectural iconoclasm was a very clear warning and prelude to the later aggressions towards the Legation Quarter.

That time had arrived on June 14, when the Boxers reached Peking.[27] Vice-consul Adrien de Mélotte de Lavaux (1874–1942) describes how riotous noises emerged from the city; the Belgian envoys remained in their legations and spent the day waiting, concerned that the turmoil would get out of hand. The legation was situated on a street corner and to get a better view of the situation, minister-resident Joostens, secretary Leopold Merghelynck (1874–1912), *valet de chambre* William and two Austrian soldiers assembled on the roof as a make-shift look-out point. From both sides, a crowd with torches came walking to the legation, with the intention to burn it down. "Jusqu'a minuit, notre legation demeure en paix," de Mélotte de Lavaux recalls, "a ce moment, une troupe de gens portant des torches allumées debouche vers la gauche dans la rue principale. Un autre groupe s'avance à une centaine de metres vers la droite. Nous sommes encer-clés."[28] The defenders on the roof prepared themselves to take action against the advancing threat and allegedly fired 18 shots. The surviving attackers turned back and eight bodies were retrieved from the street the next morning.[29]

The situation remained tense and various pieces of furniture, garments and the principal part of the archives were moved to the Austrian legation in case another attack would not be warded off as easily. Sleepless nights followed in guarding and defending the legation. Meanwhile, barricades and posts were erected by the international troops to create a line of defence around the Legation Street. Because of the Belgian legation's position far away from the core of the legations, the building was difficult to defend and not included in the protected area. Fol-lowing the proposal of the other legations, the Belgian legation was evacuated on the 16th of June. Three carts were loaded with provisions and together with the staff moved to the Austrian Legation. For the Belgian diplomats, it felt like giving up their fatherland: "Ce déménagement ... nous attriste," de Mélotte de Lavaux recalls, "nous avons l'impression d'avoir été chassés de notre territoire national. Désormais, nous ne sommes plus que des sans patrie, pour ainsi dire."[30]

The infamous ultimatum by Zongli Yamen was made on the 19th of June: the entire diplomatic community was given 24 hours to evacuate the legation quarter and travel to Tientsin to avoid any further unrest and calamity. While at first agreeing to the proposal, things changed when the German head of legation Baron von Ketteler was murdered at the Northern end of Ha Ta Men street in the vicinity of the Belgian legation, while on his way to Zongli Yamen.[31] As a result, the diplomatic community decided to stay in Peking: women, children and missionaries were to be hosted in the British legation, which was the easiest to defend. The attack started when the ultimatum ended: June 20, 1900, 4 PM. Already the next day, the first legation building was attacked, the indefensible Belgian legation.[32] Mélotte recounts:

> le 21 juin fut un jour particulièrement triste pour les Belges. Ils assistèrent de loin à l'incendie, irremediable cette fois, de leur légation. Le magnifique bâtiment de la légation d'Autriche périt à la même date et de la même manière. Notre mobilier, nos vêtements, notre linge, une part notable de nos archives, en un mot presque tout ce que nous possédions … fut pillé ou brûle par haine de l'Etranger.[33]

The next day June 22, the Dutch and Italian legations also went up in flames. Attempts are made to set fire to the British Legation as well but are repelled, although the neighbouring buildings are consumed by the fire. As the outer line of defence fell and, together with the Austrian legation, the Belgian possessions are lost, the staff seeks refuge in the French legation.[34] As two-thirds of the Legation Quarter will gradually be lost to the Boxers, the British legation became the central point of life in the besieged quarter.[35] The siege goes on for 55 days and on August 14, International forces arrive to liberate the Legation Quarter where only the British and parts of the French Legation were still standing, although heavily damaged. The Boxers almost succeeded in their aim to wipe out the foreign presence in Peking by means of architectural iconoclasm. The destruction of the Belgian legation shocked the Belgian Parliament and Ministry of Foreign Affairs, as well as the broader population, as the event was widely covered in the Belgian media. The special report by journalist Collin would pay particular attention to the destroyed legation building and its later reconstruction.[36] On a picture of the ruins of the Belgian legation, Joostens and Merghelynck are posing with the Belgian flag in what once used to be the *salon de reception*: notwithstanding the considerable material losses, the diplomats kept their spirits high (Figure 8.2).[37]

The subsequent negotiations and final settlement on January 6, 1901 were the legal basis for the further development of the Legation district.[38] It would be placed under the exclusive administration of the legations, which meant that no Chinese residents were allowed to reside in or enter the legation district without authorisation. Reinforced walls were erected, surrounded by a 150-metre glacis that served as a protective buffer. The various legations were all housed in this fortified settlement and were given significantly expanded premises and barracks for the mission guard, which would from then on be permanently present. Socially and administratively, it became more like a present-day gated community, with its own police, public services and community life.[39]

The Belgian legation itself moved to a building inside the legation district. The location was that of the former palace of Prince Su-Tong, a well-known Boxer. Considerations and symbols of location were very prominent in the remembrance of the Boxer Rebellion: taking the place of this prominent boxer

FIGURE 8.2   Joostens and Merghelynck posing in the former *salon de reception* of the Belgian Legation in Peking, November/December 1900.

was like a personal victory and revenge for the destruction of the former Belgian legation building.[40] One could say that the destruction of the legation building was a blessing in disguise. The indemnities and subsequent expansion of the Legation site meant a considerable upgrade for the Belgian Legation.[41] It provided them with the opportunity to design and build a new legation building from scratch, tailored to their liking. While the previous legation building certainly was a needed luxury and made the arrival and performance of the legation staff much more comfortable, it was not up to par with the size and splendour of other legations in China, especially the reception rooms and limited space were the source of some complaints by the diplomats.[42] Moreover, security and the ability to defend themselves better in case of a new attack became major points of interest, as well as housing the Belgian legation guard.[43] The new location in the Legation Quarter and closer to the other powers also meant a boost for their status and position compared to the other diplomatic representatives, underlining the direct competition and comparison that took place in building the new Legation Quarter.[44] Indeed, the constellation of compounds designed in national interpretations of neo-styles started to resemble more and more an international world exhibition. The Rue des Legations in Peking gradually became the diplomatic version of the *Rue des Nations*.[45]

While the first generation of the legations was housed in rented or purchased Chinese palaces and residential dwellings, they nonetheless became the symbol for the foreign diplomatic influence in Peking, and a target for the Boxers. The large-scale destruction would spark already ongoing debates in Belgium and directly lead to a more thoughtful and self-conscious approach to location and representation. The construction of the Belgian legation in Peking would be Belgium's first, independent building project. The Belgian legation in Peking proved to be a test case for the conceptualisation of diplomatic architecture and for later acquisition projects abroad. For the first time, thought was given to how Belgian diplomatic architecture could be used as an instrument of identity building and representation. During this process, the Ministry of Foreign Affairs was able to experience first-hand that a permanent diplomatic building stock not only had advantages but could also become a political target in times of unrest. It was the architectural iconoclasm by the Boxers that revealed the symbolic and representational value of diplomatic architecture to the Belgian government.

Damaged Goods: Lumumba's Assassination and the Political Fallout for Belgium and its Embassy Patrimony

Sixty-one years following the Boxer Rebellion, the Belgian diplomatic patrimony once again turned into a site of iconoclastic attacks. These attacks were intrinsically linked to King Leopold II's colonial legacy. Imbued with the idea that Belgium needed to acquire colonies, the Belgian monarch turned the resource-rich territory of Congo into his personal possession in 1885. A harsh economic system of forced labour was put into place, resulting in an enormous loss of life.[46] In 1908, amidst growing international outcry for the atrocities in Congo, the Belgian state took over control of Congo by turning the private property into a state-administered colony. Against the backdrop of the decolonisation of Africa and Asia following the Second World War and the growing call for self-rule in the Belgian colony, Congo gained its independence on June 30, 1960. As the first Congolese Prime Minister Patrice Lumumba tried to diminish Belgian influence in his country, the Belgian political-economic elite was worried that Belgian mining companies in the Congolese province of Katanga would be nationalised. The Belgian government supported Katanga's secession from Congo, thus undermining the political authority of Lumumba.[47] Simultaneously, Belgium took action to remove Lumumba from office by supporting a coup that placed him under house arrest. Worried that Lumumba might still pose a threat to its economic interests, Belgium greenlighted his transfer to Katanga's secessionist regime where he was executed on January 17, 1961.[48] Lumumba's death fuelled anti-Belgian sentiments across the globe and mass demonstrations were organised in front of Belgian diplomatic and consular missions in over 60 capitals in February 1961.[49] Most demonstrations were peaceful, but in the case of the Belgian embassy in Sydney, individuals painted the anti-Belgian slogan "Lumumba Murderers, Get Out of the Congo" on the garden wall to tarnish the country's reputation. While discussing the best method to remove the paint with the concierge, the wife of the Belgian diplomat ridiculed the entire incident in an interview with the Australian newspaper *The Daily Mirror*: "It seems someone read newspaper accounts of slogan paintings in other countries and suddenly realised that nothing had been done here. However, it is a little late. Mr. Lumumba has been dead for a few days."[50] Following the publication of the article, the Belgian diplomat notified Brussels that his wife had been wilfully misquoted by the "communist-leaning" journalist who wanted to add fuel to the fire.[51] This comment is exemplary for the way in which Belgian diplomats framed the string of anti-Belgian demonstrations in the wake of the assassination of Lumumba. If they did not like the content of an article, the newspaper in question was quickly labelled as a communist-oriented media outlet. Such comments need to be seen against the backdrop of the strong anti-colonial rhetoric coming from the Kremlin. In doing so, Moscow aimed to win over the hearts and minds of newly independent countries.[52] Against this backdrop, Brussels framed the incidents through the invariably distorting lens of the Cold War. Ministry officials and diplomats were convinced that the Kremlin was behind the anti-Belgian demonstrations to further tarnish the country's reputation on the international stage.[53] This line of thought was reinforced by two violent attacks on the Belgian embassies in the communist countries of Poland and Yugoslavia. On February 15, 1961, large demonstrations were organised in front of the Belgian embassy in Warsaw. These demonstrations initially started out as peaceful protest, but it did not take long before hundreds of agitators turned the embassy into a site of iconoclasm. The Belgian coat of arms was pulled from the façade and smashed to smithereens. The mob also stormed into the embassy and wreaked havoc on the interiors. Red paint was smeared on the walls to symbolise that Belgium had blood on its hands. Furthermore, the furniture was thrown out of the window and the archival records were set on fire. The police did arrive on the scene prior to the attack, but stood by idly as the rioters breached the gate and trespassed the embassy grounds. As the Polish state was ought to protect foreign diplomatic missions on its territory, this passive attitude was a grave violation of the immunity awarded to diplomats and their premises. Since antiquity, rulers have granted immunity to foreign diplomats residing on their territory, but this was mainly granted on an ad hoc basis.[54] This made diplomats very dependent on the goodwill of the sovereign in question to adhere to the principle of diplomatic immunity. It was only in 1961 that the United Nations anchored the core principle of diplomatic immunity in international law through the ratification of the *Vienna Convention on Diplomatic Relations*.[55] Unfortunately for Belgium, the convention was only signed in April of that year, two months after the violent attack on the Belgian embassy in Warsaw. As the Belgian Ministry of Foreign Affairs filed a complaint with the Polish government for the inadequate security at the embassy, the Polish state poured additional oil on the fire in its reply to Brussels. They left out any reference to the attack itself and only stated that the peaceful "… manifestations reflètaient une indignation profonde et justifiée de la population polonaise pour la politique aggressive belge dirigée contre l'indépendance de la République du Congo."[56] The Belgian ambassador in Warsaw also notified Brussels that the Polish press discussed the peaceful manifestations, but left out any reference to the subsequent attack on the embassy building.

The Belgian embassy in Yugoslavia also served as a scene of architectural iconoclasm. As the news of Lumumba's assassination spread across Belgrade, 30.000 demonstrators gathered at the Square of Marx and Engels in support of the slain Congolese prime minister on February 14, 1961. Following the demonstration, several hundred protestors marched towards the Belgian embassy to avenge Lumumba's death. At the time, the Belgian embassy in Belgrade was located in a walled plot in which the residence and embassy offices were situated in two separate buildings. Upon arriving at the embassy, rioters flipped the embassy's car and threw large rocks through the window of the ambassador's study. They made their way into the embassy and inflicted grave damage to the doors, walls, and ceilings. In addition to trashing the interiors, some rioters seized the attack as an opportunity to make a quick buck off their presence in the embassy's lavishly furnished interiors by taking the paintings, tapestries, silverware and clothing with them on their way out. Furthermore, rioters also accentuated their takeover of the Belgian embassy by putting up a placard with the image of Patrice Lumumba on the embassy's façade. In doing so, they turned the embassy from an architectural embodiment of Belgium into both a commemorative space and locus of protest for Lumumba's murder (Figure 8.3).

In contrast to the attack in Warsaw, the Yugoslav authorities did try to protect the Belgian embassy from the rioting masses. Police officers set up a roadblock to shield off the embassy premises, but they were heavily outnumbered and had to retreat. Some 40 police officers were wounded as hundreds of assailants stormed the checkpoint. Furthermore, the attack on the Belgian embassy in Belgrade was not censored in the national press as was the case in Warsaw. The leading Yugoslav newspaper *Politika* showed photographs of the attack.[57] In addition, the Yugoslav authorities formally apologised for the attack and financially compensated Belgium for the damage suffered to its embassy whereas the Polish regime did not even acknowledge that an attack had taken place. The constructive attitude of the Tito regime did, however, not help to alter the perception of the

FIGURE 8.3 The ambassador's study in Belgrade littered with rocks and debris, 1961.

Belgian authorities, as ministry officials believed that the Yugoslav regime had orchestrated the attack to be in the good books of Moscow. In retrospect, the assumption of Brussels that the attacks were orchestrated by communist leaders was a narrow-minded understanding of the turn of events. The international outrage was also felt in countries affiliated with the Non-Aligned Movement. This alliance of decolonised Afro-Asian countries opted to remain unaligned during the Cold War. It sought strength by unity among former colonies in order to not become a pawn in the struggle between the White House and the Kremlin.[58] As the fight against (neo-)colonialism was the hallmark of the Non-Aligned Movement, Lumumba's assassination fuelled anti-Belgian sentiments among its member states.

The Indian Prime Minister Jawaharlal Nehru, for instance, slammed Belgium for its actions in Congo and dubious role in the murder of Lumumba.[59] The strained Belgian-Indian relations became very tangible in the streetscape of New Delhi as anti-Belgian manifestations were organised. On February 14, 1961, the peaceful protest escalated as 60 African exchange students attacked the Belgian embassy offices in New Delhi. Reflecting the bipolar lens by which Brussels framed the attacks, the Belgian Ministry of Foreign Affairs reasoned that the Communist Party of India had run a smear campaign against Belgium which had incited the African students.[60] The students could enter the embassy unopposed as the municipal police, in a somewhat clumsy turn of events, made their way to the ambassadorial residence instead of going to the embassy offices. The rioters could smash all the windows with rocks and the telephone installation was damaged beyond repair. The students also targeted the most tangible symbols representing Belgium as the national coat of arms and the state portrait of the Belgian King Baudouin were struck down and smashed into pieces. Surprisingly, the Belgian ambassador reported back to Brussels that the damage was only minimal. This may not come as a surprise, as the ambassador already held his work environment in low esteem. He reasoned that the African students were most likely stunned that the Belgian embassy offices were housed in a building with the architectural appearance of an 'African cabin'.[61] In addition to showcasing a racially prejudiced attitude towards the African students involved, the ambassador's comments are exemplary for the sarcastic tone frequently used by Belgian ambassadors to complain about their diplomatic housing. The New Delhi embassy may have been somewhat below the standard of the diplomatic corps, but this was not the case for the Belgian purpose-built embassy in Cairo. Completed in 1930, the Beaux-arts embassy featured a white façade with sculptural ornamentation and classical architectural elements such as balustrades. The reception room was lavishly decorated and featured a bronze bust of the Belgian King Albert I. By the time of Lumumba's death in February 1961, Egypt was governed by President Nasser who was one of the leading figures of the Non-Aligned Movement. Framing Lumumba's assassination as yet another example of western neo-colonialism, Nasser joined his ally Nehru in criticising Belgium's foreign policy in Congo. As rumours of Lumumba's death began to circulate in Cairo on February 13, 1961, some 200 students pelted the embassy's façade with rocks and smashed several windows. The municipal police arrived immediately and set up roadblocks to shield off the Belgian embassy. As the news of Lumumba's death was confirmed the next day, it remained surprisingly quiet at the embassy, standing in stark contrast to the attacks in Belgrade and New Delhi. The Belgian embassy personnel did, however, not breathe a sigh of relief as they believed that the Egyptian government used the day to covertly plan an attack on the embassy. In retrospect, there is reason to believe that the Egyptian authorities did have a hand in the violent incidents that would transpire on February 15, 1961. In the early hours of that day, the Egyptian police lifted the roadblocks and only seven unarmed police officers were posted in front of the Belgian embassy. Much to the surprise of the Belgian embassy staffers, local photographers and camera crews took up position on the other side of the street with their lenses focused on the Belgian embassy, indicating that something newsworthy was about to happen very soon. Less than an hour later, their lenses captured how 2,000 rioters armed with axes turned the Belgian embassy into a scene of architectural iconoclasm. The skeleton police crew quickly retreated as the assailants began to breach the embassy gates. The Belgian ambassador briefly considered throwing tear gas grenades at the mob, but eventually ordered to evacuate the embassy. By means of placing a ladder against the garden wall, the ambassador together with his wife and diplomatic staff fled to the nearby Canadian embassy just minutes before the assailants breached the main entrance.[62] As the architecture and interior decoration were designed as a whole to represent Belgium abroad, the assailants vented their rage on specific symbolic objects that were displayed in the embassy's interior. The ambassador's rich book collection was torn while the furniture was severely damaged and thrown out of the windows. Furthermore, rioters plunged the bronze busts of King Albert I from its marble plinth. The assailants also tore down the state portrait of King Baudouin and replaced it with a picture of Lumumba to accentuate their takeover of the Belgian embassy. What happened next pales in comparison with the aforementioned attacks. A group of rioters went to the embassy's garage and came across several jerry cans which they used to set the Belgian embassy ablaze. Only after a huge smoke cloud filled the air, the municipal police returned to the scene triggering the demonstrators to disperse. By the time the fires were finally extinguished, the white exteriors of the embassy were covered with a black residue and the interiors were severely burnt (Figure 8.4).

Already on the evening of the attack, the Egyptian TV network showed footage of the attack in local movie theatres. The propaganda film with the telling title *How the Arabs set fire to an embassy* glorified the attack as a righteous retribution for Lumumba's death.[63] Furthermore, the state-owned newspaper *Al Ahram* stated that the attack symbolised the ongoing struggle of Egypt against Western imperialism.[64] The strained Belgian-Egyptian ties reached their zenith as Nasser did not condemn the attack nor offer any apologies to Belgium, which Tito had done for instance. Consequently, the Belgian Ministry of Foreign Affairs broke

FIGURE 8.4   The Belgian embassy in Cairo set ablaze, February 15, 1961.

off diplomatic relations with Egypt. Such a move was highly exceptional for Belgium, but was welcomed by the Belgian press. *Le Soir*, for instance, indicated that it would be inappropriate for a civilised country such as Belgium to have an embassy in a country that was run by a "*dictateur hystérique*" as Nasser who could not even protect the lives of diplomats and their premises (Figure 8.5).[65]

It is, however, striking to notice that Brussels did not take any action to improve the security of its embassy patrimony abroad. Just one year after the attack in Warsaw, the embassy moved to the reconstructed Mniszech palace that was destroyed during the Second World War. Judging by the violent incidents which had transpired the previous year in the Polish capital, one would assume that design alterations would have been made to beef up security. The newly acquired neoclassical palace could, however, easily be entered from the street side and there were no bars on the windows. As such, Brussels saw the political fallout as a temporary phenomenon. When the dust had settled, Belgian embassy buildings could once more serve as a venue for peaceful encounters with the local population.

Conclusion

In times of political turmoil, diplomatic buildings often become a target by predilection of populist assaults aiming to attack foreign political regimes on

FIGURE 8.5 The bust of King Albert I lying next to its marble plinth at the Cairo embassy, 1961.

distance by means of architectural iconoclasm. The Belgian diplomatic premises were no exception. In both the case of the Boxer Rebellion and the Lumumba assassination, the popular rage was redirected towards the Belgian diplomatic premises and widely covered by international media. Notwithstanding Belgium's neutral status in the 1900s and its conciliatory foreign policy in the post-war period, its neo-imperial and neo-colonial foreign policy triggered widespread discontent. There is a fundamental difference in the comparison of both cases: while in China, Belgium was part of a conclave of neo-imperial powers who saw unlimited opportunities in exploiting China, Belgium was the main protagonist in the case of the murder of Lumumba. However, the main outcome was the same; large crowds assembled in front of Belgian diplomatic missions to express their outrage. This expression could take on many forms: peaceful protests, defiling the exteriors, plundering, vandalising the interiors, and in some extreme cases, even the destruction of the diplomatic premises.

The assailants interpreted the diplomatic buildings as the embodiment of the Belgian state on foreign soil, which had to be held accountable for its actions. In case of absence of the representatives themselves, the crowd redirected their rage on the buildings that represented the Belgian state in a foreign context. This was a surprise for the Belgian Ministry of Foreign Affairs, as they did not fully apprehend how the representational function could be translated into a political target. Both incidents shocked the Ministry but its response was diverse. Whereas security and the defence against possible further attacks were taken into account in the design process of the new Belgian legation in China, the Lumumba affair did not prompt the Ministry to enhance its security. Even though the Ministry of Foreign Affairs did not fully comprehend the potential of its missions abroad as a political target, both cases showed that in times of turmoil, diplomatic buildings often turn into sites of architectural iconoclasm. This is a dynamic that shows uncanny similarities to the Insurrection at the Capitol in 2021 and underlines that diplomatic architecture, essentially state buildings abroad, are also susceptible to being framed as a political target. This unforeseen role as a tool of retaliation adds to the interpretation of diplomatic buildings as multi-layered symbolic architectural settings. As such, when analysing a country's national diplomatic patrimony abroad, state actors are not the only ones that have the power and means to attribute meaning to diplomatic architecture and its interior decoration. Attacks and the subsequent destruction as well, or even more so, serve as key moments that expose the fluctuating and multi-layered meaning of diplomatic architecture.

Notes

1 "Statement by President George W. Bush on Insurrection at the Capitol, January 6, 2021," George W. Bush Presidential Center, accessed October 2, 2021, https://www.bushcenter.org/about-the-center/newsroom/press-releases/2021/statement-by-president-george-w-bush-on-insurrection-at-the-capitol.html.
2 "Bush Urges End to Cartoon Violence," *The New York Times*, accessed June 17, 2020, https://www.nytimes.com/2006/02/08/world/americas/bush-urges-end-to-cartoon-violence.html.
3 Ron Robin, *Enclaves of America: The Rhetoric of American Political Architecture Abroad 1900–1965* (Princeton, NJ: Princeton University Press, 1992); James Stourton, *British Embassies: Their Diplomatic and Architectural History* (London: Frances Lincoln, 2017); Fabien Bellat, *Ambassades françaises du XXe siècle* (Paris: Editions du patrimoine. Centre des monuments nationaux, 2020).
4 Jane Loeffler, *The Architecture of Diplomacy: Building America's Embassies* (New York: Princeton University Press, 2011), 260.
5 Mark Bertram, *Room for Diplomacy: Britain's Diplomatic Buildings Overseas 1800–2000* (Reading: Spire Books, 2011), 447.
6 Robert Bevan, *The Destruction of Memory. Architecture at War* (London: Reaktion Books, 2016), 91.
7 Rik Coolsaet, *België en zijn buitenlandse politiek, 1830–2015* (Leuven: Van Halewyck, 2014), 21–50; 451–67.
8 Kristine Kolrud and Marina Prusac, "Introduction: Whose Iconoclasm?" in *Iconoclasm from Antiquity to Modernity*, ed. Kristine Kolrud and Marina Prusac (Farnham: Ashgate, 2014), 1.
9 Kolrud and Prusac, "Introduction: Whose Iconoclasm?", 6–7.
10 The authors would like to thank PhD researcher Gert Huskens for directing us towards the necessary source materials and sharing our enthusiasm for destroyed Belgian legation and embassy buildings.
11 Michael J. Moser and Yeone Wei-chic Moser, *Foreigners within the Gates: The Legations at Peking* (Chicago: Serindia, 2007), 2, 11; Diplomatic Archives of Belgium (DAB) 172.III Chine 1897–1898: Les puissances en Chine, report "La Chine au point de vue de ses engagements internationaux, approx. 1898".
12 The diplomats originally had their eyes on the site of the former Imperial Summer Palace, *Yuanming Yan*, which was tragically destroyed by foreign troops during the Second Opium War. The Chinese government declined this request and suggested an alternative location near the Southern Wall. Moser, *Foreigner within the gates*, 15–16; "Boxer Uprising," MIT visualising cultures, accessed June 25, 2021, https://visualizingcultures.mit.edu/boxer_uprising_02/bx2_essay01.html.

13 Moser, *Foreigner within the Gates*, 13–16.

14 Peter Fleming, *Die Belagerung zu Peking: zur Geschichte des Boxer-Aufstandes* (Frankfurt am Main: Eichborn, 1997), 2–4.

15 It should be noted that even though Belgium was technically a neutral, small power in this time period, it instrumentalised this label in order to obtain concessions and agreements with China. As a result, its neo-imperialist presence and activities in China are far from neutral. For the local government and population, the Belgian state was just as much part of the conclave of neo-imperialist and colonialist powers that were continuously weakening the Chinese sovereignty and economy, leading up to the general unrest in China and the Boxer uprising from 1900. For more information on the Belgian activities in China, please refer to Ginette Kurgan-van Hentenryk, *Léopold II et les groupes financiers belges en Chine: la politique royale et ses prolongements (1895–1914)* (Bruxelles: Palais des Académies, 1972); Jens Vermeersch, "Het buitenlands beleid van België tegenover China, 1919–1949," *Journal of Belgian History BTNG-RBHC* 20, 3–4 (1989): 317–398.

16 Moser, *Foreigner within the Gates*, 15–16; "Boxer Uprising," MIT visualising cultures, accessed June 25, 2021, https://visualizingcultures.mit.edu/boxer_uprising_02/bx2_essay01.html.

17 Moser, *Foreigner within the Gates*, 2.

18 Chia Chen Chu, *Diplomatic Quarter in Peiping*, unpublished dissertation (Ottowa: University of Ottawa, 1944), 14.

19 DAB, 234, personnel file Comte de Noidans-Calf, correspondence between Favier and minister-resident Serruys of September 27, 1875 and between minister-resident de Noidans-Calf and minister of Foreign Affairs Frère-Orban of March 18, 1880. At first, the Belgian Ministry of Foreign Affairs pays 210 and later on 224 taëls per trimester to use the legation building, or 6500 Belgian francs per year. Because of the shortage and subsequent high real estate prices, it will be the Ministry who will pay the rent for this building. This is an exception at the time, as Belgian diplomats were supposed to find and finance their own accommodation while on mission.

20 Het Handelsblad, *Per telefoon – onze gezantschappen*, December 27, 1898, 1.

21 DAB, 108, Missions Belges en Chine, extensive correspondence between the Belgian legation and the Belgian Ministry of Foreign Affairs is conducted regarding the culprits, motives and required debt to be paid to the families of the victims.

22 As the telegraph lines were cut, it was very difficult for the Belgian Ministry of Foreign Affairs to grasp what was going on in China. Luckily for them, Cartier de Marchienne became, on his way to Europe for vacation, stranded in Shanghai and assumed the role of communicator and that of chargé d'affairs ad interim. Luce Claeys-Bouuaert, *Le Baron Emile de Cartier de Marchienne: Missions diplomatiques en Chine et aux Etats-Unis (1898–1922),* unpublished dissertation (Louvain-la-Neuve: UCL, 1977), 75–76.

23 Translation of the quote: "The walls were covered with xenophobic posters reporting the supposed wrongdoings of foreigners. The watchful crowd gathered at the crossroads to read and comment on them." Adrien de Mélotte de Lavaux, *Les derniers jours d'une légation* (Liège, Imprimeries Nationales des Militaires Mutilés et Invalides, 1925): 36.

24 The connection by train from Peking is then interrupted, but communication between Tientsin and Peking remains possible via the telegraph lines. Until 11 June, when these too are cut off. Adrien de Mélotte de Lavaux, *Les derniers jours d'une légation*, 35–40.

25 The idea of extraterritoriality and ports opened to trade also created friction, as did the foreigners who developed separate neighbourhoods with recreational facilities in for example Tientsin and Peking. In addition to the concentration of foreigners in the capital and concessions, the whole country was riven and divided not only by the fictional spheres of influence that the foreign representatives divided among themselves as a kind of abstract fictional layer added to the reality of China but also by the

railway lines, trade routes and telegraph lines that literally had the whole country in their grip. Moser, *Foreigner within the Gates*, 43–44.

26 James Hoare, *Embassies in the East: The Story of the British Embassies in Japan, China, and Korea from 1859 to the Present* (London: Routledge, 2015), 34; "Summer retreats: Fengtai, Kuling and Beidaihe," Room for Diplomacy, Mark Bertram, accessed June 25, 2021, https://roomfordiplomacy.com/beijing-5-summer-retreats/.

27 L'Indépendance Belge, *Echos et Nouvelles – Souvernirs*, January 14, 1927, 1.

28 Translation of the quote: "Until midnight, our legation remained in peace. At that moment, a group of people carrying lighted torches came out to the left into the main street. Another group advances about 100 metres towards the right. We are surrounded." de Mélotte de Lavaux, *Les derniers jours d'une légation*, 48.

29 Victor Collin, *Un reportage Belge en Extrême Orient (guerre internationale de 1900–1901)* (Antwerpen: De Cauwer, 1901), 82; de Mélotte de Lavaux, *Les derniers jours d'une légation*, 48.

30 Translation of the quote: "This move … saddens us. We feel as if we have been driven out of our national territory. Now we are just people without a fatherland, so to speak." de Mélotte de Lavaux, *Les derniers jours d'une légation*, 49–50.

31 Moser, *Foreigner Within the Gates*, 55–56.

32 Gazette de Charleroi, *Chronique du Jour – Pékin,* September 21, 1900, 1.

33 Translation of the quote:

> 21 June was a particularly sad day for the Belgians. They witnessed from afar the fire, this time irreversible, of their legation. The magnificent building of the Austrian Legation perished on the same date and by the same means. Our furniture, our clothes, our linen, a significant part of our archives, in a word almost everything we owned … was looted or burned out of hatred for the foreigners.

de Mélotte de Lavaux, *Les derniers jours d'une légation*, 60.

34 de Mélotte de Lavaux, *Les derniers jours d'une légation*, 60–61.

35 Moser, *Foreigner within the gates*, 57–59.

36 The siege and following destruction of the legation news was widely covered in the Belgian newspapers like Het Laatste Nieuws, La Meuse, Journal de Charleroi, … In Het Laatste Nieuws, updates on the legations and their possible destruction made front page news at July 4, 6, 14, 17, 22 and 7; August 1, 2, 3 and 9, 1900.

Due to the problematic communication and cut telegraph lines, it was difficult to separate trusted news sources from (deliberately) false messages meant to confuse and slow down international cooperation. At one point, some British newspapers (Daily Mail, Daily Express) reported the death of Joostens. It was only when the first telegram by Joostens arrived in Brussels, that the Chamber of Representatives and Ministry of Foreign Affairs had any certainty about his wellbeing and that of the rest of the staff. News about his survival was published triumphantly in the Belgian Newspaper on August 9 and 10, 1900. Although the news of Joostens' death eventually proved to be a mistake, the destruction of the Belgian legation was not.

Collin, *Un reportage Belge en Extrême Orient, 137;* Moser, *Foreigner Within the Gates,* 61; Parliamentary Debates of the Belgian Chamber of Representatives, session of July 24, 1900.

37 Gert Huskens and Idesbald Goddeeris, "Maurice Joostens en het Bokserprotocol: marionet op het diplomatieke theater?", Master Thesis (KU Leuven, 2016), 60, https://repository-teneo-libis-be.kuleuven.e-bronnen.be/delivery/DeliveryManager Servlet?dps_pid=IE7050145&.

38 Chia Chen Chu, *Diplomatic Quarter in Peiping*, 24.

39 Moser, *Foreigner Within the Gates*, 94–98.

40 Vingtième siècle, *Retour de Chine, Interview de M. L Merghelynck,* December 12, 1901; Moser, *Foreigner within the gates*, 86–87; Huskens and Goddeeris, "Maurice Joostens en het Bokserprotocol: marionet op het diplomatieke theater?" 104.

41 Just like the other legation, the Belgian legation would receive considerable reparations, namely 8.484.345 taels or 31.175.000 Belgian francs. This was approximately 1.9% of the total amount of indemnities required from the Chinese government; DAB 10.562 Indemnité Boxer, report on the agreed upon indemnities for (1) The Belgian State, (2) The diplomatic staff in Peking and Tientsin and (3) Belgian nationals and companies residing in China, 1901; Moser, *Foreigner within the gates*, 86, 90.

42 DAB, 234, personnel file Comte de Noidans-Calf, correspondence between Comte de Noidans-Calf and Minister of Foreign Affairs Frère-Orban on the limited size of the rooms and shortage of salons to host receptions and parties, March 26, 1880; DAB, 108.IV, complaint from minister Charles De Vinck in Peking to Minister of Foreign Affairs Favereau about the bad location, limited space and security issues of the Belgian Legation, October 9, 1898 and December 23, 1898.

43 DAB, 108.V Mouvements xénophobes – Boxers, series of correspondence between the Belgian Legation in Peking and the Belgian Ministry of Foreign Affairs concerning the reconstruction of the Legation Building and the need for soldiers and ammunition to ensure their safety.

44 Huskens and Goddeeris, "Maurice Joostens en het Bokserprotocol: marionet op het diplomatieke theater?" 103.

45 The main street of the world exhibitions were often named 'Rue des Nations', which located the national pavilions of the participating countries. They showcased what at the time was regarded typical national architecture of the participating countries, for example the Exposition Universelle 1900 in Paris, France. The comparison between these two sites of national representation has been previously also made by prof. dr. Thomas Coomans in the historical note "The Former Belgian Legation Building at Beijing: Its Origin, Meaning and Use," February 12, 2012.

46 Adam Hochschild, *King Leopold's Ghost: A Story of Greed, Terror and Heroism in Colonial Africa* (London: Pan Books, 2012), 150–66.

47 Ludo De Witte, *De moord op Lumumba: Kroniek van een aangekondigde dood* (Tielt: Kritak, 2020), 42.

48 De Witte, *De moord op Lumumba*, 205–254.

49 DAB, 18.678 P. Lumumba – Décès 1961 Manifestations – Protestations, Préliminaires, 5–7.

50 DAB, 14.152 Australie 1962 Série générale – dossier général, Réactions australiennes décès Lumumba, attachment II, newspaper clipping from *The Daily Mirror* of February 20, 1961.

51 DAB, 14.152, Réactions australiennes décès Lumumba, February 20, 1961, p. 2.

52 Peter Calvocoressi, *World Politics since 1945* (Harlow: Pearson, 2009), 767.

53 DAB, 18.678, Préliminaires, 9.

54 Randall Lesaffer, "De Opkomst en de Ontwikkeling van de Permanente Diplomatie. Diplomatieke onschendbaarheid en de Opkomst van het Moderne Volkenrecht," in *Diplomatieke Cultuur*, ed. Peter Van Kemseke (Leuven: Leuven University Press, 2000), 38.

55 United Nations, Vienna Convention on Diplomatic Relations 1961, article 22.

56 DAB, 18.678, Préliminaires, 13.

57 DAB, 18.678, Newspaper clipping from *Politika* of February 15, 1961.

58 Calvocoressi, *World Politics since 1945*, 770.

59 Pieter De Messemaeker, "Tussen Kasjmir en Congo. Belgisch-Indiase Politieke Contacten onder Nehru," in *Het Wiel van Ashoka. Belgisch-Indiase Contacten in Historisch Perspectief*, ed. Idesbald Goddeeris (Leuven: Lipsius, 2013), 210.

60 DAB, 18.678, Préliminaires, 25.

61 DAB, 13.935 Belgique-Inde 1957–1961, Télégramme 21 Dégâts à la Chancellerie, 2.

62 DAB, 14.806 Belgique-Egypte et R.A.U. 1955–1964, Incendie notre ambassade, rapport Iweins d'Eeckhoutte, 1961, 7.

63 DAB, 18.678, Préliminaires, 18.

64 DAB, 18.678, Préliminaires, 18.
65 Le Soir, *Une décision qui s'imposait. La Belgique a rompu ses relations diplomatiques avec la R.A.U*, February 26, 1961, 1.

Bibliography

Bellat, Fabien. *Ambassades françaises du XXe siècle*. Paris: Editions du patrimoine. Centre des monuments nationaux, 2020.

Bertram, Mark. *Room for Diplomacy: Britain's Diplomatic Buildings Overseas 1800–2000*. Reading: Spire Books, 2011.

Bevan, Robert. *The Destruction of Memory. Architecture at War*. London: Reaktion Books, 2016.

Calvocoressi, Peter. *World Politics since 1945*. Harlow: Pearson, 2009.

Chen Chu, Chia. *Diplomatic Quarter in Peiping*. Unpublished dissertation. Ottowa: University of Ottawa, 1944.

Claeys-Bouuaert, Luce. *Le Baron Emile de Cartier de Marchienne: Missions diplomatiques en Chine et aux Etats-Unis (1898–1922)*. Unpublished dissertation. Louvain-la-Neuve: UCL, 1977.

Collin, Victor. *Un reportage Belge en Extrême Orient (guerre internationale de 1900–1901)*. Antwerpen: De Cauwer, 1901.

Coolsaet, Rik. *België en zijn buitenlandse politiek, 1830–2015*. Leuven: Van Halewyck, 2014.

de Mélotte de Lavaux, Adrien. *Les derniers jours d'une légation*. Liège, Imprimeries Nationales des Militaires Mutilés et Invalides, 1925.

De Messemaeker, Pieter. "Tussen Kasjmir en Congo. Belgisch-Indiase Politieke Contacten onder Nehru." In *Het Wiel van Ashoka. Belgisch-Indiase Contacten in Historisch Perspectief*, edited by Idesbald Goddeeris, 197–212. Leuven: Lipsius, 2013.

De Witte, Ludo. *De moord op Lumumba: Kroniek van een aangekondigde dood*. Tielt: Kritak, 2020.

Fleming, Peter. *Die Belagerung zu Peking: zur Geschichte des Boxer-Aufstandes*. Frankfurt am Main: Eichborn, 1997.

Hoare, James. *Embassies in the East: The Story of the British Embassies in Japan, China, and Korea from 1859 to the Present*. London: Routledge, 2015.

Hochschild, Adam. *King Leopold's Ghost: A Story of Greed, Terror and Heroism in Colonial Africa*. London: Pan Books, 2012.

Huskens Gert and Idesbald Goddeeris. "Maurice Joostens en het Bokserprotocol: marionet op het diplomatieke theater?". Master thesis. KU Leuven, 2016.

Kolrud Kristine and Marina Prusac. "Introduction: Whose Iconoclasm?" In *Iconoclasm from Antiquity to Modernity*, edited by Kristine Kolrud and Marina Prusac, 1–14. Farnham: Ashgate, 2014.

Kurgan-van Hentenryk, Ginette. *Léopold II et les groupes financiers belges en Chine: la politique royale et ses prolongements (1895–1914)*. Bruxelles: Palais des Académies, 1972.

Lesaffer, Randall. "De Opkomst en de Ontwikkeling van de Permanente Diplomatie. Diplomatieke onschendbaarheid en de Opkomst van het Moderne Volkenrecht." In *Diplomatieke Cultuur*, edited by Peter Van Kemseke, 37–50. Leuven: Leuven University Press, 2000.

Loeffler, Jane. *The Architecture of Diplomacy: Building America's Embassies*. New York: Princeton University Press, 2011.

Moser, Michael J. and Yeone Wei-chic Moser. *Foreigners within the gates: the legations at Peking.* Chicago: Serindia, 2007.

Robin, Ron. *Enclaves of America: The Rhetoric of American Political Architecture Abroad 1900–1965.* Princeton: Princeton University Press, 1992.

Stourton, James. *British Embassies: Their Diplomatic and Architectural History.* London: Frances Lincoln, 2017.

Vermeersch, Jens. "Het buitenlands beleid van België tegenover China, 1919–1949." *Journal of Belgian History BTNG-RBHC* 20, 3–4 (1989): 317–398.

9

SOCIAL INFRASTRUCTURE AND DISINTEGRATION, STATECRAFT AND DEMOCRACY. MAKING AN EXAMPLE OF BROADWATER FARM ESTATE

Alfie Peacock

Introduction

The Capitol Riot in January 2021 represent one of the most globally reported 'political acts' of recent times. Yet a brief survey of Western politics (particularly the US and UK, the latter being where this chapter draws its case study) indicates that the recent shift in the Western political consciousness – and its ever-widening Overton window – represented by the Capitol Riot, was particularly significant in the few years leading up to it: the UK elections; the Covid-19 pandemic; George Floyd's murder and the subsequent riots and protests; and the actioned Brexit initiation, name just a few of the pivotal moments of the previous two years.

During this period, the awareness and recognition of 'institutional racism' in the UK has increased,[1] albeit at the same time as xenophobic and racist sentiments, attitudes, or denialism.[2] As an example: both of these binary viewpoints tend to manifest in private homes, or public bars and social spaces across nations, and of course, in cyberspace. But it is when shared views and beliefs are collectively, and publicly, expressed in an urban space that ripples and reactions form. Whether that be a diplomatic space in the case of the Capitol Riot in January 2021 in the US, or a residential complex in the case of Broadwater Farm Estate in October 1985 in the UK as examined here; governments cannot turn a blind eye to these events. Actions have reactions.

The focus of this chapter is to explore actions and reactions which surrounded the 1985 riots in North London, and partially explore how these compare more recently with the UK-wide riots of 2011 and the subsequent policy decisions thereafter. Examining the Broadwater Farm Estate (BWFE or The Farm) in a place specific, political, and social framework, this text furnishes the argument for how both protests and urban space can be malleable toys for politicians

DOI: 10.4324/9781003272076-13

and political actors. In this case particularly: a housing estate is engulfed by rioting, and in the aftermath, the spatial organisation became implicated and thus mouldable. This housing estate in particular became a testbed for alterations, by academics and politicians alike, seeking to draw determinist conclusions, or rhetorically loaded remedial works, which they hoped would extinguish the likelihood of future conflict between citizens and the state.

The riot which occurred on the premises of the estate was instigated by the death of Cynthia Jarrett, a local black mother who collapsed and died as the police raided her home, near Broadwater Farm, on October 5, 1985.[3] The events which proceeded the following day began as protests on the nearby Tottenham High Road but ended in the penning in of an angered group within the boundary of The Farm, culminating in the killing of the Metropolitan Police Officer Keith Blakelock. This event was situated in the context of hostile race relations between police and citizens, especially after decades of prejudicial employment, and housing opportunities.[4] The narratives which followed the event were predominantly simplistic assessments of an inherently complex social and political context. This eventually culminated in the removal of particular spatial configurations on the estate, as these were declared in academia and government as a causation of the troubles.

Since the public housing project's completion in 1973, governmental and bureaucratic reorganisation has perpetuated within and around the site boundary in Wood Green, Tottenham, North London. From these, new circumstances, perceptions, and classifications have formulated as the public realm, spatial premise, and political fabric of the estate have been continuously resewn over its lifespan. Housing a population between 3,000 and 4,000 people,[5] the international style orthogonal blocks were controversial in conception for ocular and spatial reasons. Now, its dominant perception is centralised by a singular event; and this, I will argue, should not be the sole object with which to evaluate and conclude upon a place and space.

It is when the riot is retold in isolation, without nuance and context, that it is opportune for some to rush to all-damning conclusions of both a place and its inhabitants. With this in mind, I will contextualise the life of BWFE without continuously mentioning its most notable tale. By exploring specifically how social infrastructure, disintegration, statecraft, and democracy all play significant roles in its existence both pre- and post-1985.

I will argue that state-led disintegration was one of the numerous reasons why residents at a certain juncture exercised political action to take agency over their surroundings four years prior to the riots of 1985. This was a partial reaction to a lack of social infrastructure, which led this same set of residents demanding the means to support themselves through self-organisation, democracy in a participative sense. The statecraft and democracy themes are intrinsically ever-present, but specifically dissected in the latter part of the essay. Statecraft and democracy firstly refer to the fluctuating relationship between the people who dwell in public housing and the governmental state, in the context of BWFE. Lastly, how does statecraft work in conjunction with research in relation to The Farm: How does the state usurp research and orchestrate change as a response to significant cultural events? Which tropes were used in the 1980s, and which are used today?

The Architectural and Planning Assessment

The estate is made up of 27 (mainly clustered and interconnected in threes) medium-rise blocks. Constructed from the Danish Larsen-Nielsen panel system concrete, The Farm also contains two identical 18-storey towers and the main Tangmere Ziggurat formed building (Figure 9.1).

The cast-in-situ (partially removed and repurposed) main deck level is raised around three meters from the ground plain. The project, once completed, instantly suffered from its poor construction practices[6] as John Boughton lays out in his extensive 'Municipal Dreams' blog. Government relied largely on the industrialised production of public housing, favouring speed over quality and precision.[7]

The speculation to develop a sports arena adjoining a lido on the land entitled Broadwater Farm began ten years before the public housing estate opened completely in 1973. Planning documents reveal newspaper clippings describing the allotments site purchase as a *"white elephant for housing"*[8] which were eventually proven correct, as nothing but housing was built on the land. The scheme's

FIGURE 9.1   3D Model of the estate looking north-east.

FIGURE 9.2 Tangmere (Ziggurat building) facing north from ground level, looking up at the entry sequence formerly accessible from the central 'shopping precinct'.

inhabitable zones are entirely raised onto a deck level due to the River Moselle running underneath the carparks on the ground floor; concreted over for fear of flooding, which has yet to occur.[9]

The primary purpose of the site became about rehousing local people whose terraced back-to-backs were deemed as slums by the Local Authority (LA).[10] The site itself was already partially owned by the LA, but it acquired the rest via Compulsory Purchase Orders (CPOs), describable perhaps as a (partially, not entirely or conclusively) violent act of statecraft. Similarly, the political will for slum clearance accelerated in post-war Britain immensely between 1955 and 1985 where 1.5 m properties were demolished.[11] If you shift your view forward to the political tentacles of today: both Government and Local Authorities are still exercising their powers to enable CPOs and demolition, in the process of urban – and particularly public housing/council estate – renewal. Similar state apparatus is being exercised in the present moment: as The Farm is in the process of CPOs and decanting, occurring on two 'structurally unsound blocks' sanctioned in 2018 on the estate.[12] A lot of the significant moments reflected upon in this paper occurred in one of those blocks, being Tangmere, conceived as the shopping precinct of the estate: but becoming its hub of social infrastructure (Figure 9.2).

Social Infrastructure and Disintegration

Julie Brown confines the definition of 'social infrastructure' and its use in an architectural and planning context: *"The definition of social infrastructure is broad and includes schools, health centres, leisure and recreation facilities, libraries, community centres, religious facilities, local shops, open spaces, transport and utility services and emergency services".*[13] Returning to the conception of The Farm (a development which as aforementioned concentrates almost 4,000 people) the architects and planners of the scheme were conscious that social infrastructure was necessary for the adequate functioning and cohesion of the place; giving provisions for amenities and services within the original scheme in Tangmere. Denis Dilon and Bryan Fanning make clear that these *"essentials for making the estate into a living community"*[14] were discarded for financial reasons. *"The shops, pub, laundrette and doctors and dentists surgery... were cut from the scheme due to cost".*[15] Schools however did eventually form on the northern edge of the estate, but these initially missed the provision for both pre-infant (<4) and post-junior (11>) facilities.

'The Broadwater Farm Inquiry Report' (post-1985 riots, released in 1986) in the chapter entitled *'The Estate and Its people'*[16] holds insights from the initial thinkers and formulators behind the scheme. One being John Murray of the LA's Building Design Service, who explained that only the shops in Tangmere were realised but: *"things are cut out, and what is cut out is thought to be the froth or the icing on the cake. And these will always be things like pubs and community centres".*[17] As the report then makes clear, the decision to install a Tenants' Association clubroom was an *ad-hoc* afterthought, approved by the council in December 1972 and installed underneath one of the walkway decks on Willan Road – below the active social deck level and away from the few amenities provided.

There were more alarming conditions than the siting of the Tenants Association building; its admissions policy discriminated residents of colour. The inquiry report goes onto explicitly state that *"Before 1981...[BWFE] offered nothing to young black people except a home. They were effectively excluded from the social club. They had no other facilities on the estate".*[18] Clasford Stirling who was pivotal in the events which proceeded the early 1980s, explains how *"I went for a membership and I was turned away".*[19] In 1981, a census shows that *"42% of the residents of BWFE had heads of households who were born in the new Commonwealth".*[20] In 1981, the (still, all-white) Tenants Association attempting to install a small Police Station on BWFE became the catalyst in trying to change relations and the dynamics of powerbroking, culminating in the creation of the Broadwater Farm Youth Association (YA) Co-op.[21]

The YA's spatial formation came about within three weeks in 1981, as described by the post-riot's inquiry document[22]; renovating the abandoned fish and chip shop situated in the Tangmere precinct with an initial grant of £300 (£1140 in today's buying power).[23] Over the following three to four years the shop outgrew capacity and with the financial backing of, in particular, the regional statecraft body the Greater London Council (GLC), and various charitable and inter-governmental organisations, funding was released to convert a derelict shop in the corner of the Tangmere precinct as the main YA hub (Figure 9.3).

In the space of five years: *"the YA set up a number of co-operative enterprises; a community laundrette, a food and vegetable co-operative, a hairdressing salon, a photographic*

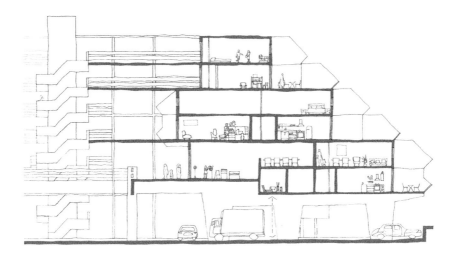

FIGURE 9.3 Tangmere Section drawing showing shop units and housing separation.

workshop, and a sewing workshop.[24] Alongside this, a day nursery and library was formed on a nearby road by the sister organisation, the Mothers Project. As laid out in the Lord Gifford Enquiry, this placed due pressure onto the Tenants Association to thereafter form a new constitution and a new committee which balanced residents' ethnicities reflectively,[25] the Tenants Association and Youth Association coexisted until restructuring occurred in the early 1990s.[26]

It is critical to contextualise the historical notion of an all-white Tenants Association into a wider cultural setting of the UK when The Farm started its life in the 1970s: the British Government and media were tactful in creating a pervasive sense that it was those who were new to arrive to Britain who were making their populations lives difficult, particularly during the commonwealth transition from British colonial power.[27] Legislative changes cemented and antagonised prejudice, as the UK government tightened and racialised its commonwealth citizenship criteria in both the 1960s and 1970s.[28] This fear mongering was espoused by the Conservative opposition leader of 1978, Margaret Thatcher: *"People are really rather afraid that this country might be swamped by people with a different culture"*.[29] Thatcher then won a large majority in the election the following year. Nevertheless, this legislative othering was not concentrated solely on the politically right: both major political parties favoured stringent restrictions on commonwealth citizen's rights,[30] despite net migration being entirely negative throughout both decades.[31]

In Lindsey German and John Rees' book *A People's History of London*, the chapter entitled *'Migrant City'* depicts a continuous battle in the post-war years between anti-fascists in solidarity with new citizens, against those riled up by the likes of Oswald Mosley and Enoch Powell.[32] Conflicts which followed a similar sequence of events throughout the 50s, 60s, and 70s, gave rise to a resentment between the London Metropolitan Police, those new communities, (which found themselves under the cosh of both policy and public opinion at the time) and a more established (but not indigenous) London community. This antagonisation went onto morph and shift continuously in terms of site and strength.

The concepts of integration are manifold, and in the case of Broadwater Farm: the scheme has to integrate with its context, the tenants with the scheme, the tenants with each other, and this triangulation was purposefully unravelling from its inception. High crime rates were a reality on the estate at the time of the police station proposal, but when an estate lacks social infrastructure, the installation of a police station would have been met with hostility when money could have instead been spent on improving socio-economic and building fabric deficiencies which were also relatively seismic. Dolly Kiffin (the initiator of the Youth Association alongside Clasford Stirling) reflected on its origins in a 1988 Channel 4 documentary called 'Scenes from The Farm' about the YA's inception:

> I don't see how they could just put in a police station, when they don't do anything for the people, have anything for the people who are growing up here, the youths here... I thought that the community should step in, and see what they could do, to help.[33]

Statecraft and Democracy

As mentioned, almost all of the YA enterprises in the 1980s were situated within the Tangmere deck-level shops; these initiatives were led by and for the residents but were predominantly facilitated by either the regional GLC or the LA; receiving their finance from the national Government. It's important to contextualise these bodies of governance, and the fact that different entities existed in parallel at polar ends of the political spectrum. So whilst the national government of the 1980s was Margaret Thatcher's Conservatives, the GLC was run by Ken Livingstone (future Labour London Mayor before Boris Johnson) and the LA overseeing Broadwater Farm was an overwhelmingly Labour majority delegation. Statecraft is and was evidently fragmented and factional: the GLC was abolished by the Thatcher government in 1986,[34] as all of their powers were delegated downwards to the local London borough authorities.

Bernie Grant was the LA leader in the early 1980s, before becoming the constituencies Member of Parliament in 1987 (featuring on a panel alongside Kiffin in the aforementioned documentary). He was hugely influential in brokering between the parliamentary government in Westminster and the LA in Haringey. He rallied (up until his death in 2000) for the rights of local citizens who were being accused of the murder of PC Blakelock, in a case embroiled in tampered evidence and subsequent false imprisonments.[35] Grant became a trusted and authoritative vessel with which to orchestrate the changes to the estate required, remaining in the communicative network of The Farm after taking up his role in Parliament.

Within The Farm's LA, Haringey Council: changes to their structures of governance developed rapidly during the 1980s. Jeremy Corbyn (Leader of the Labour Party 2015–2020) was the chair of the planning committee for Haringey until becoming an MP in 1983.[36] He employed John Murray to work in the LA architect's department, a co-founder of the New Architecture Movement.[37] In the first half of the decade, alongside fellow internal support, Murray created 'multi-disciplinary area-based design teams accountable to area committees'.[38] One of those areas being The Farm with its committee being the YA. Due to national attention following the events in October 1985, an £80m estate action programme was assigned solely for the estate's use. Alongside this, two architects were being trained specifically for the site (alongside 14 others in the borough),[39] and local labour was used for all the works on the estate, visible to TV audiences in the documentary mentioned.

The political context in the 1980s – relative to BWFE – exhibits the complexity and multifaceted nature of the state as an instrument; multiple entities making polar uses of the apparatus available to them, to either concentrate power upwards or downwards, depending on their own political stance. In the context of The Farm during the heydays of the Youth Association and John Murray's BDS team, democracy was – on certain occasions – being exercised; if by democracy, one means the participative relations between state entities and citizens as positive and productive.

John Murray believed in questioning the normative role of architects and their relationship – or lack of one – with the user,[40] and did this within the state apparatus, by manipulating the power dynamics and formula most frequented in these scenarios. However, as the Youth Association and BDS wound down its operations in the early 1990s; the material, spatial, and redemptive output of the projects on BWFE thereafter could be attributed to a series of design parameters which had already pervasively moved from academia into government departments, and 'beyond the control' of those most directly involved.

Utopia on Trial and Secured By Design (SBD)

Jeremy Till alludes to this in an essay entitled '*Architecture of the impure community*', where he discusses a stylistic and socially distinct typology which arose in the late 1980s and early 1990s in the UK: 'community architecture'. Understandably Till is sceptical towards this generic and reductively named typology. A book released in 1987 called *Community Architecture: How People Are Creating Their Own Environment* by Nick Wates and Charles Knevitt is the target of Till's hostility, in particular its supposedly apolitical foundations and subsequent championing by Prince Charles (it seems that the movement centred around a particular RIBA president at the time, and an unstatesmanlike quote from the Prince whilst discussing the hyperbolic notion of 'no-go urban areas').[41] Till describes 'community architecture' to be seen as the saviour of social malaise; antidotally nullifying those social issues which require, not long-term investment and social empowerment, but "*suburban form*"[42]: beige brick buildings, isolated from their context.

This cynical branding was undoubtedly easy to apply to the conditions of Broadwater Farm, mainly due to the fact that organisations such as the YA were attempting to infrastructurally support their community six years before the Wates and Knevitts book was released. Not all of Till's critique applies so neatly to The Farm, however, due to the particular conditions in the LA and the YA at the time. Till explains the background to this movement:

> the political climate of the 1980s made a retreat into the purified idea of community understandable… Where the disempowering of local government cut off what could have been the only source of funding for the establishment of communities in the real, and not the ideal, sense of the word.[43]

The only reason that this doesn't entirely apply to BWFE was due to the post riots funding and the social infrastructure that emerged from 1981. Working within such an unsupportive government framework was hard fought for by the political actors mentioned, in national, regional, and local frameworks.

Till then references the estate in question:

> There is something obscene about Wates & Knevitt's use of Broadwater Farm as an architectural nemesis and the subsequent redemptive status of community architecture. Their argument is one of architectural determinism inasmuch as the spatial structure of a housing estate is seen as the prime factor in causing social unrest… To promote, say balcony access over chronic unemployment as the cause for social unrest is symptomatic of a determinist approach to architecture in which the built form is argued to have a direct causal effect on social behaviour.[44]

This determinist approach which Till alludes to was part of an emerging architectural, geographical, and social zeitgeist at the time which moved its way from academia into the Thatcher government, and then funnelled back down into local government accordingly. The approach was determinist in the sense that social policy was not to be associated with the malaise felt by people with regard to their circumstance; instead, it was primarily a spatial and architectural fault, and the fault of post-war council estates in particular.

This zeitgeist was initiated across the Atlantic, with Till mentioning Oscar Newman's Defensible Space theory[45] as central to the idea of 'community architecture'. Newman theorised a process of public to private spatial reconfiguration as a remedy for crime in urban areas, using modernist mass housing as a piñata in his work in 1972.[46] It took over a decade to cement itself in the UK, in the year 1985, being a particularly eventful one for The Farm: in February Princess Diana visited,[47] the riots occurred in October; and in-between these two notable moments; Alice Coleman's 'Utopia on Trial'[48] was released. Oscar Newman's work 13 years previous gave her similar study the referential weight to implement it in a British context.

The book's quantitative and deterministic research was initially funded by a private foundation, but three years after its release, plus a half-hour meeting with the PM in 1988,[49] Coleman was swung into a government department with a £50m budget in order to test her ideas of crime and its links in public housing. They were unfinished and scrapped by the time Thatcher's grip on power slipped two years later, but nevertheless, the legislative legacy was secured. The ideas of Coleman, despite their criticism,[50] spread into the vacuum of policy makers and architect's design guides today, causing indirect effects on The Farm's subsequent redevelopments post-riots.

These redevelopments centred around the removal of The Farm's walkways, and alongside the conversion of the Tangmere shopping precinct; shops were converted into flats as the deck levels are almost all but removed or refashioned into balconies (Figures 9.4 and 9.5).

'The Enterprise Centre' (one of the community architecture projects fitting Tills description) is infilled underneath the last relic of the walkways, but never surmounted to the achievements of its predecessor's co-op formations, despite its comparatively more robust appearance. The Centre received huge support initially, but with scarce funding over the last two decades; the manager position being made redundant to a voluntary role[51]; alongside empty shops and a poor relationship with the LA has led to it potentially facing demolition, alongside the Tangmere and Northolt blocks.

FIGURE 9.4 The Tangmere precinct in 2019. Shop units were converted to flats. They have since been decanted and boarded up as demolition approaches.

FIGURE 9.5 The Enterprise Centre in 2019. Infilled under the moss-filled walkway relic.

The removal of the walkways and subsequent privatisation of space on The Farm was not in direct reference to Alice Coleman's seminal work, but there proved to be a subliminal linkage. *Utopia On Trial* focused on other estates of the same spatial features, and similar social deprivation and crime statistics, made – at the time – the association a tacit one. Coleman never mentioned The Farm directly in her thesis, and perhaps that fact directly shows how insidious this thesis then became, alongside her ideological companions beforehand. There were more direct authoritative criticisms: the Metropolitan Police claimed, even before the riot, that the estate was unpoliceable[52] due to the territorial usage of the walkways (exhibited and well documented particularly on the night of 6 October 1985).

Alongside the desocialisation of space in this (and numerous other) social housing estate(s) was a series of securitisations. The grounding process meant that BWFE blocks were no longer accessible from the now non-existent deck level, therefore concierge units were infilled into the stair cores of most blocks, with a manned security desk alongside it.

All social infrastructure additions were seen as separate and formally and stylistically distinctive to their modernist counterparts (Figure 9.6).

Till discusses these spatial reconfigurations thereafter as one which should induce sociability, not inhibit it. "*If community architecture genuinely embodied a community one would expect that it would result in a radical spatial reconfiguration, in particular that of the relationship of the public realm to the private*".[53] It is suggestable that this was the case for The Farm, but just not in the direction which he sees as favourable, that is, the minimisation of collective social space (Figure 9.7).

The spatially vast walkways were undoubtedly unloved prior to their removal, but the reversal that they were a reason for crime, as opposed to the backdrop for

FIGURE 9.6 A view towards Tangmere showing a new entrance on ground level. The walkways once spanned and connected the housing from above.

crime, is part of a pervasive discourse; one which has mutated further in today's political climate.

An outsourcing occurred in relation to the legacy of Alice Coleman's work: its mandatory impact of shaping the production of space in Britain today within the planning process of all new developments nationwide. Anna Minton in her essay *'The Paradox of Safety and Fear'* details how this has progressed since its statecraft debut at the end of the Thatcher tenure:

> Heavily promoted by geographer Alice Coleman… 'defensible space' paved the way for Secured by Design… The government-backed policy started life in 1989 and led to police officers being trained as crime prevention design advisors… describing itself as the 'official UK Police flagship initiative combining the principles of designing out crime with physical security', Secured by Design is now an independent private company funded by 480 companies selling security products that meet its standards, which are today a condition of planning permission on all new development in the UK and in particular for housing, schools and public buildings.[54]

The oversight of these principles through swathes of anonymous private companies, and their ensuing valorisation of legislative output, is telling of the complexity which allows these schemes to go about their business unscrutinised. The overarching aim remains to ensure that spatial 'safety' (but in reality – non-communal means of space) is a prerequisite to any realised building project. Some of the advice can seem rather common sensical, but it encompasses a fear-driven biased approach to the production of space, which sees crime (and

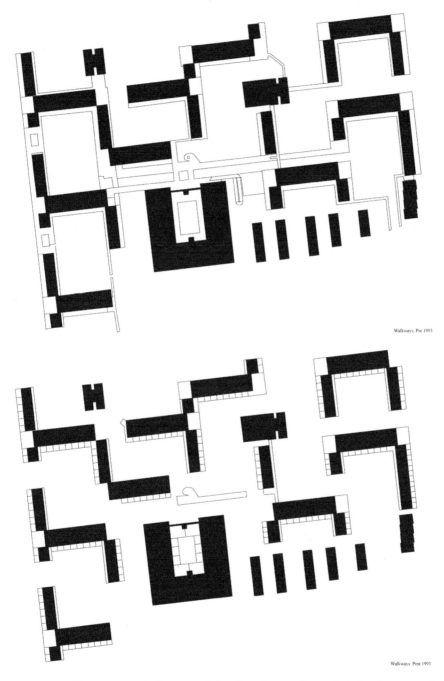

Walkways. Pre 1993

Walkways. Post 1993

FIGURE 9.7 Figure-ground diagram of the Broadwater Farm deck level, pre- and post-spatial reconfigurations.

thus social deprivation) as something which architects have the power to simply 'design out'.

2011 London Riots

During the closing segment of this chapter, it is a belated point in which to mention the more recent and much larger 2011 London riots. The relation to The Farm in particular is because Mark Duggan was a resident at points of his life, and this has since led to subsequent misinformation from legislative influencers. This event was initiated by depressing similarities to the one occurring 36 years previous, but the response thereafter was of a vastly different legislative ilk. Beginning on August 4, 2011, Mark Duggan was shot and killed by police on Ferry Lane, Tottenham.[55] The accounts of what happened that day have been told countless times, and from varying standpoints. The court case which eventually followed and attempted to bring clarity to the sequence of events proved mixed and contradictory: despite the police claiming Duggan was armed 'forensic evidence did not support that, and other expert evidence'[56] believes that to be incorrect.

Much like the events which occurred in 1985, Tottenham High Road was once again the platform for protests the following day, before turning violent as the evening progressed. Due to new means of digital connectivity and the 24-hour news cycle, over the ensuing three days, riots were mirrored all across the country. It can be briefly speculated that what followed nationwide was not a coherent and reactionary response to the killing of Mark Duggan, nor entirely a reaction towards the relationship between police and ethnic minorities in Britain. Although it can be said with some clarity that the protests in Tottenham alone which occurred the following day were, and what developed from that does not coexist with the initial anger.

The 2011 riots have since been used to increase the fuel for the legitimisation of scorn towards council estates more widely, well documented by Tom Slater in his paper *"The Invention of the 'Sink Estate': Consequential Categorization and the UK Housing Crisis"*. Slater dissects the accuracy of a series of think tank publications by 'The Policy Exchange', alongside its questionable *"claims of independence… this 'educational charity' was founded by three Conservative MPs"*.[57] Slater details the farfetched discourse of their publications relating to housing provision under similar criticisms which Alice Coleman faced 25 years previous, of *"environmental determinism, it is a reversal of causation"*.[58] The tropes have changed since Coleman; however, the writers of these publications discard the empirical weight of case studies and opt for 'baseline' assertions instead.[59]

In relation to The Farm those baseline assertions become part of an ideological assault to generate reclassifications and amnesia. Slater is keen to dispel their myths and expose the perverse construction of them. *"The Estate We're In: Lessons From the Front Line, written by crime journalist Gavin Knight, author of a 'non-fiction' book entitled Hood Rat"*.[60] A report from 2014, which features this shockingly poorly researched excerpt: *"Let us state the obvious: the [2011 England] riots did not start in a street of Georgian houses... The riots started on a social housing estate – Broadwater Farm Estate in Tottenham, to be exact"*.[61] As Slater makes clear, no rioting occurred on the premises of BWFE in 2011. If this was journalistic incompetence then it could be forgiven for its inconsequential outcomes, but this is the work of a Think Tank which feeds prejudices and misinformation to government administration.

In 2016, Cameron constructed (with the help of the Think Tank operators) his legislative remedial work: in the form of '100 sink estates' to be regenerated, with The Farm being within that list.[62] The legislative denigration is clear, as Slater mentions: *"the 2016 Housing and Planning Act in England and Wales, which allows social housing estates to be reclassified as 'brownfield sites' – a category normally reserved for contaminated ex-industrial land"*.[63] Since Cameron's resignation in June 2016, the policy has not been pursued in full; although the process of reducing, removing, and discarding council estates and social tenancies is still a chronic issue in the UK.

The complex landscape of estate regeneration still encompasses The Farm today, and it is not solely an operation undertaken by the governing Conservative party; many Labour Local Authorities and previous Labour administrations have discriminated against citizens' rights to either keep their council homes, or obtain another in their area.[64] This is well covered by writers such as Anna Minton, David Madden, and Peter Marcuse to name a few. It seems as though building security provision, and not the security of tenure, has developed into one of the priorities of housing production.

Conclusion

Broadwater Farm Estate, whether from a left or right-wing perspective, has always been a referential source with which to make an example or political point of, and there are at least four in this paper: the need for social infrastructure as a prerequisite to any housing project, the state-led disintegrative effects which then reverberate on the ground, the fluctuating ideology of statecraft and the simultaneous exercises in democracy.

The different political response by both Government and LA in the aftermath of both 1985 and 2011 riots speaks volumes about in which direction our political discourse has accelerated towards. This is not to suggest that all political actors in the 1980s were favourable of a holistic approach to The Farm's future, but enough active and resonating voices were. It would also be naive to suggest that the remedial works which followed the Youth Association and BDS collaboration came without compromise, on ethos, budgets, management, and quality. Similarly no doubt, to the compromises made in the 1960s when BWFE was planned and procured.

The state apparatus always chooses to act as either facilitator, paternalist, or violent actor, and sometimes all three coexist at once. The political actors under the state umbrella all hold personal autonomy, but deeper legislative frameworks dictate the fluidity of how they can act within that system. Housing turnover and regenerative processes cannot, in my opinion, solve crime or destitution as Coleman, Newman, and now the Policy Exchange would quantitively state. Nor will it work for The Farm, as it will only move that discontent into privacy, or into the next town or city. The positive aspects of what occurred on BWFE were always cut short, it takes long-term planning and funding to be able to provide genuine provision, and when actors pass and move on, this all too often abruptly ends.

Broadwater Farm sits in a symbolic duality: on one hand, an example of what can be achieved when people are funded to self-organise, and on another, a physical representation of the social and political disintegration from national government, of either red or blue. As much as social infrastructure can provide resilience for housing estates, it is futile without long-term localised management and maintenance programmes; these are the foundations.

Notes

1 Tony Sewell, "The Report of the Commission on Race and Ethnic Disparities," *GOV. UK*, accessed 16 October 2021, https://www.gov.uk/government/publications/the-report-of-the-commission-on-race-and-ethnic-disparities.

2 Ben Quinn and Nazia Parveen, "Historian David Olusoga Joins Academic Criticism of No 10's Race Report," *The Guardian*, 2 April 2021, sec. World news, accessed 16 October 2021, https://www.theguardian.com/world/2021/apr/02/historian-and-hundreds-of-academics-attack-no-10s-race-report.

3 Gareth Parry, John Ezard, and Andrew Rawnsley, "Policeman Killed in Riot," *The Guardian*, 7 October 1985, sec. UK news. accessed 16 October 2021, https://www.theguardian.com/uk/1985/oct/07/ukcrime.garethparry.

4 Lindsey German and John Rees, *A People's History of London* (London: Verso Books, 2012). 246.

5 "West Green E00010470 - UK Census Data 2011." Unknown Services, Good Stuff IT, accessed 31 October 2019, http://www.ukcensusdata.com/west-green-e00010470.

6 John Boughton. "The Broadwater Farm Estate, Tottenham, Part I: From 'Holiday Camp' to 'Dumping Ground'?" Municipal Dreams (blog), 7 November 2017, accessed 31 October 2019, https://municipaldreams.wordpress.com/2017/11/07/broadwater_farm_part_i/.

7 Richard Nelsson, "The Collapse of Ronan Point, May 1968 - in Pictures." *The Guardian*, 16 May 2018, accessed 31 October 2019, https://www.theguardian.com/society/-from-the-archive-blog/gallery/2018/may/16/ronan-point-tower-collapse-may-1968.

8 London Borough of Haringey, "Online Planning Applications." Last modified 5 April 2005, accessed 31 October 2019, http://www.planningservices.haringey.gov.uk/portal/servlets/ApplicationSearchServlet?PKID=71383.

9 Paul Talling, "London's Lost Rivers - River Moselle (Aka Moselle Brook)," London's Lost Rivers - Book and Walking Tours by Paul Talling, accessed 17 October 2019, https://www.londonslostrivers.com/river-moselle.html.

10 Boughton, 'The Broadwater Farm Estate, Tottenham, Part I'.

11 Stuart Lowe, "The Impact of Post-War Slum Clearance in the UK." Social Work, University of York, accessed 11 November 2019, https://www.york.ac.uk/spsw/news-and-events/news/2012/breaking-up-communities/.

12 Unknown BBC, "Broadwater Farm Estate Tower Blocks at Risk of Collapse," *BBC News*, 21 June 2018, sec. London, accessed 31 October 2019, https://www.bbc.com/news/uk-england-london-44566230.

13 Julie Brown and Austin Barber, "Social Infrastructure and Sustainable Urban Communities." *Proceedings of the Institution of Civil Engineers - Engineering Sustainability* 165, no. 1 (March 2012), 100. https://doi.org/10.1680/ensu.2012.165.1.99.

14 Denis Dillon and Bryan Fanning, *Lessons for the Big Society: Planning, Regeneration and the Politics of Community Participation* (London: Routledge, 2016), 1.

15 Dillon and Fanning, 2.

16 Tony Gifford, *The Broadwater Farm Inquiry: Report of the Independent Inquiry Into Disturbances of October 1985 at the Broadwater Farm Estate, Tottenham, Chaired by Lord Gifford* (London: Karia Press, 1986), 14.

17 Gifford, 16.

18 Gifford, 24.

19 Gifford, 23.

20 Gifford, 22.

21 Gifford, 24.

22 Gifford, 25.

23 "£300 in 1981 → 2019 | UK Inflation Calculator," Unknown, accessed 13 November 2019, http://www.in2013dollars.com/uk/inflation/1981?amount=300.

24 Gifford, *The Broadwater Farm Enquiry*, 29.

25 Gifford, 29.

26 Peter Antwi, "The Active Community, Broadwater Farm Estate (BWFE), London." PDF Regenerate-uk.org 7_london (28 February 2008), accessed 13 November 2019, https://web.archive.org/web/20080228054558/http://www.regenerate-uk.org/downloads/7_london.pdf.

27 Maya Goodfellow, *Hostile Environment: How Immigrants Become the Scapegoats* (London: Verso Books, 2019), 87.

28 Goodfellow, 87.

29 Unknown, *Corporate Watch, UK Border Regime: A Critical Guide* (Place of publication not identified: Corporate Watch, 2018). 20.

30 Goodfellow, *Hostile Environment*, 87.

31 Long-Term International Migrants, UK - Office for National Statistics," GOV.UK, accessed 8 December 2019, https://www.ons.gov.uk/peoplepopulationandcommunity/populationandmigration/internationalmigration/bulletins/longterminternationalmigrantsuk/2017.

32 German and Rees, *A Peoples History*, 244.

33 Melissa Llewelyn-Davies, Broadwater Farm Estate, London, UK. "Scenes from the Farm," Allegra Film for Channel 4, 1988, 46 mins. https://www.youtube.com/watch?v=F7bcYu6CODI.

34 Esther Webber, "The Rise and Fall of the GLC." *BBC News*, 31 March 2016, sec. London, accessed 8 December 2019, https://www.bbc.com/news/uk-england-london-35716693.

35 David Rose, "David Rose Meets Winston Silcott." *The Observer*, 18 January 2004, sec. Politics, accessed 8 December 2019, https://www.theguardian.com/politics/2004/jan/18/ukcrime.race.

36 John Murray, Concrete Action "Interview. Concrete Action and Architectural Workers, John Murray – co-arch-ive," Audio Recording/Transcription, November 2017, accessed 8 December 2019, https://co-arch-ive.net/interviews/john-murray/.

37 "Broadwater Farm Building Design Services," London Borough of Haringey, accessed 6 November 2019, https://www.haringey.gov.uk/sites/haringeygovuk/files/broadwater_farm_bulding_design_team.pdf.

38 London Borough of Haringey, "Broadwater Farm Building Design Services."

39 Murray and Concrete Action, "Interview."

40 Tatijana Schneider and Jeremy Till, "Spatial Agency: New Architecture Movement." Catalogue, Spatial Agency, accessed 6 November 2019, https://www.spatialagency.net/database/new.architecture.movement.nam.

41 Jonathan Hill and Jeremy Till, "Architecture of the Impure Community," in *Occupying Architecture: Between the Architect and the User* (London: Routledge, 2005), 67.

42 Hill and Till, 65.
43 Hill and Till, 64.
44 Hill and Till, 66.
45 Oscar Newman, *Creating Defensible Space* (US: DIANE Publishing, 1996) n.d., 126.
46 Anna Minton. "The Paradox of Safety and Fear: Security in Public Space," *Architectural Design* 88, no. 3. (2018): 84–91, 87. https://doi.org/10.1002/ad.2305.
47 "Broadwater Farm Exhibition," Odin Biddulph, accessed 14 November 2019, http://www.broadwaterfarm.info/2010/08/blog-post.html.
48 Alice Coleman, and King's College (University of London) Design Disadvantagement Team, *Utopia on Trial: Vision and Reality in Planned Housing* (London: H. Shipman, 1985).
49 Jane M. Jacobs and Loretta Lees. "Defensible Space on the Move: Revisiting the Urban Geography of Alice Coleman: Defensible Space and the Urban Geography of Alice Coleman," *International Journal of Urban and Regional Research* 37, no. 5 (September 2013): 1559–1583, https://doi.org/10.1111/1468-2427.12047.
50 Jacobs and Lees, "Defensible Space on the Move."
51 Biddulph, "Broadwater Farm Exhibition."
52 Elizabeth Hopkirk, "Design of Broadwater Farm Estate Criticised at Old Bailey." *Building Design*, accessed 25 November 2019, https://www.bdonline.co.uk/design-of-broadwater-farm-estate-criticised-at-old-bailey/5067091.article.
53 Hill and Till, "Architecture of the Impure Community," 65.
54 Minton, "The Paradox of Safety and Fear," 87.
55 "England Riots: Maps and Timeline," *BBC News*, 15 August 2011, accessed 25 November 2019, www.bbc.co.uk/news/uk-14436499.
56 Vikram Dodd, "Mark Duggan's Death: Two Shots Fired and Two Conflicting Stories," *The Guardian*, 8 January 2014, sec. UK news, accessed 25 November 2019, https://www.theguardian.com/uk-news/2014/jan/08/mark-duggan-death-london-riots.
57 Tom Slater, "The Invention of the 'Sink Estate': Consequential Categorisation and the UK Housing Crisis," *The Sociological Review*, 66, no. 4 (1 July 2018): 877–897, 855. https://doi.org/10.1177/0038026118777451.
58 Slater, 886.
59 Slater, 886.
60 Slater, 889.
61 Slater, 889.
62 David Cameron, "Estate Regeneration: Article by David Cameron," GOV.UK, accessed 31 October 2019, https://www.gov.uk/government/speeches/estate-regeneration-article-by-david-cameron.
63 Slater. "The Invention of the Sink Estate," 891.
64 Geraldine Dening and Simon Elmer, "Mapping London's Estate Regeneration Programme," Architects for Social Housing (ASH), 10 September 2017, Accessed 11 November 2019, https://architectsforsocialhousing.co.uk/2017/09/10/mapping-londons-estate-regeneration-programme/.

Bibliography

Antwi, Peter. 'The Active Community, Broadwater Farm Estate (BWFE), London'. PDF. Regenerate-uk.org/downloads/7_london.pdf, 28 February 2008. https://web.archive.org/web/20080228054558/http://www.regenerate-uk.org/downloads/7_london.pdf.

Beckett, Andy. 'The Right to Buy: The Housing Crisis That Thatcher Built'. *The Guardian*, 26 August 2015, sec. Society. https://www.theguardian.com/society/2015/aug/26/right-to-buy-margaret-thatcher-david-cameron-housing-crisis.

Biddulph, Odin. 'Broadwater Farm Exhibition'. Accessed 14 November 2019. http://www.broadwaterfarm.info/2010/08/blog-post.html.

Boughton, John. 'The Broadwater Farm Estate, Tottenham, Part I: From "Holiday Camp" to "Dumping Ground"?' *Municipal Dreams* (blog), 7 November 2017. https://municipaldreams.wordpress.com/2017/11/07/broadwater_farm_part_i/.

'Broadwater Farm Estate Tower Blocks at Risk of Collapse'. *BBC News*, 21 June 2018, sec. London. https://www.bbc.com/news/uk-england-london-44566230.

Brown, Julie, and Austin Barber. 'Social Infrastructure and Sustainable Urban Communities'. *Proceedings of the Institution of Civil Engineers - Engineering Sustainability* 165, no. 1 (March 2012): 100. https://doi.org/10.1680/ensu.2012.165.1.99.

Cameron, David. 'Estate Regeneration: Article by David Cameron'. GOV.UK. Accessed 31 October 2019. https://www.gov.uk/government/speeches/estate-regeneration-article-by-david-cameron.

Coleman, Alice, and King's College (University of London) Design Disadvantagement Team. *Utopia on Trial: Vision and Reality in Planned Housing.* H. Shipman, 1985.

Dening, Geraldine, and Simon Elmer. Architects for Social Housing (ASH). 'Mapping London's Estate Regeneration Programme', 10 September 2017. https://architectsforsocialhousing.co.uk/2017/09/10/mapping-londons-estate-regeneration-programme/.

Dillon, Denis, and Bryan Fanning. *Lessons for the Big Society: Planning, Regeneration and the Politics of Community Participation.* Routledge, 2016.

Dodd, Vikram. 'Mark Duggan's Death: Two Shots Fired and Two Conflicting Stories'. *The Guardian*, 8 January 2014, sec. UK news. https://www.theguardian.com/uk-news/2014/jan/08/mark-duggan-death-london-riots.

German, Lindsey, and John Rees. *A People's History of London.* Verso Books, 2012.

Gifford, Tony. *The Broadwater Farm Inquiry: Report of the Independent Inquiry Into Disturbances of October 1985 at the Broadwater Farm Estate, Tottenham, Chaired by Lord Gifford.* Karia Press, 1986.

Goodfellow, Maya. *Hostile Environment: How Immigrants Become the Scapegoats.* Verso Books, 2019.

GOV.UK. 'The Report of the Commission on Race and Ethnic Disparities'. Accessed 16 October 2021. https://www.gov.uk/government/publications/the-report-of-the-commission-on-race-and-ethnic-disparities.

Hill, Jonathan, and Jeremy Till. *Occupying Architecture: Between the Architect and the User.* Routledge, 2005.

Hopkirk, Elizabeth. 'Design of Broadwater Farm Estate Criticised at Old Bailey'. Building Design. Accessed 25 November 2019. https://www.bdonline.co.uk/design-of-broadwater-farm-estate-criticised-at-old-bailey/5067091.article.

Jacobs, Jane M., and Loretta Lees. 'Defensible Space on the Move: Revisiting the Urban Geography of Alice Coleman: Defensible Space and the Urban Geography of Alice Coleman'. *International Journal of Urban and Regional Research* 37, no. 5 (September 2013): 1559–83. https://doi.org/10.1111/1468-2427.12047.

Llewelyn-Davies, Melissa. 'Scenes from the Farm'. Allegra Film for Channel 4, 1988. https://www.youtube.com/watch?v=F7bcYu6CODI.

London's Lost Rivers - Book and Walking Tours by Paul Talling. 'London's Lost Rivers - River Moselle (Aka Moselle Brook)'. Accessed 17 October 2021. https://www.londonslostrivers.com/river-moselle.html.

Lowe, Stuart, Social Work University of York, Heslington, York, and Yo10 5dd. 'The Impact of Post-War Slum Clearance in the UK'. University of York. Accessed 11 November 2019. https://www.york.ac.uk/spsw/news-and-events/news/2012/breaking-up-communities/.

Minton, Anna. 'The Paradox of Safety and Fear: Security in Public Space'. *Architectural Design* 88, no. 3 (2018): 84–91. https://doi.org/10.1002/ad.2305.

Murray, John. Concrete Action and Architectural Workers. John Murray – co-arch-ive. Audio Recording / Transcription, November 2017. https://co-arch-ive.net/interviews/john-murray/.

Nelsson, Richard. 'The Collapse of Ronan Point, May 1968- in Pictures'. *The Guardian*, 16 May 2018, sec. Society. https://www.theguardian.com/society/from-the-archive-blog/gallery/2018/may/16/ronan-point-tower-collapse-may-1968.

Newman, Oscar. 'Creating Defensible Space', n.d., 126.

Parry, Gareth, John Ezard, and Andrew Rawnsley. 'Policeman Killed in Riot'. *The Guardian*, 7 October 1985, sec. UK news. https://www.theguardian.com/uk/1985/oct/07/ukcrime.garethparry.

Quinn, Ben, and Nazia Parveen. 'Historian David Olusoga Joins Academic Criticism of No 10's Race Report'. *The Guardian*, 2 April 2021, sec. World news. https://www.theguardian.com/world/2021/apr/02/historian-and-hundreds-of-academics-attack-no-10s-race-report.

Rose, David. 'David Rose Meets Winston Silcott'. *The Observer*, 18 January 2004, sec. Politics. https://www.theguardian.com/politics/2004/jan/18/ukcrime.race.

Schneider, Tatjana, and Jeremy Till. 'Spatial Agency: New Architecture Movement'. Catalogue. Spatial Agency. Accessed 6 November 2019. https://www.spatialagency.net/database/new.architecture.movement.nam.

Slater, Tom. 'The Invention of the "Sink Estate": Consequential Categorisation and the UK Housing Crisis'. *The Sociological Review* 66, no. 4 (1 July 2018): 877–97. https://doi.org/10.1177/0038026118777451.

Spicker, Paul. 'Poverty and Depressed Estates: A Critique of Utopia on Trial'. *Housing Studies* 2, no. 4 (1 October 1987): 283–92. https://doi.org/10.1080/02673038708720608.

Unknown. CORPORATE WATCH. *UK BORDER REGIME: A Critical Guide*. Place of publication not identified: CORPORATE WATCH, 2018.

Unknown. 'England Riots: Maps and Timeline'. *BBC News*, 15 August 2011. //www.bbc.co.uk/news/uk-14436499.

Unknown, London Borough of Haringey. 'Broadwater Farm Building Design Services'. Accessed 6 November 2019. https://www.haringey.gov.uk/sites/haringeygovuk/files/broadwater_farm_bulding_design_team.pdf.

Unknown. London Borough of Haringey, I. T. S. 'Online Planning Applications: Haringey Council', 5 April 2005. http://www.planningservices.haringey.gov.uk/portal/servlets/ApplicationSearchServlet?PKID=71383.

Unknown. '£300 in 1981 → 2019 | UK Inflation Calculator'. Accessed 13 November 2019. http://www.in2013dollars.com/uk/inflation/1981?amount=300.

Unknown, ONS. 'Long-Term International Migrants, UK - Office for National Statistics'. Accessed 8 December 2019. https://www.ons.gov.uk/peoplepopulationandcommunity/populationandmigration/internationalmigration/bulletins/longterminternationalmigrantsuk/2017.

Unknown. Services, Good Stuff IT. 'West Green E00010470- UK Census Data 2011'. UK Census Data. Accessed 31 October 2019. http://www.ukcensusdata.com/west-green-e00010470.

Webber, Esther. 'The Rise and Fall of the GLC'. *BBC News*, 31 March 2016, sec. London. https://www.bbc.com/news/uk-england-london-35716693.

10

GERMANIA-ON-THAMES

Murray Fraser

Prologue

The Capitol Riot on January 6, 2021 was an attempted coup that singled out the emblem of US democracy for an unelected seizure of power. Recordings depict an intense, jujitsu-like grapple over the building's entrances and symbolic staterooms.[1] On one side the defending police, on the other a populist, ultra-nationalist mob incited by former-US President Donald Trump. Part-planned, part-anarchic, the riot used a crucial spatial strategy for insurrectionists, the linear march to/invasion of a provocative location. In the White House, Trump watched television coverage to judge whether the Capitol attack was successful, utilising social media to influence events. Earlier, he had deployed the second crucial spatial strategy, a collective oratorical rally in Washington DC's Mall. As reincarnation of an ancient mode of human assembly – modernised by combining built form, embodied event and mediated representation – the epitome of rallies is usually cited as Nazi Germany, specifically at Nuremberg. However, this chapter looks to another city rarely associated with populist ultra-nationalism – London, Britain's capital – to see how the political rally was reshaped in the 1930s as a spatial expression of Fascist ideology (Figure 10.1).

The chapter focusses on two rallies by the British Union of Fascists (BUF) in rival exhibition centres in west London: the first on June 7, 1934 at Olympia, and the second on July 16, 1939 in Earl's Court. In showing how the BUF's tactics under Sir Oswald Ernald Mosley – an aristocrat known privately as "Tom" and publicly as a would-be demagogue styling himself "The Leader"[2] – changed architecturally, links are made to Fascism in Italy and Germany, and to innovations in US corporate capitalism which were absorbed into the framework of the declining British Empire. Elsewhere in the 1930s, with his health deteriorating in a Fascist jail, Antonio Gramsci scrutinised the workings of cultural hegemonic

DOI: 10.4324/9781003272076-14

FIGURE 10.1 Sir Oswald Mosley addressing the July 1939 British Union rally in Earl's Court.

struggle.[3] Through his analysis of why Italy had accepted Benito Mussolini, Gramsci argued that citizens needed to engage in a continual "War of Position" which involved every facet of life under (state-enforced) capitalism. He used a spatialised military metaphor to portray this War of Position as a gradualist counter-hegemonic attack on the trenches and ramparts of dominant ideology.

While debates about architectural ideology tend usually to suggest a dilemma for left-wing architects working within capitalism,[4] with Gramsci being an oft-quoted theoretical touchstone, it can be argued that 1930s British Fascists too were engaged in their own War of Position over architectural aesthetics and building technology. Gernot Böhme defines the latter not as individual apparatuses but as a dispersed, interconnected network he calls "technification." Within the War of Position, technification is essentially disruptive. Böhme points out, for instance, the frequent struggle over how technological innovations are implemented: "Once installed, they function independently of their creators' intentions. New users can devise entirely new usages."[5] Böhme argues that due to the uncontrollable, invasive impact of technification, architecture becomes about the "aesthetics of atmospheres" that it creates both externally (socio-urbanistically) and internally (socio-psychologically).[6] Building exteriors transmit symbolic messages – a process extended during the interwar period by artificially illuminated night-time façades – while the emotive atmospheres of interior spaces, similarly technologically enhanced, merge visual/objective and spatial/subjective feelings through bodily sensory experience. As Walter Benjamin wrote when observing that architecture is experienced collectively by people in states of distraction: "Buildings are received in a twofold manner: by use and by perception. Or better: tactilely and optically."[7] It is a view echoed in current Deleuzian theories of "architectural affect" within the capitalist processes of subjectification.[8]

What, then, were the links between architecture and 1930s British Fascism? Roger Griffin has led a historiographical switch from focussing on Fascist organisations to a broader comparison of populist ultra-nationalism across interwar Europe. This means treating Fascism more as an interlocked, polarising ideology rather than as individual movements, thereby studying the influences of Italy/Germany/Spain on adjacent authoritarian regimes or with countries that adhered to parliamentary democracy like Britain. For this comparative account, Griffin calls for the inclusion of architectural history:

> much would be gained by examining on a nation-by-nation basis any architectural plans or projects for urban renewal conceived in fascist movements that never succeeded in seizing power, and in particular, any cases of modernist architects being drawn even marginally into the orbit of fascism.[9]

Furthermore, as Thomas Linehan observes, there is a need to spatialise British Fascism.[10] This chapter addresses both points, and it does so less by looking at architects' creative authorship and more by examining the adaptation – however temporarily – of buildings as sites of Lefebvrian spatial contestation.[11]

The chapter hence traces architecture's role in transformations in Fascist tactics between Olympia and Earl's Court, both venues built for business rather than politics. Without power, there was never likely to be a British Fascist building programme like in Mussolini's Italy or Hitler's Germany. Thus, in comparative terms, the argument here is that whereas in Italy and Germany the links to architecture were primarily state-controlled (although not exclusively), in Britain, any connections arose through opportunistic distortions of leaks and fissures within Anglo-American "free-market" capitalism. While 1930s' British architectural culture held generally firm against Mosleyite Fascism, innovative building technologies indeed became embroiled. This was exemplified by the BUF's appropriation of the rebuilt Earl's Court Exhibition Centre, reportedly the world's most technologically advanced building. Designed by a US architect, Charles Howard Crane, it was constructed from 1936 to 1937 by Hegeman-Harris, a New York contractor erecting much of Manhattan's Art Deco-style Rockefeller Center. In creating novel and unknown conditions, it was the opportunities opened by sites like Earl's Court that Fascists seized upon to host mass rallies to promote Oswald Mosley as their demagogic leader. Tellingly, the location of Earl's Court in a marginal, lower-class area helped to underline and increase the challenge being made to the established political classes in Westminster. Presaging the Capitol rites, this aestheticisation of politics by Mosley turned it into a mass spectacle – not previously at all a British way of doing politics – and the manipulation of architectural space was vital for this transformation.

As Griffin notes, Fascism had its own distinctive narrative about modernity.[12] Speaking for the BUF, *The Blackshirt* magazine trumpeted: "Fascism is modern nationalism – and something. Fascism is not a foreign importation. It is a world idea."[13] In balancing nationalist sentiment with internationalism, Mosley used remarkably similar language to that of European Modernist architects, as seen in his 1932 book, *The Greater Britain*:

> In every town and village, in every institution of daily life, the will of the organised and determined minority must be struggling for sustained effort. The Modern Movement, in struggle and in victory, must be ineradicably interwoven with the life of the nation.[14]

Mosley believed this "Modern Movement" could revive Imperial Britain. Hence, Fascism was not merely ultra-conservatism, but a modernised variant distinguished by revolutionary zeal. The name derived from the Latin "fasces," referring to the bundled-wooden-rods-and-axe symbol of Etruria and Ancient Rome that Mussolini's party adopted as an icon of imperial power. Griffin argues that the hopes of Mussolini, Hitler, Mosley and their ilk were palingenetic, imagining the rebirth of a "national community" to implement social cleansing after years of decline.[15] Fascists were at odds with traditional conservatives, criticising "old gang" parties as ineffectual. Their definitions of "national community" were populist, identifying territory with ethnicity and cultural belief: by asserting "purity," doctrines were racist to varying degrees in hatred for perceived inferiors such as Jews, Muslims, African-Americans, etc. To achieve palingenetic change, Fascists wished a strong militaristic state to wield ultimate collective power, while contradictorily cosying up to corporate businesses for personal gain. Scared of influence from intellectuals, Fascists fuelled anti-elite sentiments, instilling among the populace a fear of being controlled by ruling groups (while aiming to exercise that very power themselves).

Interwar Fascism came in different varieties. Mussolini's Fascists seized power in Italy in 1922, being cultish and statist but lighter on racist rhetoric. Hitler's Nazi Party, governing Germany after he became Chancellor in January 1933, thrived upon anti-semitism. Neither Italy or Germany possessed major overseas empires like Britain and France, and it was their efforts to redress this lack which dragged into the mix other nations like the USA and Soviet Union. Richard Overy proposes re-dating the Second World War to 1931–1945 and terming it "The Great Imperial War."[16] He argues that imperial territorial ambitions left unresolved by the First World War triggered geopolitical shockwaves during the 1930s: Italy's African campaign, Germany's annexing of "Lebensraum" in central/ eastern Europe, and Japan's seizure of Manchuria. With the USA in economic ascendancy, British Fascists believed it was imperative to protect the imperial economy: by the late-1930s, due to global recession after the Wall Street Crash and the implementation of protective tariffs, nearly half of Britain's imports and exports were now with its colonies, while two-thirds of overseas investment was in those territories.[17]

The Earl's Court rally in July 1939, just six weeks before hostilities, was a fruitless attempt to oppose war with Nazi Germany and Fascist Italy. Nonetheless, as Julie Gottlieb observes, the BUF's attempts to copy Hitler signalled a modernised, media-driven politics that became mainstream after the Second World War. In *The Marketing of Megalomania*,[18] Gottlieb pinpoints Mosley as the bridgehead of Americanised politics reliant upon cinema, celebrity, male egocentricity, provocative rhetoric and adoration by "fans," all of them Trumpian antecedents. Indeed, "Britain shall be great again" was a BUF lyric, presaging Donald Trump's 2016 election slogan, "Make America Great Again."[19] Mosley's favourite mantra was "Britain First," paraphrasing the "America First" slogan which Trump later resurrected.

At Earl's Court, Mosley stood upon a 7-metre tower, high enough to sense power over a 20,000-strong audience claimed as the largest-ever indoor political meeting. Mosley was framed by a giant Union Jack flag and uniformed "Blackshirt" guards, speaking into a capacious hall washed by floodlights and with bodies as rows of pinpoints in space. It was a political spectacle born in Hollywood and finessed in the mid-1930s by Joseph Goebbels, Albert Speer and Leni Riefenstahl on Nuremberg's Zeppelin Field. Riefenstahl's indebtedness to Hollywood, notes Kracauer, stemmed from seminal Weimar Germany films like Fritz Lang's *Die Nibelungen* and *Metropolis*, with their screenplays by Thea von Harbou (Lang's wife, and a committed Nazi after their divorce).[20] Walter Benjamin's seminal 1936 essay, *The Work of Art in the Age of its Technological Reproducibility*, was intended as explicit warning that Fascism was appropriating the potential revolutionary medium and power of cinema – although not mentioning Riefenstahl's *The Victory of Faith* and *The Triumph of the Will*, those were his targets.[21] Identifying cinema as the quintessential perceptual/cultural form under capitalism, Benjamin felt it had revolutionised art's previous qualities (unique, auratic, ritualistic, outside everyday life) through a novel expressive mode (profane, multiple, montaged, repeatable, cutting directly into people's lives). Art's meaning and purpose were thus altered from meditating upon the sacred to celebrating the proletarianisation of the urban masses, whom Benjamin pointed out were the "human material" that Fascism sought to capture/control in its desire for power. As Guy Debord wrote later in *The Society of the Spectacle*, this was "the proletariat [both] as subject and representation."[22]

Everyday aestheticisation under capitalism, says Böhme, as an adaptation of Debord's critique, leads to a new architectural paradigm of designing "stage settings," which are then manipulated by various groups to affect how audiences perceive and receive visual/spatial atmospheres.[23] Architecture is hence not simply the preserve of elite professionals designing "pure" new buildings, but includes everyone in daily life involved in creating atmospheric aesthetics.

Adopting Böhme's formulation, this chapter is organised into three acts in architectural stage-sets reframed by populist ultra-nationalists. The first is Olympia in June 1934, followed, in the second act, by the British Union's rally at Earls Court in July 1939. To understand these events, however, other 1930s factors are woven in – including concerns about Britain's faltering empire, and the ideological divisions that led a handful of architects to become embroiled in Mosleyite Fascism. Similarly, the impact of US technologies destabilised British architectural beliefs during that decade. What emerges is an uncertain, opportunistic vision of Modernism very different ideologically to that imagined by left-wing interwar architects.

The final act takes place on May 23, 2014 in another stage-set – the "Hoy and Helmet" pub in South Benfleet, Essex – with the UK Independence Party leader, Nigel Farage, posing for a photo-opportunity holding a pint of beer while ringed by England flags and corporate signage (Figure 10.2). Farage is a transatlantic missionary for US ultra-nationalism, a cheerleader priding himself on personal connection with Donald Trump (especially after Trump became US President). But what is the situation of right-wing populism in Britain today? After decades of failure by parties like the National Front and British National Party, causing them to downgrade tactics such as street marches, spatial manipulation is now orchestrated through digital communication systems.[24] "I wouldn't be here if I didn't have social media," admitted Trump while still President.[25]

Hardt and Negri speak of a neoliberal corporate "empire" that uses digital communications to conquer minds and pockets, never attempting anything messy like invading other lands.[26] Thus, as ultra-nationalists, Trump and Farage

FIGURE 10.2 Nigel Farage with a pint in a pub in South Benfleet, Essex in May 2014.

rely upon US-based transnational media companies to spread Neo-Fascist ideology. In the online realm of Twitter and fake website news, Farage's manipulation of the "normal" image of cheery-white-bloke-in-a-pub-with-a-pint assisted Britain's departure from the European Union in the 2016 Brexit referendum. While questioning whether the far-right seam has really declined in Britain, it clearly has morphed. The architectures and atmospheres are entirely different. Mosleyite Fascism was about state control and imperial territory; today, in the 2020s, Neo-Fascism feels corporate and trans-spatial.

Act 1, Stage-Set: Olympia 1934

The Aesthetic of Fascism, aka the (Other) Modern Movement

In his 1936 essay, Benjamin declared (Figure 10.3):

> Fascism attempts to organise the newly proletarianized masses while leaving intact the property relations which they strive to abolish. It sees its salvation in granting expression to the masses – but on no account granting them rights … *The logical consequence of fascism is an aestheticizing of political life.*[27]

FIGURE 10.3 Photograph of the audience and hyper-attentive security staff at the BUF rally in Olympia in June 1934.

Twentieth-century media innovations were, by being recorded and widely distributed and repeated, turning politics into art:

> The change noted here in the mode of exhibition – a change brought about by reproduction technology – is also noticeable in politics. *The crisis of democracies can be understood as a crisis in the conditions governing the public presentation of politicians* ... This results in a new form of selection – selection before an apparatus – from which the champion, the star, and the dictator emerge as victors.[28]

Even if it proved "a watery English stew ... compared to Italian Fascism,"[29] the initial inspiration for Mosley's party was Mussolini's Italy with its ideology and iconography taking much from Futurism (a movement already partially known in Britain through Percy Wyndham Lewis' Vorticist paintings and writings). Mosley himself began as a young star in the Conservative Party, before going Independent, then switching to the Labour Party as a Fabian Socialist and becoming a junior minister in Ramsay MacDonald's 1929 National Government. He absorbed Keynesian principles of state intervention. But, dissatisfied with the government's unemployment policies, Mosley quit to form the New Party and subsequently the British Union of Fascists from October 1932 – not Britain's first or only Fascist party, but the most organised.

The BUF's emulation of Italian Fascism was mainly banal, creating a plethora of uniforms, badges, banners and other accoutrement.[30] Mosley however also appreciated Mussolini's wider cultural vision. In 1934, one adherent claimed: "I have it on authority that under Fascism a Ministry of Fine Arts would be one of the first things created."[31] The belief was that the Elizabethan era had been Britain's "Golden Age" (Shakespeare and all that), and thus needed reviving. An ex-Communist, E.D. Randall, became Britain's "poet of fascism," using *The Blackshirt* and *Fascist Week* to argue that cultural struggle was as vital as political struggle in fighting for the racial existence of British people. "The extent of a nation's biological energy is manifest in the nature of its patriotism, which is the basis of its culture," wrote Randall. "When the flame of the spirit wanes and patriotism becomes gross and false, and is exploited to base ends, culture in consequence loses its animation and its individuality."[32] Randall felt that culture was "super-racial," able to transcend its roots to create a nobler civilisation.[33] Thus, notable figures in the arts and sciences would be elected to the second chamber of a Fascist parliament to reinvigorate "national culture."[34]

Here it is also worth mentioning Oswald Mosley's architectural forays. In late 1926, Mosley's first wife, Cynthia Curzon – daughter of an American heiress and George Curzon, a former Viceroy of India and Foreign Secretary – purchased a medieval house, Savehay (Savay) Farm, near Denham in Buckinghamshire, as their weekend retreat. They had it revamped and extended by Clough Williams-Ellis, then just embarking upon his most famous project, the Italianate holiday village of Portmeirion in north Wales. Williams-Ellis was the brother-in-law of John Strachey, a close associate of Mosley's in the Labour Party.[35] Cynthia Mosley was another ardent Socialist and briefly a Labour MP in her own right. Through her family connections, Mosley also came to know Edwin Lutyens, saying of the latter: "He was a great droll as well as a gifted architect."[36] In 1933, Mosley commissioned Lutyens (plus the latter's son, Robert) to design a pink travertine marble tomb at Savehay Farm following Cynthia's sudden death from peritonitis.[37]

E.D. Randall likewise admired Italian Fascism, including its architecture and town planning. In spreading the word, he was ably helped by Anne Brock Griggs, wife of a British Fascist architect (Figure 10.4).[38] Her role for the BUF included liaising with the Italian Consulate, notably Ambassador Dino Grandi (then channelling funds to Mosley), to publicise Mussolini's architectural achievements to a British audience.[39] It was a relatively easy task given that Italian precedents had long entranced British architects and intellectuals. During the 1930s, architectural journals wrote extensively about Fascist Italy, with sympathetic reviews by critics like John Gloag or the openly anti-semitic Philip Morton Shand.[40] Tours to Italy took in recent buildings and exhibitions, as in the 1933 Architectural Association trip organised by its secretary, Frank Yerbury – an avid photographer of Modernist buildings and enthusiastic about Italian Fascist architecture.[41] Alister MacDonald, architect-son of Labour's first prime minister, met Mussolini when

FIGURE 10.4 Sir Oswald Mosley with Anne Brock Griggs on the day of the "Battle of Cable Street," October 4, 1936.

travelling in Italy in the early-1930s, and worked briefly on an unbuilt Milanese skyscraper.[42]

However, British admiration extended only up to a point: in the end, Italy was regarded as too southern European and *sui generis*. T.S. Eliot described Fascism as "an Italian regime for Italians, a product of the Italian mind."[43]

Architecture and Empire

The specific British problem that worried Mosley was imperial decay. Late Victorian certitude had been rocked during the Second Boer War by worries about health of the population stock, especially the working classes. The 1904 British Physical Deterioration Report epitomised the clamour for greater "national efficiency."[44] Spectres of decline had been raised by the likes of Macaulay and Jerrold, a pessimistic mood echoing Oswald Spengler's broader prediction about the end of western civilisation.[45] Conversely, nationalistic writings that emphasised British cultural superiority also proliferated, including *A History of Architecture on the Comparative Method* (1896 onwards) by Banister Fletcher senior/junior.[46] By the mid-1930s, Britain's imperial reality felt extremely vulnerable. The dilemma for Mosleyites was how to balance protection for the British Empire with support for Italy's and Germany's right to carve their own empires. Dissension in India and other colonies also posed problems for the imperial order, yet, as Anne Orde notes, an even greater challenge came from the USA, which by the inter-war era had clearly become the world's wealthiest nation.[47] The paradox was that while the interwar British Empire reached its zenith in territory and population – around one-quarter of the world's total for both, the largest empire ever – it was imploding due to America's ascendancy. In 1938, French surgeon/anthropologist Robert Briffault could write a book teasingly titled *The Decline and Fall of the British Empire*.[48]

This formed the context for 1930s British architecture, of which only a sketch can be given here due to its sheer diversity. There were around 12,000 architects in Britain by 1939 amid a population of 48 million (one architect for every 4,000 people).[49] Most architects were middle-class/middle-road Conservatives or Liberals, albeit with growing numbers of Socialists and Marxists among younger practitioners and students. The latter included Communist Party members (then averaging 10,000–18,000), such as Colin Penn, active in the Association of Architects, Surveyors and Technical Assistants. Other Marxist sympathisers like the architectural historian John Summerson preferred to stay independent: he said he was committed to historical materialism as an intellectual method, yet abhorred politics.[50] Furthermore, the right/left divide remained fluid. The Social Credit movement, for instance, which included the ex-Fabian Socialist housing architect, Arthur Penty, exemplified the rightwards drift, with Penty now championing Mussolini.[51]

Numerous forces were pressing towards increased professionalisation: the 1930s Registration Acts, more architectural schools, more colonial architecture positions, etc. Aesthetically, many styles were in play, such as Neo-Georgian, Arts and Crafts, and even Late-Gothic Revival. The hitherto influence of imperialist thought was waning, turning the key ideological debate among British architects – like in much of interwar Europe – into that of tradition (nationalism) versus modernity (internationalism). Defenders of tradition included Albert Richardson, head of the Bartlett School of Architecture and champion of the Neoclassical "Grand Manner," and Reginald Blomfield, outspoken author of *Modernismus* (1934).[52] Those favouring modernity and internationalism were not only the acolytes of continental Modernism but also those who regarded Art Deco – or, rather, streamlined Moderne – as being most up-to-date.

Poised somewhere between tradition and modernity was stripped Classicism, commonplace for 1930s civic architecture. Americanised steel framing (instead of solid masonry) meant more buildings could now afford to use clip-on stone cladding panels, typically white Portland stone, while advances in heating/ventilating systems enabled floor-plans to become deeper. This technological blend saw the appearance in interwar London of large "iceberg" buildings which novelists and poets liked to portray as sinister Fascist/totalitarian monoliths. George Orwell famously used his office – Room 101 in the BBC headquarters, by Val Myer and team – as the torture room in *1984*, a dystopian novel whose "Ministry of Truth" invoked Charles Holden's Senate House for London University.[53] However, such barbs were misguided. Stripped Classicism in other interwar democracies (e.g., France, Sweden, USA) was equally hard to distinguish stylistically from buildings in Fascist Italy or Nazi Germany.[54] And when similar architectural forms in Britain were built in brick instead, the allusions made were not to Fascism but – as with Reginald Uren's Hornsey Town Hall (1934–1935) – to Dutch or Scandinavian Modernism.

In other words, the BBC headquarters or Senate House were not "fascist" in the way of Nuremberg's Nazi Congress Hall or Albert Speer's New Chancellery in Berlin. What Orwell and other writers were criticising said less about architectural aesthetics and more about their distaste for the imposition of vast corporate institutions into the urban scene, with another much-criticised example being Holden's London Transport headquarters. Stripped Classicism is of interest for other reasons. David Frazer Lewis notes that thin stone cladding tended towards sculpture-like abstraction in facades.[55] Indeed, Alan Powers describes Holden's earlier British Medical Association building, of 1908, as "classicism reduced to geometric shapes."[56] To alleviate formal simplification, interwar architects commissioned sculptors to add symbolism via freestanding stone figures or low-relief panels. Summerson denounced this as "the unnatural union of the two arts," while others were uglier in their criticisms.[57] Jacob Epstein, American-Jewish and truly loathed by Mosleyite Fascists, was Britain's most famous interwar sculptor, being repeatedly lambasted for breaking taboos about depicting human anatomy.[58] Another reason for writers like Orwell to hate "icebergs" was their testimony to the incursion of US Beaux-Arts "City Beautiful" planning. Beginning with 1920s designs by American architects like Harvey Corbett's

Bush House and Thomas Hastings' Devonshire House, the approach spread during the 1930s when financial hardship prompted US architects to diversify into Britain, the world's second-largest economy – key examples being John Russell Pope's Tate Museum Sculpture Galleries (1933–1937) and Duveen Gallery for the British Museum's Elgin Marbles (1936–1939).[59] In turn, many British architects were enthralled by American civic design. Holden, for one, had visited the USA in 1913, and Edwin Lutyens, who greatly enjoyed his 1925 US trip to collect the American Institute of Architects' Gold Medal, also altered direction – Alison Smithson subsequently berating him for helping "the Americanisation of our cities through monstrous office-blocks with hideous plans."[60]

For those British architects who viewed continental Modernism as the proper future, growing impact was demonstrated by copious joint-articles in *The Architect and Building News* from 1926 to 1932 by Howard Robertson (text) and Frank Yerbury (photography),[61] and by Frederick Etchells' 1927 translation of Le Corbusier's *Vers Une Architecture*. Crucial too, with Europe lurching to right, was an influx of Jewish and Socialist/Communist architects fleeing persecution or else seeking a more receptive environment. Sometimes their move to Britain was a stepping-stone to the USA, *pace* Walter Gropius and Marcel Breuer; others like Berthold Lubetkin and Ernő Goldfinger stayed on. However, the presence of continental emigres must not be exaggerated. Until 1939 there were about 25 refugee architects from Nazi Germany with labour permits in Britain. The crunch came in early-1939, with the RIBA rapidly setting up a refugee committee to process a surge in applications.[62] Also important for British Modernism were children-of-empire like Amyas Connell and Wells Coates, active in the first swathe of British houses in this mode and with Coates instrumental in founding the Modern Architecture Research (MARS) Group in February 1933 as a CIAM offshoot.[63] Tokyo-born but Canadian by parentage, Wells Coates waxed lyrical on steel-framing: "the wall, no longer an essential part of structure, becomes (truly considered) an expression of its thermal and other insulating functions – to include or exclude the light, the view, the weather, or the public."[64] To make the case that Modernism was intrinsically British, two oft-quoted forerunners were the sparse domestic architecture of Georgian/Regency Britain and the truth-to-materials Arts and Crafts which Nikolaus Pevsner evoked when linking William Morris to Walter Gropius.[65] It enhanced Modernism's acceptance by private clients and businesses, or for municipal/philanthropic showcases like the De La Warr Pavilion, London Zoo, Finsbury Health Centre, Kensal House and Peckham Health Centre.

Two Architects: James Burford and Marshall Arnott Sisson

A pair of architects who joined the British Union of Fascists were James Burford (1894–1967) and Marshall Sisson (1897–1978). Burford was a Neoclassicist appointed by Richardson as a tutor at the Bartlett School of Architecture, running its evening classes. Initially, designing war memorials, he gradually embraced Italian Rationalism, typified by Westwood (1935) in Gerrard's Cross.[66] Writing also for journals, Burford held a fundamentalist view of architectural design: "It is a question of race, of blood; in the true historical sense, of Culture."[67] Sisson, a few years younger, was Burford's star student at the Bartlett, and, after winning a Duveen Scholarship in 1927 to work with John Russell Pope in New York, went on to design, *inter alia*, two all-brick Modernist houses in Cambridge and a white-rendered villa in Cornwall, Gull Rock House.[68]

What attracted Burford and Sisson to Mosleyite Fascism? One possibility was the Bartlett School's position within University College London. Due to institutional complexities, having merged with the school at King's College London, the Bartlett was rehoused from late-1913 in a block that was also to contain the newly-formed Department of Eugenics and Applied Statistics.[69] The latter was run by the statistician, Karl Pearson, protégé of Frances Galton, founder of "Eugenics" – a pseudo-science later notorious as the basis for racial eradication policies, especially Nazi Germany.[70] Indeed, in his retirement dinner speech in 1934 Pearson said his work was not the culmination of Eugenics research:

> No, that lies in the future, perhaps with Reichskanzler Hitler and his proposals to regenerate the German people. In Germany a vast experiment is at hand and some of you may live to see the results. If it fails it will not be for want of enthusiasm ...[71]

One might expect Mosley's party to be Eugenicists, but that was not so.[72] Likely this was because the BUF never had a scientific policy, preferring racial theories based on culture rather than biology, and because Eugenics was already a broad-based middle-class movement supported by "old gang" figures like Winston Churchill and George Bernard Shaw.[73] Nor was there a close connection between Eugenics and the Bartlett School of Architecture, only uncomfortable overlaps. These two UCL departments were near-identical twins in a Neoclassical wing funded and built by the same benefactor, and both were designed by the head of the architecture school, Frederick Moore Simpson. Furthermore, Pearson bred dogs in a stable block behind the Bartlett School which was replaced in 1930 by a new structure by Simpson (completed by his architect-son).[74] These were not ordinary dogs, but Pekingese which Pearson reared to make them pure-white and short-haired.[75] If one could control genetics for a "new race" of dog, then one could breed racially purer humans: Pearson believed the British government could thereby make all the Empire's people white.

Aside from wondering whether on hot days, with windows open, Bartlett tutors/students were distracted from Neoclassical reveries by the barking of genetically purified dogs, there had to be a different cause for Burford and Sisson's Fascist conversion. Working together on certain projects, their entry in the 1933 De La Warr Pavilion competition for Bexhill-on-Sea was specially commended. Its L-shaped plan was stiffly axial, not a patch on Serge Chermayeff and Eric Mendelsohn's fluid winning design, which, opening in 1935, is arguably Britain's finest interwar building. However, qualitative judgements mattered little to

Burford and Sisson. They were incensed that "foreign" architects were taking this job from British architects, especially as the winners were a Russian/Chechen Jew (albeit naturalised) and a German Jew.

Piqued, they joined the British Union of Fascists and became embroiled in a letter campaign in *The Architects' Journal (AJ)*. On January 26, 1934 – likely tipped off before the De La Warr decision was announced – *Fascist Week* launched an attack on the prospect of foreign architects winning: "Britons, not aliens, shall carry out the task!"[76] After the *AJ* praised Chermayeff and Mendelsohn's scheme, in the February 15 issue came a curt letter from Henry Thomas (Tom) Brock Griggs – architect-husband of Anne Brock Griggs – asking to reprint the *Fascist Week* article "in fairness to the many Fascist architects."[77] The *AJ* did so. In the following issue was another letter from Brock Griggs and a sour-grapes note from Burford claiming there was "strong public protest at the result of this competition. The public generally will not discriminate between the design and its author." This anti-Jewish jibe prompted the *AJ*, puzzled by these Fascist architects, to taunt Mosley by asking which style he would adopt if victorious: "Will the Leader prefer banker's Classic or builder's Tudor?"[78] After further squabbles in *AJ* between Burford and De La Warr, two responses were published on April 19, one from BUF Director of Policy, Alexander Raven Thomson (grandson of Scottish architect Alexander "Greek" Thomson). "Fascism will make no endeavour to enforce some particular style of architecture as an authoritative ruling," he said, adding that they welcomed concrete-and-glass Modernist designs. The other letter, from "a number of Fascist architects," concurred, arguing for revived traditionalism but using contemporary forms: "That is where Fascism and vital modern architecture join hands. Both, in objective, are revolutionary, in the sense that revolution implies change and growth."[79]

Things quietened down, but reignited on January 10, 1935 when Serge Chermayeff and Jim Richards – *AJ*'s assistant-editor, a Marxist and anti-Fascist marcher – published a satire titled "A Hundred Years Ahead: Forecasting the Coming Century."[80] It imagined a future in which, emulating many dictatorships across Europe, Britain elected a Fascist government in 1965 which proceeded to build bunker-like structures "rooted in fear," prior to a Socialist revolution in 1983. The BUF's publicity chief, A.K. Chesterton, wrote to complain, triggering further letters including again from Brock Griggs. In the February 14 issue, the *AJ*'s editors drew a halt. It was an episode which confirmed that British architects were generally immune to Fascist ideology. Burford and Sisson soon quit the BUF. Retreating to the countryside, both took up building conservation, with Sisson becoming an establishment figure. Yet following his death, even a sympathetic early-1980s piece sighed that being a Blackshirt "is, unfortunately, the only aspect of his life that many people now remember him for."[81]

The Olympia Debacle

Olympia was the rival to Earl's Court as an American-style exhibitions and entertainments centre. Opening in 1886, a year before Earl's Court, it possessed two older halls – the original Grand Hall, with iron-and-glass barrel-vaulted roof, and National Hall, a 1920s replica.[82] In the late-1920s, with Earl's Court in decline, Olympia's owners appointed Joseph Emberton to revamp the venue. He restored the existing halls, adding a new frontage – dramatically floodlit at night[83] – in the "business architecture" mode he was using convincingly elsewhere for the Royal Corinthian Yacht Club, Simpsons on Piccadilly and Blackpool Pleasure Beach. Emberton's particular talent lay in fusing continental Modernism with flowing Art Deco/Moderne (Figure 10.5).

Emberton was also highly alert to Modernist discourse. "Steel and concrete are materials of a new age," he declared. "... Beauty needs no adornment and a building which is 100% efficient for its purpose is beautiful."[84] Elsewhere he said: "'Functionalism' is the new word in building. Everything should express its function 100 percent ... That is why I like this modern economy – it is moral and even aesthetic. It has a purifying influence which nothing else has."[85] This emphasis on purification was again stated in a 1931 lecture in which Emberton claimed his Olympia design:

> ...was the result, not of any effort to be modernistic, but of imperative needs, of the building's purpose, and of strict regulations in the shape of fire escape facilities. He believed that a building should be as impersonal as

FIGURE 10.5 Drawing by Henry Thomas Brock Griggs of the new Olympia façade by Joseph Emberton (aquatint and dry point, 1929).

possible, for he did not think that any man's personality was big enough to be expressed in the street in the form of a utilitarian building.[86]

He disapproved of sculptors like Jacob Epstein "affixing slabs of emotion to a utilitarian building."[87] Such talk positioned Emberton as an innovator, with one newspaper declaring that "the construction of the Empire Hall at Olympia, has marked something like an architectural epoch."[88]

Emberton boldly proclaimed Olympia as "the most up-to-date building in London."[89] His boosterism invoked two aspects that clients appreciated: scale and speed. A press release said it was "the biggest building in the Empire. All records are being broken for speed of construction."[90] Erected from 1929 to 1930, 84 engineers worked on its multi-storey steel frame and Portland stone cladding.[91] Emberton further enlarged Olympia from 1933 to 1935 by creating another entrance onto Addison Road and near-doubling its exhibition space to 93,000 square metres – making it Europe's largest exhibition venue, albeit still behind New York's Madison Square Gardens.[92] He also designed a six-storey reinforced-concrete car park with 1,000 spaces, completed in February 1937. This made it ideal for events like the International Motor Show or the British Industries Fair's Dominions and Colonial exhibition: "a vast shop window of British goods … set before the buyers of the country and of overseas markets."[93]

The British Union of Fascists appreciated great pomp and circumstance, the two features of Mosley's preferred venues like the Royal Albert Hall. Their Olympia rally on June 7, 1934 marked the high point of the party's membership, some 40–50,000 people, with Mosley enjoying strong press support such as the "Hurrah for the Blackshirts!" editorial by the *Daily Mail's* proprietor, Lord Rothermere.[94] Around 10,000 people filled Olympia's Grand Hall under its daylit barrel-vaulted roof, with photographs showing an old-style rumbustious political event with bodies packed together willingly in an agitated throng. The rally however descended into chaos with Mosley's "Biff Boys" violently beating many of the anti-Fascist protestors, Jewish or Communist, and female BUF members attacking women hecklers. A few weeks later came Hitler's *Night of the Long Knives*. There was widespread condemnation in Britain's parliament and society of Fascist violence, and erstwhile sympathisers like Rothermere abandoned Mosley. Backlash from Olympia proved disastrous, with BUF membership plunging to about 5,000.

Not only *The Architects Journal* believed Mosley insignificant after Olympia: historians confirm that centrist and leftist architects chose to ignore the BUF.[95] Given his setback, Mosley decided to realign by embracing the harder, racist variant in Hitler's Germany.[96] In June 1936 came a relaunch as the British Union of Fascists and National Socialists, with a new symbol of a flash-within-a-circle. The much-mythologised *Battle of Cable Street* on October 4, 1936, in which 100,000 Jewish, Socialist and Communist opponents prevented Mosley's Fascists from marching through the extensively Jewish district of Whitechapel, despite police protection for the Fascist marchers, exemplified a confrontation in politicised public space that was raw and visceral. In wake of Cable Street, the government banned quasi-military organisations and the wearing of military uniforms in public. Mosley was satirised by PG Wodehouse in *The Code of the Woosters* (1938) as Roderick Spode, pompous leader of the comically useless Saviours of Britain, aka the "Black Shorts." Brickbats aside, the BUF turned instead towards a new architectural aesthetic evoking Nazi display and cinematography.

Act 2, Stage-Set: Earls Court 1939

The Nazi Aesthetic

If originally fascinated by Mussolini, the British Union of Fascists and National Socialists (from 1937 simply the British Union) now embraced a line closer to Nazi Germany (Figure 10.6). Spectacle was amplified in their rallies, a trend already seen in mid-1936 at the Albert Hall, the last they were allowed to hold there. One of their virulently anti-semitic propagandists, William Joyce (later "Lord Haw Haw"), said that it "could not bear unfavourable comparison with the greatest manifestations … in Nüremberg."[97] In 1937, E.D. Randall visited the Nazis' "Degenerate Art" exhibition in Munich, praising its total repudiation of the "Bourgeois Bolshevism" of Modernist painting.[98] For architecture, however, the question was more complex. Barbara Miller Lane notes there never was an official Nazi architectural style, and indeed Martin Kitchen comes closest when observing that "Hitler's sole interest in architecture was its effect."[99] Aesthetic consistency was secondary, as Albert Speer admitted: "Ideology was apparent in

FIGURE 10.6   Photograph of the British Union's rally held in the main arena of Earl's Court in July 1939.

the definition of the commission, but not in the style of its execution."[100] Instead, a range of styles from Neo-Vernacular to Neoclassical were used, including Modernism in buildings for Hermann Göring's Luftwaffe or in some Nazi industrial structures. Each style offered distinctive associations and meanings, expressing, through their own forms, an interpretation of modernity for the New World Order. Griffin is therefore right to observe that Fascists were not regressive traditionalists in regard to architecture, although he stretches things too far in arguing that the stripped Classicism used for Fascist public buildings (or in other 1930s countries of whichever political hue) should be called "rooted modernism" to indicate it was an alternative, hybrid form to "iconoclastic, experimental" Modernism.[101] It seems better to accept the real difference that contemporaries saw between stripped Classicism and Modernism, while also acknowledging the contradictions, overlaps, provisionality and slipperiness inherent in the classification of all architectural styles. A similar conclusion is reached by Neal Shasore in his recent book, *Designs on Democracy*, which shifts the historiography of British interwar architecture away from descriptions of the "battle of the styles" while still recognising the very deep ideological split between Traditionalists (nationalists) who favoured stripped Classicism, and Modernists (internationalists).[102]

What was certainly evident to all during the 1930s was the weight placed upon architecture in Hitler's Germany. Thus, despite leading Nazis' fondness for a line from a 1933 play, *Schlageter* – best translated as "When I hear 'culture' … I reach for my revolver" – they were deeply immersed in cultural struggle. British Fascism followed suit. "The most distinctive way that [Mosleyite] fascism implemented its palingenetic designs was through culture," notes one scholar.[103] With the BUF now looking increasingly towards Nazi Germany, their architecture and housing spokesperson, Anne Brock Griggs, changed her rhetoric. In May 1936, she wrote in *Action*: "Adolf Hitler was by profession an architect. Now he has begun the tremendous task of building a new civilisation."[104] Her claim was rather misleading. Hitler had been rejected twice from studying painting at the Viennese Academy of Fine Arts, and although he briefly considered becoming an architect, he chose not to.[105] Nonetheless, his immense admiration for Paul Ludwig Troost and Gerdy Troost, and then for Albert Speer – spending hours discussing designs for the Third Reich's putative new world-capital, Germania – was palpable. In Hitler's mind, it was he who made the crucial design decisions, and thus followers could believe their Führer was an architect.[106] Oswald Mosley and Anne Brock Griggs thus now recognised the political potential of architecture, yet with no opportunity to erect any buildings, how could the British Union play out its strategy?

Along with Joseph Goebbels as propaganda minister, Hitler had implored his favourite filmmaker, Leni Riefenstahl, to find ways with Speer to heighten the Nazi imaginary at the 1930s Nuremberg rallies. Riefenstahl's films set the tone cinematically, whereas, for Speer, his arrangement of upward-shining floodlights to create illusory colonnades was intended as a dramatic expression of what was labelled "*Lichtarchitketur* [architecture of light]" or "*Architektur der Nacht* [night architecture]." The source for Speer's lighting designs was the USA, where floodlights were first used in 1933 for quasi–architectural effect at Chicago's "Century of Progress" exhibition.[107] Thus, despite Speer's spartan Neoclassical buildings for the Third Reich, such as Berlin's New Chancellery, his contribution to the "aesthetics of atmospheres" at Nuremberg was his creative peak – notwithstanding Leon Krier's claim of Speer as a first-rank architect.[108] Historians also stress the extent to which Speer's buildings relied on forced labourers who were worked to death, or else involved displacing communities of Jewish citizens sent to extermination camps, all to glorify Germania.[109]

Given his closeness to Hitler, there was a flurry of British interest when Albert Speer was asked to alter the interiors in the German Embassy at Carlton House Terrace, overlooking the Mall.[110] The reality however was mundane. Speer travelled to London twice in late-1936 and early-1937 for site inspections but also said that the redecorations were in fact being designed by the wife of the German ambassador, Joachim von Ribbentrop. Urban legends spread about swastika decorations, whereas there was only a muted motif, as a quasi-Greek key pattern, in one parquet floor. In terms of Nazi architecture in Britain it was underwhelming, somewhat like other instances of influence in 1930s Britain – of which links to German industrialists by the manager of an industrial estate in Gateshead, and the open admiration for the Nazi's autobahn system, were the most substantive.[111] Intriguingly, in the run up to war in July 1939, the conservative architect, town planner and critic, Arthur Trystan Edwards, suddenly made efforts to contact an official in the German Embassy to express admiration for Hitler's housing policies, no doubt a self-promoting and self-preserving tactic just in case Nazi Germany successfully invaded Britain.[112]

Technologies of Display at Earl's Court

Americanised technological innovations (steel-framing; artificial lighting; air-handling systems) enabled taller buildings with deeper floor plans, in turn pumping up the scale of London's civic and commercial buildings from the early 20th century. This included the development of Kingsway before the First World War, with, as Mark Crinson notes, strong imperial links.[113] In 1919, the Air Ministry moved into one of its buildings, Adastral House, where Tom Brock Griggs later worked.

By the late-1930s, however, the apogee of deep plans was Earl's Court Exhibition Centre.[114] Faced with Olympia's resurgence, a consortium had leased Earl's Court with the aim of blowing their competitor out of the water. They appointed Charles Howard Crane, a noted Detroit theatre, cinema and commercial architect. He had sailed over to Britain in 1932 after realising his bleak prospects during America's "Great Depression." After selecting Gordon Jeeves as his British partner, Crane designed various cinemas including the Gaumont Theatre (1936–1937) on a busy corner of London's Holloway Road.

Crane's design for Earl's Court was his major commission, a masterclass in site maximisation (Figure 10.7). To the west, the plot was constrained by a railway

Design & Construction, April, 1937

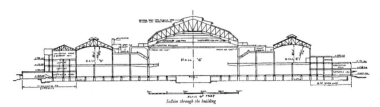

4. Sectional Diagram showing Central Hall and Side Halls.

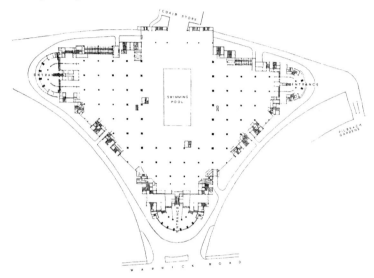

5. The Ground Floor (Main Plan).

6. General View of the Scheme (from a model).

FIGURE 10.7 Plan and model of Earl's Court Exhibition Centre.

cutting, while two curved residential streets created a triangular shape which Crane covered completely. There were three entrances, one at each corner. Photographs of the reinforced-concrete structure of the main Warwick Road entrance, before tile-cladding, make it feel like a civic building in Fascist Italy, or even a Michigan cinema. As a giant triangular box, with its plan 180-metres-deep in places, the building provided a main central arena (107 ×76 metres, 35 metres tall) plus two smaller side-halls. A crucial decision was to avoid rooflights, making these halls entirely dependent on artificial lighting and ventilation. It created a black box, a gigantic sound-stage, a Plato's cave into which any image or ideology could be projected. As a behemoth to outdo Olympia, with state-of-the-art retractable swimming pool in the main arena, and parking for 2000 cars, Earl's Court was routinely called the largest reinforced-concrete building in Europe, the world's largest exhibition centre and one of the biggest buildings anywhere. A newspaper explained that "the arena is longer and more than twice as wide as a standard football field."[115] The building contained 130,000 square metres of floor space, only surpassed by the Rockefeller Center – prompting Crane to argue that the higher ceilings in Earl's Court made it volumetrically larger than its New York rival.[116]

A shares issue was announced in July 1935 to erect the new Earl's Court and remodel its old Empress Hall (accessed via a railway bridge) into an ice-hockey stadium. The contractor was Hegeman-Harris of New York, heavily involved in the Rockefeller Center. Hegeman-Harris employed no American labourers, instead using local subcontractors. Structural engineers were Mouchel, experts in Hennebique-style concrete, and the mechanical consultant was a rising British star, Oscar Faber. Because the site sat over six railway lines, several of them underground, groundworks were entrusted to Sir Robert McAlpine Ltd, builders of many of Britain's largest reinforced-concrete structures (Wembley Stadium, Dorchester Hotel, etc). Building started in July 1935 and aimed to finish by Christmas 1936. That proved over-ambitious: construction took until mid-1937, with costs rising to £2 million primarily due to complicated foundations. The rush to complete saw 3,000 workers on site and many accidents and injuries, including two deaths. Material shortages caused delays, as did strikes by bricklayers and electricians, while neighbours complained about night-time noise.[117]

Earl's Court was conceived as a technological miracle for 1930s Britain and could claim plausibly to be the world's most advanced building (Figure 10.8). Relying entirely on electricity for lighting and heating, Faber calculated its demand as equivalent to a town of 75,000 people. Illuminating the main arena were 416 high-powered Mazdalux floodlights by British Thomson-Houston, part of the Associated Electrical Industries consortium. These floodlights permitted any hue of colour-wash.[118] Because the arena was so vast, Faber designed an ingenious system using American high-velocity, cannon-like blowers to distribute heated/cooled air over long distances, offering unimagined thermal control. Fellow engineers were impressed, with one observing "it would be the pioneer of quite a number to be introduced to this country."[119]

FIGURE 10.8 Promotional drawings and photographs of Earl's Court Exhibition Centre under construction.

The reopening event at Earls' Court, in September 1937, was the Chocolate and Confectionery Show, followed by the International Motor Show, lured away from Olympia – as were the Dominions and Colonial displays for the British Industries Fair, and Ideal Homes Show.[120] By then, however, Earl's Court Ltd was in financial difficulties, having lost £90,000 in its first year. It went into receivership in early July 1939, a glitch within capitalism that Mosley eagerly exploited.[121]

On July 16, only ten days after Earl's Court went bust, the British Union – effectively banned from all major London venues – quickly hired its main arena after hearing that another event was cancelled (Figure 10.9). The scale and lighting allowed an indoor Nazi-style pageant, with the audience sitting in rows and Mosley on his stepped-profile tower. Newspapers called it "the largest indoor meeting ever held in any country," while the British Union boasted that Earl's Court is "much larger than the Madison Square Hall, New York, or the Deutschland Hall, Berlin."[122] A renowned pro-German appeaser wrote approvingly in his diary: "The hall was laid out à la Nuremberg."[123] Attendees were mesmerised, with one telling his local newspaper: "I was impressed at the amazing spectacle, decorous and disciplined, with perfect organization. It might have been in Berlin or Rome for the unison and regimentation that prevailed."[124] Britain's press mostly downplayed the event because the Peace Rally Movement was perceived as veiled Nazi propaganda, yet some newspapers referred to the theatricality:

FIGURE 10.9 *Action*, no. 177 (July 15, 1939), front cover article about the Earl's Court rally to be held the next evening.

> Sir Oswald Mosley … dwarfed on top of a yellow tower, with pink lights casting a halo around him, to-night thundered a denunciation of Jewry to an audience which three-parts filled the 30,000 seats in Earls Court … Limelights from the roof of the hall followed him as he walked to the platform.[125]

However, the *Daily Mirror*'s columnist remained unimpressed:

> The tension was whipped up by the triumphal entry of standard bearers in true Nazi style … And slowly, with remarkable poise, Oswald Ernald Mosley climbed to the top of the immense rostrum. The High Priest pinnacled on his own altar … Every trick, every device, to add to the drama of the scene I have experienced before. Hitler. Fifteen years ago Hitler first started it. To-day Mosley copies it. To anybody who has seen this sort of thing in Germany, Earls' Court was an imitation, with all the lack of fire that is the hallmark of meticulous, unimaginative mimicry.[126]

Even if an imitation, the Nuremberg-esque show at Earl's Court confirmed Benjamin's comment about Fascism as the aestheticising of politics. Its aim was to make the British Union audience feel like a mass community – seduced by partaking in a collective performance that prioritised aesthetics and minimised socio-economic change, focussing their attention on the spectacle of their own control, rather than anything being said. There were two reasons why Mosley's party was now putting so much emphasis on the "architecture of affect." One was pragmatic: with British newspapers ignoring the British Union, and with the BBC from 1935 operating a ban on Mosley, they needed to find alternative publicity routes. Yet the second, more sinister reason came from Adolf Hitler himself. In *Mein Kampf*, Hitler stressed the value of the persuasive atmospheres of big meetings whereby attendees "succumbed to the magic influence of what we might designate as 'mass suggestion'."[127] In his opinion, crowded rallies represented the most effective way for Fascism to inspire and cement loyalty. Susan Buck-Morss sees this "double role" of mass audiences – being both the subject being acted on and simultaneously the willing observers of their own manipulation, analogous to Lacan's "mirror stage" in psychology – as "the genius of Fascist propaganda," creating a cultural phantasmagoria that conceals the agency of its leaders.[128]

At Earl's Court, the Hitlerite atmospheric effect was achieved through tactile and optical means which created something akin to a cinematic dream sequence: the bank of flags/banner/emblems draped behind Mosley, his towering perch, the halo of pink light around him when speaking, the immensity of the crowd controlled through the rational efficiency of the arena's layout, and the spotlights accentuating Mosley and his "troops" when entering and leaving the hall. As Debord later observed: "Fascism is a cult of the archaic completely fitted out by modern technology."[129] The idealistic, if misguided, hopes of British Union members were being cynically manipulated by this realignment of politics with aesthetics through technification. Or, as Benjamin wrote, "a compelling urge towards new social opportunities is being clandestinely exploited in the interests of a property-owning minority."[130] Interwar British Fascism hence represented a class-based appropriation and distortion of the heroic, democratic aspirations of Modernism.

Two Architects: Henry Thomas Brock Griggs and William Vernon Coupland

The Earl's Court rally coincided with the British Union's brief revival, with membership up to around 22,500 on eve of war.[131] No attendance record was kept, but the event would have attracted virtually all British Union members, including any architects: "Most of the audience were respectable middle-class citizens who sported fascist badges."[132] Burford and Sisson had long departed, so were other architects involved? There were clearly those in the profession interested in Mosley, for *The Blackshirt* in February 1935 announced a BUF meeting purely for architects.[133] A later list by the "Friends of Oswald Mosley" reveals that two architects were interned in 1940 during the sweep-up of about 750

British Union members, a move the government felt necessary to suppress potential traitors.[134] With 12,000 architects, yet only one Fascist internee per 64,000 people, one would not have expected any architect internees. Given there were two of them, nearly 20 times above the national norm (albeit based on a tiny statistic), it is worth noting who they were.

One we have met before. Tom Brock Griggs (1900–1981), an accountant's son, came from a wealthy background and grew up partly in Gidea Park, a model housing estate in Essex.[135] He joined the Royal Flying Corps late in the First World War, then decided to become an architect, completing his studies in 1924. For reasons unknown, he successfully submitted an aquatint of Emberton's Olympia to the Royal Academy's 1930 Summer Show: maybe it had been commissioned as a publicity image.[136] Brock Griggs joined the Air Ministry as an Architectural and Civil Engineering Assistant (Grade II) in September 1933, specialising in airport design, having just joined Mosley's party. His internment files describe him as "fanatically a Fascist before the war," and "an ardent National Socialist." Brock Griggs felt Hitler had "done a wonderful job … in raising Germany from the dust to a first-rate power." He claimed to have told the Air Ministry about being a Fascist, with them merely asking him not to mention it publicly nor to become active in the BUF. Brock Griggs lived with his wife, Anne, at Bramerton Street in Chelsea. Near to King's Road, it was a few blocks from the "Black Building," the brick-built former women's teaching college which served as the BUF's headquarters and training centre for its paramilitary Fascist Defence Force from 1933 to 1935, and where he was a regular if secretive visitor. In August 1939, expecting a clampdown on the British Union, Brock Griggs wrangled a transfer with the Air Ministry to Singapore. Soon he was in trouble after writing a letter to the *Straits Times* describing Nazi Germany as his "blood-brothers." He was swiftly sent home and arrested on June 27, 1940.

Before his aberration in Singapore, Tom Brock Griggs had mostly refrained from voicing his Fascist beliefs – save for the few lapses when writing to *The Architects' Journal*, and an essay in *The Blackshirt* proposing state-run slum clearance.[137] It left the path open for his wife, Anne Brock Griggs (1905–1972). Daughter of a barrister, she was highly intelligent yet rabidly anti-semitic, as befitting a paid BUF staff member. After joining in 1933, she became Women's Propaganda Organiser, then Chief Women's Organiser (Southern), then for the whole country. "She was one of Mosley's intimates, and attended meetings of the inner cabinet of the movement," noted her internment records.[138] In May 1936, she travelled to Germany to help orchestrate the party's shift towards Nazism; soon after, Mosley married his second wife, Diana (nee Mitford), in Goebbels' Berlin sitting room, with Hitler guest-of-honour. Anne Brock Griggs stepped up the vilification of British Jews, using the pages of *Action* to savage the Viennese Jewish émigré architect, Michael Rosenauer, "and others of his tribe."[139] Meanwhile, she extolled Nazi architecture, including a gushing account of visiting Berlin's Olympic Stadium – this corresponding to growing coverage of German buildings in British journals by the late-1930s.[140]

Anne Brock Griggs was a skilled orator whom Mosley selected to stand in the LCC's East End elections in 1937, although like their other candidates, she lost badly. She was a proficient writer, penning essays for *Fascist Quarterly* and *Action's* "Women's Page" on "female" issues (wages for mothers, healthcare, sanitation, housing design, etc). In 1935 she wrote *Women and Fascism: Ten Important Points — You Have the Vote Yet are Still Powerless*, which claimed Fascism offered "freedom" for women. Emulating housing campaigners like Elizabeth Denby, two manifesto items stated: "Slums will be abolished," and "Organized national planning [of] decent homes at economic rents within 3 years."[141] These might seem progressive policies, especially when added to her call for the training of more female architects. In fact, her aim was to define appropriate lines of women's work, subordinate to men[142] — although, significantly, Brock Griggs envisaged architecture, Hitler's "profession," within the female sphere.

On May 23, 1940, Anne Brock Griggs was interned in London's Holloway Prison — the same as Lady Diana Mosley (and later Sir Oswald Mosley) — but was released by December to care for her daughters. She was offered factory work, frequently discovering the need to move on once colleagues learned of her past. Tom Brock Griggs remained intractable, voicing pro-Nazi opinions that saw him transferred to Peveril camp, toughest of all, on the Isle of Man. At a secret meeting there in August 1942, hosted by another zealot who believed Hitler was Jesus Christ's Second Coming, Brock Griggs was among those shouting "Heil Hitler!" and giving the Nazi salute.[143] Transcripts from his release appeal paint an unpleasant picture of this most unrepentant Fascist.

Little is known about the second architect internee, William Vernon Coupland (1895–1958). Yorkshire-born, a solicitor's son, he qualified in 1920 and entered partnership in Richmond-upon-Thames with William Couch.[144] In 1931, Couch retired. Coupland became the sole partner yet kept the joint name. He designed Neoclassical commercial buildings and some Art Deco/Moderne apartment blocks in Brixton, yet his speciality was houses or small estates in London's southwest suburbs in muted Arts-and-Crafts manner. Coupland's standout design was a white-rendered two-storey house (since extended) in Ailsa Road in Twickenham, dated 1935, designed not in the traditionalist style of neighbouring dwellings, but Art Deco/Moderne — and with what seems a disguised SS logo within the zig-zag pattern on its front door (Figure 10.10).

Partly this bold design was down to the client, Ernest Arthur Ireland, a surveyor for British Thomson-Houston (the company supplying the Earl's Court floodlights); he wished to portray himself as a man of modernity, eyes on the future. It offered a rare opportunity for Coupland, a secretive figure who from 1934 was a spare-time Fascist in the local BUF chapter.[145] He was however never more than a mid-ranking member, being interned at the Ascot camp, the softest option. Coupland's penance included clearance work after Liverpool air-raids. He returned to architecture after the war, under the radar. In 1991, when Bridget Cherry updated Nikolaus Pevsner's volume in the *Buildings of England* series, she described the Ailsa Road design as a "modernistic intruder" on its street.

FIGURE 10.10 Photographs of the front façade of 46 Ailsa Road in the 1970s.

Cherry was obviously unaware that Coupland had been a Fascist internee – something which might well have interested Pevsner, who was briefly interned in 1940 as an "alien" in a Liverpool camp, and whose name was on the Nazi's "Most Wanted" list for when they conquered Britain.[146]

Act 3, Stage-Set: "Hoy and Helmet" pub, South Benfleet, Essex 2014

The British Union rally at Earl's Court showed that indoor events could be effective even if public confrontations like Cable Street were not. One might imagine the outbreak of war would have ended British Fascist activities, but no. As Joe Kerr recounts, when Berthold Lubetkin and fellow Communists erected a bust of Lenin in Finsbury in May 1942, celebrating the Anglo-Soviet Treaty, the statue required 24-hour police protection – the only one – to save it from Fascist desecration.[147] After 1945, many Fascists resurfaced, including ex-internees, meaning that post-war developments were partly about old-timers. Oswald Mosley created the Union Movement but soon retrenched to Ireland, then Paris, before returning to try to make capital following the 1958 Notting Hill riots. New parties were formed, notably the National Front in the 1970s and British National Party in the 1980s, led by unremarkable men whom Graham Macklin calls "Failed Führers."[148]

Post-war British Fascists engaged in widespread violence and intimidation, increasingly targeting those from the West Indies or Indian subcontinent. They revived the tactic of anti-immigration street demonstrations, as incited by racist rhetoric from a Conservative politician, Enoch Powell. The nadir was the National Front's "Battle of Lewisham" march/rally in July 1977, but, as before, Fascist demonstrations were repeatedly neutralised by larger presences of left-wing activists (this author included). Musicians like the Clash, Steel Pulse or the Specials supported Rock Against Racism in the late-1970s, a tributary of the broader Anti-Nazi League.[149] Music, linked to protests about South African apartheid, was an effective agent in nullifying Fascist events. Likewise, Fascist parties proved ineffective in local and national elections.

Yet into the 21st century, there remains a seam of British Neo-Fascism using dog-whistle phrasing and misinformation to tap into fears and prejudices among the wider population, as Brexit showed. Britain's leading ultra-nationalist is Nigel Farage, who posed for his usual white-bloke-in-a-pub-with-a-pint photo in the "Hoy and Helmet" pub in South Benfleet, Essex on May 23, 2014. Celebrating his UK Independence Party performing its best-ever in local elections, he used the British public house as a new sensory atmosphere through which right-wing populism can appeal to working-class, racist voters. In this Essex pub, one can bedeck a bar with Union Jacks in an environment surrounded by alcohol, expressing undeclared Islamophobia by doing so. Farage's photo created a stage-set specifically to appeal to old-style "Little Englanders" who hate immigration and indeed almost everything about the contemporary globalised world. Yet if the photographic image of a privileged public space for white British citizens is now an Essex pub, then Farage realises that, as an update of the 1930s Fascist aestheticisation of politics, the image needs to be distributed via trans-spatial social media and other digital formats.

British Neo-Fascism has thus retreated from overt proclamation in buildings and streets, where, in the War of Position, it can be more easily opposed. Instead, it abuses the largely unregulated social media platforms that Donald Trump and US "cyberfascist" groups have harnessed. Fascism is therefore flirting once more off corporate capitalism, like it did at the Earl's Court Exhibition Centre in 1939. Is contemporary architecture immune from far-right populist views? Not if one listens to Leon Krier's apologia for Albert Speer, or else to a figure like Patrik Schumacher, partner in Zaha Hadid Architects, who has been accused – in, for instance, calling for poorer citizens to be relocated out of central London so only the wealthy live there – of "being an extreme example ... of how far architecture can tend toward a populist, right-wing politics."[150] Or there is Bjarke Ingels misquoting Nietzsche to claim the latter was "unfettered by moral outcomes. He went beyond what people considered reasonable in order to create new values."[151] Ingels worked briefly for Rem Koolhaas, about whom there have long been concerns that his cynical, in-your-face realism could only lead to an emptying out of architectural meaning, facilitating the corporatisation of architecture.[152]

Flirting with Neoliberalism is no joke, with its hold over architecture being criticised by many academics.[153] Notable practitioners around the world oppose its workings, whether Peter Barber (Britain), Anne Lacaton or Doina Petrescu (France), Teddy Cruz (USA) or Rahul Mehrotra (India). It is important to resist the assimilation of corporate Neo-Fascism under Neoliberalism, spread by fear and the supposed "need" for social control. Michael Hardt and Antonio Negri describe this as a new kind of all-pervasive, non-territorial "empire" that slowly smothers the world, being "formed not on the basis of force itself but on the basis of the capacity to present force as being in the service of right and peace."[154] Deleuze and Guattari argue that Neoliberalism blocks any image different to the normalised through what they term "microfascism," a repressive technique used "to stifle every little thing, every suspicious face, every dissonant voice."[155]

Yet we also need to recognise why Donald Trump and his ultra-nationalist supporters failed in the Capitol Riot. In abandoning the trans-spatial networks of social media – where Trump had free reign due to the disruptive nature of new technology – and instead presenting themselves in real space within the Capitol, they were defeated. Now they have retreated again into the digital realm, lining up investors for a right-wing populist social media channel, Truth Social, to enable them to say whatever they want "without discrimination on the basis of political ideology" – the latter of course being precisely what they are engaged in.[156] Thus, the War of Position still rages hard. If there is a danger in the focus on "affect" and the "aesthetics of atmospheres," it is the reduction in attention to the invisible workings of cultural hegemony. As 1930s British Fascism shows, especially now we are experiencing increasing dematerialisation through digitalisation, resistance must again be through the presence of bodies in space as the means to oppose right-wing populism, a Neo-Fascism that seeks to divide societies so that a few exploitative billionaires can accumulate more resources and power than they can handle. Architecture of counter-hegemony is needed more than ever.

Acknowledgements

In writing this chapter, I am especially grateful to those scholars who read an earlier draft and offered their invaluable comments and suggestions, namely Eva Branscome, Mark Crinson, Adrian Forty, Julie Gottlieb, Elizabeth McKellar and Neal Shasore. Others who were kind enough to offer information and advice about various aspects were Marcus Alexander, Joe Cain, Graham Cairns, Valeria Carullo, Elizabeth Darling, Alborz Dianat, Andrew George, John Gold, Roger Griffin, David Haney, Kaye Heron, Maria Kiladi, Ian Klinke, Tom Quick, Amy Spencer, Paul Velluet, Adam Walls and Steven Woodbridge. Librarians and archivists who helped a lot include Justine Sambrook and Anthony Wilkinson at the RIBA Library, Chris Loftus at the University of Sheffield's Special Collection and Archives, Lara Bond at the London Borough of Richmond's Local Studies Library and Archive, and Dave McCall at the Imperial War Museum London.

Notes

1 Jamie Roberts (director), "Four Hours at the Capitol," *BBC* 2 (October 20, 2021).
2 The account here of Sir Oswald Mosley and 1930s British Fascism is largely taken from the following books and texts written by those from all sides of politics: Claudia Baldoli, "Italian Fascism in Britain: The *Fasci Italiani all'Estero*, the Italian Communities, and Fascist Sympathisers during the Grandi Era (1932–1939)," PhD thesis, London School of Economics (2014): 111; Colin Peter Cook, "Towards a Greater Britain: A Political Biography of Oswald Mosley, 1918–1947," PhD Thesis, Oxford Brookes University (2000); Nigel Copsey, *Anti-Fascism in Britain* (London and New York: Routledge, 2017); Stephen Dorril, *Blackshirt: Sir Oswald Mosley and British Fascism* (London: Viking, 2006); James Drennan, *B.U.F.: Oswald Mosley and British Fascism* (Quakertown, PA: Antelope Hill Publishing, 1934/2020); Julie V. Gottlieb, *Feminine Fascism: Women in Britain's Fascist Movement* (London: I.B. Taurus, 2000/03); Julie V. Gottlieb and Thomas P. Linehan (eds), *The Culture of Fascism: Visions of the Far Right in Britain* (London and New York: I.B. Taurus, 2004); Julie V. Gottlieb, "The Marketing of Megalomania: Celebrity, Consumption and the Development of Political Technology in the British Union of Fascists," *Journal of Contemporary History* 41, no. 1 (2006): 35–55, https://doi.org/10.1177/0022009406058671; Julie Gottlieb, "British Union of Fascists," *Oxford Dictionary of National Biography Online*, 24th May 2008, https://doi.org/10.1093/ref:odnb/96364; Roger Griffin, *The Nature of Fascism* (London and New York: Routledge, 1993); Thomas Norman Keeley, "Blackshirts Torn: Inside the British Union of Fascists, 1932–1940," MA Thesis, Simon Fraser University (1998); Jon Lawrence, "Fascist Violence and the Politics of Public Order in Britain: The Olympia Debate Revisited," *Historical Research* 76, no. 192 (2003): 238–267; Jon Lawrence, "Why Olympia Mattered," *Historical Research* 78, no. 200 (2005): 263–272; Gary Love, "What's the Big Idea? Oswald Mosley, the British Union of Fascists and Generic Fascism," *Journal of Contemporary History* 42, no. 3 (July 2007): 447–468; Graham

Macklin, "Onwards Blackshirts! Music and the British Union of Fascists," *Patterns of Prejudice* 47, no. 4–5 (2013): 430–457; Michael Mann, *Fascists* (Cambridge: Cambridge University Press, 2004); John Millican, *Mosley's Men in Black: Uniforms, Flags and Insignia of the British Union of Fascists 1932–1940 and Union Movement* (London: Sanctuary Press, 2020); Oswald Mosley, *Fascism for the Million* (London: Sanctuary Press, 1936/2019); Oswald Mosley, *My Answer* (London: Sanctuary Press, 1946/2019); Oswald Mosley, *My Life* (London: Sanctuary Press, 1968/2019); Sybil Oldfield, *The Black Book: The Britons on the Nazi List* (London: Profile Books, 2021); Martin Pugh, "The British Union of Fascists and the Olympia Debate," *The Historical Journal* 41, no. 2 (1998): 529–542; Martin Pugh, *Hurrah for the Blackshirts! Fascists and Fascism in Britain Between the Wars* (London: Cape, 2005); Martin Pugh, "The National Government, the British Union of Fascists and the Olympia Debate," *Historical Research* 78, no. 200 (2005): 253–262; Bret Rubin, "The Rise and Fall of British Fascism: Sir Oswald Mosley and the British Union of Fascists," *Intersections* 11, no. 2 (2010): 323–380; Michael A. Spurr, "'Living the Blackshirt Life': Culture, Community and the British Union of Fascists, 1932–1940," *Contemporary European History* 12, no. 3 (2003): 305–322; Richard Thurlow, *Fascism in Britain: From Oswald Mosley's Blackshirts to the National Front* (London and New York: I.B. Taurus, 1987/98).

3 Antonio Gramsci, *Selections from the Prison Notebooks* (New York: International Publishers, 1971).

4 This was the challenge laid down to architects in Manfredo Tafuri, *Architecture and Utopia: Design and Capitalist Development* (Cambridge, MA and London: MIT Press, 1973/76) and Manfredo Tafuri, *Theories and History of Architecture* (London: Granada, 1968/80). It was the intention of US "post-critical" architectural theory to deny the relevance of any such debates, yet the challenge proved vapid. The most important contributions remain: Hilde Heynen, *Architecture and Modernity: A Critique* (Cambridge, MA and London: MIT Press, 1999); Fredric Jameson, "Architecture and the Critique of Ideology," in *The Ideologies of Theory* (London: Verso, 2008), 344–471.

5 Gernot Böhme, *Invasive Technification: Critical Essays in the Philosophy of Technology* (London: Bloomsbury, 2008/2012), 17.

6 Gernot Böhme, *Atmospheric Architectures: The Aesthetics of Felt Spaces*, ed. Tina Engels-Schwarzpaul (London: Bloomsbury, 2013/2017); Gernot Böhme, *The Aesthetics of Atmospheres*, ed. Jean-Paul Thibaud (London and New York: Routledge, 2017); Gernot Böhme, *Critique of Aesthetic Capitalism* (Berlin: Mimesis International, 2017); Tonino Griffero, "Critique of Aesthetic Capitalism: A Short Interview with Gernot Böhme," *Mimesis International*, accessed September 15, 2021, http://mimesisinternational.com/-a-short-interview-with-gernot-bohme-author-of-critique-of-aesthetic-capitalism/. See also Christian Borch (ed.), *Architectural Atmospheres: On the Experience and Politics of Architecture* (Basel: Birkhauser, 2014), 43–89.

7 Walter Benjamin, "The Work of Art in the Age of its Technological Reproducibility: Second Version," in *Selected Writings, 3: 1935–1938*, ed. Howard Eiland and Michael W. Jennings (Cambridge, MA: Harvard University Press, 2006), 120.

8 The key texts by Gilles Deleuze and Felix Guattari are *Anti-Oedipus (L'Anti-Oedipe) [Capitalism and Schizophrenia I]* (London: Bloomsbury, 1972/2013) and *A Thousand Plateaus (Mille Plateaux) [Capitalism and Schizophrenia II]* (Minneapolis, MN: Minnesota University Press, 1980/87). Many contemporary architectural historians/theorists have taken up these ideas, with the most notable being: Douglas Spencer, *The Architecture of Neoliberalism: How Contemporary Architecture Became an Instrument of Control and Compliance* (London: Bloomsbury, 2016); Marko Jobst and Helene Frichot (eds.), *Architectural Affects after Deleuze and Guattari* (Abingdon and New York: Routledge, 2021).

9 Roger Griffin, "Building the Visible Immortality of the Nation: The Centrality of 'Rooted Modernism' to the Third Reich's Architectural New Order," *Fascism* 7 (2018): 42.

10 Thomas P. Linehan, "Cultures of Space: Spatialising the National Front," in *Cultures of Post-War British Fascism*, ed. Nigel Copsey and John E. Richardson (London and New York: Routledge, 2015), 49–67.

11 Walter Benjamin, *The Arcades Project*, translated by Howard Eiland and Kevin McLaughlin (Cambridge, MA and London: The Belknap Press of Harvard University Press, 1999); Susan Buck-Morss, *The Dialectics of Seeing: Walter Benjamin and the Arcades Project* (Cambridge, MA and London: MIT Press, 1989); Henri Lefebvre, *The Production of Space* (Oxford: Blackwell, 1974/91).

12 Griffin, "Building the Visible Immortality of the Nation": 9–44. See also: Roger Griffin, "'This Fortress Built Against Infection': The BUF Vision of Britain's Theatrical and Musical Renaissance," in *The Culture of Fascism*, ed. Gottlieb and Linehan, 45–65.

13 *The Blackshirt*, no. 20 (30th December 1933–5th January 1934): 3.

14 Oswald Mosley, *The Greater Britain* (London: Greater Britain Publications, 1932), 25.

15 Griffin, *The Nature of Fascism*.

16 Richard Overy, *Blood and Ruins: The Great Imperial War 1931–1945* (London: Allen Lane, 2021).

17 Overy, 19, 26–29.

18 Gottlieb, "The Marketing of Megalomania": 35–55. For a similar proposition about what was happening in Nazi Germany see: Nicholas O'Shaughnessy, *Marketing the Third Reich: Persuasion, Packaging and Propaganda* (Abingdon: Routledge, 2018).

19 The BUF songs, "Mosley!" and "Britain Awake!," received their first public performance at a 10,000-strong rally in the Royal Albert Hall on April 22, 1934: "Two Fascist Songs: Publication for Royal Albert Hall Meeting," *The Blackshirt*, no. 52 (April 20–26, 1934): 3; W.J. Leaper, "Leader's Inspired Speech: A Hallowed Memory to Blackshirts," *The Blackshirt*, no. 53 (April 27– May 3, 1934): 1.

20 Siegfried Kracauer, *From Caligari to Hitler: A Psychological History of the German Film* (Princeton, NJ and Oxford: Princeton University Press, 1947/2004): 91–95, 149–152, 162–164, 248, 272, 296–303. For more about *Die Nibelungen* (1924) and *Metropolis* (1927), and the three set designers that Lang used on both films – Erich Kettelhut, Otto Hunte and Karl Vollbrecht – see Dietrich Neumann (ed.), *Film Architecture: Set Designs from Metropolis to Blade Runner* (Munich and New York: Prestel, 1996): 74–79, 94–103.

21 Benjamin, "The Work of Art in the Age of its Technological Reproducibility," 101–133. For the links of the essay to Fascism, see: Böhme, *The Aesthetics of Atmospheres*, 31–32; Susan Buck-Morss, "Aesthetics and Anaesthetics: Walter Benjamin's Artwork Essay Reconsidered," *October* 62 (Autumn 1992): 3–41; Peter Osborne, "Walter Benjamin," *Stanford Encyclopedia of Philosophy* (January 18, 2011, revised October 14, 2020), accessed December 15, 2021, https://plato.stanford.edu/entries/benjamin/.

22 Guy Debord, *The Society of the Spectacle* (New York: Zone Books, 1967/95), 47.

23 Böhme, *Atmospheric Architectures*, 157–166; Böhme, *The Aesthetics of Atmospheres*, 135–140.

24 The account here of post-war fascism in Britain is taken mainly from: Copsey and Richardson (eds), *Cultures of Post-War British Fascism*; Copsey, *Anti-Fascism in Britain*; Graham Macklin, *Very Deeply Dyed in Black: Sir Oswald Mosley and the Resurrection of British Fascism After 1945* (London: I.B. Taurus, 2007); Graham Macklin, *Failed Führers: A History of Britain's Extreme Right* (London and New York: Routledge, 2020); David Renton, "The Attempted Revival of British Fascism: Fascism and Anti-Fascism 1945–51," PhD thesis, University of Sheffield (1998); David Renton, *Fascism, Anti-Fascism and Britain in the 1940s* (Basingstoke: Macmillan, 2000); David Renton, *Never Again: Rock Against Racism and the Anti-Nazi League 1976–1982* (London and New York: Routledge, 2019); Thurlow, *Fascism in Britain*.

25 Donald Trump as quoted in: James Clayton, "A Year on, has Trump Benefitted from a Twitter Ban?" *BBC News Online* (January 12, 2022), accessed January 14, 2022, https://www.bbc.co.uk/news/technology-59948946.

26 Michael Hardt and Antonio Negri, *Empire* (Cambridge, MA: Harvard University Press, 2000).

27 Benjamin, "The Work of Art in the Age of its Technological Reproducibility," 120–121.

28 Benjamin, 128 (f. 23).

29 John Gunther, *Inside Europe* (New York and London: Harper and Brothers, 1936), 265.

30 Millican, *Mosley's Men in Black*. For analysis of the Blackshirt's clothing aesthetic, see: Philip M. Coupland, "The Black Shirt in Britain: The Meaning and Function of Political Uniform," in *The Culture of Fascism*, ed. Gottlieb and Linehan, 100–115.

31 Henry B. Rayner and Robert Stevens, "Fascism and Ministry of Fine Arts," *Musical Times* 75, no. 1098 (August 1934): 737–738. See also: M.B. Wallace, "An Artistic Renaissance," *Fascist Week*, no. 22 (April 13–19, 1934): 4.

32 E. D. Randall, "The Flame of Fascism: Discarding the Selfish Futilities of Individualism," *Fascist Week*, no. 11, (January 19–25, 1934): 4.

33 E. D. Randall, "Fascism and Culture: True Place of Creative Genius," *The Blackshirt*, no. 48 (March 23–29, 1934): 1.

34 E. D. Randall, "Fascism and Culture": 1.

35 Stephen Dorril, *Blackshirt*, 103; Mosley, *My Life*, 123.

36 Mosley, *My Life*, 136.

37 Buckinghamshire Gardens Trust Research and Recording Project, "Understanding Historic Parks and Gardens in Buckinghamshire: Savay Farm, Denham" (March 2017), accessed February 26, 2022, https://bucksgardenstrust.org.uk/wp-content/uploads/2016/10/Savay_Farm_Denham.pdf; Dorril, *Blackshirt*, 239; Robert Skidelsky, *Oswald Mosley* (New York: Holt, Rinehart & Winston, 1975), 298.

38 She was christened Margaret Helen Anna, with the third forename sometimes being spelled as Ann, or else with her surname hyphenated as Brock-Griggs.

39 Theo Lang, "Mussolini, a Man of the Twentieth Century: Building a New Nation," *The Blackshirt*, no. 94 (February 8, 1935): 8. See also: Claudia Baldoli, "Anglo-Italian Fascist Solidarity?: The Shift from Italophilia to Naziphilia in the BUF," in *The Culture of Fascism*, ed. Gottlieb and Linehan, 147–148, 151; Francesca Billiani, *Fascist Modernism in Italy: Arts and Regimes* (London: Bloomsbury, 2021); Julie Gottlieb, "Britain's New Fascist Men," in *The Culture of Fascism*, ed. Gottlieb and Linehan, 89; Flavia Marcello, "Building the Image of Power: Images of *Romanita* in the Civic Architecture of Fascist Italy," in *Brill's Companion to the Classics: Fascist Italy and Nazi Germany*, ed. Helen Roche and Kyriakos Demetriou (Leiden: Brill, 2017): 325–369. DOI: https://doi.org/10.1163/9789004299061_015; Flavia Marcello, "Forma urbis Mussolinii: Vision and Rhetoric in the Designs for Fascist Rome," in *Brill's Companion to the Classics: Fascist Italy and Nazi Germany*, ed. Roche and Demetriou: 370–403.

40 Indicating the growth of interest within 1930s British journals, see: "A Children's Holiday Centre, Santa Severa, Italy," *The Architect and Building News* (October 16, 1936): 75–77; "The Military Centre at Grappa," *The Architect and Building News* (December 25, 1936): 380–381; Pier Luigi Nervi, "Reinforced Concrete Aeroplane Hangar in Italy," *The Architect and Building News* (September 16, 1938): 320; "Periodicals, July Anthology: Italy," *The Architects' Journal* (August 17, 1939): 249–250; "School of Mathematics, Rome," *The Architectural Review* (November 1936): 204–206; "Some Recent Italian Buildings," *The Architectural Review* (June 1940): 193–194; Valeria Carullo, "Lo Sguardo D'Oltermanica sul Moderno," *Domus* (January 2017): 28–31.

41 Francis [Frank] Rowland Yerbury, "The AA Excursion, 1933 – Italy, Old and New," *Architectural Association Journal* 49, no. 562 (December 1933): 207–223.

42 Anon, "Alister Gladstone MacDonald (or Alistair Gladstone MacDonald)," *Dictionary of Scottish Architects Biography Report*, accessed October 18, 2021, http://www.scottisharchitects.org.uk/architect_full.php?id=202048.

43 Thomas Stearns Eliot, as cited in Leslie Susser, "Right Wings over Britain: T.E. Hulme and the Intellectual Rebellion against Democracy," in *The Intellectual Revolt against Liberal Democracy, 1870–1945*, ed. Zeev Sternhell (Jerusalem: 1996), 371. See also: Dan Stone, "The English Mistery, the BUF, and the Dilemmas of British Fascism," *The Journal of Modern History* 75, no. 2 (June 2003): 336–358.

44 Bentley B. Gilbert, "Health and Politics: The British National Deterioration Report of 1904," *Bulletin of the History of Medicine* 39, no. 2 (March–April 1965): 143–153.

45 Richard Overy, *The Morbid Age: Britain Between the Wars* (London: Allen Lane, 2009); David Skilton, "Contemplating the Ruins of London: Macaulay's New Zealander and Others," *Literary London: Interdisciplinary Studies in the Representation of London* 2, no. 1 (March 2004), accessed on October 18, 2021, http://www.literary-london.org/london-journal/march2004/skilton.html; Blanchard Jerrold and Gustav Dore, *London: A Pilgrimage* (London: John Murray, 1871); Oswald Spengler, *Der Untergang des Abendlandes (The Decline of the West)* (Berlin: Albatross Verlag, 1918/1922/2007).

46 Murray Fraser and Catherine Gregg (eds.), *Sir Banister Fletcher's Global History of Architecture* (London: Bloomsbury, 2020), xi–xxxviii.

47 Murray Fraser with Joe Kerr, *Architecture and the "Special Relationship": The American Influence on Post-War British Architecture* (London and New York: Routledge, 2007), 39–122; Anne Orde, *The Eclipse of Great Britain: The United States and British Imperial Decline, 1895–1956* (Basingstoke and London: Macmillan, 1996).

48 Robert Briffault, *The Decline and Fall of the British Empire* (New York: Simon and Schuster, 1938); Edward Gibbon, *The History of the Decline and Fall of the Roman Empire* (London: Strahan and Cadell, 1776–1789).

49 Charlotte Benton, *A Different World: Emigré Architects in Britain, 1928–1958* (London: RIBA Heinz Gallery, 1995), 70.

50 Canadian Centre for Architecture, Wells Coates Fonds, 30: 21, 23 (1/2) 22 (publications) B.20.1.03, *Proceedings of the Architectural Association General Meeting*, Tuesday 22nd March 1938, p. 456]. See also: Michela Rosso, "John N. Summerson and Tales of Modern Architecture," *The Journal of Architecture* 5, no. 1 (2000): 65–89. Based also on email correspondence from Elizabeth McKellar, formerly at the Open University, to author (December 30, 2021).

51 John Patrick Carswell, *Lives and Letters: Literary Reminiscences* (London: New Directions, 1978), 148; Andrew Saint, "Wright and Great Britain," in *Frank Lloyd Wright: Europe and Beyond*, ed. Anthony Alofsin (Los Angeles, CA: University of California Press, 1999), 131–146.

52 Reginald Theodore Blomfield, *Modernismus* (London: Macmillan, 1934). See also: David Dean, *The Thirties: Recalling the English Architectural Scene* (London: RIBA Drawings Collection/Trefoil Books, 1983), 36–38; William Whyte, "The Englishness of English Architecture: Modernism and the Making of the International Style, 1927–1957," *Journal of British Studies* 48, no. 2 (April 2009): 450–451, 458.

53 Ashley Maher, "'Three-Dimensional' Modernism: The Language of Architecture and British Literary Periodicals," *Journal of Modern Literature* 43, no. 1 (Fall 2019): 71–93. https://doi.org/10.2979/jmodelite.43.1.05; Ashley Maher, *Reconstructing Modernism: British Literature, Modern Architecture and the State* (Oxford: Oxford University Press, 2020), 159–160, 205–209.

54 See for instance the fascinating comparisons in Diane Ghirardo, *Building New Communities: New Deal America and Fascist Italy* (Princeton, NJ: Princeton University Press, 1989).

55 David Frazer Lewis, "The Ideal of Architecture as Sculpted Mass during the Interwar period," *Sculpture Journal* 25, no. 3 (2016): 343–360. https://doi.org/10.3828/sj.2016.25.3.5. See also: Sarah Crellin, "Let There be History: Epstein's BMA House Sculptures," *Modern British Sculpture*, ed. Penelope Curtis and Keith Wilson (London: Royal Academy of Art, 2011), 36–42.

56 Alan Powers, "Holden, Charles (Henry)," Oxford Art Online/Oxford University Press, 2003. https://doi.org/10.1093/gao/9781884446054.article.T038611. See also: Ted Ruddock, "Charles Holden and the Issue of Tall Buildings in London, 1927–47," *Construction History* 12 (1996): 83–99.

57 John Newenham Summerson (J.N.S.), "All Sorts of Sculpture," *The Architect and Building News* (December 27, 1935): 381.

58 For a typically brutal Fascist attack on Epstein, see: The Archer, "Self-Portraiture," *Action*, no. 77 (August 7, 1937): 14.

59 Murray Fraser (with Joe Kerr), *Architecture and the "Special Relationship"*, 93–103, 105–107.

60 Brian Hanson, "Singing the Body Electric with Charles Holden," *The Architectural Review* (December 1975): 350; Alison Smithson, "The Responsibility of Lutyens," *RIBA Journal* (April 1969): 150; Richard Simpson, "Classicism and Modernity: The University of London's Senate House," *Bulletin of the Institute of Classical Studies* 43 (1999): 41–95.

61 A selection taken from around 200 original joint articles was published as Howard Robertson and Francis Rowland Yerbury, *Travels in Modern Architecture* (London: Architectural Association, 1989). See also: Jasmine Benyamin, "Hoarding Knowledge: F.R. Yerbury and Howard Robertson's Records of the Modern Movement," paper at Association of Collegiate Schools of Architects Annual Meeting (2016), accessed on November 24, 2021, https://www.acsa-arch.org/proceedings/Annual%20Meeting%20Proceedings/ACSA.AM.104/ACSA.AM.104.49.pdf.

62 Charlotte Benton, *A Different World*, 33–106; Valeria Carullo, "Island of Last Hope: Refugee Architects on the Brink of the Second World War," online lecture to 2021 Art History Festival, September 21, 2021; David Dean, *The Thirties*, 136–137.

63 John R. Gold, *The Experience of Modernism: Modern Architects and the Future City, 1928–1953* (London: E and FN Spon, 1997), 120–140, 145–163; John R. Gold. "'A Very Serious Responsibility'? The MARS Group, Internationality and Relations with CIAM, 1933–39," *Architectural History* 56 (2013): 249–275. https://doi.org/10.1017/S0066622X00002501. See also: Elizabeth Darling, *Re-Forming Britain: Narratives of Modernity before Reconstruction* (London and New York: Routledge, 2007): 42–44, 118–125, 172–174; Elizabeth Darling, "Institutionalizing English Modernism 1924–33: From the Vers Group to MARS," *Architectural History* 55 (2012): 299–300. https://doi.org/10.1017/S0066622X0000137; Elizabeth Darling, *Wells Coates* (London: RIBA Enterprises, 2012).

64 Wells Coates, "Response to Tradition," *Architectural Review* (November 1932): 168. For F.R.S. Yorke's approach, see: Francis Reginald Stevens [F.R.S.] Yorke, "The Facing of Steel and Concrete Buildings," *The Architectural Review* (November 1932): 161–164.

65 Charles Reilly, *Scaffolding in the Sky*; Nikolaus Pevsner, *Pioneers of the Modern Movement: From William Morris to Walter Gropius* (London: Penguin, 1936/1991); Joseph Sharples, Alan Powers and Michael Shippobottom, *Charles Reilly and the Liverpool School of Architecture, 1904–1933* (Liverpool: Liverpool University Press, 1996); Whyte, "The Englishness of English Architecture": 441–465.

66 "Westwood," Windsor Road, Gerrard's Cross, Buckinghamshire, designed (1935) by James Burford', *The Architect and Building News* 144 (November 15, 1935): 104. See also: Jeremy Gould, *Modern Houses in Britain, 1919–1939* (London: Society of the Architectural Historians of Great Britain, 1977), 37.

67 James Burford, "Old Wine in New Bottles," *The Architectural Review* (September 1930): 131–134.

68 "A House at Cambridge: Designed by Marshall Sisson, 1934," *The Architectural Review* (December 1932): 266–268; "House at Carlyon Bay, Cornwall, 1934: Marshall Sisson," *The Architectural Review* (December 1936): 306–307; James Bettley, "Marshall Sisson, 1897–1978," *Transactions of the Royal Institute of British Architects* 1/2 (1982): 93–100; James Bettley, "Sisson, Marshall (Arnott)," *Oxford Art Online*,

2003, accessed September 8, 2021, https://doi.org/10.1093/gao/9781884446054. article.T079021; Louise Campbell, "A Call to Order: The Rome Prize and Early Twentieth-Century British Architecture," *Architectural History* 32 (1989): 143; David Dean, *The Thirties*, 24–26, 103, 130, 134; Gould, *Modern Houses in Britain*, 13, 14, 38, 39, 42, plates 10 + 41.

69 Sir Herbert Bartlett's donation was not offered as cash, but as the forfeited costs of building works by Bartlett's firm, including a notional 10% profit. See: University College Committee (University of London), minutes of meeting on January 12, 1912, item 51: "Report of Sub-Committee on Arrangements in Connection with Gift of £30,000 for College Buildings", 47; Amy Spencer, "University College London: An Architectural History, 1825–1939," PhD thesis, University College London (2021): 239–248, 277–278.

70 The excellent research by UCL professor, Joe Cain, and assistant, Maria Kiladi, has compelled UCL to rename the Pearson Building and Galton Lecture Theatre. See: Legacies of Eugenics website, accessed September 28, 2021, https://legacies-of-eugenics.org/about/; Francis Galton, *Memories of My Life* (London: Methuen, 1908), 321. Also quoted in Karl Pearson, *The Life, Letters and Labours of Francis Galton* (Cambridge: Cambridge University Press, 1914/1924/1930), 223–224.

71 Filon, Louis Napoleon George, George Udny Yule, Harald Westergaard, Major Greenwood, and Karl Pearson, *Speeches Delivered at a Dinner Held in University College, London in Honour of Professor Karl Pearson, 23 April 1934* (Cambridge: privately printed at the University Press, 1934), 23.

72 David Redvaldsen, "'Science must be the Basis': Sir Oswald Mosley's Political Parties and their Policies on Health, Science and Scientific Racism 1931–1974," *Contemporary British History* 30, no. 3 (2016): 368–388. https://doi.org/10.1080/13619462.2016.1144511.

73 Lyndsay Andrew Farrall, *The Origins and Growth of the English Eugenics Movement* (London: UCL Department of Science and Technology Studies), STS Occasional Papers no. 9, 1969/1985/2019, preface to 1985 edition. See also: M. Eileen Magnello, "The Non-Correlation of Biometrics and Eugenics: Rival Forms of Laboratory Work in Karl Pearson's Career at University College London, Part 2," *Historical Science* 37 (1999): 123–150; Overy, *The Morbid Age Wars*, 93–135.

74 University College Committee (University of London), minutes of meeting on January 3, 1933/November 5, 1929/December 3, 1929/January 7, 1930/January 3, 1933; UCL Special Collections, PEARSON 4/11; Correspondence regarding animal house (1929–30) in PEARSON 4/27; "Block Plan of University College, London (1935)," UCL Special Collections: HISTORICAL DOCUMENTS 7/10/9, accessed October 14, 2021, https://cpb-eu-w2.wpmucdn.com/blogs.ucl.ac.uk/dist/1/541/files/2019/07/hist_docs_7_10_box_9.jpg; *The Builder* (July 17, 1931): 98, 110; Henry Law Jackson, *Lewis's 1844–1944: A Brief Account of a Century's Work* (London: H.K. Lewis, 1945), 73–76; Tom Quick, "The Making of a New Race in the Early Twentieth Century Imperial Imaginary," *The Historical Journal* 63, no. 5 (2020): 1252–1254.

75 Quick, "The Making of a New Race": 1231–1256. See also: "Pekingese Dogs kept at UCL by Karl Pearson," Pearson Archive, UCL Special Collections: PEARSON 7/158/2.

76 'A British Architect', "Alien Architects Invade Britain," *Fascist Week*, no. 12 (January 26–February 1, 1934): 7. The matter arose again in "Alien Architects," *Fascist Week*, no. 14 (February 9–15, 1934): 4.

77 Henry Thomas Brock Griggs, letter to the editors of *The Architects' Journal* (February 15, 1935): 244. It was accompanied by two letters reprinted from a Bexhill newspaper, with one of those being the response from Earl De La Warr, Mayor of Bexhill Council; Letters to the editors from Wesley Dougill, D.L. Bridgwater, Henry Thomas Brock Griggs, James Burford and A.G. Gibson to *The Architects' Journal* (February 22, 1935): 278–279; Letters from Earl de la Warr, James Burford, Wesley Dougill and J. Lewis Wonersley to the editors of *The Architects' Journal* (March 5, 1934): 351. See also: "The De La Warr Pavilion, Bexhill – 1," *The Architect and Building News* (December 20, 1935): 343–347; Charlotte Benton, *A Different World*, 47–48; David Dean, *The*

Thirties, 133–135; Anthony Jackson, "The Politics of Architecture: English Architecture 1929–1951," *Journal of the Society of Architectural Historians* 24, no. 1 (March 1965): 97–107; Russell Stevens and Peter Willis, "Earl de La Warr and the Competition for the Bexhill Pavilion, 1933–34," *Architectural History* 33 (1990): 135–166; Whyte, "The Englishness of English Architecture": 447.

78 "A Question to Sir Oswald Mosley," *The Architects' Journal* (February 22, 1934): 269.

79 Two letters to the editors, one of them signed 'By a number of Fascist architects', and the other from Alexander Raven Thomson, Deputy Director of Policy, British Union of Fascists, *The Architects' Journal* (April 19, 1934): 566–567.

80 Serge Chermayeff and James Maude Richards, "A Hundred Years Ahead: Forecasting the Coming Century," *The Architects' Journal* (January 10, 1935): 79–86; Letter to the editors from Arthur Kenneth Chesterton, *The Architects' Journal* (January 17, 1935): 120; Letters to the editors from A. Croft, C.H. Stoney and Keith Aitken, *The Architects' Journal* (January 24, 1935): 159–160; Letters to the editors from Arthur Kenneth Chesterton, 'Anti-Fascist', D.V.W.P., J.H. Madge, 'Progressive Architect', F. Wickham, and response from Serge Chermayeff and James Maude Richards, *The Architects' Journal* (January 31, 1935): 188–190; Letters to the editors from Cyril Adler, Arthur Kenneth Chesterton, Robert Townsend, Henry Thomas Brock Griggs and James MacQuedy, *The Architects' Journal* (February 14, 1935): 263–264; 'Architect', "Outlook Unsettled," *The Blackshirt*, no. 97 (March 1, 1935): 7; "Homes for Britons: How Democracy Diddles the Workers," *The Blackshirt*, no. 169 (July 18, 1936): 5; Gavin Stamp, "Richards, Sir James Maude [Jim] (1907–1992)," *Oxford Dictionary of National Biography Online* (2005), accessed October 28, 2021, https://www.oxforddnb.com/view/10.1093/ref:odnb/9780198614128.001.0001/-odnb-9780198614128-e-51298/version/1.

81 Bettley, "Marshall Sisson": 97.

82 *The Architect and Building News* (January 24, 1930): 130–137; *The Architect and Building News* (October 3, 1930): 455, 468–469; *The Architect and Building News* (January 9, 1931): 74–76; *The Architects' Journal* (April 8, 1937): 601–606; *The Architectural Review* (April 1930): 319–320; Felix Brittain (ed.), *Olympia: A Souvenir Review Commemorating the Golden Jubilee 1887–1937* (London/Cheltenham: Edward J Burrow and Co, 1937); David Dean, *The Thirties*, 93, 111–112, 125, 133; Historic England, "Grand Hall and Pillar Hall, Olympia Exhibition Centre," Listed Building Description, 2003/2018, accessed October 14, 2021, https://historicengland.org.uk/listing/the-list/list-entry/1096048; Rosemary Ind, "A Style of His Own," *Building Design* (February 14, 1975): 14–16; Rosemary Ind, *Emberton* (London/Berkeley, CA: Scolar Press, 1983); Matthew Whitfield, *Olympia Exhibition Centre Research Report* (London: Historic England, 2018). See also the full planning application by Olympus Property Holding Limited submitted to London Borough of Hammersmith and Fulham, ref. 2018/03100/FUL (October 11, 2018): 50–51.

83 John Compton, "The Night Architecture of the 'Thirties," *The Journal of the Decorative Arts Society* 4 (1980): 40–47.

84 Anon, "Hundred Per Cent Beautiful: Architect Defends Modern Buildings," *Liverpool Echo* (November 9, 1932): 13.

85 *Sheffield Independent* (July 20, 1933): 1.

86 *Staffordshire Sentinel* (March 13, 1931): 8.

87 Anon, "The London Letter," *Aberdeen Press and Journal* (July 13, 1929): 6.

88 *Staffordshire Sentinel* (January 27, 1930): 6.

89 *Staffordshire Sentinel* (April 24, 1929): 8.

90 Anon, "The Biggest Building in the Empire", *Atherstone News and Herald* (September 6, 1929): 7.

91 Anon, "The Biggest Building in the Empire": 7.

92 Anon, "Olympia to be Bigger: Colossal Extension to be Built," *West London Observer* (February 24, 1933): 3.

93 *Staffordshire Sentinel* (August 5, 1930): 4.

94 Viscount Rothermere, "Hurrah for the Blackshirts!," *Daily Mail* (January 15, 1934): 10.

95 Email correspondence from Elizabeth Darling, Oxford Brookes University, to author (December 20, 2021); Email correspondence from John Gold, Oxford Brookes University, to author (July 30, 2021); In-person interview with Neal Shasore at the London School of Architecture (July 5, 2021).

96 Pugh, *Hurrah for the Blackshirts!*, 166–167; Robert Skidelsky, "Great Britain," in *Fascism in Europe*, ed. Stuart Joseph Woolf (London: Routledge, 1968/81), 273; Thurlow, *Fascism in Britain*, 91–99; Gerry Webber, "Patterns of Membership and Support for the British Union of Fascists," *Journal of Contemporary History* 19 (1984): 575–606.

97 William Joyce, "Searchlight over Britain," *Action*, no. 6 (March 26, 1936): 10.

98 E.D. Randall, "Bourgeois Bolshevism," *Action*, no. 103 (February 5, 1938): 7.

99 Martin Kitchen, *Speer: Hitler's Architect* (New Haven, CT and London: Yale University Press, 2015), 50; Barbara Miller Lane, *Architecture and Politics in Germany, 1918–1945* (Cambridge, MA: Harvard University Press, 1968); Barbara Miller Lane, "Architects in Power: Politics and Ideology in the Work of Ernst May and Albert Speer," *Journal of Interdisciplinary History* 17, no. 1 (Summer 1986): 183–310. See also: Iain Boyd Whyte, "National Socialism and Architecture," in *Art and Power: Europe under the Dictators*, ed. Dawn Ades (London: Hayward Gallery, 1995): 258–269; Iain Boyd Whyte, "National Socialism, Classicism, and Architecture," in *Brill's Companion to the Classics: Fascist Italy and Nazi Germany*, ed. Roche and Demetriou (Leiden: Brill, 2017): 404–434. DOI: https://doi.org/10.1163/9789004299061_016; Griffin, "Building the Visible Immortality of the Nation"; Despina Stratigakos, *Hitler at Home* (New Haven, CT and London: Yale University Press, 2015); Robert Taylor, *The Word in Stone: The Role of Architecture in National Socialist Ideology* (Berkeley, CA: University of California Press, 1974); Jochen Thies, *Hitler's Plan for Global Domination: Architecture and Ultimate War Aims* (New York and Oxford: Berghahn Books, 1967/2012).

100 Albert Speer, *Spandau Tagebucher* (1975), 202 – as quoted in Kitchen, *Speer*, 32.

101 Roger Griffin, "Building the Visible Immortality of the Nation," *Fascism* 7 (2018): 41–43.

102 Neal Ethan Shasore, *Designs on Democracy: Architecture and the Public in Interwar London* (Oxford: Oxford University Press, 2022).

103 Peter Richard Pugh, "A Political Biography of Alexander Raven Thomson," PhD thesis, University of Sheffield (2002): 27.

104 Anne Brock Griggs, "May-Day in Germany: A Leader Speaks to His People," *Action*, no. 13 (May 14, 1936): 6.

105 Hitler had never completed his school certificate and he certainly didn't want to return to school to obtain the necessary qualifications to study architecture. See: Alan Bullock, *Hitler: A Study in Tyranny* (New York: Harper and Row, 1962/71), 4–7; Gunther, *Inside Europe*, 1–2; Adolf Hitler, *Mein Kampf*, translated by Ralph Manheim (Boston, MA and New York: Houghton Mifflin, 1925/27/71/99), 17, 19, 20, 35, 124.

106 For a personal account by Speer of his relationship with Hitler, see: Albert Speer, "Preface/Foreword," in Leon Krier, *Albert Speer: Architecture, 1932–1942* (Brussels: Archives D'Architecture Moderne, 1985), 9–10, 213–214. For an example of the repeated claim by Nazi officials that Hitler was an architect, see the quote made by his personal adjutant Fritz Wiedemann in James J. Fortuna, "Fascism, National Socialism, and the 1939 New York World's Fair," *Fascism* 8 (2019): 203. For an account of Gerdy Troost's relationship with Hitler, see: Stratigakos, *Hitler at Home*, 107–146, 187–193.

107 Sandy Eisenstadt, "A Century of Progress International Exhibition – Chicago, Illinois – 1933," in *Architecture of the Night: The Illuminated Building*, ed. Dietrich Neumann (Munich/London: Prestel, 2002), 164–165.

108 Dietrich Neumann, "Lichtarchitektur and the Avant-Garde" and "Neue Reichskanzlei – Berlin – 1939," in *Architecture of the Night*, ed. Neumann, 46–47, 174–175; Albert Speer, *Inside the Third Reich: Memoirs by Albert Speer* (New York: Macmillan, 1970), 59. See also: Paul B. Jaskot, *The Architecture of Oppression: The SS, Forced Labor and the Nazi Building Economy* (London: Routledge, 2009); Kitchen, *Speer*; Krier, *Albert Speer*. Krier's misguided book was slightly revised and

republished in 2013 by Monacelli Press but without the "Preface/Foreword" by Albert Speer (instead a new "Foreword" was written by Robert Stern); Sharon Macdonald, "Words in Stone? Agency and Identity in a Nazi Landscape," *Journal of Material Culture* 11, no. 1–2 (2006): 108–110; Sharon Macdonald, *Difficult Heritage: Negotiating the Nazi Heritage in Nuremberg and Beyond* (London: Routledge, 2008); Taylor, *The Word in Stone*.

109 Jean-Louis Cohen, *Architecture in Uniform: Designing and Building for the Second World War* (Montreal/Paris: Canadian Centre for Architecture/Editions Hazan, 2011), 127–128; Jaskot, *The Architecture of Oppression*; Kitchen, *Speer*, 4–5, 38–39, 72–100.

110 Alan J. Clark, "Notes on the History of Nos. 6, 7, 8 and 9 Carlton House Terrace, with a List of Known Occupants, 1829–1967," *Notes and Record of the Royal Society of London* 47, no. 2 (July 1993): 297–303; Albert Speer, *Inside the Third Reich*, 108. For another outcome of this same story, see also: Martin Bailey, "The German Museum Paintings Secretly Sold by the British Government in 1946," *The Art Newspaper Online* (May 31, 2007), accessed October 17, 2021, https://www.theartnewspaper.com/archive/the-german-museum-paintings-secretly-sold-by-the-british-government-in-1946.

111 David Matless, *Landscape and Englishness* (London: Reaktion Books, 1998/2016), 90–93; Sam Wetherell, *Foundations: How the Built Environment made Twentieth-Century Britain* (Princeton, NJ and Oxford: Princeton University Press, 2020), 35. For other examples, see also: Greig Watson, "The Chilling Day the Swastika Flew Beside the Union Jack," *BBC News Online* (September 2, 2021), accessed on October 12, 2021, https://www.bbc.co.uk/news/uk-england-nottinghamshire-58341335.

112 Wellcome Collection Archives, Eugenics Society Archives, SA/EUG/D.101: Letter from Carlos Paton Blacker, Honorary Secretary of the Population Investigation Committee, LSE, to Dr Henry Sigismund-Sizzo Fitzrandolph, Press Attache, German Embassy (July 3, 1939); Letter from Carlos Paton Blacker to Arthur Trystan Edwards (July 3, 1939); Letter from Henry Sigismund-Sizzo Fitzrandolph to Carlos Paton Blacker (July 4, 1939), accessed February 24, 2022, https://wellcomecollection.org/works/dkdeanrb. I am indebted to Neal Shasore for drawing my attention to this reference.

113 Mark Crinson, *Architecture and the End of Empire* (London and New York: Routledge, 2003), 5–7.

114 This account of Earl's Court is taken from: "The New Earls Court," *Building* (May 1937): 192–198; "The New Earls Court," *Building* (September 1937): 343–346; Robert J. Siddall, "Achievement in the Construction: Creation in the Colossal," *Design and Construction* (April 1937): 217–222; "The £1,250,000 Plan to Make Earl's Court the World's Largest Centre for Exhibitions: A Pictorial Forecast," *Illustrated London News* (July 20, 1935): 134–135; "The Completion of the Biggest Building in the World: Remarkable Details of the New Earl's Court Exhibition" and "The New Earl's Court: Some Facts and Figures," *Illustrated London News* (July 20, 1935): 404–405, 410; B. Bennison, "The New Earl's Court," *The Illustrated Sport and Dramatic News* (July 30, 1937): 236; Oscar Faber and J.R. Kell, "Earls Court Exhibition Mechanical Equipment," *Journal of the Institute of Heating and Ventilating Engineers* 6, no. 61 (March 1938): 29–53; Royal Borough of Kensington and Chelsea/London Borough of Hammersmith and Fulham, "Earls Court Exhibition Centre 1 and 2: EARLS COURT REDEVELOPMENT SITE, London SW5 – Museum of London Archaeology, Report on a Standing Building Survey" (July 15, 2016); Royal Borough of Kensington and Chelsea/London Borough of Hammersmith and Fulham, "EARLS COURT REDEVELOPMENT SITE, London SW5 – Museum of London Archaeology, An Assessment of the Signage from Earls Court 1" (October 10, 2016).

115 *Linlithgow Gazette* (November 4, 1938): 4; Anon, "The 1937 Earl's Court Takes Shape," *The Sphere* (April 10, 1937): 69.

116 *Westminster and Pimlico News* (September 3, 1937): 5.

117 Anon, "Earls Court Exhibition: Limitation on Night Work," *Westminster and Pimlico News* (May 29, 1936): 3; Anon, "Remaking Earls Court Exhibition: Complaints about Noise of Demolition Work," *Westminster and Pimlico News* (June 19, 1936): 8. In terms of accidents on the Earl's Court building site, see for instance: "Earl's Court Exhibition Buildings: L.C.C. Report on Recent Accident," *The Builder* (December 1936): 1019.

118 *Rugby Advertiser* (August 27, 1937): 9.

119 Oscar Faber and J.R. Kell, "Earls Court Exhibition Mechanical Equipment," *Journal of the Institute of Heating and Ventilating Engineers* 6, no. 61 (March 1938): 51.

120 Russell Hayes, *Earls Court Motor Show: An Illustrated History* (Stroud: The History Press, 2016), 9–19; Deborah Sugg Ryan, *Ideal Homes, 1918–1939: Domestic Design and Suburban Modernism* (Manchester: Manchester University Press, 2018).

121 *Yorkshire Post and Leeds Intelligencer* (July 7, 1939): 16.

122 As quoted in Mosley, *My Answer*, 56. See also: Oswald Mosley, *Britain First: The Earls Court Peace Rally* (London: Black House Publishing, 2012).

123 Admiral Sir Barry Domvile's diary entry on July 16, 1939, as quoted in Pugh, *Hurrah for the Blackshirts!*, 286. See also Stephen Dorril, *Blackshirt*, 456–258.

124 J.F. Broadhurst, "At Earl's Court," *West Middlesex Gazette* (July 22, 1939): 4.

125 Anon, "20,000 hear Mosley attack Jewry," *Birmingham Daily Gazette* (July 17, 1939): 7.

126 'Cassandra', "The Blackshirt Caesar": 12.

127 Hitler, *Mein Kampf*, 478–479.

128 Buck-Morss, "Aesthetics and Anaesthetics": 38.

129 Debord, *The Society of the Spectacle*, 77.

130 Walter Benjamin, "The Work of Art in the Age of its Technological Reproducibility," 115.

131 Webber, "Patterns of Membership and Support": 575–606.

132 Thurlow, *Fascism in Britain*, 86–87. See also: National Archives, HO/144/21281/142–146, 150–154, "Special Branch Report" (July 16, 1939); Copsey, *Anti-Fascism in Britain*, 65; Pugh, *Hurrah for the Blackshirts!*, 286.

133 "Architects," *The Blackshirt*, no. 95 (February 15, 1935): 2.

134 The Friends of Oswald Mosley, "The Defence Regulation 18B: British Union Detainees' List," November 2008, accessed September 15, 2021, https://www.oswaldmosley.com/wp-content/uploads/2017/05/18b-Detainees-List.pdf.

135 The biographical information on Henry Thomas Brock Griggs here is based on: National Archives, AIR/79/1661/183920, "Henry Thomas Brock Griggs" (1918–28); National Archives, KV 2/4165, "Henry Thomas BROCK-GRIGGS, Ann BROCK-GRIGGS, British Fascists" (March 16, 1936–June 11, 1942); National Archives, KV 2/4166, "Henry Thomas BROCK-GRIGGS, Ann BROCK-GRIGGS: British Fascists" (February 25, 1943–August 3, 1962); various RIBA Kalendars from the 1920s and 30s; *London Gazette* (May 7, 1937): 2991; genealogical material from Ancestry.com and Findmypast.com; Alfred William Brian Simpson, *In the Highest Degree Odious: Detention Without Trial in Wartime Britain* (Oxford/New York: Oxford University Press, 1995), 202.

136 Royal Academy of Arts, *Exhibition Catalogue* (1930), 60, 112, dry point and aquatint.

137 Henry Thomas Brock Griggs, "Clear the Slums! Do Not Perpetuate Chaos," *The Blackshirt*, no. 95 (February 15, 1935): 10. He also wrote in appreciation of T.E Lawrence ("Lawrence of Arabia"), who he claimed to have met: Henry Thomas Brock Griggs, "Lawrence and Leadership," *The Blackshirt*, no. 110 (May 31, 1935): 7.

138 National Archives, KV 2/4165, "Henry Thomas BROCK-GRIGGS, Ann BROCK-GRIGGS, British Fascists" (March 16, 1936–June 11, 1942); National Archives, KV 2/4166, "Henry Thomas BROCK-GRIGGS, Ann BROCK-GRIGGS: British Fascists" (February 25, 1943–August 3, 1962). See also: Gottlieb, *Feminine Fascism*, 57–74, 95–96, 102, 116, 124–128, 130–132, 150, 170, 236, 271, 287–288.

139 Anne Brock Griggs, "Anne Brock-Griggs describes the Building of a Super Race," *Action*, no. 15 (May 28, 1936): 7. She was glowingly introduced to the members of Oswald Mosley's party in "British Union Personalities: No.3 – Anne Brock Griggs," *Action*, no. 40 (November 21, 1936): 8.

140 Anne Brock Griggs, "May-Day in Germany: A Leader Speaks to His People," *Action*, no. 15 (May 14, 1936): 6; Anne Brock Griggs, "Stirring Berlin Scenes," *Action*, no. 25 (August 6, 1936): 7. In terms of coverage in British architectural journals, see: Francis [Frank] Rowland Yerbury, "In Germany Now – (I)," *The Architect and Building News* (May 5, 1933): 141–143; Francis [Frank] Rowland Yerbury, "In Germany Now (II)," *The Architect and Building News* (May 12, 1933): 163; "German Naval Monument near Kiel," *The Architect and Building News*, October 16, 1936): 58–59; "New German Chancellery," *The Architects' Journal* (July 27, 1939): 125; "Periodicals, July Anthology: Germany," *The Architects' Journal* (August 17, 1939): 248–249; "Modern Germany: Lecture at Hastings School of Art," *Building* (October 16, 1936): 748; "Architecture and Revolution," *Building* (January 1937): 1; Christian Ranck, "Housing Today in Germany," *Building* (November 1937): 486–488; "A Country House near Hamburg: Architect, Carl Hermann," *Building* (July 1939): 294; Arnold Whittich, "Architecture of the Third Reich," *Building* (July 1941): 170; "The Olympic Games Buildings, Berlin", *Design and Construction*, (August 1936).

141 Anne Brock Griggs, *Women and Fascism: Ten Important Points: You Have the Vote Yet are Still Powerless* (London: BUF Publications, 1935); British Union of Fascists, "Fascism means Freedom for British Women," 1935, UCL Institute of Education Archive, UWT/D/251/2, accessed on November 8, 2021, https://nuwtarchiveioe. files.wordpress.com/2011/12/uwt_d_251_2-3.jpg; Elizabeth Denby, *Europe Re-housed* (London: George Allen and Unwin, 1938). For examples of the promotion of architecture and the training of women architects by the British Union, see: R. Saw, "Fascism and Our Cultural Heritage: Beauty must be Protected for Britain," *The Blackshirt*, no. 64 (July 13, 1934): 6; E.C. Cornforth, "The Twilight of British Culture," *The Blackshirt*, no. 80 (November 2, 1934): 8; 'Architect', "Working Class Housing," *The Blackshirt*, no. 95 (February 15, 1935): 11; "100 Per Cent British Buildings," *The Blackshirt*, no. 134 (November 15, 1935): 4; Anne Brock Griggs, "Give Us Sunshine Homes," *Action*, no. 1 (February 21, 1936): 11; Rosalind Raby, "Beautiful Work at Women Architects' Exhibition," *Action*, no. 1 (February 21, 1936): 11; "The Thatched Roofs of Old England," *Action*, no. 48 (January 16, 1937): 4; Michael Penty, "Farewell to Old England: Desecration of Town and Countryside," *Action*, no. 77 (August 7, 1937): 3; Nellie Driver, "Woman and Her Home," *Action*, no. 103 (February 5, 1938): 14; Anne Brock Griggs, "Women can be Real Revolutionaries," *Action*, no. 112 (April 9, 1938): 14; Keith Tyler, "Britain Will Live Again in Beauty," *Action*, no. 172 (June 10, 1939): 16.

142 Janet Dack, "Cultural Regeneration: Mosley and the Union Movement," in Copsey and Richardson (eds), *Cultures of Post-War British Fascism*, 17–18; Gottlieb, *Feminine Fascism*, 71–72, 93–135.

143 The behaviour of Tom Brock Griggs at the Peveril camp meeting at Peel in the Isle of Man is described in: Renton, *Fascism, Anti-Fascism*, 43. See also: Simpson, *In the Highest Degree Odious*, 132, 176–177, 202 (f. 21).

144 For information about William Coupland's life and practice history: London Borough of Richmond, Local Studies Library and Archive (online), "Couch and Coupland," accessed on September 25, 2021, https://richmond.spydus.co.uk/ cgi-bin/spydus.exe/ENQ/OPAC/ARCENQ?ENTRY_NAME= BSandENTRY=couch+and+couplandandENTRY_TYPE=KandNRECS= 10andSORTS=SQL_REL_ARCandSEARCH_FORM=%2Fcgi-bin% 2Fspydus.exe%2FMSGTRN%2FOPAC%2FBSEARCH_ARC%3 FHOMEPRMS%3DARCPARAMSandISGLB=0andGQ=couch+and+coupland; various interwar *RIBA Kalendars*; Joshua Abbott, *A Guide to Modernism in Metro-Land*

(London: Unbound, 2020), 104; Dictionary of Scottish Architects, "Couch and Coupland" (2016), accessed on October 4, 2021, http://www.scottisharchitects.org. uk/architect_full.php?id=408722; Dictionary of Scottish Architects, "John George MacGruer" (2016), accessed on October 4, 2021, http://www.scottisharchitects. org.uk/architect_full.php?id=403582; "Flats, Brixton Hill: Designed by Couch and Coupland," *The Architects' Journal* (October 5, 1939): 445–449; Anon, *West London Observer* (December 15, 1935): 10; *London Gazette* (May 21, 1957): 3056; *London Gazette* (December 20, 1963): 10512; *London Gazette* (January 24, 1964): 816; Biographical Entry – Personal name: William Edward Couch (1877–1942), RIBA Library.

145 Email correspondence about the Richmond-Upon-Thames chapter of the British Union of Fascists from Dr Steven Woodbridge, then Senior Lecturer in History, Kingston University, to the author (September 13, 2021). See also: "Local Fascists visit Streatham," *Richmond Herald* (July 21, 1934): 14; Steven Woodbridge, "Fascism in Richmond: A Brief History," *Richmond History Journal* 26 (May 2005): 34–36.

146 Nikolaus Pevsner and Bridget Cherry, *London: Northwest (Buildings of England Series),* 1991, p. 436; Oldfield, *The Black Book,* 219–221. Listed as no. 118, his name was misspelled as "Nikolaus Prevsner, Dr." See also: Charlotte Benton, *A Different World,* 77–87; Susie Harries, *Nikolaus Pevsner: The Life* (London: Chatto and Windus, 2011), 258–282.

147 Joe Kerr, "Lubetkin and Lenin's Bust: Unlikely Allies in Wartime Britain," in *Strangely Familiar: Narratives of Architecture in the City,* ed. Iain Borden, Joe Kerr, Alicia Pivaro and Jane Rendell (London: Routledge, 1996), 16–21.

148 Macklin, *Failed Führers.*

149 Renton, *Never Again*; David Widgery, *Beating Time: Riot 'n' Race 'n' Rock 'n' Roll* (London: Chatto and Windus, 1986).

150 Jobst and Frichot (eds), *Architectural Affects,* 2. See also: Jonathan Prynn, "Top architect blasts 'free-riding' tenants living in council housing in London and says they should be moved, to make way for HUS staff," *Evening Standard Online* (November 26, 2016); accessed December 14, 2021, https://www.standard.co.uk/ news/london/top-architect-blasts-freeriding-tenants-living-in-council-houses-in-central-london-and-says-they-should-be-moved-a3404711.html; Aaron M. Renn, "Architect Patrik Schumacher: "I have been depicted as a Fascist'," *Guardian Online* (January 27, 2018), accessed December 14, 2021, https://www.theguardian.com/cities/2018/jan/17/architect-patrik-schumacher-depicted-fascist-zaha-hadid.

151 Bjarke Ingels as quoted in Jan-Carlos Kucharek, "Reason in Madness," *RIBA Journal* (March 2016): 92.

152 Murray Fraser, "Beyond Koolhaas," in *Critical Architecture,* ed. Jane Rendell, Jonathan Hill, Murray Fraser and Mark Dorrian (London and New York: Routledge, 2007), 332–339.

153 See for example: Kenny Cupers, Catharina Gabrielsson and Helena Mattsson, *Neoliberalism on the Ground: Architecture and Transformation from the 1960s to the Present* (Pittsburgh, PA: University of Pittsburgh Press, 2020); Peggy Deamer, *The Architect as Worker: Immaterial Labour, the Creative Class, and the Politics of Design* (London: Bloomsbury, 2015); Spencer, *The Architecture of Neoliberalism.*

154 Hardt and Negri, *Empire,* 15.

155 Gilles Deleuze and Felix Guattari, *Two Regimes of Madness* (New York: Semiotext(e), 2006), 137.

156 "Trump Social Media Firm Says It Has Raised $1bn," *BBC News Online* (December 5, 2021), accessed on December 6, 2021, https://www.bbc.co.uk/news/business-59538590. See also: Roger Griffin, "Mussolini Predicted a Fascist Century: How Wrong Was He?," *Fascism* 8 (2018): 1–8.

Bibliography

Benjamin, Walter. "The Work of Art in the Age of Its Technological Reproducibility: Second Version." In *Selected Writings, 3: 1935–1938*, ed. Howard Eiland and Michael W. Jennings. Cambridge, MA: Harvard University Press, 2006.

Böhme, Gernot. *Atmospheric Architectures: The Aesthetics of Felt Spaces*, ed. Tina Engels-Schwarzpaul. London: Bloomsbury, 2013/2017.

Böhme, Gernot. *Invasive Technification: Critical Essays in the Philosophy of Technology*. London: Bloomsbury, 2008/2012.

Copsey, Nigel, and John E. Richardson (eds). *Cultures of Post-War British Fascism*. London and New York: Routledge, 2015.

Crinson, Mark. *Architecture and the End of Empire*. London and New York: Routledge, 2003.

Darling, Elizabeth. *Re-Forming Britain: Narratives of Modernity before Reconstruction*. London and New York: Routledge, 2007.

Dean, David. *The Thirties: Recalling the English Architectural Scene*. London: RIBA Drawings Collection/Trefoil Books, 1983.

Debord, Guy. *The Society of the Spectacle*. New York: Zone Books, 1967/95.

Dorril, Stephen. *Blackshirt: Sir Oswald Mosley and British Fascism*. London: Viking, 2006.

Fraser, Murray, with Joe Kerr. *Architecture and the "Special Relationship": The American Influence on Post-War British Architecture*. London and New York: Routledge, 2007.

Gold, John R. *The Experience of Modernism: Modern Architects and the Future City, 1928–1953*. London: E and FN Spon, 1997.

Gottlieb, Julie V. *Feminine Fascism: Women in Britain's Fascist Movement*. London: I.B. Taurus, 2000/03.

Gottlieb, Julie V. "The Marketing of Megalomania: Celebrity, Consumption and the Development of Political Technology in the British Union of Fascists." *Journal of Contemporary History* 41, no. 1 (2006): 35–55.

Gottlieb, Julie V., and Thomas P. Linehan (eds). *The Culture of Fascism: Visions of the Far Right in Britain*. London and New York: I.B. Taurus, 2004.

Gramsci, Antonio. *Selections from the Prison Notebooks*. New York: International Publishers, 1971.

Griffin, Roger. "Building the Visible Immortality of the Nation: The Centrality of 'Rooted Modernism' to the Third Reich's Architectural New Order." *Fascism* 7 (2018): 42.

Griffin, Roger. *The Nature of Fascism*. London and New York: Routledge, 1993.

Hardt, Michael, and Antonio Negri. *Empire*. Cambridge, MA: Harvard University Press, 2000.

Kitchen, Martin. *Speer: Hitler's Architect*. New Haven, CT and London: Yale University Press, 2015.

Kracauer, Siegfried. *From Caligari to Hitler: A Psychological History of the German Film*. Princeton, NJ/Oxford: Princeton University Press, 1947/2004.

Krier, Leon. *Albert Speer: Architecture, 1932–1942*. Brussels: Archives D'Architecture Moderne, 1985.

Macdonald, Sharon. *Difficult Heritage: Negotiating the Nazi Heritage in Nuremberg and Beyond*. London: Routledge, 2008.

Macklin, Graham. *Failed Führers: A History of Britain's Extreme Right*. London and New York: Routledge, 2020.

Maher, Ashley. *Reconstructing Modernism: British Literature, Modern Architecture and the State*. Oxford: Oxford University Press, 2020.

Miller Lane, Barbara. *Architecture and Politics in Germany, 1918–1945.* Cambridge, MA: Harvard University Press, 1968.

Neumann, Dietrich (ed.). *Architecture of the Night: The Illuminated Building.* Munich/London: Prestel, 2002.

Orde, Anne. *The Eclipse of Great Britain: The United States and British Imperial Decline, 1895–1956.* Basingstoke and London: Macmillan, 1996.

Overy, Richard. *Blood and Ruins: The Great Imperial War 1931–1945.* London: Allen Lane, 2021.

Overy, Richard. *The Morbid Age: Britain Between the Wars.* London: Allen Lane, 2009.

Pugh, Martin. Hurrah for the Blackshirts! Fascists and Fascism in Britain Between the Wars. London: Cape, 2005.

Renton, David. *Fascism, Anti-Fascism and Britain in the 1940s.* Basingstoke: Macmillan, 2000.

Renton, David. *Never Again: Rock Against Racism and the Anti-Nazi League 1976–1982.* London and New York: Routledge, 2019.

Shasore, Neal Ethan. *Designs on Democracy: Architecture and the Public in Interwar London.* Oxford: Oxford University Press, 2022.

Speer, Albert. *Inside the Third Reich: Memoirs by Albert Speer.* New York: Macmillan, 1970.

Stratigakos, Despina. *Hitler at Home.* New Haven, CT and London: Yale University Press, 2015.

Thurlow, Richard. *Fascism in Britain: From Oswald Mosley's Blackshirts to the National Front.* London and New York: I.B. Taurus, 1987/1998.

11

THE PORNOGRAPHIC SCENE OF INSURRECTION

On *Disimaging* the Architecture of Democracy from the Imagery of Potemkin Steps to the Reimaging of the Capitol Riot

Nadir Lahiji

In his short book, simply entitled *Trump,* Alain Badiou reserves a damning label for the 'new political figures': 'democratic fascism'. It is 'a paradoxical but effective designation', he asserts. 'After all', he says, 'the Berlusconis, the Sarkozys, the Le Pens, the Trumps, are operating inside the democratic apparatus, with its election, its oppositions, its scandals, etc.'.[1] Some years prior to this book, Badiou had published another slim volume rendered in English as *The Pornographic Age.* In the latter, he vigorously took issue with the word 'democracy' and provocatively characterized our age as 'pornographic'.[2] The figures of 'democratic fascism' perfectly fit this 'pornographic age' and are one of the most scandalous of these figures that sat at the centre of the reactionary insurrection that stormed the Capitol building in Washington, D.C. on January 6, 2021. As is to be expected in the *pornographic age*, the tele-techno-media networks did not miss any chance to produce and transmit photographs and videos of this incident, in thousands.[3]

In this essay I adopt Badiou's thesis in his *The Pornographic Age* to claim that the *spectacle* of the insurrection on January 6, 2021 amounts to a *pornographic* instance which exposes the inherent *crisis* in the institutions of 'liberal democracy'. For this purpose, I invoke Badiou's notion of '*disimage*' to not only challenge this political system of representation, but *also* the architectural *emblems* sheltering it. According to Badiou, the order of representation is fundamentally the 'order of the image'. To understand 'the regime of images', he contends, 'A real analysis of the images of the present age' must be undertaken.[4] For him the 'pompous emblems of power' in the name 'democracy' constitutes the 'image of the present'. He goes on to crucially state that 'The result is that, for us, any advance within the images of the present age is largely the attempt to grasp what has no image. The Present of the present has no image. We must disimage, disimagine'.[5]

DOI: 10.4324/9781003272076-15

Building on this, here I want to make an attempt to dramatically contrast the *reactionary* scene on the Steps of the Capitol to a *revolutionary* scene staged on another famous flight of Steps belonging to another era in the Twentieth Century. By the latter I mean the powerful cinematographic scene of the Odessa Steps in Sergei Eisenstein's landmark film *The Battleship Potemkin*. We have therefore two mediatic opposed scenes: The one that *cinematographically* reconstructs an actual *revolutionary* event, and the other a *reactionary* insurrection *photographically* recorded. In political and aesthetic terms, the two scenes have an opposite impact on the *perceptual apparatus* of the *human sensorium* resulting in two different *political subjectivity*.

In the case of the Capitol Steps, a two-fold *disfiguration* can be discerned, namely, at the levels of the *political* and *architectural*. The 'spectacle', as invoked above, on both levels, can be conceptualized in relation to *photography* in the age of *technological reproducibility,* to invoke Walter Benjamin's term. In this age, our perception of buildings is mediated and conditioned by their *photographic* reproduction. Thus, our perception of the 6 July 2021 incident on the Capitol building is ultimately *mediated* by its photographic *reproduction*—even if we were happened to be actually present on the scene. This is because in the age of *technological reproducibility* 'Everything begins with reproduction'. In this conceptual framework, 'photography' must be understood as having a far more significance than being just a technology of image production. It is not a platitude to say that 'one should see things not only from one's own point of view, but also from the point of view of others'. According to Kojin Karatani, it is the notion of *parallax* which can explain this phenomenon.[6] The camera, in its difference from the traditional 'mirror image', is a technological device producing this 'parallax view'. This notion defines the dialectical mediation between the subjective and objective viewpoints grounded in *the other*. Such is, therefore, the epochal effect of *photography* as the image of the *other*. In political terms, we can say that the insurrection on January 6, 2021 at the Capitol building with its photographic reproductions is an instance of *memento mori*. This *death* is mediated through *photography*.

With these preliminary remarks, I can now come to present the two contrasting scenes, which chronologically can be ordered as 'before' and 'after' the *pornographic age*. They are as follows:

Scene One: The *Revolutionary* Scene of the Odessa Steps –
    cinematographically critiqued
Scene Two: The *Reactionary* Scene of the Capitol Steps –
    philosophically grounded

Scene One

As the *mise-en-scène* is an interrelation of people in action, so the *mise-en-cadre* is the pictorial composition of mutually dependent *cadres* (shot) in a montage sequence.

—*Sergei Eisenstein, Film Form: Essays in Film Theory*[7]

I call the Scene One a 'proletarian scene'.[8] Before the 'proletariat' enters our 'consciousness' it has to be *seen*. But it *cannot* be seen with the naked eye. To come to visibility, it must be submitted to the technological apparatus of the camera. In the age of cinema, the proletariat must be *photographed* to come into being, to become visible. It must therefore become an *image* first—read *phenomenon*. It is an image, *but* it reveals that it is more than an image that is not given to sensible intuition— nowhere given to experience. In the *transcendental* sense, it must be conceived in a *parallax* relationship to the masses.[9] Here I employ the resources of critical philosophy to examine the class *consciousness* of the proletarian masses. But we must go to cinema, to Plato's Cave again, as Badiou says, to see its *cinematic* presentation, its '*new realm of consciousness*'. The 'proletarian masses' are on the move and their *movement* cannot be seen if not through a technological operation called *cinematography*. Recall that the word *cinema* is originally derived from the French *cinématographe*, which 'comes from the Greek *kinema* meaning movement (hence the popular term *the movie*). So, the word *cinémato* plus the suffix *graphe* means variously imagining, tracing, or writing movement'.[10] In his 1932 essay *A Course in Treatment*, Sergei Eisenstein made the following remarks about the notion of 'cinematography':

> To build cinematography, starting from the "idea of cinematography," and from abstract principles, is barbarous and stupid. Only by a critical comparison with the more basic early forms of spectacle is it possible to master critically the specific methodology of the cinema.[11]

And further: 'The art of cinematography is not selecting a fanciful framing, or in taking something from a surprising camera-angle'.[12]

Historically, in order to capture the proletarian masses in *movement,* we have to go to the famous Odessa Steps. Not to the *actual* steps but to the image of them in Eisenstein's *The Battleship of Potemkin*—the classic revolutionary cinema, par excellence. It is in this film that the 'masses' come to their *phenomenal* visibility, or the visibility of their *image*, staged by Eisenstein's great art of *montage*. Only after seeing the specific sequences of the Odessa Steps in this film, can one submit the notion of the 'proletariat masses' to philosophical-theoretical and political scrutiny.

In his 'Reply to Oscar A. H. Schmitz', published in 1927, Walter Benjamin intervened in the debate about the *Potemkin* at the time and took the occasion to raise several important points that he would later take up again in his *Artwork* essay. Discussing the political notion of 'proletariat' and 'consciousness', Benjamin foregrounded the notion of technology linked to the aesthetic and political in film and brought up the 'superiority' of the Russian revolutionary cinema, interestingly in a positive comparison with the American slapstick comedy. The 'target' of both is 'technology', he said.

> This kind of film is comic, but only in the sense that the laughter it provokes hovers over an abyss of horror. The obverse of a ludicrously liberated

technology is the lethal power of naval squadrons on maneuver, as we see it openly displayed in *Potemkin*.[13]

He noted that 'The international bourgeois film, on the other hand, has not been able to discover a consistent ideological formula. This is one of the causes of its recurrent crises'.[14] In this case, 'For the complicity of film technique with the milieu that essentially constitutes a standing rebuke to it is incompatible with the glorification of the bourgeoisie'.[15] Benjamin continues by making an important point central to my concern here:

> The Proletariat is the hero of those spaces that give rise to the adventures to which the bourgeois abandons himself in the movies with beating heart, because he feels constrained to enjoy "beauty" even where it speaks of the annihilation of his own class. The proletariat, however, is a collective, just as these spaces are collective spaces. And only here, in the human collective, can the film complete the prismatic work that it began by acting on that milieu. The epoch-making impact of *Potemkin* can be explained by the fact that it made this clear for the first time. Here, for the first time, a mass movement acquires the wholly architectonic and by no means monumental (i.e., UFA) [Universum-Film AG] quality that justifies its inclusion in film. No other medium could reproduce this collective in motion.[16]

Benjamin called *Potemkin* 'a great film' and 'a rare achievement' and further wrote:

> To protest against it calls for the courage born of desperation. There is plenty of bad tendentious art, including bad socialist tendentious art. Such works are determined by their effects; they work with tired reflexes and depend on stereotyping. This film, however, has solid concrete foundations ideologically; the details have been worked out precisely, like the span of a bridge;

lyrically concluding that 'The more violent the blows that rain down upon it, the more beautifully it resounds. Only you touch it with kid gloves do you hear and move nothing'.[17] Here I should mention that among the notions that Benjamin employs in this essay, and that he would pick up again to discuss later in his *Artwork* essay, is the notion of 'collectivity', characteristically a feature of the 'proletariat', that he links to the 'collective urban space' that film would forever explode.

In his 1934 essay, *Through Theatre to Cinema*, Eisenstein wrote

> No screen had ever before reflected an image of collective action. Now the conception of "collectivity" was to be pictured. But our enthusiasm produced a one-sided representation of the masses and the collective;

one-sided because collectivism means the maximum development of the individual within the collective, a conception irreconcilably opposed to bourgeois individualism. Our first mass film missed this deeper meaning.[18]

Further, he remarked: "'individuality within the collective," the deeper meaning, demanded of cinema today, would have found entrance almost impossible if the way had not been cleared by the general concept'.[19] In the same essay, Eisenstein related his influential 'theory of montage' to the notion of 'proletariat' and wrote:

> I consider that besides mastering the elements of filmic diction, the technique of the frame, and the theory, we have another credit to list—the value of profound ties with the traditions and methodology of literature. Not in vain, during this period, was the new concept of film-language born, film-language not as the language of the film-critic, but as an expression of cinema thinking, when the cinema was called upon to embody the philosophy and ideology of the victorious proletariat.[20]

'Cinematography is, first and foremost, montage', Eisenstein declared.[21] 'Montage is conflict': 'At the basis of every art is conflict (an "imagist" transformation of the dialectical principle). The shot appears as the *cell* of montage. Therefore it also must be considered from the viewpoint of *conflict*'.[22] In his 1929 essay, *A Dialectic Approach to Film Form*, Eisenstein attempts to bring 'philosophy' to 'art', the philosophy of 'dialectical materialism' to art as conflict. He wrote:

> *Thus*: The projection of the dialectic system of things
> into the brain
> *into creating abstractly*
> *into the process of thinking*
> yields: dialectic method of thinking;
> dialectic materialism— PHILOSOPHY.
> *And also:*
> The projection of the same system of things
> while creating concretely
> while giving form
> yields: ART.[23]

In an essay written in the same year entitled *Methods of Montage*, Eisenstein discusses 'montage principle' and distinguishes between '*Metric Montage*', '*Rhythmic Montage*', '*Tonal Montage*', and '*Overtonal Montage*'. He then adds a 'higher category' to the list and calls it '*Intellectual Montage*' that he bases on his recollection of 'Lenin's synopsis of the fundamental elements of Hegelian dialectic'.[24] Intellectual montage, he says, is 'montage not of generally physiological overtonal sounds, but of sounds and overtones of an intellectual sort: i.e., conflict-juxtaposition of accompanying intellectual affects', concluding that

> The intellectual cinema will be that which resolves the conflict-juxtaposition of the physiological and intellectual overtone. Building a completely new form of cinematography—the realization of revolution in the general history of culture; building a synthesis of science, art, and class militancy.[25]

Filming the Revolutionary Collective

With this brief discussion on the principle of montage we can now come to the Odessa Steps—also named the 'Potemkin Steps'.[26] The stairs are a formal entrance into the city from the direction of the sea and are the best known symbol of Odessa.

> The stairs were originally known as the Boulevard steps, the Giant Staircase, or the Richelieu steps. The top step is 12.5 meters (41 feet) wide, and the lowest step is 21.7 meters (70.8 feet) wide. The staircase extends for 142 meters, but it gives the illusion of greater length. The stairs were so precisely constructed as to create an optical illusion. A person looking down the stairs sees only the treads and the risers are invisible; whereas a person looking up sees only risers, and the treads are invisible.[27]

We are further informed that the original 200 stairs were designed in 1825 by Italian architect Francesco Boffo and St. Petersburg architects Avraam I. Melnikov and Pot'e.

> The staircase cost 800,000 rubles to build. In 1837, the decision was made to build a "monstrous staircase", which was constructed between 1837 and 1841. An English engineer named John Upton supervised the construction. Upton had fled Britain while on bail for forgery. Upton went on to oversee the construction of the huge dry-docks constructed in Sevastopol and completed in 1853. As erosion destroyed the stairs, in 1933 the sandstone was replaced by rose-grey granite from the BOH area, and the landings were covered with asphalt. Eight steps were lost under the sand when the port was being extended, reducing the number of stairs to 192, with ten landings.[28]

The pivotal sequence of Part 4 of *The Battleship Potemkin* takes place on the Odessa Steps and might be claimed to be 'the most famous single sequence of images in the history of world cinema, and especially of silent montage cinema'.[29] The sequence is also notable for its 'poetic license' as it does not follow the actual historical event of the munity, which took place on the battleship. In this sense, as Richard Taylor notes, the Odessa Steps sequence is the 'paradigm of *pars pro toto*.[30] Part 4 begins with the title 'That memorable day the city lived one life with the rebellious battleship'.[31]

As Taylor points out, the descent of the pram down the Odessa Steps 'is probably the most famous image' of *The Battleship of Potemkin*. Taylor writes:

> The device of using the suffering of a child to move the audience has been much imitated, although Eisenstein, unlike so many of his imitators, leaves the sufferings of this particular baby to our imagination, rather than depicting it in graphic details.[32]

The next famous shot, also much imitated, is the case of 'extreme close-up' showing the face of the 'schoolmistress' or the 'nurse': 'Her pince-nez are now awry on her nose, the right lens shattered as her right eye bleeds. Her mouth gapes in horror'.[33] In his 1929 essay *The Dramaturgy of Film Form* (*The Dialectical Approach to Film Form*), Eisenstein cited this scene as an instance of 'logical montage'. He wrote: 'Representation of a spontaneous action, Potemkin. Woman with pince-nez. Followed immediately—without a transition—by the same woman with shattered pince-nez and bleeding eye. Sensation of a shot hitting the eye'.[34] It must be noted that, as Taylor reminds us, Potemkin's characteristic feature is the application of 'Eisenstein's principle of the montage of attraction', as 'objects are chosen for associations that will resonate with the audience'.[35] Taylor brings out the notion of 'seeing' and the ambiguity of 'pince-nez' in *Potemkin* and nicely observes that, in contrast to the doctor who examines the rotten meat with his pince-nez, when the 'schoolmistress' on the Odessa Steps

> wears pince-nez, these present her clarity of vision: hence, to restore the "proper order of the society" the Cossack has to slash, not just her face, but also her pince-nez, in order to destroy both her vision and her life.[36]

A number of things in Eisenstein's film caused reaction and debate in subsequent decades, as Taylor notes, namely the question of the historical authenticity of the mutiny on the ship, the role of montage, mass and the individual, the purpose of revolutionary art, etc. But:

> with amazing keenness Eisenstein observes nature, the human face, the machine. He listens with sensitivity to the very breathing of the ocean's depths. He loves material objects. He knows that revolution *is not an individual but the mass* and he is searching for the language to express mass emotions.[37]

Scene Two

The present of the present has no image. We must disimage and disimagine.
—Alain Badiou, *The Pornographic Age*[38]

Badiou's *The Pornographic Age* is the translation of the original French titled *Pornographie du temps présent* that appeared in 2013.[39] In this book, Badiou offers a reading of Jean Genet's play, *The Balcony*, the first version of which was published in 1956.[40] Among many great 'small' books of Badiou, this one stands out for its brief, dense and provocative argument. I examine Badiou's diagnosis of the present age and bring out its political and architectural implications for my discussion of the reactionary scene on the Capitol building. Badiou forcefully asserts the essential connection that exists between 'pornography' and the 'times' or the 'age' in which we live now.[41] As he writes, 'to conceive of the present' is the proper task of philosophy. The crux of his argument comes to this: Not only *pornography* defines the essence of the present time, but there is a connection between 'pornography' and 'democracy'. As he claims, 'Democracy' has now become the 'dominant political watchword or symptom of our age', for which he offers his powerful critique.[42] I begin by discussing Badiou's critique of 'democracy', what he terms as the 'fetish of democracy'. The relevance of this critique of democracy to the scene on the Capitol as the seat of 'liberal democracy' will be spelled out later.

The Fetish of Democracy

The term 'democracy' is attached to the capitalist parliamentary 'representative' system, the very obsession of our contemporary 'democrats' in the contemporary political system. This is the crux of Badiou's novel argument in his *The Pornographic Age* against the tired term 'democracy'. Analysing Genet's play, *The Balcony*, and discussing the 'regime of images' and 'power', along with the character of 'The Police Chief' as Phallus understood in Jacques Lacan psychoanalytical theory, Badiou poses these questions:

> What names are put into play in the philosophical comedy of the present, of our present? What are today's pompous emblems of power? What is its untouchable value? How is it that there is an unfortunate presence of the present? To my eyes, the principal name is 'democracy'.[43]

He elaborates on the name 'democracy' as follows:

> To avoid any misunderstanding, let us agree that the word 'democracy' does not cover any theory, or fiction, of a shared power of the *demos*, of an effective sovereignty of the people. It will only be a question of the word 'democracy' in so far as it designates a form of the State and all that goes with it. It is a constitutional category, a juridical hypothesis. It is a form of public liberties, supposedly protected by the constitution and animated by the electoral process. It is a form of the 'Rule of Law [*l'État de droit*], to which all the so-called Western powers lay claim, as those countries that

live in the shelter of those powers try to do, or, as their clients, pretend to agree to.[44]

He further reflects that

> To make the comedy of images exist today is thus, almost inevitably, to treat the name "democracy" for what it is: the Phallus of our present. To win, beyond the monotonous presence of our everyday life, the life of a true present, requires the courage to go beyond the democratic fetish as we know it. Jean Genet's *The Balcony* can serve as the preliminary operator.[45]

Badiou explains that the subject of the play is what is at stake in the expression 'images of the present age'. 'In fact, Genet's text asks explicitly what becomes of images when the present is disorder'.[46] 'For Genet', he continues, 'it is riots or revolution; for us, it is undoubtedly the Arab Spring, the movement of the Indignados, at the same time, as that of the crisis of capitalism and its deleterious effects in Europe'.[47]

Before *The Pornographic Age*, Badiou had discussed the concept of 'democracy' extensively on two other occasions.[48] In 'Democratic Emblem', which appeared in *Democracy in What State?*, Badiou 'brackets' the word *democracy,* as he puts it, in order to 'make the Platonic critique of democracy comprehensible'.[49] He begins by saying that 'Despite all that is devaluing the word *democracy* day after day and in front of our eyes, there is no doubt that this word remains the dominant emblem of contemporary political society'.[50] Contesting this emblem he says:

> before one can even begin to apprehend the reality of our societies, it is necessary, as a preliminary exercise, to dislodge their emblem. The only way to make truth out of the world we're living in is to dispel the aura of the word *democracy* and assume the burden of not being a democrat and so being heartily disapproved of by "everyone" (*tout le monde*)

adding that 'in the world we're living in, *tout le monde* doesn't make any sense without the emblem, so "everyone" is democratic. It's what you could call the axiom of the emblem'.[51] He makes clear that our concern must be rather *le monde,* that is,

> the world that evidently exists, not tout le monde [everybody], where the democrat (Western folk, folk of the emblem) hold sway and everyone else is from another world—which, being other, is not a world properly speaking, just a remnant of life, a zone of war, hunger, walls, and delusions.[52]

He henceforth turns to Plato, to the 'moment in philosophy', as he puts it, 'when the democratic emblem was first dislodged', to book 8 of *Republic*. He informs us that Plato employed the term *demokratia* to discuss the organizing affairs of the polis, serving as its 'constitution'. He notes that Lenin also said the same thing to the effect that 'democracy is no more than a particular form of State'.[53] But, Badiou explains,

> both Plato and Lenin are more interested in the subjective impact of this State form than they are in its objective status. Thought must shift the focus from the legal framework to the emblem or from democracy to the democrat. The capacity of the democratic emblem to do harm lies in the subjective type it molds; and, not to mince words, the crucial traits of the democratic type are egoism and desire for petty enjoyment.[54]

Badiou points out that Plato was convinced that 'democracy would not save the Greek polis, and in fact it didn't', and goes on to say,

> Dare one assert that democracy will not save our beloved West either? Indeed; I daresay it won't, and I would add that this brings us right back to the ancient dilemma: *either we reinvent communism or we undergo some invented form of fascist barbarity*[55]
>
> *[emphasis mine]*

Badiou further explains that despite Plato's 'aristocratic reactionism', his critique of democracy holds an independent, even a 'bivalent force'. 'On the one hand', Badious writes, 'it is aimed at the essence, the reality, of the democratic form of State, on the other hand, at the constitution of the subject—*homo democraticus*—in a world thus formalized'. He goes on to say that he wishes to retain Plato's 'two theses' and extend his argument beyond the world of polis, namely, '1. The democratic world isn't really a world; 2. The only thing that constitutes the democratic subject is pleasure or, more precisely, pleasure-seeking behavior'.[56] In elaboration, he points out that

> Plato is a sure and perceptive guide to the panorama of modern society, which is a weave of three motifs: the absence of world, the democratic emblem as subjectivity enslaved to circulation, and the imperative of universal adolescent pleasure seeking.[57]

With these reflections on 'bracketing around the authority of the word *democracy*', Badiou concludes that

> we can go right back to the literal meaning of democracy if we like: the power of people over their own existence. Politics immanent in the people and the withering away, in open process, of the State. From that perspective, we will only ever be true democrats, integral to the historic life of peoples, when we become communists again.[58]

In 'Speculative Disquisition on the Concept of Philosophy', published in his *Metapolitics,* Badiou returns to his philosophical analysis of the word 'democracy', this time contesting it more vigorously in specific relation to State and politics.[59] He begins by observing that in the aftermath of the collapse of 'socialist States' the West entered into the humanitarian crusade with the word 'democracy' as an organizing principle of a consensus. He characterizes 'democracy' in this context as an *authoritarian opinion*, meaning that it is forbidden 'not to be a democrat'. Any subjectivity suspected of not being a democrat, Badiou says, 'is 'regarded as pathological'. This by itself 'elicits' as Badiou contends, 'the philosopher's critical suspicion precisely in so far as it falls within the realm of public opinion and consensus', given the fact that since Plato, 'philosophy has stood for rupture with opinion, and is meant to examine everything that is spontaneously considered as *normal*'.[60] He brings up Lenin again to say that, according to him, there are two types of democracy, namely, 'bourgeoise democracy and the proletarian democracy', with the latter eventually prevailing over the former. But what is more appropriate for Badiou is Lenin's insistence on saying that '*democracy* should in truth always be understood as a *form of State*', with 'form' meaning 'a particular configuration of the separate character of the State and of the formal exercise of sovereignty', which is closer to Greek philosophy in terms of the 'power of the demos or the people; the capacity of the demos to exert coercion for itself'.[61] Badiou further reflects that the philosophical significance of 'democracy as a form of State' is that for Lenin the 'aim or idea of politics is the withering away of the State, the classless society, and therefore the disappearance of every form of State, including, quite obviously, the democratic form'.[62] Reminding us that this might be called 'generic communism' whose principle was put forward in Marx's *1844 Economic and Philosophical Manuscript*, Badiou explains that:

> Generic communism designates an egalitarian society of free association between polymorphous labourers where activity, rather than being governed by status and social or technical specialization, is governed by the collective mastery of necessities. In such a society, the State as an authority separate from public coercion is dissolved. Politics, which is the expression of the interest of social groups, and whose aim is conquest of power, is itself dissolved.[63]

If one represents philosophy as the 'ultimate aim of politics', and if as Lenin said, the 'ultimate aim is the withering away of the State', or

> again, if the ultimate aim of politics is said to be the in-separate authority of the infinite, or collective self-realization as such, then, in respect of this supposed aim—which is *the* designated aim of politics as generic communism—"democracy neither is, nor can it be, a philosophical category.[64]

'Why?', Badiou immediately explains that: 'Because democracy is a form of the State; because philosophy evaluates the ultimate aims of politics; and because this aim is also the end of the State, and so too the end of all relevance for the word "democracy"'.[65] He further remarks:

> In terms of this hypothetical framework, the only adequate *philosoph-ical* word for evaluating the political is possibly the word 'equality', or 'communism', but certainly not the word 'democracy'. For this word re-mains bound by tradition to the State and to the form of the State.[66]

Badiou goes on to say that in our present situation, that is, 'our parliamentary States', the *subjective* relation to the question of the State 'is governed by three norms: the economy, the national question and, precisely, democracy'.[67] After briefly explaining these three norms and stating that currently the 'State submits itself to the above threefold politics, rather than of *politics* in general'.[68] He writes:

> So much for the hypothesis that politics aims to determine the good State. What we end up with, at best, is 'democracy' as possible category of a particular politics—parliamentarianism—which provides no decisive rea-son why 'democracy' should be retrieved, captured as a philosophical concept.[69]

By coming back to his initial question arising from his major hypothesis, Badiou writes that,

> if 'democracy' is conjoined to *mass*, one indeed presumes that the aim of politics is generic communism, from which it follows that 'democracy' is not a philosophical category. This conclusion is empirically and concep-tually borne out by the fact that on the question of mass democracy it is impossible to distinguish democracy from dictatorship. This is obviously what has enabled Marxists to hold on to the possibility of using the expres-sion 'dictatorship of the proletariat'. However, it is important to understand that what facilitated subjective valorization of the word 'dictatorship' was precisely the existence of points of reversibility between democracy and dictatorship which assumed the historical figure of mass democracy, or revolutionary democracy, or romantic democracy.[70]

At the end Badiou offers a definition:

> Democracy could thus be defined as that which authorizes a placement of the particular under the law of the universality of the political will. In a certain way, "democracy" names the political figure of the conjunction between particular situations and a politics. In this case, and in this case alone, "democracy" can be retrieved as a philosophical category, as from

now on it comes to designate what can be called the effectiveness of politics, or politics in its conjunction with particular stakes. Understood in this way politics is clearly freed from its subordination to the State.[71]

Based on Badiou's analysis above, we are now in a better position to understand his critique of 'democracy' in *The Pornographic Age*. There he writes: 'Since the idea of revolution has disappeared, our world is merely that of resumption of power, under the consensual and pornographic image of market democracy'.[72] And further:

> They propose a regulated and decent capitalism, a non-pornographic capitalism, an ecological capitalism, and always more democracy. They demand, in short, a comfortable capitalism for all: a capitalism with a human face. Nothing will emerge from these chimeras. The only dangerous and radical critique is the political critique of democracy, because the emblem of the present age, its fetish, its phallus, is democracy.[73]

The Reign of Image and the Phallic Fetish of Our Time

Returning to his reading of Genet's *The Balcony*, Badiou begins with a reference to Jacques Lacan's analysis of the play in his Seminar V, *Formations of the Unconscious* (1957–1958).[74] In that Seminar Lacan told his audience that Genet's play is a 'Comedy' and goes on to define it as follows: 'Comedy embraces, gathers and takes enjoyment from the relationship with an effect that has a fundamental relation to the signifying order, namely the appearance of this signified called the phallus'.[75] Emphasizing the word 'appearance' [*apparition*] in Lacan's definition, Badiou writes:

> Tragedy is the majestic melancholy of destiny: it says that the Truth is in the past. Comedy is always, on the contrary, a comedy of the present, because it makes the phallus appear, that is, to say, the authentic symbol of this present. The theatre alone points out the comical appearance of what power is in the present, and thus opens it to derision. In every tragedy, we see the dark melancholy of power. In every comedy, we see the farcical semblant.[76]

Based on his reading of Lacan, Badiou states that his 'goal' is to 'find the register of the *philosophical* comedy of the present' and goes on to name it as 'the speculative Phallus' of the present.[77] He points out that 'the power [*puissance*] of comedy is to show that, beneath its pompous emblems, naked power [*pouvoir*] cannot dissimulate its ferocity or its emptiness forever'.[78] Badiou poses these questions: 'What are today's pompous emblems of power?', 'What is its untouchable value?', and 'How is it that there is an unfortunate presence of the present?'. His answer: 'The principal name of it is democracy'.[79] To prevent any misunderstanding, he reminds us that his use of the word 'democracy', as cited above, does not refer to any 'theory, or fiction, of a shared power of *demos*, of an effective sovereignty of the people', that it rather 'designates a form of State and all that goes with it'.[80]

Contained in the 'comedy of images' that reigns today, Badiou asserts that the name 'democracy' is 'what it is: the Phallus of our present'.[81] And the task is to go beyond this 'democratic fetish'. It is here that Badiou takes Genet's play as his guide. And it is mainly because '*The Balcony* confronts the reign of images with the real of revolt'.[82] Lacan in his Seminar, referring to the characters in *The Balcony*, had pointed out that

> we see the bishop, the judge and the general posited there before us on the basis of the question—what is it really like to enjoy the status of a Bishop, a Judge or a General? This explains the device by which this balcony is nothing other than what is known as a "house of illusion", a brothel.[83]

For Badiou, the brothel is 'a figure of order as the order of images' and, to reiterate, *The Balcony* 'confronts the reign of images with the real of revolt'. He points out that in the 1950s Genet saw what is absolutely visible now:

> [W]hat reveals the hidden ferocity of power is the proliferation of the obscenity of images, which is to say, the fusion, at all levels, including the cultural and political, of the potentially sophisticated arousal of a desire with the vulgarity of commercial propaganda. The brothel is the theatrical place of this fusion: that which presents there the object of desire, in costume and adorned, is immediately convertible into cash. The brothel is the place where the average price of desire is evaluated and fixed. It is the market of images.[84]

Against these 'images' inside the brothel, there is a 'real' on the outside. In our time, as Badiou reminds us, there is the revolt—not revolution—among all sorts of workers mainly outside of the 'Western brothel', like the Arab Spring. In the outside is the 'figure of the real, the figure of life. It is the pure present, either as a fit of rage or as infinite patience'.[85] We learn that Genet's play is about the 'existence or absence' of desire that, as Lacan said, would not be a 'semblant'. A desire by the rule must be animated, as Badiou puts it, by 'the real' and not by 'images'. What is it that makes this desire a problem, Badiou asks. Offering an eloquent answer he says, 'Well, politically, it is a desire for revolution, which would bring about the real equality of all humanity', and putting it in his own philosophical terms, a desire for politics, science and art, that 'every authentic desire concerns the absoluteness of its object'.[86]

With the explorations of Badiou's thesis above, I can now return to my main concern for a tentative conclusion. In sharp contrast to Genet's play, the revolutionary *agency* in *The Balcony* is nowhere to be seen when we come to the scene of January 6, 2021 on the Steps of Capitol. Here that revolutionary messenger has degenerated into a reactionary figure of 'democratic fascism'. By no means should we assume that the *pornographic* scene of the insurrection on the Steps of Capitol, brutally pushed itself to the empty Chambers inside, was confined to the reactionary crowd storming the edifice of 'democracy' from the *outside*. On the contrary. The pornographic scene taking place outside is an extension of the inside, the very political 'deliberative' body of the so-called 'representatives' system in 'liberal democracy'—the very seat of the 'capitalist parliamentarianism', to put it in Badiou's terms. What we witnessed was *disfiguration* on two interconnected levels: architecture and politics. By the term 'disfiguration' here I mean literally 'defacement' of *'appearance'* or 'deforming', which in a higher conceptual meaning in the context of Badiou's thesis can be named as the 'obscene deformation'. Together, they must both be *disimaged* and *disimagined*. It is here that the word 'democracy' in its contradictory association with 'liberalism' comes under critical scrutiny; the inherent contradiction between 'freedom' and 'equality' under 'liberal democracy' is irresolvable. I may point out here that its genealogy in fact goes back to 'Athenian Democracy'. As Kojin Karatani in his remarkable *Isonomia and the Origins of Philosophy* informs us:

> Modern democracy is a composite of liberalism plus democracy, that is to say liberal democracy. It attempts to combine, therefore, two conflicting things, freedom and equality. If one aims for freedom, inequalities arise. If one aims for equality, freedom is compromised. Liberal democracy cannot transcend this dilemma. It can only swing back and forth like a pendulum between poles of libertarianism (neoliberalism) and social democracy (the welfare state).[87]

The 'liberal democracy', as Karatani puts it, always is capable of producing demagogues and tyrants. In Badiou's words, it is capable to produce scandalous figures of 'democratic fascism'.

I imagine that one day a revolutionary filmmaker will take up Eisenstein's great art of *montage* to *reconstruct* the pornographic scene of January 6, 2021 to *cinematographically* record the actual reactionary insurrection on the Steps of Capitol in par with Eisenstein's memorable scene of the Odessa Steps in *The Battleship Potemkin*. Once this film is made, it will then make us see not the *essence* but the *Schein* (semblance-appearance) of a political ideology that is veiled by an architectural ideology, an *illusory* political and aesthetic image waiting to be *disimaged* and *disimagined*.

Notes

1 See Alain Badiou, *Trump* (Cambridge: Polity, 2019), 13. Badiou prefaces his remarks by pointing out that 'It is often said that these new political figures—Trump, to be sure, but many others in the word today—resemble the fascists of the 1930s. There is indeed a certain resemblance. But, alas, there is also a major difference: today's new

political figures do not have to confront the powerful and intractable enemies who were the Soviet Union and the communist parties', 12–13.

2 Alain Badiou, *The Pornographic Age*, trans. and ed. with afterword, A. J. Bartlett and Justin Clemens (London: Bloomsbury, 2020).

3 The 1 July 2021 issue of the *New York Times* published a short video in which it documented thousands of video footages showing minute by minute take-over of the Capitol Building on 6 January 2021, see https://www.nytimes.com/2021/06/30/us/jan-6-capitol-attack
takeaways.html?action=click&module=Top%20Stories&pgtype=Homepage

4 Alain Badiou, *The Pornographic Age*, 2.

5 As the translators of Badiou's work explain, here Badiou invokes the French neologisms '*désimager*' and '*désimaginer*' in which the prefix '*dé*' (*des*) 'has the general force of reversal, splitting, separation or dissemination'. Alain Badiou, *The Pornographic Age*, 7.

6 For this see Kojin Karatani, *Transcritique: On Kant and Marx* (Cambridge: The MIT Press, 2003).

7 Sergei Eisenstein, *Film Form: Essays in Film Theory*, ed. and trans. Jay Leyda (San Diego: Harcourt, 1949, 1977), 16.

8 For my reflections on this scene, I partially draw on a chapter in my *Architecture, Philosophy and Pedagogy of Cinema: From Benjamin to Badiou* (New York: Routledge, 2021).

9 For the term 'parallax' see Kojin Karatani, *Transcritique: On Kant and Marx*.

10 See Christopher Kul-Want, 'Introduction' in his edited *Philosophers on Film, from Bergson to Badiou: A Critical Reader* (New York: Colombia University Press, 2019), 3.

11 Sergei Eisenstein, *Film Form: Essays in Film Theory* (San Diego: Harcourt, 1977), 86.

12 Eisenstein, 92.

13 Walter Benjamin, 'Reply to Oscar A. H. Schmitz', 17. The editors note that Oscar Adolf Hermann Schmitz was 'a playwright and essayist', who maintained a 'close contact with the circle around Stefan Georg', and that 'Benjamin's reply to Schmitz exemplifies the tenor of the argument over *Battleship Potemkin*', 19.

14 Walter Benjamin, 'Reply to Oscar A. H. Schmitz', 17–18.

15 Benjamin, 18.

16 Walter Benjamin, 'Reply to Oscar A. H. Schmitz', 18. The editors provide a brief information about the term UFA (Universum-Film AG):

> the largest firm in the German film industry, was founded in 1917. Vertically integrated, UFA owned everything from machine shops and film laboratories to production and distribution facilities. It was acquired by the Hugenberg Group in 1927, nationalized by the German Reich in 1936–1937, and dismantled by the Allies in 1945
>
> 19

17 Benjamin, 19.

18 Sergei Eisenstein, *Film Form: Essays in Film Theory*, 16.

19 Eisenstein, 17.

20 Eisenstein, 17. Eisenstein further remarks that

> Stretching out its hand to the new quality of literature—the dramatics of the subject—the cinema cannot forget the tremendous experience of its earlier periods. But the way is not back to them, but forward to the synthesis of all the best that has been done by our silent cinematography, towards a synthesis of these with the demands of today, along the lines of story and Marxist-Leninist ideological analysis. The phase of monumental synthesis in the images of the people of the epoch of socialism—the phase of socialist realism
>
> 17

21 Eisenstein, 20.

22 Eisenstein, 38.

23 Eisenstein, 45.
24 Eisenstein, 81. He gives the categories of Lenin's synopsis of Hegelian dialectics in the following:

> These elements may be presented in a more detailed way thus: ... 10) an endless process of revealing *new* aspects, relationships, etc. 11) an endless process of deepening human perception of things, appearances, processes and so on, from appearance to essence and from the less profound to the more profound essence. 12) from co-existence to causality and from one form of connection and interdependence to another, deeper, more general. 13) recurrence, on the highest level, of known traits, attributes, etc. of the lowest, and 14) return, so to say, to the old (negation of the negation) ...
>
> *81*

25 Eisenstein, 82–83.
26 The famous battleship took its name from the Russian soldier and statesman, Prince Grigory Potemkin. He was given the responsibility to build the Black Sea Fleet under Catherine the Great (who ruled over Russia from 1762 to 1796). He was one of the favourites of Her Majesty, the Empress. It was anecdotally reported that, to impress her, Potemkin ordered the construction of a 'sham village' in order to give the false impression of rural prosperity when she was to travel to Crimea in 1787: so the famous term 'Potemkin village'. It is noteworthy to mention here that this term became the title of an essay by the architect Adolf Loos in 1898, in which he sarcastically ridiculed his contemporary architects in the city of Vienna for putting historicist facades on their designed buildings hence falsifying their actual historical time.
27 I have adopted the description from Wikipedia, see https://en.wikipedia.org/wiki/Potemkin_Stairs.
28 https://en.wikipedia.org/wiki/Potemkin_Stairs.
29 See Richard Taylor, *The Battleship Potemkin* (London and New York: I. B. Tauris, 2000), 35. For my description of the film and its reception I am mainly relying on this informative text.
30 Taylor, 35.
31 Taylor, 35.
32 Taylor, 48.
33 Taylor, 50.
34 Cited by Taylor, 50.
35 Taylor, 62.
36 Taylor, 62.
37 In Taylor, 72. Taylor devotes many pages of his book to discuss the history of the reception of the *Potemkin* that I do not have space here to discuss.
38 Alain Badiou, *The Pornographic Age*, 7.
39 Alain Badiou, *Pornographie du temps présent* (France: Fayard, 2013). The actual length of Badiou's text in the English edition is no more than 20 pages to which the editors of the volume have contributed a very helpful 44-page 'Afterword' entitled 'Minus Something Indefinable', followed by an additional commentary by William Watkin. For my reflections I heavily draw on a chapter in my recent *Architecture in the Age of Pornography, Reading Alain Badiou* (New York: London, 2021).
40 Jean Genet, *The Balcony*, trans. Bernard Frechtman, revised edition (New York: Grove Press, 1966).
41 See A. J. Bartlett and Justin Clemens, 'Minus Something Indefinable', in Alain Badiou, *The Pornographic Age*, 22.
42 A. J. Bartlett and Justin Clemens, 'Minus Something Indefinable', 22. As they further point out,

> Moreover, it is bound up with how "pornography" has become the dominant genre: pornography incites the uptake of new technologies as it moves from being

> marginal to a billion-dollar industry by enforcing an absolute prohibition on the prohibition of image
>
> *23*

43 Badiou, *The Pornographic Age* 3.
44 Badiou, 3–4.
45 Badiou, 4.
46 Badiou, 2.
47 Badiou, 2.
48 See Alain Badiou, 'A Speculative Disquisition on the Concept of Democracy', in Alain Badiou, *Metapolitics*, trans. with intro. Jason Barker (London and New York: Verso, 2005), and Alain Badiou, 'The Democratic Emblem', in Giorgio Agamben et al. *Democracy in What State?*, trans. William McCuaig (New York: Columbia University Press, 2011).
49 Badiou, 'The Democratic Emblem', 15.
50 Badiou, 6. He further remarks:

> An emblem is the "untouchable" in a symbolic system, a third rail. You can say what you like about political society, display unprecedented "critical" zeal, denounce the "economic" horror," you'll always earn pardon as long as you do so in the name of democracy. The correct tone is something like: "How can a society that claims to be democratic be guilty of this or that?" Ultimately you will be seen to have judged society in the name of its emblem and therefore itself. You haven't gone beyond the pale, you still deserve the appellation of citizen rather than barbarian, you're standing by at your democratically assigned place. Be seeing you at the next election,
>
> *6*

51 Badiou, 6–7.
52 Badiou, 7.
53 Badiou, 8.
54 Badiou, 8.
55 Badiou, 8–9. I might say here that in this statement of Badiou I cannot find any stronger affirmation of the alleged 'perplexing' dictum in the Walter Benjamin *Artwork* essay almost 70 years ago, where he best put the dilemma: either *politicization of art* by communism or *aesthetization of politics* by fascism.
56 Badiou, 9.
57 Badiou, 12. Further:

> His thesis is that any society matching the description is on the road to ineluctable disaster, because it is incapable of organizing a discipline of time. Plato puts a famous ironic tribute to the existential anarchy of contented democrats and their "beautiful, youthful, mode of government" in the month of Socrates,
>
> *12.*

> Here Badiou cites a long passage of his own 'translation' of Plato's *Republic*, published later.

58 Badiou, 15.
59 See Alain Badiou, 'A Speculative Disquisition on the Concept of Democracy', in *Metapolitics*, trans. and intro. Jason Barker (London and New York: Verso, 2005).
60 Badiou, 78. Badiou notes that

> If "democracy" names a supposedly normal state of collective organization or political will, then the philosopher demands that we examine the norm of this normality. He will not allow the word to function within the framework of authoritarian opinion. Everything consensual is suspicious as far as the philosopher is concerned.
>
> *78–79*

61 Badiou, 79.
62 Badiou, 79.
63 Badiou, 79–80. Badiou further adds that 'Thus, every communist politics strives for its own disappearance by striving to abolish the separate form of the State in general, even the State that declares itself to be democratic', 80.
64 Badiou, 80.
65 Badiou, 80.
66 Badiou, 80.
67 Badiou, 83.
68 Badiou, 84.
69 Badiou, 85.
70 Badiou, 89–90.
71 Badiou, 90.
72 Alain Badiou, *The Pornographic Age*, 16.
73 Badiou, 17.
74 Jacques Lacan, *Formation of the Unconscious: The Seminar of Jacques Lacan, Book V*, ed. Jacques-Alain Miller, trans. Russel Crigg (Cambridge: Polity, 2017).
75 Lacan, 246.
76 Alain Badiou, *The Pornographic Age*, 3.
77 Badiou, 3.
78 Badiou, 3.
79 Badiou, 3.
80 Badiou, 3–4.
81 Badiou, 4.
82 Badiou, 4.
83 Jacques Lacan, *Formation of the Unconscious*, 247.
84 Alain Badiou, *The Pornographic Age*, 5.
85 Badiou, 5.
86 Badiou, 6. In terms of his philosophy, Badiou says,

> in poetry, a sublime desire, by which a particular language, worked in its depths, rises to a level of universal clarity; in mathematics, a desire for intellectual beatitude, which alone procures the certainty of having resolved an extremely difficult problem and offering solution to all; in love, a desire that the experience of life, in all its domains, be more intense and precise as two than when alone. Such are the desires that, to touch on their real, must clear themselves of numerous images
>
> 6

87 See Kojin Karatani entitled *Isonomia and the Origins of Philosophy*, trans. Joseph A. Murphy (Durham and London: Duke University Press, 2017), 16.

Bibliography

Agamben, Giorgio et al., *Democracy in What State?* trans. William McCuaig (New York: Columbia University Press, 2011).
Badiou, Alain, *Metapolitics*, trans. with intro. Jason Barker (London and New York: Verso, 2005).
Badiou, Alain, *The Pornographic Age*, trans. and ed. with afterword, A. J. Bartlett and Justin Clemens (London: Bloomsbury, 2020).
Badiou, Alain, *Trump* (Cambridge: Polity, 2019).
Eisenstein, Sergei, *Film Form: Essays in Film Theory*, ed. and trans. Jay Leyda (San Diego: Harcourt, 1949, 1977),
Genet, Jean, *The Balcony*, trans. Bernard Frechthman, revised edition (New York: Grove Press, 1966).

Karatani, Kojin, entitled *Isonomia and the Origins of Philosophy*, trans. Joseph A. Murphy (Durham and London: Duke University Press, 2017).

Karatani, Kojin, *Transcritique: On Kant and Marx* (Cambridge: The MIT Press, 2003).

Kul-Want, Christopher, ed. *Philosophers on Film, from Bergson to Badiou: A Critical Reader* (New York: Colombia University Press, 2019).

Lacan, Jacques, *Formation of the Unconscious: The Seminar of Jacques Lacan, Book V,* ed. Jacques-Alain Miller, trans. Russel Crigg (Cambridge: Polity, 2017).

Lahiji, Nadir, *Architecture in the Age of Pornography, Reading Alain Badiou* (New York: London, 2021).

Lahiji, Nadir, *Architecture, Philosophy and Pedagogy of Cinema: From Benjamin to Badiou* (New York: Routledge, 2021).

Taylor, Richard, *The Battleship Potemkin* (London and New York: I. B. Tauris, 2000).

IMAGE CREDITS

Figure 10.1   University of Sheffield Library Archives, Special Collections, BU_8_1_11
Figure 10.2   Facundo Arrizabalaga/EPA/Shutterstock
Figure 10.3   ANL/Shutterstock
Figure 10.4   Daily Herald Archive/Getty Images
Figure 10.5   Scolar Press/Routledge
Figure 10.6   Picture Post Collection, Humphrey Spender/Getty Images
Figure 10.7   Architectural Design/John Wiley & Sons
Figure 10.8   Illustrated London News/Mary Evans Picture Library + RIBA Collections
Figure 10.9   British Online Archives, British Union of Fascists Collection
Figure 10.10 Courtesy of Marcus Alexander

INDEX

Note: *Italic* page numbers refer to figures and page numbers followed by "n" denote endnotes.

Taylor & Francis eBooks

www.taylorfrancis.com

A single destination for eBooks from Taylor & Francis
with increased functionality and an improved user
experience to meet the needs of our customers.

90,000+ eBooks of award-winning academic content in
Humanities, Social Science, Science, Technology, Engineering,
and Medical written by a global network of editors and authors.

TAYLOR & FRANCIS EBOOKS OFFERS:

A streamlined
experience for
our library
customers

A single point
of discovery
for all of our
eBook content

Improved
search and
discovery of
content at both
book and
chapter level

REQUEST A FREE TRIAL
support@taylorfrancis.com

 Routledge
Taylor & Francis Group

 CRC Press
Taylor & Francis Group